Michael Timm

September 1999

PORTFOLIO

2001

PORTFOLIO
2001

INFORMED INVESTING
IN THE NEW MILLENNIUM

JOHN KATZ

RANDOM HOUSE
BUSINESS BOOKS

First published in 1999 by Random House Business Books
Random House, 20 Vauxhall Bridge Road,
London SW1V 2SA

Random House Australia (Pty) Limited
20 Alfred Street, Milsons Point, Sydney,
New South Wales 2061, Australia

Random House New Zealand Limited
18 Poland Road, Glenfield,
Auckland 10, New Zealand

Random House South Africa (Pty) Limited
Endulini, 5a Jubilee Road, Parktown 2193, South Africa

Random House UK Limited Reg. No. 954009

Papers used by Random House UK Limited are natural,
recyclable products made from wood grown in sustainable forests.
The manufacturing processes conform to the environmental
regulations of the country of origin.

ISBN 0 7126 7930 8

Typeset in Garamond by MATS, Southend-on-Sea, Essex
Printed and bound in Great Britain by
Creative Print and Design (Wales), Ebbw Vale

Companies, institutions and other organizations wishing to make bulk
purchases of any business books published by Random House should
contact their local bookstore or Random House direct:

Special Sales Director
Random House, 20 Vauxhall Bridge Road,
London SW1V 2SA

Tel 0171 840 8470   Fax 0171 828 6681

www.randomhouse.co.uk
businessbooks@randomhouse.co.uk

DEDICATION

Portfolio 2001 is dedicated to my wife Adrienne whose loyalty, encouragement and support made it possible.

ACKNOWLEDGEMENTS

My children, family and friends have, as always, been great encouragers and enablers. Giuseppe Ciardi, the most brilliant and inspired global investor I have been privileged to know and his colleagues at Park Place Capital started me on the road to professional money management. My editor, Simon Wilson, patiently steered me through the long and challenging paths that led to the concept of *Portfolio 2001* reaching the printing press. My friend Tony Taylor, a businessman, acted as my sounding board and read draft versions for years. His practical down to earth suggestions and straightforward criticisms proved invaluable. Andrew Hine efficiently solved all computing problems and challenges and set up and managed my web sites including **www.Portfolio2001.com**

A NOTE ON SOURCES

Market Unbound - Unleashing Global Capitalism published by John Wiley and Sons and written by Lowell Bryan and Diana Farrell, both senior McKinsey global business advisors, is a lucid explanation of the background to the era of explosive growth we are living through. I have read many other outstanding books on investing and have enjoyed access to well presented company specific research which all contributed directly and indirectly to content in *Portfolio 2001*. However, by 1998 I decided that the integrity of my research thesis depended on whether investors could in fact find the information they needed to be savvy using the Internet, without the privilege of starting, as I had, with top investment house research. The result is that the information sources I should acknowledge now are in the Webliography, chapter nine. They include the leading Internet booksellers who provide on line reviews of their books. **Portfolio2001.com** will also include an extensive and up to date reading list for investors.

Important disclaimer and note on investment advice

Portfolio 2001 includes research and analysis on a list of investing prospects. However, the opinions and commentary are those of the author and it is the responsibility of the reader to do his/her own further research and form his/her own conclusions about investments. Therefore no information or content in the book should be read as or regarded as investment advice.

Care has been taken to ensure that facts and figures quoted are accurate but neither the author nor the publisher warrant the accuracy of any information and accept no responsibility for inaccuracies.

Readers should verify current facts and figures at the time they are considering making investments and seek assistance from regulated financial advisors wherever appropriate before making investments.

CONTENTS

INTRODUCTION

High rewards and low risk

Must high rewards inevitably mean high risks for investors?

The coupling of high reward with high risk was at one time fixed in my mind like a sacred mantra. More recently I have learned that even sacred mantras pass their sell-by dates and can be misleading. In the information age and the heyday of global capitalism, the simple and welcome truth is that the combination of high rewards and low risks is neither an obvious contradiction nor a speculative idea. Surprisingly, the best growth investments I could find for my *Portfolio 2001* – targeting exceptionally high rewards – were picked from the world's best blue chip companies.

Over the closing decades of the twentieth century big business has been reinventing itself as lean, mean and very profitable. The world's top companies that dominate global markets have become both models of business efficiency and vigorous innovators. Add to this the fact that some recent whiz-kid start-ups have evolved as flagship and cash-rich global technology enterprises, and we find a range of great investing opportunities among the world's best companies.

It would be all too easy to make money if successful investing only required picking great names. Opportunities have to be well researched and, after shares are bought, investors should never take their eye off the risk-reward relationship, even if they started with a favourable purchase price. Research, Risk and Reward are the three Rs of investing, and the investing strategy and research focus behind *Portfolio 2001* is directed at investing at low risk for potentially high rewards.

Research: the bedrock of money management

Professional investors only act with all available information at their fingertips. They maintain costly on line connections for current market prices and data, initiate reports on target investments in-house and call in research prepared by specialist teams in investment banks and stock brokers. For example, a report on a bioscience company will be prepared with the assistance of scientists in the relevant disciplines. However, excellent as the standards of research can be for professionals, what private investors receive is often at the other extreme – thin on substance and oversimplified.

The research presented in this book, on the other hand, does evaluate the kind of comprehensive material which professionals rely on, but it is written for private investors in jargon-free language. Also, while even the best research for professionals can be motivated to encourage a sale, my work is entirely independent. When I require the advice of an expert, I consult an independent, usually an academic.

In the 1990s the private investors world has changed dramatically for the better as the barriers to the free flow of information have been falling. Real-time market information and comprehensive fundamental and technical analysis are now easily accessible to everyone on the Internet, data is broadcast and televised, and quality financial publications appear on the Internet and in traditional print form. These information resources make it possible for you to approach investing the same way as professionals – but at negligible cost. The élite of the investing world are now those who choose to become the best informed, rather than the privileged few insiders in the know. Information superhighways cross national barriers and time zones; private investors can scan the globe to find the world's best opportunities.

The research presented in this book starts by explaining what makes each business tick. I go on to suggest potential share prices and earnings to the year 2001, spell out each company's growth story, examine its competitive advantage, look at what competitors and peers are doing, and discuss management and corporate culture. My research also points the way to analysis of revenues, cash flows, margins, share splits, dividends, share buy backs, and key items of financial performance and technical indicators.

Growth shares with double digit earnings potential

Why have I chosen this particular set of *Portfolio 2001* companies? I picked the target investments by starting with a 'top down' research overview to identify the countries and sectors best positioned to benefit from the global conditions and trends expected into the early years of the twenty-first century. Then I switched to 'bottom up' research directed at analysing individual prospects on their fundamental strengths to find the best investing opportunities.

Before I worked on individual companies, two core require-ments defined those I should consider. First, a focus on long-term value meant I would only look at growth companies which are the best investments if they can be held for a reasonable time. As long as they earn more profits they become intrinsically more valuable, and shareholders also benefit from the compounding effect of increased earnings year after year. If markets retreat generally and equity prices fall overall, investors can still expect that the increased value of successful growth companies will be recognized sooner or later on the markets, and their shares will be appropriately repriced.

My second core requirement was for exceptional earnings per share growth, and I only looked at targets where I could identify the prospect of compound earnings growth of above 10 per cent at some stage early in the twenty-first century. After completing my own research, I then looked for confirmation of my earnings estimates from leading analysts.

Beyond these two core requirements mentioned, I introduced further screening criteria to select the world's best shares and I only looked at blue chips with impeccable financials. To take advantage of the vast new world markets, the company had to be global, and, to be sure that competitive advantages could be sustained, I only looked at the dominant global franchises or businesses in their sectors.

My investment targets are divided into two groups, 'Innovators' and 'Global Profit Harvesters'. Of course, there are overlaps. Many of the Global Profit Harvesters are great Innovators, and all the Innovators are very profitable. However, the distinction defines two identifiably different growth opportunities.

The Innovators have proprietary technologies and unique development plans which should radically influence their future earnings, while the Global Profit Harvesters are so entrenched as the dominant global franchises in their sectors, or as global empires, that their future profits will be influenced most by the strength and sustainability of world economic growth.

The Innovators

The Innovators have been drawn essentially from three sectors: Life Sciences; Technology including Communications; and Millennial Niche Opportunities. Scientific advances in the fields of molecular biology, genetics and immunology over the last few decades have been so profound that the life sciences are likely to challenge the physical sciences for dominance in the new century. While bio-technology companies offer the promise of high reward they only do so with the certainty of high risk. However, by identifying a blue chip pharmaceutical company with strong biotechnology interests, the astute investor can tap into the potentially exceptional rewards of a cutting-edge technology without shouldering the full risk.

The world's leading life sciences companies have strategies based firmly on innovation, and, supporting their global pharma-ceutical resources, they own or control leading-edge biotechnology companies, usually in the United States. Life Sciences companies also benefit from chains of research alliances with academic institutions and commercial organizations. Through their wide-spread research efforts they share the high costs of the research to devise the medicines of the future.

Information Technology is still the big growth story of our times. Only a quarter of a century ago, Intel started the digital revolution with its microprocessor technology, and changed forever the way the world works. An investor who staked $2,300 for a thousand Intel shares when it went public in 1971 would now have a holding worth over $2 million after sixteen share splits.

Computers, microprocessors, software, the Internet and communications are to investors at the end of the twentieth century what gold mines were at the beginning. Some technology shares have already performed dizzying acrobatics, and the show would appear to be far from over. With the seemingly endless growth in microprocessor capacity, the personal computer is being continuously redefined. Its biggest use in the future is likely to be connecting people to information and to each other. Videophones with colour screens which run off our PCs, and wireless phones which connect with displays on screens could shortly be as much part of our furniture as a colour TV is today. Microsoft and Intel, two of the world's most successful innovators with others in the industry are set on growing Internet use with powerful new hardware, software and content.

In the 1960s, Marshall McLuhan coined the term 'global village' to describe a future world girded by mass communication networks. That vision is now becoming the reality of the networked society. Its growth well into the twenty-first century will extend from entertainment and leisure to employment and applications in education, health care, shopping and banking, and will be spurred by emerging technologies including digital TV and satellite communications.

The millennial celebrations, televised to a world audience of over four billion people, promise an early bonus to investors in entertainment, media and communications companies. Other businesses are also in line to make exceptional profits from the millennial celebrations, and I have pinpointed specific opportunities in travel, gifts and entertainment. Among them champagne producers and their shareholders are in line to enjoy vintage years in 1999, 2000 and possibly 2001 as well.

The Global Profit Harvesters

The Profit Harvesters span a wide range of industries and services from aircraft engines to deodorants. What they have in common is that they are all global enterprises, and have had years when they have minted money in the growing free enterprise global environment. As long as the world economy remains positive, they can be expected to do better and better well into the twenty-first century and perhaps even beyond. However, they are also more vulnerable if the global economic climate changes for the worse.

The Profit Harvesters include dominant energy and resource suppliers, retailers, and the great global consumer and capital equipment brands. The investing targets among the Profit Harvesters are proxies for their industries and for the global economy, and they include household names like Shell, Unilever and Caterpillar.

I have also recognized Profit Harvesters among global banks, insurers and financial service providers. The global financial services industry is consolidating and restructuring and leading companies are positioning themselves to benefit both from managing the prodigious savings and wealth of the greying baby boomers in the well-developed economies and from new opportunities in emerging markets. Financial shares are a useful balance in *Portfolio 2001* as they are often more modestly priced growth opportunities than leading-edge growth companies.

Buying and selling shares of blue chip companies in countries other than your own should not present serious difficulties. The world's equity markets are globalized and it should be straight-forward to buy shares in any of the world's main markets using your local broker or high street bank. However, if they cannot give you the services you need, or if their charges are unacceptable, you will find listings of brokers who will value your business in Part Two which puts you in the driving seat on the investor information highways. Professional investors are now accustomed to thinking global and acting local and you can do the same.

The global picture – a warning

Economic crises can cloud the horizon and threaten the global economic framework on which strong equity markets depend. In 1977, several Asian countries reversed a dramatic growth spurt, currencies collapsed and rescue packages had to be put in place by the International Monetary Fund. Russia's economy imploded in 1998, and Japan entered 1999 still grappling with an entrenched economic decline which it is trying to reverse.

Global economic and political resolve to foster conditions for stability in emerging markets averted a financial catastrophe of epic proportions in 1998 and, by the turn of the century, investors hope they can look forward to a global economy which is more mature and less opportunistic than the early 1990s proved to be. However, changed conditions may yet lead to a red alert for everyone with funds requiring them to review their investments and strategies. Equity investing generally may not be advisable in dangerously volatile times and, as an ongoing part of the investing process, investors must be aware of risks arising from currency exposure in investments. Currency changes can never be ignored as they influence earnings. Ford is hurt when the dollar rises too steeply against the euro so that Volkswagens can be sold in the US cheaper than Fords. British Airways feels pain when the pound rises against the US dollar because airline fares are based on dollar prices; and Scotch whisky sipped on the waterfront in Cape Town costs more each time the South African rand sinks deeper.

However, currency can also introduce reward opportunities. At times we can use the relative currency neutrality of major global enterprises to spread risks, and currency exposure can also support a decision to buy a share or to sell it. I approach currency as an investment dynamic that can reduce risks and increase rewards.

Research and monitoring

Can you phone your broker now, buy any of the shares that you fancy in *Portfolio 2001*, and be sure to sell in two years' time at a good profit? Even if the odds look as if they are in your favour, the answer is NO. The subject of this book is investing, not speculating. *Portfolio 2001* is a research list and not a shopping list.

To make sure that the prospects in *Portfolio 2001* can be researched using comprehensive easily accessible information, I have chosen only companies whose shares are traded in the United States of America as American Depository Receipts, with the exception of company number 51, discussed in the closing chapter.

A disciplined approach treats investing as a process which will lead to buying shares in the best opportunities at the right time. Equally important are monitoring, managing and at times selling investments with a focus on the crucial low-risk high-reward relationship: code name r&R.

www.portfolio.2001 will update the information on prospects in this book continuously and serve as your convenient information resource for updating information and accessing further research.

No matter how great a prospect looks at the time you invest, investing can never be a one-way bet: 'low risk' does not and never will mean 'no risk'. In the capitalist world risk is in the system.

PART ONE

Global

Growth

Investing

—

1

Investing in the Heyday of Global Capitalism

Every man, as long as he does not violate the laws of justice,
is left perfectly free to pursue his own interests his own way,
and to bring both his industry and capital into competition
with those of any other man or order of men.

Adam Smith on how free markets work

There is no saying no, no, no to globalization

When in November 1990 Margaret Thatcher was ousted overnight as the Prime Minister of Great Britain, the world was shocked. She was the icon of Great Britain's market forces led economic renaissance and even thought of as the leader who put the Great back in Great Britain. However, the iron lady was not for turning, or for bending, and her uncompromising attitude to European Monetary Union (EMU) brought about her downfall. Her famous answer to any talk of a European Central Bank was 'no, no, no' but, even with all her power and influence, she could not afford to say that. The issue of European monetary union was bigger than her.

The socialist historian Eric Hobsbawn discusses the evolving global society in his book *The Age of Extremes – the Short Twentieth Century* and warns that 'for many purposes, notably in economic affairs, the globe is now the primary operational unit and older units such as the national economies defined by the politics of territorial states are reduced to complication of trans national activities . . . Perhaps the most striking characteristic of the end of the twentieth century is the tension between this accelerating process of globalization and the inability of both public institutions and the collective behaviour of human beings to come to terms with it.'

In the heyday of global capitalism following the end of the cold war, entrepreneurs and investors everywhere were on the move, chasing opportunities to share in the peace dividend. World exports grew 70 per cent over a decade, reaching a staggering $5 trillion in 1996. Free trade and enterprise started to span the globe and everyone wanted to be on the freeway.

Technology revolutionized communications and the flow of ideas and transport shrunk the globe. The concept of a global village started to become a reality.

In the wake of the fall of the Russian communist system, globalization of opportunity opened the floodgates for a surge in trade and investment. Led by the United States, the world became almost a free trade zone and the United States and Europe started harvesting the peace dividend.

The long road to the peace dividend

A quick glance back over some of the misfortunes of this century will remind us that global prospects for peace and prosperity have not always looked promising. The First World War started in 1914, and in 1917, before it had ended, the Russian Communist Revolution overturned Tsarist Russia and installed a central command economic order. This ideological alternative to free trade endured for more than half a century and, until the fall of the Berlin Wall in 1989, economics and politics globally were polarized by the ideologies of capitalism and communism.

When the First World War ended in 1918, Europe was faced with unparalleled devastation, yet the Armistice sealed at Versailles in 1918 failed to address post-war economic reconstruction. This failure carried with it the seeds of future conflicts.

The reverberations of the Wall Street crash of 1929 and the great depression of the 1930s followed. Then, in 1933, Hitler came to power in Germany, with fanatical policies that flourished in the fertile soil of German post-war economic ruin and hyperinflation. Hitler's rise to power started the countdown to the Second World War which was waged in Europe from 1939–45 and in the Pacific from 1942–45.

Economic accords reached at the end of the Second World War at a conference in Bretton Woods in America followed and put a new economic plan in place to rebuild Europe and Japan physically and economically. The Bretton Woods accords were pragmatic, well structured and worked. The United States provided a lifeline and the lion's share of the capital to rebuild post-war Europe and Japan, and national governments accepted the financial disciplines of the plan and undertook to rebuild as a condition of receiving the aid.

The United States Federal Reserve controlled the issue of dollars, the primary reserve currency, and effectively acted as the central banker for most of the world. Fixed exchange rates were set for currencies which were pegged to the US dollar and, through the US dollar to some extent to gold, and the arrangements were implemented in the American post-war Marshall plan for Europe and the Dodge plan for Japan.

Japan and Germany rebuilt their economies and soon prospered, and from the 1950s a period of considerable wealth expansion followed in America. Between 1950 and 1971 its gross domestic product (GDP) increased by 2.2% a year, making Americans collectively the wealthiest nation in the world by 1971.

The decade of the 1970s, by contrast, was a time of economic stagnation, increased taxation and high inflation. In 1971 the Western world was pressured by the Organisation of Petrol Exporting Countries (OPEC) for higher prices and this, with other factors, led to a formal US dollar devaluation. Then, in 1973, a second oil shock was experienced as OPEC hit the US and Europe with an oil embargo, resulting in an increase of 400 per cent in the price of crude oil and causing predictable damage to the Western economies.

The pegged currency links established at Bretton Woods and the $ link with gold have since disappeared, but the US dollar remains the world's dominant currency. In the 1980s under President Ronald Reagan, the direction of the American economy turned positive again. The growth rate rose from 2.7% to 3.75%, and inflation was halved from 7.74% to 3.65%. Prosperity returned and Wall Street soared. An era of less government, deregulation and lower taxes encouraged a cycle of re-investing and American industry took giant steps forward and won back its productive leadership and competitiveness.

Meanwhile, Margaret Thatcher's government in the United Kingdom stimulated economic revival, greatly helped by North Sea Oil revenues and her passion for privatization, deregulation and lower taxes.

American Resurgent

By the end of the 1980s, the American economy was buoyant and the total commitment to free trade and a free society was vindicated. America's net worth has continued to grow. Figures to 1990 show the net wealth of Americans as $16.5 trillion (ie $16,500,000,000,000 – $16.5 thousand billion) following a steady rise over the last fifty years. By 1991 the GDP of America reached almost $5 trillion while at the same time the GDP of the Soviet Union stagnated at under $500 billion, or less than one tenth of the US figure.

There was another great turnaround year for America in 1997. Median family income bounced back to its pre-recession peak of $37,000 (and has been rising since then):

Median Household Income: 1967–1997

(In 1997 dollars)

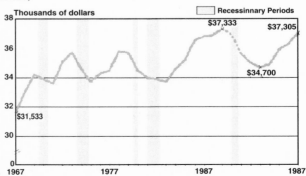

Source: Census Bureau March Census Population Survey

Strength in its economy and pragmatism in its politics enabled the US to tackle its erstwhile chronic budget deficit, and by 1998 America moved from running budget deficits to running surpluses. But remarkable as this watershed achievement was, 1998 will be remembered by investors and economists instead as the year when the Asian economic crisis threatened global growth and the year when Russia's economy imploded. Global stock markets collapsed and a menacing domino effect threatened where one collapse would initiate the next. Political leaders and economists realized that they were staring at a looming global depression. Again American wealth helped to avoid the disaster. By 1998 Americans were so prosperous that adopting a 'shop till you drop' mode they spent sufficient money on imported goods to keep many emerging market afloat.

Stopping the slide into another great world depression

Currency and stock market losses in many global markets, particularly in Asia, were devastating, as reflected in these charts drawn in April 1998:

Selected Asian economies: Bilateral US dollar exchange rates and equity prices

(Logarithmic scale: January 1998-100)

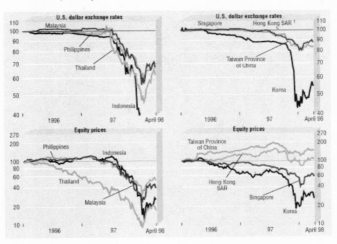

Sources: Bloomberg Financial Markets, LP. International Finance Corporation and Reuters.

Note: [1]Pegged to US dollar

The spotlight moved from economic collapse in emerging countries to the prospect of an awesome depression or slump in the major industrial economies. The agenda changed from supporting IMF rescue packages and bale-outs – with doses of traditional medicines to get the ailing countries back on track – to preventing the world sliding into another great depression by reshaping the financial structures of the entire global economy.

The great depression of the 1930s was exacerbated by a vicious circle of competitive devaluations, high interest rates and asset deflation. World economic growth was stifled by these forces and a well-known spider's web diagram, published by the League of Nations in 1934, shows how relentlessly the web closed in:

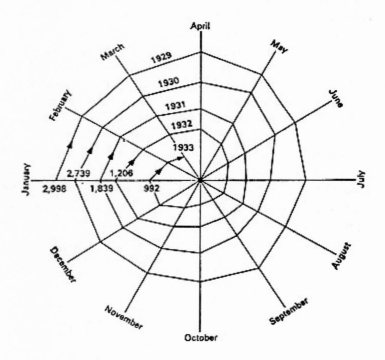

(In millions of dollars)

Source: League of Nations, Monthly Bulletin of Statistics, February 1934, p.51.

From a high of nearly £3,000 million in January 1929, trade spiralled steadily down to less than $1, 000 million in March 1933.

Global cooperation since the end of the cold war has benefited from economic and financial management becoming more the domain of economists than politicians. Until 1998, the main focus was on containing inflation and working towards long-term sustainable growth. Faced with a global crisis, the leading industrial nations in the G7 and the OECD (Organization for Economic Cooperation and Development), with the support of the World Bank and the IMF, responded to the threat of a meltdown with a concerted policy of reducing interest rates. Their decisive response appears to have headed off the worst-case scenarios which threatened, and the risks of damaging recessions in the US and Europe now appear to be low. The challenge still remains, however, on whether what has been done will be sufficient to rekindle global growth.

The IMF and the World Bank, who had put together multi-billion dollar rescue packages for Asian countries and Brazil in 1997 and 1998, remained proactive, revising expectations for global economic growth downwards three times in a year. The December 1998 forecast of the World Bank predicted global growth of a mere 2 per cent for a second year. The Japanese economy was expected to shrink again, projections for the robust US economy were set at only 1.8 per cent and the Euro zone was expected to achieve 2.4, more in line with former expectations. By 2000, global growth was projected to recover to 3 per cent, and to progress again in future.

Global Growth Slows
World GDP

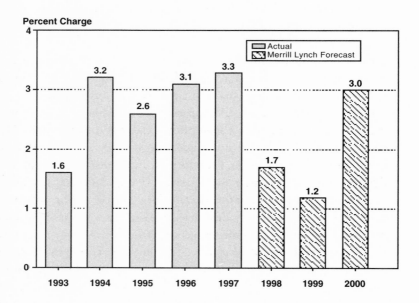

Source: County Source Data, Merrill Lynch

The year 2000 as an approximate turning point for the global economy

The year 2000 serves as an approximate marking point for the emergence of a truly global economy, according to Professor Lau in her book *The Emergence of a Global Economy*. The increasing mobility of capital unleashed a wave of global capitalism that rapidly accelerated the globalization of the world's entire economy for goods, services and labour. Not surprisingly, the years surrounding this transition were extraordinarily turbulent as national governments struggled with how to work in harmony with an overwhelmingly powerful global capital market, and faced the difficulties of curtailing popular entitlement programmes. However with the collective leadership of the major nations of the time, such as Germany, Japan and the United States, working with international agencies, calamity was avoided and the stage was set for several decades of economic growth unparalleled in human history.

And, at the centre of this process was the global capitalist. Far from being the villain envisioned by Karl Marx in his famous book *Das Kapital*, the global capitalist has been the hero of this fundamental economic transformation.

This is an extract from a lecture said to have been read to a live student population at Adam Smith University in Shanghai, China, in 2020. The Professor Lau quotation is of course fictional. The authors, Lowell Bryan and Diana Farrell, invented her to bring home to readers the core themes of their book *Market Unbound*, where they describe a wave of global capitalism, rapid economic growth and integration of the world's economy. On the road most of the signposts they saw pointed the right way, that is to global prosperity.

However, the authors recognized there could be times when all global forces would have to work together effectively to make sure the world economy did not derail. Since they stared disaster in the face in September and October 1998 the industrialized nations have been pulling together and they have an agenda to improve financial systems in future, aimed squarely at preventing a recurrence of the 1997 and 1998 collapses. They should have acted earlier to head off disaster, but in 1998 they were reminded that without global growth prosperity in their own countries was an illusion. The primary economy is now the global economy.

Global risks and global opportunities

Debating the 'what went wrong' questions of 1997 when global trade started to fall off and Asian economies were first affected, 'what went wrong' in 1998 when Asian economies collapsed, and 'what went wrong' in 1998 when Russia's débâcle threatened the stability of the global economic system would make the subject for another whole book. However, useful factual analysis, current and archive, is available on the web sites of the World Bank and the IMF, and lucid commentary on current global economic issues is often available on the site of the Brookings Institute, an American public policy think tank. www.worldbank.org www.imf.org www.brookings.org
The economist Neil Roubeni has a full chronology of the crisis with extensive commentary on www.roubeni.com

Economists and historians dwell on the 'what went wrong' question while we, as investors seeking new opportunities, will be asking 'what is going right now?' While initiatives were launched in 1998 which should lead to a better world financial order in future, the world's economic problems were not solved instantly and there are no magic buttons that any nation, group of nations or organizations can press.

Global capital markets have formidable power gained from the size and momentum of the global economy, and these forces will influence nations to give up their monopolies on running their own economies, setting tax rates and even printing their own money – the point where Margaret Thatcher drew the line. Conceptually and practically, free trade requires that nations who want to share in free markets must keep to the club rules and abolish the restrictive regulations that protect domestic markets. While these are developments which mature over years and decades, 1998 taught us that a global free world economy will have to be nurtured and protected and global economic cooperation can be mobilized to steer the world economy more safely.

Put simply, we cannot escape the global economy and its risks because the countries we live in can face economic hardship as a result of problems elsewhere in the world. We are involved in IMF bale-outs and World Bank rescue packages because the countries we live in support their funding packages and our investments are in the national pot. From the national pot they are exposed to the global pot.

In the real world, to husband money responsibly let alone profitably, we have to come to terms with the global economy. Many wish they could look after their nest eggs in the confines of familiar and cosy domestic national structures, but they will delude themselves if they think they can. The response 'no, no, no' will not keep out risks; it will increase them – and it may close the door to the best opportunities in one of the most exciting times, if not *the* most exciting time, in the world's history – and to a share in the post cold war peace dividend.

The arrival of the euro investing opportunity

European Monetary Union (EMU) became a reality in January 1999 as eleven European nations joined the first wave of membership and adopted a single currency, the euro. They also accepted a single monetary policy set by the European Central Bank (ECB), based in Frankfurt.

The euro is now the official currency of Germany, France, Italy, Austria, Finland, Ireland, Spain, Portugal, the Netherlands, Belgium and Luxembourg. The currencies of the individual countries are fixed denominations of the euro. The next step is that the countries' domestic currencies will be completely replaced by euro notes and coins scheduled for 2002. The ECB is already conducting monetary policy in the new 'Euroland' with the objective of currency and price stability.

The global economic benefits of EMU could be substantial. EMU should be a catalyst for stronger European growth through increased cross border European trade, and increased global stability could come from greater currency stability through the euro.

There are also risks. Countries with long histories of independence, different levels of prosperity, cultures and languages will have to toe a uniform economic line which may not suit everyone all the time. Europeans are less likely than Americans to move to other areas of their own country to find work, and are even less likely to migrate to other European countries if there is no local employment. Europe's chronically high unemployment could become a significant problem to EMU and make it difficult to sustain one monetary policy for all of Euroland. Politically the euro is still controversial – political pressures could increase if individual nations feel that they will be better off managing their own economies.

EMU is part of the new global economic order and on the positive side the build up to a meaningful convergence of the European economies has already taken place. Starting from this secure foundation the chances are that European economic and monetary union will work for the benefit of the world's developed and emerging economies. On the negative side the euro has been a depreciating currency since its inception and to economists and investors who subscribe to the theory that strong currencies and strong economies run in tandem, the prospects for the euro have become increasingly worrying.

As Europe becomes a level corporate playing field, private investors have been among the first group to find new opportunities. The equity cult has taken off. Fixed income savings, the traditional choice of Europeans, lack the vigour and excitement of owning shares and, in any event, at current low rates of interest, they are unattractive.

Pensions will drive demand for the world's best shares

The US state funded pension entitlement was developed on a population projection of six workers per retiree, and in twenty-five years' time there will only be 1.89. The eerie number 1.89 spooks American politicians and economists, and even more eerie numbers spook other countries in the developed world where the burden of funding state pensions will become unsupportable by the employed population early in the new century.

People are living longer and have smaller families and the problem will not just disappear. Either, we won't get paid our state pension and medical care entitlements or, the next generation will be taxed blind to contribute the money that the governments don't have.

No one knows quite how the pensions time bomb will be defused. National governments may bend the rules, borrow money to fund consumption, run increased deficits to pay us and take on running the gauntlet of the global capital markets. Or, global growth could bring enough prosperity to help solve the problem.

The growth opportunity is the compelling option. Pension funds are already soaking up more and more shares of the great blue chips; and, many of the companies are themselves buying back their own shares all the time. The world's best shares still hold the promise of being the great investing opportunity of our times. Technology, capital and enterprise should usher in the unprecedented growth opportunity the world has been expecting and needs – what writers have been calling the long boom. The time to start preparing for the opportunity is now.

Indeed, the opportunity of investing in top shares is so compelling that President Clinton has opened the debate in the US on allowing increased investing in equities by state-managed pension funds, which could have a dramatic impact on demand and on equity prices.

Exciting prospects

As the new century dawns 'Professor Lau's predictions' – for decades of economic growth on a scale never known before – should come true. European Monetary Union represents the most dramatic change to the international monetary system since the US went off the gold standard in 1971 and ushered in the era of flexible exchange rates. Bryant and Farrell estimate that in 1992 the world's liquid financial stock was some $30 trillion, about double the GDP of the OECD nations. In the year 2000, projections are that it will be some $90 trillion, about three times the GDP of these countries, and there is no pre-set limit on the extent of funds which can come into the system. The baby-boomers in the developed world are accumulating prodigious savings, expected to account for $12 trillion of money over the next decade, which could be invested through the financial system into the world economy, fuelling growth on an unprecedented scale. The money exists to invest in growth once investors feel confident again about the security of opportunities outside their borders.

The arithmetic of equity investing has never been more attractive. We expect that money in the bank is safer, but it produces precious little return. We are paid a high rate of interest only when inflation is high and the currency is depreciating, and, after adjusting for inflation and currency devaluation, in real value terms we only achieve a few percent return. When inflation is low, banks pay a low rate of interest which again, after adjusting for inflation, leaves at best a few percent a year. In deflationary conditions, investors at times even pay to have national banks hold their funds safely – as has recently happened in Japan.

Protecting our assets while winning a worthwhile return on our money is challenging. When we look for higher returns, we take on more exposure to the risks of the global economy, and are more exposed to market forces and the volatility of markets.

A winning team: you, the information age and the global economy

When interest rates are falling, investors can do exceptionally well buying fixed-income long-term securities because, although the interest rate paid may be low, after rates fall the capital value of the bond will be greater when it is sold. Ironically in 1998, when Wall Street scaled new heights, the lowest risk investment with an assured high return would have been long-dated government bonds because interest rates fell.

Low interest rates make equities more appealing and there are scores of opportunities: emerging markets, small companies, value investing, special situations managed funds and even hedge funds. *Portfolio 2001* focuses on a small spectrum of opportunities: blue chip global growth companies including the great innovators who are leading the technology and life sciences revolution.

Exciting things are happening in the world. China has over one and a quarter billion people and India has almost one billion. Together they account for almost half the world's population, and they are urbanizing and modernizing. While China is still technically a communist country, since the 1980s it has followed capitalist oriented market reforms, and increasingly works as part of the global free enterprise economy. The growth potential of China and India is overwhelming as their stunted economies and dismal standards of living must be uplifted, transformed and modernized.

Lucent will probably be supplying China with telephone exchanges and IBM is certain to be providing computers running Microsoft software, probably with Intel chips. Glaxo has launched a major new drug in China before launching it elsewhere and LVMH is already marketing its range of luxury goods there.

Some of the prospects in *Portfolio 2001* already have track records of breathtaking investor returns, but they are not sure bets and will not be exempt from setbacks if the global economy does not come back to life vigorously.

Intellectual Capital

Market capitalizations of companies in today's world relate to the value of their intellectual property. Microsoft, America's most valuable company, has a market value of over $500 billion. Rising stars like Yahoo as internet information service providers have reached market values of $30 billion, the same as the 100-year-old Reuters at the time.

There is a case to make that many valuations of intellectual capital have gone over the top, and that the investments are anything but safe bets at such high valuations. Far from arguing against this proposition I support it, but I would find it difficult to say that at a third less, or a half less, I would still be negative. Intellectual capital has become the most valuable resource of our times and this fact puts the focus on the most important question we all have to answer as investors in the information age: are we recognizing and using the value of our own intellectual assets?

As an investor, you have only one safe bet: you yourself – and the better informed you are, the greater your chances of investing successfully. This book will not tell you to go and buy Microsoft today or Pfizer next week because any investment you make can only be low risk and high reward if you pay the right price at the time. This book will give you something much more valuable than a buying list. It will show you how to harness the resources of the information age to work for you and empower you to find opportunities and anticipate risks.

2

PICKING THE WORLD'S BEST SHARES

*I was asked the other day about United States competitive-
ness and I replied that I don't think about it at all. We at
NCR think of ourselves as a globally competitive company
that happens to be headquartered in the United States.*
Jonathan Schnell, *N Y Newsday* 1993

The world's top global companies are the investing domain of
pension funds and insurance companies. Therefore, many private
investors take for granted that it must be too late to buy them and
expect the best returns. This conclusion is misguided as top shares
are bought and held by institutions when they offer the best combination of perceived risk and reward.

The fundamental headline strengths of top global growth companies make them attractive to professional and private investors.
These include:

1 *Predictable earnings*: Market dominance, competitive advantage,
well-established brands and entrenched growth plans nurture
growing revenues, high profit margins, increasing earnings per
share and strong operational cash flows.

2 *Global players*: The global economy is more important than any local economic interest and generally companies that operate globally have achieved greater earnings growth and better investor returns than domestic companies. Brokers and analysts at investment banks will research and analyse these companies and their forecasts will be published.

3 *Market dominance*: Vice-like grips on markets, and having the resources to exploit them, lead to economies of scale that give them access to a global labour pool for lowest cost manufacturing and subcontracting, which entrenches them as the most competitive suppliers.

4 *Innovation and setting the standards*: There was a time when global leaders survived by living off their big brand names and reputations, but this era ended in the 1980s. Success in the current economic climate follows setting new global standards and benchmarks for efficiency and productivity. Corporate cultures of innovation have been built and Research and Development priorities are funded by significant investments that build future product leadership.

5 *Here today and here tomorrow*: Profits have grown in the past and can be expected to grow in future. Profitability is underpinned by management remuneration and incentives at levels that attract the world's most talented people.

6 *Financial strength*: Following years of strong profits and cash flows they have the cash funds to implement ambitious growth plans without diluting shareholder interests. It is unlikely that they will make calls on shareholders for more funds to finance new opportunities and it is likely that they will initiate share buy back programmes which enhance value for shareholders.

Finding buying opportunities

Making a case for the attractions of top companies is easy, but finding buying opportunities at rational prices will certainly be challenging. The legendary global investor and billionaire, the late Sir James Goldsmith, is credited with the saying 'When you can see a bandwagon coming you have missed it.' Shares in the world's top companies have produced staggering price rises over the last decade, but the fact that a share looks expensive at any time should not discourage you from studying the company, putting a rational value on it, following it on the market and waiting for a future buying opportunity.

In Chapter 3, on Strategy, I concentrate on a patient research and investing process that will lead you to recognize various opportunities. Markets are likely to remain volatile: shares trade in ranges, many companies are neglected by the market at times, and all share prices are affected by the flow of funds in and out of sectors and markets. Opportunities also come repeatedly when markets over-react to current events and shares are oversold.

When you have determined rational prices for the shares on your shopping list, you can act decisively. You may see a buying opportunity at ruling prices, or you may opt for a strategy of waiting for an opportunity at a lower price in the share's trading range. You may decide to wait for a correction if you think market valuations are too high generally and, if you are prepared for market volatility, you will have an even greater chance of finding opportunities. Buying well will involve some hard work, but what is unusual about that? Rewards usually only come if we are prepared to work for them.

Innovators and Global Profit Harvesters

In the listing which follows, fifty-one companies are presented, categorized as Innovators, Millennial Niche Opportunities, Global Financial Services and Global Profit Harvesters. No successful company today could be a leader if it were not innovative, and the millennial niche companies, financial service and global profit harvesters have all been vigorous and at times brilliant innovators. What makes the profit harvesters distinct from innovators from an investor perspective is that innovators are less dependent on the prevailing economic conditions and are more able to make their own fortunes with new technologies. Global profit harvesters are companies that are heavily dependent on general economic prosperity to achieve revenue and earnings growth.

10 LIFE SCIENCES

UNITED STATES
1: MERCK
2: PFIZER
3: JOHNSON & JOHNSON
4: ABBOTT
5: MEDTRONIC
6: BAXTER
7: MONSANTO

UK
8: SMITHKLINE BEECHAM
9: GLAXO WELLCOME

SWITZERLAND
10: NOVARTIS

5 INFORMATION TECHNOLOGY

UNITED STATES
11: MICROSOFT
12: INTEL
13: IBM
14: SUN MICROSYSTEMS

GERMANY
15: SAP AG

5 TELECOMMUNICATIONS

UNITED STATES
16: LUCENT
17: TEXAS INSTRUMENT
18: CISCO SYSTEMS
19: MOTOROLA

CANADA
20: NORTEL

10 MILLENNIAL NICHES

UNITED STATES
21: BERKSHIRE HATHAWAY
22: GE
23: TIFFANY
24: TIME WARNER
25: OMNICOM
26: BOEING
27: AMERICA ON LINE

FINLAND
28: NOKIA

UNITED KINGDOM
29: VODAFONE AIRTOUCH

FRANCE
30: LVMH

10 GLOBAL FINANCIAL SERVICES

UNITED STATES
31: CHARLES SCHWAB
32: MORGAN STANLEY DEAN WITTER
33: J.P. MORGAN
34: MERRILL LYNCH
35: CITIGROUP
36: CAPITAL ONE FINANCIAL

NETHERLANDS
37: ING GROUP

SWITZERLAND
38: AIG
39: ALLIED ZURICH

FRANCE
40: AXA

10 GLOBAL PROFIT HARVESTERS

UNITED STATES
41: DISNEY
42: CATERPILLAR
43: WAL-MART

JAPAN
44: SONY

UNITED KINGDOM
45: THE GAP
46: GILLETTE
47: RIO TINTO (RTZ)

UK/NETHERLANDS
48: UNILEVER
49: ROYAL DUTCH
    PETROLEUM (SHELL)

GERMANY
50: VOLKSWAGEN

VENTURE CAPITAL
UNITED KINGDOM
51: 3i GROUP

Buy shares in global companies but not from anywhere in the world

In selecting the portfolio, I found that top down research favoured companies quoted on the world's major stock exchanges, mainly due to liquidity and transparency, and it led to a strong bias towards companies quoted on Wall Street, including ADRs (Amercian Depository Receipts). *Portfolio 2001* presents a wide spectrum of opportunity, including companies from the United States, Britain, France, Germany, Switzerland, Canada, the Netherlands, Japan and Finland.

United States – Wall Street

Wall Street is likely to remain the equity market where most of us want to make investments. Geographically it is the street in Manhattan where the New York Stock Exchange is situated but when we talk about Wall Street we mean all the American stock exchanges and their financial establishments in a package. Wall Street is the home of Merck, Pfizer, Microsoft, Lucent, IBM, Disney Coca-Cola and other top global franchises.

Wall Street is also the world's largest and most liquid market, with the greatest transparency and investor protection, and it is the world's largest global market. Over a thousand foreign companies trade on Wall Street as American Depository Receipts. To all practical purposes owning an ADR is like owning the share itself, with the complexities of dealing with a company outside the United States removed. An American bank owns the foreign share and issues you an American Depository Receipt confirming that it holds shares to the value of your purchase against the certificate. Your advantage is that all your dealings are within the US and there are no foreign settlements, foreign stock exchange procedures or dividend payments outside the US. ADRs can also be traded using an American discount broker, often at a fraction of the cost that would apply to the same transaction traded domestically with a traditional broker or bank. All the companies in *Portfolio 2001*, with the exception of 3i Group, are either American shares or are traded on Wall Street as ADRs.

America is the home of Silicon Valley and technology

investing, and the world's leading technology shares are traded on Wall Street either as US companies or as ADRs. American *Portfolio 2001* companies include the dominant global technology companies in their sectors: Microsoft, Intel, IBM, Sun Microsystems and the telephony companies Lucent, Texas Instruments, Cisco Systems, Motorola and the Canadian company Nortel. The German software company SAP AG, traded on Wall Street as an ADR, is also included as a technology prospect.

In the Life Sciences section Wall Street is again the leading market. *Portfolio 2001* companies reviewed include Merck, America's world's largest prescription drugs company, and Pfizer, the company challenging it for number one slot; Johnson & Johnson, the world's largest healthcare company; Baxter, the world's leading blood technology company; and Medtronic, the world's leading manufacturer of inplantable devices. I've also included two leading global pharmaceutical companies which are close to Merck in market share in the prescription drugs industry: the British group Glaxo Wellcome and the Swiss group Novartis. The UK's SmithKline Beecham, which is launching globally a major new drug for adult onset diabetes, completes the section.

With the exception of the French champagne and luxury goods company LVMH, traded as an ADR, the millennial opportunities selected are all American. Top of the list is Warren Buffett's Berkshire Hathaway, not only because it is Buffett's investment vehicle and he has rewarded his investors richly, but, following a merger with America's largest insurance company US Re at the end of 1998, Mr Buffett has some $23 billion in cash and fixed income securities to invest in equities and initiate another round of value creation. The world's most successful industrial conglomerate GE follows, trailed by the world's currently most unsuccessful industrial company Boeing. But watch this space. Boeing is the world's premier space engineering company and when the global economy is back on its growth course prepare for Boeing's profits to lift off. Disney is part of the psyche of the twentieth century. So is advertising and Omnicom, the world's leading advertising group, is destined for a bumper year as millennial marketing builds up.

America's most famous jeweller and gift retailer Tiffany is as fine an example as there can be of a sparkling millennium niche marketing opportunity. Among financial services companies, Charles Schwab has been flying with a fast tailwind since Internet broking started a few years ago and in November 1998 the market value of Schwab passed the market value of Merrill Lynch, the world's largest traditional brokerage although it is facing challenges.

Merrill Lynch is also among the Global Financial Services opportunities reviewed in *Portfolio 2001*, with the world's largest financial services group, Citicorp, and America's investment banking icon J. P. Morgan. The Dutch ING Group and the French group AXA are financial services conglomerates, and Allied Zurich is a Swiss/British fund management and insurance group. These European companies with their ADR shares present interesting and different opportunities to investors.

Global Profit Harvesters include The Gap, Gillette, Caterpillar and Volkswagen. The fifty-first company, British venture capital group 3i, is an opportunity for investors who expect the new century will favour entrepreneurs.

Transparency and the Internet
US law requires companies to file quarterly reports within sixty days of the end of each quarter, and these tight reporting periods result in investors being kept up to date with what the companies are doing currently as opposed to historically. Top companies often file their reports within weeks of the end of the reporting date and investors in these companies have the advantage of working with very current information. Filings made by companies listed on US stock exchanges with the government Securities and Exchange Commission (SEC) are in the public domain and accessible using several Edgar sites on the Internet listed in the Webliography.

Howard Gold, the editor of the *Wall Street Journal* on line, wrote at the end of 1997 that investing in the new century will be dominated by private investors, and the Internet will deliver the opportunity for them. Investor information for research and monitoring of US companies is the benchmark and the standards are rising all the time. For example, investment bank research is being made available through several channels.

The national perspective in the United States
Politically and economically, the United States is attractive as a country to invest in. Taxation is unlikely to rise until well into the new century, the currency and economy are exceptionally strong,

and while there are concerns about declining manufacturing output, adverse effects of the Asian crisis and instabilities in Latin America, these should concern investors when deciding whether to hold shares at all, rather than in relation to holding shares in America's top companies.

There are also well-founded concerns that Wall Street has become overvalued and the 'Bear Essentials' pages in www.portfolio2001.com, which I started as a separate web site in the second half of 1998, will continue to publish views on market valuations as a reality check for investors. Wall Street attracts the spotlight from commentators who point to overvaluation because the markets are transparent. Signposts like the price to earnings ratio for the S&P 500 (Standard and Poor) Index and the forecasts for earnings of individual S&P companies are accessible, but market overvaluation is not an isolated US problem. Overvaluation will be likely to affect all markets in the western industrialized world at the same time, and most times Wall Street will probably not be the most overvalued market.

Britain – London

Until 1999 more foreign stocks were traded in London each day than on any other single market in the world, and this may not change even after European Monetary Union (EMU). The London Stock Exchange is dominated by institutional investors who follow the best global opportunities, and the flow of these substantial funds makes London a very liquid market. London also tends to be realistically valued because fund managers working there, who do not find opportunities domestically, will look for value in other global markets.

The London Stock Exchange was a closed shop and establishment playground until its deregulation in 1986, the event that became known as 'the big bang'. Then, for the first time, foreign firms were allowed to take shares in and take over British brokerages. American investment banks were keen to enter the new market which also abolished fixed commissions and closed shop practices and London expanded dramatically. European markets will become more internationalized with European Monetary Union, but London is still well positioned to hold its leadership.

English is the main language for global commerce, London has an unsurpassed pool of skilled investment professionals, the market is liquid and efficient and it has become an established home ground for global investment banks and international brokers.

All round, London has a lot running for it as a potential market for investors. It has replaced Japan as the second largest stock exchange after the US. The market capitalization of shares traded on the London Stock Exchange is some 40 per cent greater in value than the country's GDP. Britain has historically been a home for multinational companies, and international investment and foreign income from investments are now a major contributor to British corporate revenues.

Britain is a member of the European Union, has a special relationship and close financial links with the US, and has a tradition and history of international finance and global investing.

National perspectives in the United Kingdom

International shareholders can invest through London comfortably, and with the advent of European Monetary Union the floors of the stock exchanges in the EU nations are opening up to each other. Shares in London, Frankfurt and Paris can already be traded on any of the three markets on the same terms.

As the United Kingdom has not yet joined EMU there is scope for conflict between it and its partners in the European Union who already have, and this may result in unwelcome currency volatilities. Fortunately the UK is politically stable with Prime Minister Tony Blair's New Labour government commanding an unassailable majority in Parliament. New Labour have cloned President Clinton's pragmatism, and national economic policy is middle of the road with a strong bias in favour of business and initiative. Unemployment is low, labour demands are moderate, and Britain is a petro-economy with wealth pumped out of the North Sea all day and night – even when oil prices are depressed. Expectations are that corporate and private taxation will remain stable. Since 1997 the Bank of England has also been made independent of Treasury control, able to set interest rates free from political interference.

Britain and European Monetary Union

Industrial and business leaders have tried to encourage Britain to be in the first wave of monetary union which came into effect in January 1999, but no national decision to join has yet been taken. The government is committed not to join in the life of the present parliament, which will run into 2002, unless a national referendum endorses the decision first. The parliamentary opposition, the Conservative party, following their former leader Margaret Thatcher's message of 'no, no, no', have committed themselves not to join a European single currency in any circumstances for the life of two parliaments – that is until 2007, assuming two full 5-year terms.

The nation is divided on whether to join EMU. People are concerned that monetary union really means that they will surrender fiscal control to an unelected European authority. Many are also emotionally against abandoning the British pound as their currency.

Britain may not have all the options some politicians suggest are open. The Treaty of Rome, the foundation of the European Community, provided that there should be a single currency. However, the debate continues. At grass roots many people from all walks of life follow the line of big business and see more job security and better prospects once the euro is adopted, but there are others, again from all walks of life, who view any loss of control over the nation's purse strings as an irrevocable and unacceptable loss of sovereignty. Among those who have no particular passions on the subject, there is mainly a lack of understanding on how the single European currency will work. The European Union is an association of very different and individualistic sovereign states with strong linguistic and cultural identities and diverse economic societies. They cannot even agree to a standard for an electric socket.

The United Kingdom's differences with its European partners could continue well into the new century, and could even cause frictions between the national government and the global capital market, currency volatility and volatility in equity markets.

There are several British companies in *Portfolio 2001*. Forty per cent of the companies in the FTSE 100 index do most of their business outside the UK, and often the majority of shareholders are outside the UK. The *Portfolio 2001* shares reflect the international flavour of the London Stock Exchange.

France

France joined the first wave of EMU with Germany and the Benelux countries in 1989. As a country France is among the world's most blessed and the French are among the most talented, organized and imaginative people, but some of France's social and economic problems are daunting. Public spending on welfare is too high, unemployment at over 12 per cent too high, politics is fragile, and organized labour is very powerful. Labour is also vociferous and prone to taking to the streets and disrupting services if it cannot get its own way.

France, like its wine estates, is a country best enjoyed by those who understand it. There are only two French companies in *Portfolio 2001*. Louis Vuitton Moët & Hennessy (LVMH) is an attractive millennial niche company as it controls the world's main champagne producers and has leading top end ranges of luxury items which should earn spectacular profits with the millennial celebrations; and the French global insurance conglomerate AXA is also included as a financial services opportunity.

There are many great French investing opportunities that are not included in *Portfolio 2001* because, compared to similar opportunities in other markets, valuations were unfavourable. L'Oréal, the global cosmetics group is listed as an ADR on Wall Street and would have been in the portfolio if the share price did not keep marching ahead relentlessly, dragging conventional valuation yardsticks in the dust behind it. The global hypermarketing group Carrefour's achievements are similar but Carrefour does not have an ADR listing. *Portfolio 2001* is the loser in not having these companies, and readers interested in France could spend time well studying them.

Germany

Over the next few years Germany should become an increasingly attractive market for foreign investors. The industrial base is strong, companies are well financed and the national Bundesbank conditioned the country to a regime of tight monetary management which the European Central Bank is committed to maintain.

The former Chancellor Helmut Kohl was at the very heart of

the movement for European monetary union, yet at the election in 1998, before it became a reality, he was defeated at the polls. The present Chancellor, Gerhard Schröder, and his government are no less committed to monetary union, but are not hardliners on monetarism and may find themselves at odds with the European Central Bank on this issue.

Unwelcome volatility with the European currency could emerge if passions in Germany ever get inflamed over frictions within the European Central Bank. Passions could also be aroused in 2002, the date when the Deutsche Mark will cease to be Germany's currency.

There are other problems to investing in Germany. The German capital market has not courted foreign investors, and accounting in the continental tradition is opaque. German management, particularly in the large groups, is hierarchical and transparency is often a rude word. The position is improving with the influence of foreign institutional investment over the last decades and hence calls for more glasnost. Veils are also lifted when German companies seek ADR listings and have to comply with American and international accounting and reporting standards.

The investor landscape will not change overnight in Germany. German banks still hold controlling stakes in major listed industrial groups, following investments made at the end of World War Two, and the same companies have cross holdings in the banks. These shareholding structures will have to be modernized before ensconced management structures become accountable. It will be worth waiting for because the changes will bring investing opportunities. The Daimler–Chrysler merger, with the support of Deutsche Bank, the largest shareholder in Daimler Benz, is an example of how successful entrepreneurial German business can be.

Public ownership of utilities and industries is still the norm in Germany and this means that investors can look forward to participating in several rewarding privatization opportunities.

The two German companies in *Portfolio 2001* are from very different sectors and will attract investors for different reasons. SAP AG is in the technology sector. It is the second largest software developer in the world after Microsoft, with a strong global presence, and its shares have a full listing on Wall Street. SAP applications have global dominance in software for 'mission critical applications' like banking, airline reservation and major corporate activities. Its operational and financial results have been spectacular and the share price reflected this. At the end of 1998 it felt the pinch from the global economic slowdown and the share price came out of the stratosphere, reviving the prospect of SAP as a low-risk high-reward opportunity.

Volkswagen is Europe's largest car manufacturer and a company on the move. It is the only automobile manufacturer in included in *Portfolio 2001*.

Daimler Chrysler and BMW are missing from *Portfolio 2001* and their absence calls for an explanation. BMW is an exceptional opportunity in the automotive sector. It builds cars and motorcycles the world wants and will pay for, and because demand exceeds supply it has pricing power. But the group is still unsuccessful with its Rover plant in the UK, and BMW do not have an ADR listing.

Daimler Chrysler would also have fitted well into *Portfolio 2001*, and is an alluring investment prospect as a merged global enterprise. It also has the ADR which BMW is missing and this makes it easier to research, monitor and trade. However, post the merger, exciting as the new group is as an automotive company, investors will be led by expectations of cost synergies and marketing opportunities which are less tied to the organic growth story than the focus of *Portfolio 2001* calls for.

Switzerland

The Swiss Stock Exchange is in Zurich and the country has a mature and sophisticated international banking industry. Historically, Switzerland has been a world centre for money management, and recent Federal Stock Exchange Laws have been aimed at boosting liquidity on the market and increasing transparency. However, a transition away from deeply rooted opaqueness will take time.

One of the world's largest pharmaceutical groups, Novartis, with headquarters in Basel, Switzerland is included in *Portfolio 2001*. It was formed in 1996 out of a $35 billion merger of two major Swiss pharmaceutical groups, Ciba and Sandoz. Novartis had a headstart as a company reporting to international standards when two American investment banks advised on the proposed merger and engaged the support of international investors from the outset. Novartis trades as an ADR and is likely to promote more exposure on Wall Street as it owns significant interests in the US, including control of the important biotechnology company, Chiron.

The banking sector in Switzerland is traditionally attractive, but 1998 saw disappointing performances, particularly in the wake of the Russian debt default. The *Portfolio 2001* Swiss financial opportunity is the British and Swiss group Allied Zurich, formed by a merger at the end of 1998 between the financial services business of BAT Tobacco and the Zurich Insurance Company. The group brings the focus on insurance and fund management, particularly in Europe.

Currency can be sensitive for investors in Switzerland and the Swiss franc frequently gets overvalued to the detriment of domestic companies who rely on exporting, or who earn profits in local currencies from other countries. Europeans anxious about European Monetary Union or other currency volatilities tend to regard Switzerland as a safe haven for money. The currency supply and demand imbalances that follow have, in the past, artificially affected the Swiss franc's exchange rate.

The Netherlands

The Netherlands is a straightforward country. The Dutch guilder was an even stronger currency than the German mark prior to monetary union in 1999, and company reporting and accounting is to the highest standards.

Portfolio 2001 includes the two Anglo Dutch giants, Unilever and Shell, mentioned earlier, and the ING Group, an entrepreneurial financial services and insurance company which has performed strongly. The ING Group includes the American investment bank Furman Selz and the British investment bank Barings, which together give the operation a well-established global presence and its share is listed as an ADR on Wall Street.

Japan

Japan's Stock Exchange is having its 'big bang' and deregulating in 1999, and optimists still expect that this will correspond with a normalization of economic conditions in the country. Since 1995, Japan's economy has been falling apart and a stock exchange collapse has been interrupted only by several false dawns. The Yamaichi Bank collapsed in 1997 and drained what little global investor confidence was left in the system. In 1998 there were vigorous but still unsuccessful efforts to revive consumer spending and for 1999, while economic forecasts continue to point to recession in the early part of the year, the first shoots of growth might be seen by the second half of the year.

Some economists in the US believe that the Asian miracle is yesterday's story and Japan's dismal economic performance is only reflecting this. Deflation menaces and despite the lowest interest rate structure in the world, with government yields in the range of 1% to 2%, industrial overcapacity and currency volatility threaten the manufacturing economy. There were even fears that instead of contributing to solving the Asian crisis, Japan was increasingly becoming the core problem and, until Japan's economy starts to grow again, global prosperity and prospects for global free trade are being undermined, Japan's recession could slide into a depression affecting us all.

Only a decade ago, Japanese technology and quality standards set the world's benchmarks , public finance was a model of correctness and stock market valuations reflected robust profitability. The US has now replaced Japan as the economic model with the most efficient and innovative companies, strong growth, full employment, and even a balanced budget – while Japan's massive budget deficit is rising.

At the core of Japan's problems is its banking system, destabilised by non-performing loans. In 1998 Japan took legislative steps directed at supporting banks in dire circumstances, but the banking system remains in crisis and Japan's industrial base is vulnerable. Japanese industry has been depending on an overly depreciated yen and the risk can not be ignored that the US will find itself driven to take a protectionist stance to the general detriment of the world economy.

To stimulate economic activity Japan has introduced stimulus programmes worth more than $500 billion to kick start the economy and accepted that it must deregulate, create jobs, stimulate consumer spending and generate economic growth. Investors can certainly believe in Japan's strong work ethic and organized manufacturing and marketing resources, but political determination and confirmation that the economy is being managed effectively are still missing.

Several of the world's top companies are Japanese and when the turnaround really comes, Japan will yield many exceptional new investing opportunities. However, economic and currency uncertainties discouraged the inclusion of a range of Japanese companies in *Portfolio 2001* and Sony is the only prospect. The Life Sciences company Abbott has a close connection with Japan's pharmaceutical giant Takeda, an important innovative company which readers interested in Global Pharmaceulities should certainly study.

Honda would have had a place in *Portfolio 2001* as a great automotive company, if there had been scope for another company in that sector.

Finland

Nokia is a fully global company which happens to be Finnish, and was included as the leading mobile phone handset manufacturer in the world's fastest growing industry.

Sure losers set themselves up to lose

We all know people who tell us they are always unlucky with shares, and prices are bound to tumble as soon as they buy and rocket as soon as they sell. Equities are not for everyone and before buying shares you must find and research quality investments, have the money available to commit for years, know what you are doing, and, most important of all, have the mind-set to succeed.

When I speak to friends who tell me that they always come unstuck with shares, and I try to prise out why, usually the first thing to come out is that funds for the investments were either borrowed and had to be repaid, or were taken from funds needed elsewhere, in the hope of a quick payoff. A hot tip from someone at the club, a broker, or a newspaper triggered the share purchase. We do not have to be very smart to fathom out that prices go up while hype lasts.

Our friends who get it wrong buying also get it wrong selling. They have never studied the company, don't know what is going on at grass roots, and then sell when they read a misinformed newspaper comment, hear another hot tip at the club, need the money, or get bored with the share and offload it. Then a good announcement is made, the share price goes up soon after they sell, and it turns out that the company was not all that bad after all.

Sure losers position themselves wrongly and manage investments badly. Luck has nothing to do with it. A mind-set and commitment to be well informed and to buy rationally is the prerequisite to successful investing.

Getting investing right

Picking shares yourself or investing in managed funds is not an either/or choice and many investors do both. There are times when investing through managed funds is the only way to go. If you cannot commit time to researching and monitoring a portfolio, fund managers do this part of the work for you.

Investors seeking exposure to emerging markets and technology opportunities will also be better served by funds, unless they have specialized knowledge. Funds have skilled people on the ground and information sources in emerging markets which should equip them to produce positive results, and technology funds have qualified specialists who keep up to date in a fast moving industry.

If you have not invested directly before, it must make sense to start with a small amount of capital and develop your skills and knowledge before getting too committed. You can also start by only investing time in research, and following companies and markets to get a feel of what is involved in managing a portfolio, thus getting familiar with major sectors, including technology and life sciences, by following companies before making investments.

CNN's web site **www.sandbox.net** is an excellent introduction to running a portfolio which demystifies technical terms, explains on line dealing using the Internet and allows you to run a phantom portfolio backed by all the resources of news and market analysis.

Using **www.portfolio2001.com** as a research and information base, you can instantly update with up to the minute information from the Internet. The research reports do not have a sell-by date as the top companies I have presented will take ages to dislodge from the markets they dominate, barring some global catastrophe which derails the world's economy. Your grand-children will want to buy some *Portfolio 2001* shares, unless your investments turn out to be so successful they find themselves owning them anyway.

The buck stops with you

Picking the shares you invest in means *you* take responsibility for your money and cannot pass the buck. I have a friend who has a mental process of blaming everything in life that goes wrong on someone else. This insulates her from setbacks in daily life. If she runs out of petrol, it is her husband's fault for not making sure the tank was full. If her career is not going well, it is the fault of the people at the office, and if she bought a share and lost money it would be the broker's fault. However, blaming the broker is of zero value if your money is lost.

Woody Allen once described a stockbroker as someone who invests all your money for you until there is nothing left. An investor who picks his own shares can only blame himself or herself for losses . . . or maybe we can all blame Woody Allen? Or failing him his broker? Or, invest your money in a managed fund and blame the fund manager.

Or tune in to the information age and make profitable investments.

3

A FOUR-PRONG GROWTH INVESTING STRATEGY

1. Pick the world's best companies

Currency is on the agenda

The key advantages of investing in the world's best companies are: predictable earnings, market dominance, innovation and setting the standards, here today and here tomorrow security and financial strength. These were outlined in the previous chapter, but the currency implications of holding foreign shares were not examined.

In a global economy, where commerce, industry and capital markets are globalized, currency relationships are bound to affect all investments, domestic and foreign. However, although there should not be, there is a difference in how we respond to the currency factor with domestic and foreign investments. If domestic investments go wrong because of currency, we may be inclined to sweep the losses under the carpet and conveniently blame the government or the Asian crisis or anyone we can think of. If a foreign investment goes wrong because of currency, the loss is going to stand out as if it had a big illuminated neon sign above it flashing 'currency loss', and we have to take the blame ourselves. Investors tend to be naïve about currency exposure through domestic investments and averse to all foreign investments because they fear losing money on a foreign currency.

Foreign currencies do introduce visible risks, but can be recognized and approached as a useful dynamic for investors. All investors, domestic and global, should start with currency as item one on their research and monitoring agendas, and then keep currency on the agenda.

Bring currency into the equation to your advantage

Currency volatility can be exploited by investors, moderated or even eliminated depending on the strategy followed. Generally, four different approaches to using currency are important.

The first is when the investment is motivated on its own merits and there is potentially an added currency benefit. Investors buy the foreign company and stay exposed themselves to any fluctuations in the currency. Japanese pension funds were active buyers of US and European equities over the years that the yen was weakening and will have profited from both the rise in the prices of their shares and the rise in the value of the currencies they were held in. A similar prospect of share price rises and currency gains may one day attract US-dollar-based investors into Euroland and non-US residents into the US. These investors will be taking a view on future currency outcomes and will also expect the shares they buy to appreciate in value domestically.

The second approach is where investors carry currency exposure themselves when they buy foreign shares to introduce a general spread of currency exposure in an asset portfolio. This strategy appeals particularly to people who live in countries with currencies that look weak and vulnerable. Many investors living even in Europe and the US are tempted not to have all their eggs in one basket.

The third approach is to gain currency spread through holdings in global companies.

Finally, investments in foreign companies can, at a cost, be made currency neutral. Currency neutrality can be bought by arranging forward exchange contracts that insulate investments, or can be made by borrowing the required foreign currency to fund the investments and repaying the loan when the shares are sold.

In 1996 and 1997, when the yen was falling against the US dollar, shares in top Japanese exporters were set to benefit from the yen currency weakness, but the investor's paper profit on the share was vulnerable to erosion from the falling yen. For years past, the yen could be borrowed at 1% to 2% per annum and investors had borrowed yen to buy Japanese shares and paid for the shares in yen. These investors stood to get the best of both worlds if the companies prospered, helped by the weaker Japanese currency. The shares rise in yen, and the investor banks the full profits after selling the shares and repaying the yen loan. A small currency loss when converting the profit to a domestic currency would result, and the nominal interest on the loan would have had to be paid, but practically speaking the gain would be intact and could be substantial.

Honda benefited as an exporter from the weak yen from 1996, and the following chart comparing the performance of the Tokyo Honda share and the ADR on the same share illustrates how substantial the gains were to investors who held Honda Japanese shares in yen at the time, insulated from currency loss because the yen were borrowed. The spread between the two prices on the graph reflects the currency movement for the share quoted in yen in Japan and in US dollars as an ADR. Investors who held the share in yen would have made over 60 per cent on their investments at the best point shown on the chart, while investors who held ADRs in US dollars would only have made about 30 per cent.

Comparison of Honda Shares in Japan – (Top Line) with Honda ADR (Bottom Line) 1997 to 1999

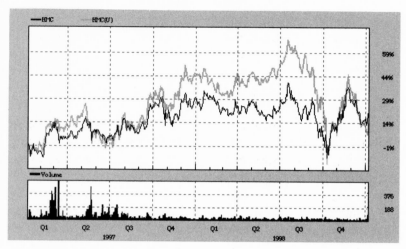

Source: J. P. Morgan adr.com

The strategy is to buy the world's best shares. Though at times currency considerations will tip the balance against making an investment in a foreign company, private investors should not slot themselves into inflexible rule-book boxes on what they will and will not do.

There is certainly a line to draw between being enterprising on the one hand and investing out of one's depth on the other, but all investors will benefit from a better understanding of currency risks and opportunities, and will find that when they want to structure investments to achieve the best currency exposure, the enabling steps can be sensibly constructed. Excellent opportunities should not be lost because the currency dynamic calls for intelligent management. In the above example, all the circumstances favoured the investor, and in hindsight the opportunity was compelling and one that should not have been missed.

2. Make informed investing decisions and safeguard investments with up-to-the-minute information

'Ignorance is not bliss – it's expensive'

This advertisement for financial services site www.thestreet.com says almost all that needs to be said in just one line. John Corzine, chief executive at the time of the investment bankers Goldman Sachs, acknowledged in a *Time* magazine interview in May 1997: 'Information is transparent today. No one generates a long term competitive edge just because they know something that someone else does not.'

The concept of equal opportunity to access information is an important social milestone, which all will agree deserves to be applauded, but private investors will be more interested in whether they can make as much money as the professionals. Can they? The answer has to be 'No ... not yet anyway.' Information gives us tools, but experienced money managers know how to use them better, and have developed skills at using information to generate immense wealth.

In the next chapter, on Research, Risk and Reward, I outline the research sequences followed in *Portfolio 2001* and then, in Part Two: In the Driver's Seat, I raise the practical subject of getting information to make buying and selling decisions, and the challenging subject of using information well.

Becoming really clever at using information as a private investor is a prospect that may sound daunting as it suggests you will be pitting your skills against the best professionals. Many of the world's most brilliant people and top earners work in investment banking and fund management. The abilities of top money managers should never be underestimated and there are lucrative branches of finance like trading in derivatives which they master. However, researching company information well with access to good information, and interpreting the information using good business sense, call more for common sense and intelligence than for exceptional brilliance.

Target compelling opportunities
Organizational structures do not guarantee the most successful

performance and even the best professional money managers are at times held back by structural limitations on how they can operate. Money managers exist to find a home for other people's savings, and waiting for the compelling opportunity is not always a practical option for them because they cannot switch the flow of funds on and off. Money streams in which *must* be invested.

Private investors are at an advantage here because they can direct their efforts and resources to finding compelling opportunities, even if it means they have to wait for the right time.

Act decisively when you should sell

Only fundamentals change the real growth prospects for the global economy, for nations and for companies. However, the media have to concentrate on the news stories of the day and air all the different points of view and sometimes everyday problems are sensationalized to sell newspapers. The herd often moves without sufficient thought and, ironically, many money managers have a reputation for following the herd and responding excessively to fuss, while informed private investors as a group have shown themselves to be more objective and are certainly more independent. They should be. They have access to all the information they need to reach balanced decisions and there will be times when the *compelling* decision is to sell a holding without delay.

When instant course changes are called for, money managers may find themselves shackled by management protocols that demand a collective decision. However, there are no inertia imperatives for alert private investors who can make a decision and act without delay. Cashing in before the storm when a major sell off is pending can mean putting more money in the bank, or when others are selling hysterically they could be giving you your buying opportunity.

3. Focus on long-term value with investments that grow earnings

The current 'rule books' for growth investing are bound to follow strategies outlined by Warren Buffett, and for good reason. He is the world's most successful stock picker, his advice is patently wise, he is articulate, and he is the world's most successful investor.

Warren Buffett communicates his investing ideas in letters to shareholders that can be read on the web site of his holding company Berkshire Hathaway www.berkshirehathaway.com (Berkshire Hathaway is a *Portfolio 2001* Millennial Niche investing opportunity.)

Portfolio 2001 follows a growth investing strategy and three of Warren Buffett's so called Golden Rules are at the core:

1: Focus on long term value

2: Stick to stocks within your circle of competence

3: Study prospects and their competitors in detail. Look at raw data not analysts' summaries. Trust your own eyes.

An investor who buys a share in a company growing its profits has a stake in both the increasing profits earned and the compounding effects of the increased profits retained in the company year after year. Arithmetically, this is a winning package, particularly when there is high growth. The downside is that, to be sure of cashing in the profits, growth investing demands long time horizons. Market sentiment towards a particular share often turns negative for reasons that have nothing to do with the company or the real grass roots events in the business world. It follows that, at times, the intrinsic value of a performing growth investment will not be reflected in the share price, even though in the long term it almost certainly will.

Investment managers like to explain why patience is necessary using the analogy that the gestation period for a baby human is nine months, and is twenty-two months for a baby elephant. Indeed, it takes time for all well-laid plans to hatch. The only time frame a growth investor can look at is years. Hence the title *Portfolio 2001* for a book first published in 1999. It can take years to build a portfolio.

The long time horizon demanded for successful growth investing is not often sweetened by the prospect of healthy dividend payments while you wait. Top growth companies usually do not pay dividends on the premise that they can do better with the money in the company, and when growth companies do pay dividends, they are usually a nominal one or two per cent.

Dell Computers, an investor's superstar at the close of the twentieth century, went public in 1994. It has never paid a dividend and probably never will. Investors will agree taking money out of the company would be a bad idea: ten thousand dollars invested in Dell in 1994 was worth almost $1 million by the beginning of 1999. Who could have done better themselves with the proceeds of dividends?

Value of $10,000 invested – Dell Computer Corporation

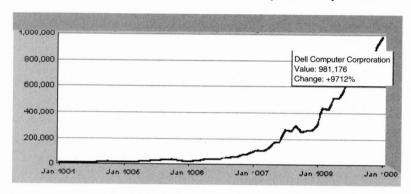

Source: www.moneycentral.com

4. Use information to make money

Investors do not need to be boffins to use the Internet, and even committed technophobes must shake off any prejudices and get on line. An Internet connection for financial information is as essential as a telephone connection if you run a business. You must have it – it's as simple as that.

There are no country barriers on information superhighways and from the comfort of our homes we can 'think global and act local' with an ordinary PC and an Internet connection.

Our computers will make us smarter when they communicate with each other on the Internet. Mine has a super brain and is a far better communicator than I am, and your computer will be the same.

Professional investors pay tens of thousands of dollars a year to use similar global financial databases to the resources we can now access at little or no cost on the Internet. It is senseless not to use a resource that gives you greater control over your investments, and you will be disadvantaged if you do not.

The Internet is the dominant, user friendly and comprehensive resource for investor information. Because so much of the information is free, investors are often suspicious and think there must be a catch somewhere. There is no catch and there is nothing sinister in the free information Internet system.

In fact, it is not provided free. Advertising revenue covers costs and also makes prodigious profits for Internet publishers. The more visitors they get to the site, the greater their advertising revenue. Unlike in print media, where for example, every extra copy of a newspaper printed increases costs, it does not cost Internet publishers any extra money to serve another customer, and all the advertising revenue after breakeven point is profit.

Yahoo has performed what seems like a miracle for investors by supplying outstanding information free on the Internet. The following chart shows how in 1998 Yahoo (YHOO) shares shot up while the shares of information industry leader Reuters (RTR) moved sideways. In January 1999, the market value of Reuters was $19.5 billion dollars and the market value of Yahoo was over $30 billion: proof, if any is needed, that supplying information on the Internet free is good business. And proof that Yahoo has performed a miracle for its own shareholders.

Comparison of Share Price Of Yahoo (YHOO) (Top Line) and Reuters PLC ADR (RTRSY) (Lower Line) for year ending 5 Jan 1999

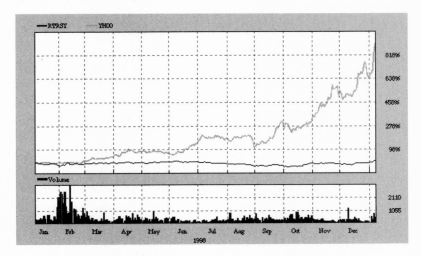

Source: J. P. Morgan adr.com

Monitoring with slaves that liberate you

The *Wall Street Journal*, Yahoo and several other web publishers will monitor portfolios and news for you free. You can get portfolio reports by e-mail and as 'custom newspapers' on line with all the news on companies you are following. I call these great free services the slaves that have liberated me. Most of the information I need is reliably gathered and delivered in a well-organized format so that I can spend my time studying and interpreting information and using it. I also get e-mails on subjects that I need to be kept up to speed on.

Corporate web sites – a new dimension in investing

Corporate web sites introduce a new dimension to investors when companies set out their stalls on the Internet and present themselves to the world as they want to be seen. As the World Wide Web is interactive, we should be able to dialogue with prospect companies any time of the day or night. The investor relations sections in corporate web sites are predictably well serviced with current results, archive information, company announcements and timetables for future announcements.

This financial data is convenient but also available elsewhere. What makes corporate WWW sites especially meaningful as a new dimension is that they can tell us about their businesses at grass roots, and show us how they present themselves to the world generally and to investors in particular.

Companies with complex messages to explain use the Internet to great advantage. Monsanto is one of the world's most innovative companies, but one of the most difficult to understand. The information they deliver on `www.monsanto.com` presents their unique technology and marketing resource and is worth a visit, if not as a potential investor, as an investment web site surfer.

Research using corporate web sites also brings the opportunity for instant comparison. A broader picture of the performance of a company can always be gained if we examine its competitors: after you look at Monsanto, you may want to visit the Swiss company Novartis, who are also active in genetic seed modification, on `www.novartis.com`

I was amused when I saw an advertisement for a new information provider who claimed his Internet information service was so complete he could offer 'inside information' without all that 'inconvenient time behind bars'. Research on the net may never make you an insider, but you can be sure that if you ignore information which others use, you are always going to be an outsider.

Top companies, particularly technology leaders like Microsoft, now open video and phone links when they host investor presentations, so that all investors have an opportunity to see the level playing field at work. Video conferencing on corporate WWW sites is set to completely transform corporate investor relations and communications, possibly within the next couple of years, depending on the limits of bandwidth capacity.

Tune into the future

The Internet is an educator and we can learn the new skills in our own time. You can start at CNN's Investment Challenge – `www.sandbox.net` from `www.cnnfn.com` It demystifies charts, explains technical terms, sets you up to run a phantom portfolio and equips you for dealing on line with an Internet broker, which is more convenient and a fraction of the cost of traditional broking.

If you browse around the learning resources on the net you will be rewarded with clear and straightforward explanations of formidable sounding terms and will cash in on the benefits of the convenience and low cost of on line investing offers.

This article by Leo Fasciocco from CNNFN's web site is headlined 'Tune into the future' and challenges investors to look ahead:

> There are two characteristics of the stock market that vary sharply with the way the average investor thinks. The first is that the stock market is a 'discounting' mechanism. The market is always looking ahead, which means that current stock prices are not really based on today's facts, but rather on perceptions about the future. The average investor is often not looking out far enough. Instead, he is enthralled with the past – in stock market parlance, old news.
>
> The second characteristic of the stock market is that it is 'dynamic'. It is always changing with changes in companies and in line with opportunities. The economy, interest rates, new technology, and international unrest are only some of the dynamics that impact the overall market and, more importantly, the fortunes of individual companies and their shareholders.

The average investor tends to cling to the static. He or she is slow to let go of past concepts and to adapt to change, which requires letting go of the old and adjusting to the new.

There are a lot of tricks you can use to adapt to these 'discounting and dynamic' characteristics of the market. The first is to try to be well informed, especially about individual companies. The second trick is to think ahead and don't get caught up in what the majority thinks. And third, don't be afraid to let go of past ideas.

4

THE
THREE RS OF
INVESTING:
RESEARCH, RISK
AND REWARD

To invest successfully you need not understand beta, efficient markets, modern portfolio theory, option pricing or emerging markets . . . Your goal as an investor should simply be to purchase, at a rational price, a part interest in an easily understandable business whose earnings are virtually certain to be materially higher five, ten and twenty years from now. Over time you will find only a few companies that meet these standards — so when you see one that qualifies you should buy a meaningful amount of stock. You must also avoid the temptation to stray from your guidelines. If you are not willing to own a stock for ten years don't even think about it for ten minutes. Put together a portfolio of companies whose aggregate earnings march upwards over the years and so will the portfolio's value.

Warren Buffett – 1997

This chapter introduces the subject of investment research, explains the approach taken in the company reports that follow later, and examines some dynamics of risk, reward, buying, selling and timing.

The research menu

Research means different things to different people. A financial accountant will scrutinize all the niceties of the figures in a set of accounts. An investment banker will have one eye on a merger or acquisition and the other on the lookout for a management buy out if the merger plan does not work. A marketing man will zoom in on products, competitive advantages and distribution networks. Value investors will weigh up the balance sheet to see if the company's shares are undervalued on the market. A technical investor may not even look at the accounts and only study charts instead. Warren Buffett looks for companies whose earnings are virtually certain to be materially higher year after year, and so should we.

Research is either 'fundamental' or 'technical'. Fundamental research concerns essentially the business's structure, operating track record, profitability and prospects. The grass roots fundamentals of major companies are entrenched and information prepared can be used for years ahead as long as it is updated. However technical research, which analyses what has happened and is likely to happen with a share's market performance is time sensitive and has a short sell-by date. *Portfolio 2001*'s research horizon is fundamental.

Technical research has been demystified on the Internet and in Part Two I introduce the subject briefly and list excellent stop-off points for technical information.

Picking a company as an investment and picking an exceptional restaurant for a three-course gourmet meal can start in similar ways. The restaurant must have a celebrated chef, an excellent reputation for its specialities, draw custom away from competitors, and be the sort of establishment we look forward to spending time at. The company in which we are thinking of becoming stake holders must have brilliant managers, an excellent track record and be the sort of business establishment we want to own a part of. The gourmet dinner menu and the research report can also be built up on similar lines. The starters should whet our appetites, the main course should be hearty and filling and the dessert suggestive.

Here is my suggested menu for a treat at Chez r&R – the low-risk high-reward research establishment. Bon appetit.

Chez r & R
Gourmet Growth Story Research Menu

Appetisers:
Fattened profit margins lightly sautéed on a bed of seasonal cash flow

The Growth Story Main Course:
Tender medallions of monopolistic pricing power stuffed with former competitors, and marinated in a rich innovative sauce of superior products
Served with a side order of volume growth and sprinkled with extra wide margins

Dessert:
Earnings soufflé— a delicious but salutary reminder that timing is everything, and that even the fastest risers can collapse quickly

A corny after dinner joke to remind of risks round every corner:

Question: What happens when an A-Class Mercedes goes round a corner?

Answer: Mercedes bends.

The bill? In what currency would you like it? The currency can make a big difference to what the growth story will really be worth in the end.

The research menu: the appetisers

Blue chip companies have strong financial resources and, though my research is not weighted to financial analysis, these three financial appetisers are delightful and can be essential:

- revenue, profit and margin growth
- a good return on equity
- a strong positive cash flow

A strong positive cash flow points to operational success and management's effectiveness in planning and controlling its operations. It also reassures investors that funds will be available for ambitious growth plans without diluting shareholders' interests through capital increases made to fund them. When companies have strong positive cash flows they build cash reserves and the opposite happens: they buy back their shares and, pro rata, the remaining shareholders come to own more of the company. Share buy back programmes for *Portfolio 2001* companies are all mentioned in the research in Part Three if they have been initiated or are expected.

The research menu: the growth story main course

The investing strategy proposed is to invest on the strength of the growth story with a focus on long-term value. The growth story is therefore the meat of the research, and concentrates on:

- management's track record
- the growth story past, present and future
- competitive advantages, and strategies to keep competitive advantage
- the sector and competitors
- the rational price for the investment

Researching and updating:

The Research reports on the companies that follow are an information resource you can easily update using current information. I have used the *Wall Street Journal* (WSJ) as my main research database; for a $59 annual subscription fee I have – at the click of a mouse – ready access to all the news from the world's leading financial newspaper updated twenty-four hours a day, a range of free portfolio and monitoring services, plus access to an extensive database of background information on most of the world's top companies. The WSJ have conveniently arranged their accumulated company information databases in briefing books on individual companies. Their background information is supported by fundamental information on profitability and earnings presented in a straightforward format, and is supported by both excellent interactive graphics and easily accessible current and archived news. For a fee, all news items in their archives can be accessed.

There are now several excellent investment information providers on the Internet with free sites. `www.dowjones.com` was launched in June 1999 by the owners of the WSJ and will meet the basic information needs of many investors.

Company web sites:

A prospect company's web site should be a good place to start or update research. Here is a print off from the web site of the clothing chain The Gap `www.gap.com` where early in 1987 I read this very simple narrative. It described a business I could understand and as I liked shopping at the Gap I was encouraged to research the company as a target investment. Time spent studying the company soon suggested that there was scope for a phenomenal investing opportunity:

> (GAP) started in 1969, when San Francisco real estate developer Donald G. Fisher tried to exchange a pair of blue jeans. He visited store after store, only to find jeans departments that were disorganised, poorly stocked, and difficult to shop. In August of that year, Fisher and his wife, Doris, created the antithesis: a jeans-only store that was neatly organised by size. The name they gave it was an allusion to the generation gap.
>
> Gap expanded rapidly – first in California and then throughout the country. Gap also began selling more than just jeans, and in 1974 it began creating its own private label clothing and accessories . . . In 1983, with 550 Gap stores already open, the company acquired Banana Republic, a two-store chain with a thriving catalogue business. Gap, Inc expanded upon the chain's established line of travel and safari wear . . .
>
> In 1985, after one of his own unsuccessful shopping trips, Gap

President Mickey Drexler found that comfortable, basic clothing for kids was virtually unavailable. His experience led to the first GapKids store, opened in 1986, featuring fashionable, not fussy, clothes appealing to parents who wore Gap clothing themselves. In addition to the kid-sized versions of Gap basics, GapKids own product development team began to design clothing in styles specifically for kids. In 1990, GapKids launched the babyGap line of infant and toddler clothing, which is now available in virtually all GapKids stores and departments. The first Gap store outside the United States opened in 1987.

This simple – almost folksy – tale from The Gap web site illustrates a key message for researchers. Information we research need not be pretentious or difficult to understand to warrant serious consideration.

I soon understood from reading company background information that The Gap was a very focused company. Further research revealed that it has also been one of the world's most successful businesses. By January 1999 The Gap had reached a market capitalization of $35 billion dollars. An investment of $10,000 made five years earlier would have grown over 600% and been worth $64,000 by that time. It is a myth that only technology companies produce mega returns; spectacular gains can be achieved by investing in conventional businesses we can all can understand. Further research I conducted on The Gap by visiting its web site, this time as a potential on line customer, reaffirmed how well they marketed their products and why they are also a successful e-trader.

Investment research can be top down or bottom up

Research starts top down with the question 'where should I invest?' Jim Slater, a notably successful British investor and author, has titled a book on investing *The Zulu Principle*. He chose the name after reading about the legendary endurance that Zulu warriors gained from single-minded dedication to physical prowess. Warren Buffett takes an approach on somewhat similar lines advising us to *concentrate* on investments we can *understand*. With the information, computing, communications, life sciences and global financial services revolutions all taking place at the same time, the choice of new investing opportunities can be bewildering. But commencing investment research need not be a daunting challenge if you first look for shares in business sectors you can understand. After you have identified these sectors from your top down research overview you will probably have in hand a list of individual companies in the sectors that interest you as prospects for detailed research. In investing jargon, you will call these prospect companies your research horizon and the next step will be detailed research on the target companies, known as bottom up research.

Before you start committing time to detailed bottom up research on companies bear in mind that research requires time. If you are over-ambitious with your list of research targets it can easily become counter-productive and you may not have the time to do justice to your enquiries. I should also warn you of a debilitating computer virus that comes from drawing too much research from the Internet known as analysis paralysis. Investing wisdom maintains that owning a basket of shares spreads risk and every portfolio should have a good few shares. But again I caution you to be on your guard. Every share you own also introduces its own risks and it takes time to monitor an investment. There is a crucial balance to strike between spreading risk over a number of investments and effectively focusing your efforts on the compelling r&R (low-risk high-reward) opportunities which will really make you money.

Building an earnings forecast

A growth investing strategy starts with the earnings forecast because earnings expectations determine valuations of shares on markets and earnings growth propels share prices. Taking a view on an earnings forecast also marks a vital threshold for investors between having information and using it effectively. Consensus forecasts built from estimates published by professional analysts are now widely available on the Internet and in other publications for all American and British shares, plus well over a thousand leading foreign shares listed as ADRs on Wall Street. In fact earnings forecasts in the US are now almost as commonplace as share price quotes and with the surge in discount and Internet investing, on line brokers make Wall Street investment bank research available to clients free or at minimal cost. Your broker should be in a position to support you with access to published research but for dyed in the wool independents, who want to be in a position to find everything themselves, the research library Multex www.multex.com sells research reports by investment banks and brokers to the public. Earnings forecasts are also published for companies outside the US but some effort may be needed to find suitable information. In Chapter 9, the Webliography, listings of good sources for earnings forecasts globally are included.

Earnings per share forecasts are calculated by dividing the net after-tax income expected for a company by the number of ordinary shares outstanding. A company that has after-tax income of a million dollars and a million shares has earnings per share of one dollar. If earnings per share grow at 12.5% per annum compound, and the number of issued shares remains unchanged, earnings per share will grow from $1 to $2.25 in five years. Making an earnings forecast at times calls for specialised knowledge but ultimately all forecasts, no matter how complex, are built primarily from three sources of information all in the public domain. The first is the company growth story and management indications, the second is the marketplace and the third is the macroeconomic environment. The growth story is the real key to forecasting earnings. Established businesses have track records which reflect past achievements and management give public indications on what they expect to achieve in future.

Start with good information. As an example Bloomberg on `www.bloomberg.com` have a well-presented earnings centre which includes past, present and future information. The Bloomberg page looks like this for Tiffany & Co:

Recommendations

Number of brokers recommending as:		Months ago	
	1	2	3
Strong Buy	4	5	5	6
Moderate Buy	11	10	10	9
Hold	4	3	3	3
Moderate Sell	0	0	0	0
Strong Sell	0	0	0	0
Mean*	1.95	1.83	1.83	1.78

*(strong buy) 1.00 - 5.00 (strong sell)

Earnings Estimates

	This Quarter (Jul 99)	Next Quarter (Oct 99)	This Year (Jan 00)	Next Year (Jan 01)
Avg Estimate	0.44	0.41	2.99	3.50
# of Analysts	15	14	19	19
Low Estimate	0.43	0.40	2.90	3.31
High Estimate	0.45	0.45	3.05	3.65
Year Ago EPS	0.37	0.34	2.50	2.99
EPS Growth	20.19%	21.77%	19.64%	17.03%

Consensus EPS Trend

	This Quarter (Jul 99)	Next Quarter (Oct 99)	This Year (Jan 00)	Next Year (Jan 01)	Long Term Growth
Current	0.44	0.41	2.99	3.50	17.17%
7 Days Ago	0.44	0.41	2.99	3.50	17.17%
30 Days Ago	0.44	0.41	2.93	3.41	17.14%
60 Days Ago	0.44	0.41	2.91	3.39	17.21%
90 Days Ago	0.44	0.41	2.87	3.50	17.21%

Earnings Growth

	Last 5 Years (Actual Growth)	This Year (Dec 00)	Next Year (Dec 01)	Next 5 Years	Price/ Earnings
TIFFANY & CO	26.50%	19.50%	17.00%	17.20%	27.80
RETAIL-JEWELRY	16.50%	21.70%	19.00%	17.20%	12.00
S&P 500	10.30%	8.10%	5.20%	7.00%	26.80

Earnings History

	Apr 99	Jan 99	Oct 98	Jul 98	Apr 98
Estimate	0.38	1.41	0.34	0.34	0.28
Actual	0.44	1.49	0.34	0.37	0.31
Difference	0.06	0.08	0.00	0.03	0.03
% Surprise	15.79%	5.67%	0.00%	8.82%	10.71%

Data provided by Zacks Investment Research www.zacks.com

Your first input when evaluating an earnings forecast is to ask questions. Ask yourself question after question until you have assembled information that you feel is secure. An obvious first question would be what management have disclosed on earnings prospects. Who are the management and how does their track record look? Do they think they will be able to maintain and even possibly increase revenues and margins and can they produce better profit margins than their competitors? What are their competitive advantages? How are the competitors doing and is there one who is doing better than your prospect? What is the exposure to emerging markets? What growth plans have been published and is the money there to implement them? What are the prospects for share buy backs? What are the risks to profits in the growth story?

The questions you ask will be different from company to company and time frame to time frame. Where it is reasonable you can raise queries with the company. You can contact the investor relations managers with your query by letter, fax, phone or through their web site, but any information you seek from a company must belong in the public domain.

You should also make comparisons to form a perspective and resources accessible on the Internet will again make this easy for you. Graphics programmes enable you to compare shares with other shares and with indexes using web sites accessible on `www.wsrn.com` Comprehensive analysis programmes like `www.marketguide.com` introduce a range of comparative data extensively analysed.

After you have questioned and compared there will probably still be questions you want answered and you should raise raise them with your brokers and other advisors. *Portfolio 2001* strategy urges you to be well-informed but you will be doing no one a favour by becoming a DIY enthusiast. Your task is to get well-informed and when the best way you can do this is by speaking to advisors and well-informed people that will be the way to go.

The growth story is the key to every earnings forecast
Studying and getting to grips with the growth story of an individual company is more meaningful than mechanically taking on board indications published by analysts. Investing is a process in which research can take months and even years. It would be glib for me to write 'study the sector' because simply getting to grips with the companies that comprise any sector will take time, particularly in fast-changing and innovative areas like life sciences and technology. Researching the marketplace and the macroeconomy again follows the route of asking question after question, but the questions are different and the answers are likely to be more obscure. An important advantage of investing in leading global companies is

that you can expect that news on all matters that affect them will be well-aired in the financial press and probably also in the mainstream press.

The Internet is an open information medium that works as the central nervous system for the investing community and as its global mouthpiece. An early and memorable example of a vociferous Internet community was in 1995 when Intel's first Pentium chip had a defect that manifested itself while processing certain advanced mathematical calculations. Intel first denied there was a problem and the Internet, which arguably owes its success to Intel and Moore's Law, erupted with thousands of complaints from Pentium users. In response to the outcry, Intel rapidly accepted that there was a fault and did what was necessary to rectify it.

Discussion forums are common on investor web sites and a range of investors from millionaires to paupers, cranks to geniuses and long-term investors to speculators and option traders all raise their queries, declaim on their causes and vent their passions. It can be tedious paging through all these comments but it will probably help to understand the investing issues in a given situation. A free service **www.companysleuth.com** even e-mails you a daily list of all the discussion forum comments on the companies you list for them to sleuth for you.

Researching the marketplace often builds understanding of the business at grass roots. I cited the example of buying at The Gap as an experience that inspires confidence in the company's merchandising skills. My own good experiences with using Microsoft software have helped make me a believer in its strengths but if I start to see computers advertised running with Linux operating systems instead of Microsoft, I will start asking questions again. In late 1998 a new generation of cellular phones supplied with prepaid cards hit the market and opened a new market potential for the cellular phone industry. For the first time, potential customers included almost every teenager in the Western world, occasional business users and those social users not in a position to secure credit contracts with cellular phone operators. In hindsight, the well-publicized success prepaid phones enjoyed was an obvious predictor of the earnings surge that followed and is continuing in the industry.

Every growth story has to be examined in the context of national and global economic conditions and this means some forecasting for national and global economies has to be addressed. All matters that affect the US and leading nations in Europe and Asia are fully discussed in the financial press and, in changing conditions, we all have to learn from day to day. Fortunately the resources available to us for information get better and better. Dr Ed Yardeni's web site **www.yardeni.com** is a magnificent presentation of accessible and well-explained economic data on the US and other leading world economies supported by illustrative charts that crystallize key information segments. Morgan Stanley Dean Witter's top economists publish their views on the events of the day every day on **www.ms.com** and Merrill Lynch's top team publish regular briefings on **www.merrill-lynch.com** The Brookings Institute public policy think tank in Washington www.brookings.org report on debates that influence global policy makers on issues such as containing volatility in emerging markets in future. The World Bank, the IMF and the OECD keep us well informed on what they are doing to manage the global economy and what they are forecasting for the future on **www.worldbank.org, www.imf.org** and **www.oecd.org.** The Webliography in Chapter 9 lists key reference sites to support economics research.

Earnings forecasts have short sell-by dates

The latest expiry date for the shelf life of any forecast will be the date of the next company report and events before then could make the forecast obsolete overnight. When considering whether a forecast needs to be revised there is a world of difference between fine tuning to accommodate changes or actually changing your mind about a company's entrenched growth prospects. Modest revisions in earnings expectations for the next quarter, half year or even a year are likely to have short term effects on the share price but need not trigger any change in investing strategy. On the other hand, if you have reviewed information that changes your overall opinion on earnings growth prospects, or if you loose confidence in the growth story, you should not invest. And if you have invested, consider selling and doing something better with your money. The risk-reward relationship could have shunted to low-reward and high-risk, the opposite of the low-reward high-risk (r&R) relationship we should have.

The earnings soufflé in the dinner menu at Chez r&R's was a

reminder that what goes up can come down and the Mercedes Bends after dinner joke introduced the crucial 'What Can Go Wrong?' question after the sumptuous dinner. As after dinner jokes are alas inclined to be, the joke was also in bad taste as Daimler Benz were quick to remedy the problems with the A-Class car that caused it to topple. But investors should not forget that no one ever expected Daimler Benz, of all companies in the world, to a launch car on the market that was potentially dangerous. Even with the greatest companies there are going to be product risk and unexpected events that necessitate our revising forecasts.

The Portfolio 2001 'what if' forecast worksheet

Research reports for companies in *Portfolio 2001* start with a 'what if' forecast worksheet that suggests future earnings per share and future market prices. For the life science and technology prospects, earnings and share prices are targeted to the year 2002 and for the other prospects to the year 2001. The information starts with the last reported year's earnings and earnings for following years are increased by an estimated earnings-per-share growth rate in line with our expectations, past performance, the indications management have recently given and the estimates analysts have published. Target prices for the share are then set by multiplying the forecast earnings by a guess at the price earnings multiple at which the share might trade in future years. This guess is made after taking into account the earnings multiple at which the share is actually trading at the time, the rate at which it is expected to grow profits, the earnings multiple at which it has traded in the past and the multiples at which other companies in the same sector trade plus a view of the direction of markets in future. As US Companies report earnings quarterly, it is possible for investors to work continuously with fresh data.

Unlike earnings forecasts price targets are not essential but as markets will value shares on potential rather than history, we are forced to take a view on how we think our shares will perform. A worksheet approach that looks at market price potential disciplines investing and will support a monitoring process. Everyone expects great things from Microsoft hence the rich multiple of over fifty times earnings its share commands. However, I would not be comfortable with an earnings multiple of fifty times current earnings, even for Microsoft, unless I think that earnings will surprise on the upside of expectations. I detail my thinking when discussing assumptions used in the worksheets for each company.

Suggesting future price to earnings ratios is far more speculative than suggesting future earnings because, even if the forecast earnings were certain (which forecasts by definition can never be) it would still be misleading to pretend that price targets are going to be accurate. To try to square the circle, *Portfolio 2001* reports give a target price range that starts with the target price and goes on to show prices 10 per cent below and 10 per cent above the target. The three prices span a range of some 20 per cent which should be a useful guide for investing and monitoring.

Earnings forecasts and guesses at market prices become dangerous if ever we think of them as cast in stone. Making the same specific 'what if' assumptions as I make in this book at some undefined future date will certainly be the wrong thing for you to do. Your 'what if' asssumptions must be refreshed and forecasts must be treated as mobile signposts on the road. They must be repositioned after all company results, news and changes in the marketplace or the economic climate. Otherwise they may point you in the wrong direction, directing you away from the promised land and straight down a precipice.

The $64,000 question: is the investment worth the risk?

If we looked at investing in 1000 Intel shares in June 1999, our research would have revealed the following profile:

	Per Share	Per 1000 Shares
Share Price 6 June 1999.	$53.25	$53,250
Estimated earnings fiscal 1999.	$ 2.33	$2,330
Price to earnings ratio	22.85.	

The share may look attractive to us because we think that Intel has good news in the pipeline, the market is going to get stronger generally and the effect of market strength could boost Intel's shares to a price to earnings ratio of about 27.5 times earnings. If so, the value of our 1000 Intel shares would rise by 22 per cent to $64,000.

The importance of the guess at market valuations gets even more telling if we compare the effect of changes in market valuation to actual performance against estimates. If Intel continues to trade at a price to earnings ratio of 27.5 times earnings and exceeds its earnings forecast by an impressive 5 per cent it will earn $2.44 per share and be priced at $67.10 reflecting a gain of almost 5 per cent. If earnings miss estimates by a disappointing 5 per cent they will be $2.21 and at 27.5 times earnings the share price will be $60.77 reflecting a loss of marginally more than 5 per cent. The effect of the deviation in earnings either way will be far less than the effect of any change in the market multiple of earnings at which share trades. You will expect when you buy an Intel share that the market will rate it in future at least as highly as when you made the purchase but there are risks that cannot be ignored. Between 1988 and 1994 Intel traded at a price to earnings ratio of below 12.6. Between 1994 and 1997 Intel's price to earnings ratio climbed to over 20 after it demonstrated strong profitability and grew earnings at above 33 per cent for five years. For 1999 analysts are expecting earnings per share growth in the range of 22.5 per cent and making a case to buy Intel at $53.25 involves a measured risk with a a a healthy upside potential as long as you will have time to let the market work for you. In any year that you invest there is probably a one in four chance of taking a loss on the market as a whole. If your investing horizon is a year or less your risk is greater and you will be gambling rather than investing. If your investing horizon extends to several years a well-timed investment in a good company made after rigorous research is likely to pay off.

Reviewing a researched investment to see if it attracts

With markets having reached all-time highs there is a tendency for commentators and analysts to look for novel measures that reveal hidden value. This accounts for some of the incredible valuations of Internet shares and a myopic approach to risk which many analysts and commentators have adopted. But even the most conservative investors often look beyond the strict limitations of conventional valuation parameters when assessing the worth of their holdings. Warren Buffett brings into the equation as an important attraction what he calls the 'internal return' an investment is earning for him. To do this he imports an accounting fiction and looks at the retained profits in a company after dividends paid to shareholders. His argument is that de facto, as the shareholder, he owns his pro rata share of undistributed profits and will eventually benefit from them even if it is only when he ultimately sells the share at a profit. In Buffett's case the subject is raised for discussion and information, not to hype the value of his assets. On the contrary, he has been a weighty critic of markets that appear overvalued.

Every investment has to be looked at on its own merits and we are bound to see attractions and disadvantages which we respond to differently. If we consider again a sensationally successful technology company like Intel, the attraction of new technology and products in the pipeline will certainly eclipse nominal dividends which Intel pays and a share of undistributed earnings. Intel is not a share for everyone, and the drawbacks and attractions of investing in Intel can be drawn with a broad brush on these lines:

On the minus side

1) Technology may not be a sector you understand and you should not be seduced into buying a share because of a historic 10,000 per cent plus appreciation over the last twenty-seven years. In the years to come, Intel will probably have some ups and downs and the 'what can go wrong?' section of my Intel report is not short.

2) A financial year is not always a meaningful time frame to measure performance for an innovative company like Intel that invests billions of dollars year after year in developing leading edge technology. In the past, Intel have invested relentlessly in both new facilities and in research and development to lift themselves out of business reversals. While new capital investments can take years before they pay off markets measure performance only in annual reporting time frames and Intel's annual results may not reflect its real world achievements. In 1998, which started with some refocusing and competitive problems, the intrinsic value of Intel was growing for much of the year while the share price was depressing.

3) Monitoring investments can become excessively time consuming and a core technology company makes the news every day.

4) With a market capitalisation of over $220 billion Intel is a leading momentum share. A rapid fall in Intel's share price could be distressing if funds flow away from the company, the technology sector, the semiconductor sector, or even the consumer sector generally.

5) Intel is vulnerable to price competition and in a severe recession could be hampered by excess manufacturing capacity.

On the plus side:
1) Intel is a brilliant innovative technology and marketing company with undisputed global leadership in microprocessor technology and has been one of the world's greatest investments. Earnings are virtually certain to be materially higher five, ten and twenty years down the line and growth is predictable.
2) Earnings should continue to grow at a healthy compounded rate and even the hypothetical internal return in Intel with dividends paid will probably exceed what money could currently earn in fixed income securities.
3) Company earnings per share are after corporation tax has been paid and as the owner of a share you only will only incur a capital gains tax liability when you sell your shares. When you own a share that performs as well as Intel has in the past appreciable gains in your wealth that accumulate are sheltered from tax.
4) As long as strong earnings are maintained the share price is likely to keep rising. Intel have thrilled investors with several share splits in the past and are likely to continue doing so.

When making investment decisions we will not all have the same expectations for Intel, or for other companies, or for markets and our circumstances, knowledge and attitudes are bound to be very different. I may be fearful of Innovators and want to invest in Profit Harvesters only. I may also expect that the baby boomers legendary savings will be invested for them by financial organisations and Morgan Stanley Dean Witter is the one to invest in because I like their track record and business model. If I think that Internet brokers will get a bigger slice of the business, I may invest in Charles Schwab instead, or I may invest in both. In spite of its high price I may also buy some shares in The Gap because I think it is such an amazing company and I think I understand what they are doing.

You may be a rocket scientist who wants to invest in innovation and you understand Intel's technology better than most brokers. After conducting your research you may even recognize more value in Intel than Wall Street does and have the confidence to back your opinion with an investment. You may also know enough about Boeing's strengths as a space age company to recognise a buying opportunity while the share is depressed. You may even have strong views about Monsanto and be convinced that genetic modification of seeds is not harmful and is essential technology to provide food for a burgeoning world population. Markets exist because we all have different expectations and priorities and for every seller, at a price there is a buyer.

Technical information

Fundamental research is essential and no investing processes and disciplines can proceed without it. Live technical data can be essential when timing investments and there are important benefits to gain from the convenience of using charts as an information source. Technical research has been demystified on the Internet. CNN's Investment Challenge site on www.sandbox.net brings the world of Internet investing, including technical research and on line dealings with discount brokers, within the reach of even novice investors. As technical data is time sensitive it is not appropriate material to include in *Portfolio 2001* reports. The subject is introduced in Chapter 7 on Using Information and in Chapter 9, the Webliography, several excellent web sites are listed.

Portfolio 2001's top down and bottom up research and web site

Your research efforts will be supported by a good range of web sites and by www.portfolio2001.com where earnings announcement and archived news on our 51 prospects will be published to update you conveniently at all times. It will also publish current technical indicators for the prospect companies. Dare I say in the idiom of our times . . . *enjoy!*

Risk

Risk dynamics

Low-risk high-reward (r&R) investing follows a commitment to recognising, managing and moderating risk wherever possible. There are five directions risk can be expected to come from which can be recognised:
1) Investor specific risks – your own strategy, skills and resources
2) Company specific and business risks
3) Risk in the system including risk in market valuations
4) Currency risks
5) The volatility of momentum shares.

Investor specific risks

You have a far better chance of making money in a casino than by buying shares if you lack the financial resources to hold them for years or if you are not sufficiently well-informed on what you are doing. Timing is also always crucial and if you buy when the market trend is moving against you, you are likely to find that far from buying bargains you have committed your money to losses that may take years to recoup. William O'Neil spells this out clearly in his book *How to Make Money in Stocks and Shares*. If a share price falls 50 per cent it has to recover 100 per cent before you break even – and how often does a share price really double? You risk your capital if you invest impulsively and if you keep churning your holdings opportunistically. You will put your holdings at risk if you 'orphan' them and stop monitoring. Risk is introduced not only when shares are bought at prices that are not rational but it can be introduced if shares are not sold when they should be at a profit or at a loss. Successful investors discipline themselves to cut their losses to protect their assets and they concentrate on making money by running with their profits. This does not mean they never sell shares that are doing well. There are times when high prices are clearly too opportunistic or vulnerable and at these times selling has to be on the agenda.

Risk is also introduced when investors throw money at markets without having an investing strategy or without an investing strategy they are managing. It need not be a growth investing strategy. Many investors will be more effective following value investing strategies, special situations, investing for high yields or other opportunities. There is no case to make that growth investing is bound to be more rewarding than value investing and you will find books and articles full of statistics that 'prove' growth has outperformed value – or vice versa. The fact is that at the end of the day investors make or lose money themselves. There is no single certain winning strategy for all markets at all times and investors can follow several strategies as long as they understand what they are doing.

Company specific risks

Portfolio 2001 is composed of big name blue-chip companies with immense financial resources but, no matter how great the name you invest in, mishaps can dent share prices.

No Daimler-Benz investor or A-Class Mercedes Benz buyer expected the car would be unsafe and prone to overturn. After the A-Class débâcle in November 1997, Daimler-Benz recalled the first 3000 A-Class models supplied and halted deliveries pending modifications to make the car safe. The share prices fell sharply as illustrated in the following chart:

DAIMLER-BENZ ADR (DAI) OCTOBER 1997 TO SEPTEMBER 1998

Chart Wall Street Journal

Investors in major companies often need only patience to ride out problems caused by mishaps and with Daimler-Benz, Europe's largest industrial company, the A-Class mishap was a high-profile setback that was never going to account for more than a than a minor part of earnings in its Mercedes Benz car division. Investors in Daimler-Benz who did not have to sell their shares while the price was depressed reaped the benefits of an investment in a superb company, particularly when Daimler-Benz went on to merge with Chrysler in 1998. By the end of 1998 Daimler's share price had performed superbly and the A-Class safety problems were all but history.

Risks in the system

Risk is in the DNA of all equity markets and is in the DNA of the free market capitalist system. It is also in the psyche of markets which have the tendency of being driven excessively at times by fear or greed. Volatility in currency, bond and equity markets, successes and failures, booms, busts and recessions, inflation and even deflation are all par for the course in the 'unfettered, unrelenting search for profit' which drives global capitalism.

In mid-1997 many investors thought that global economic growth was unstoppable and the Dow Jones Industrial average took off on a trajectory that lifted it from 7400 to 8350 in six weeks. If it remained on this track the Index would have reached 100,000 by the year 2000 – ten times the 10,000 target that bullish analysts were calling. Later in 1998 the economic crisis in parts of Asia took its toll and in September 1998 a Russian economic implosion wrought havoc with markets.

With share investments we look forward to a bright progression where increased earnings and higher market multiples gear the market ratings of shares up. Risk is the dark side and mirror image of this bright progression. When earnings fall, the price multiple at which the share trades also falls gearing the prices down. Buying an Intel share with forecast earnings of $2.33 at a price to earnings ratio of 27.5 for $64, following the '$64,000 Question' example above, introduces the risk that if Intel were to disappoint the market and grow earnings at only 15 per cent, the earnings multiple might fall to 20 or even lower. At the reduced price to earnings ratio of 20 the Intel share would be priced at $53,59 resulting in a of 15 per cent. And, perish the thought, if at the same time market sentiment moved from greed to fear and the earnings multiple fell to 15 times earnings the loss reflected would be over 35 per cent.

Regional Currency risks

In the globalized economy at times currency will be the dominant investing dynamic. Predictably it affects the fortunes of importers and exporters directly but often its effects for investors are insidious. Global enterprises like Novartis, the Swiss-based Life Sciences Group, earn significant revenues from overseas subsidiaries and at times what happens on the ground with their foreign subsidiaries gets distorted when earnings of their domestic currencies are consolidated in group results. When the Swiss franc rises, even if

Novartis's overseas operations are growing earnings admirably in local currency terms, the value of their income contribution to the group is going to be devalued in Swiss franc group accounts. And conversely, if the Swiss franc falls in value, overseas earnings will be artificially boosted in value in group accounts.

Regional problems can also affect the prospects of financial services companies severely. HSBC Group are a successful, major and well-managed global financial services and banking group with an entrenched banking infra structure in Asia. For many investors thay are seen as a proxy investment for Asia.

Predictably market reaction to Asia's economic and currency problems in 1997 decimated the share price of HSBC. After staging a rally in 1998 HSBC shares plummeted again on bad news in the region and on Russia's economic implosion, recovering only when regional prospects and market sentiment to Asia improved in 1999. The following chart shows HSBC's ADR compared to the underlying security quoted in London and Hong Kong and the volatile share movements for both securities. (Currency fluctuations did not affect the relationship of the ADR and the underlying security's price because the Hong Kong dollar was pegged to the US dollar.)

HSBC GROUP : 1997 AND 1998 : ADR AND UNDERLYING SECURITY:

RIGHT-HAND SCALE PERCENTAGE MOVE FROM 1.1.1997 to
30.12.1998. The lower scale reflects volume.

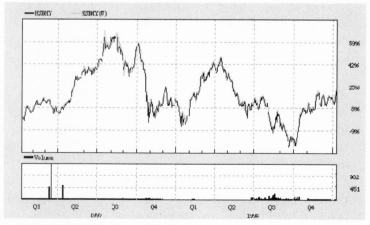

Chart www.adr.com

The countries in Asia where HSBC have operations experienced severe economic crises that were bound to affect the market rating of HSBC. When markets collapse regionally the devastation can be severe as this chart illustrating market falls in South East Asia for a year to October 1998 reveals. Korea and Thailand recorded falls at the time of almost 60 per cent:

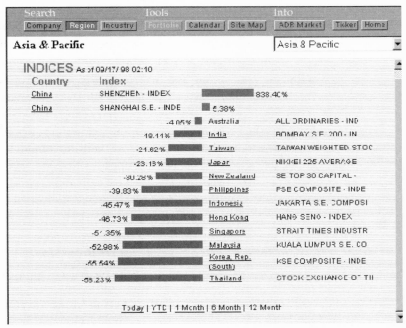

Chart **www.adr.com**

The volatility risk with momentum shares

Because they are bought and sold in high volumes by institutions and funds as they move money in and out of sectors and markets the shares of top companies are bound to be momentum shares. In addition to shares bought as investments to hold by individuals and funds, large sums of money are invested by index tracking funds in shares that make up main indexes. When money flows in to or away from the markets or sectors this exacerbates supply and demand pressures

The prices of momentum shares rise strongly when funds flow positively and fall dramatically when funds flow negatively. When investor sentiment turns negative, momentum shares are likely to be the first to fall and they can fall like lead balloons.

Most sudden falls in share prices follow market over-reaction to the news of the day. Any event which can affect markets is commented on in the financial press, the mainstream press, on TV and radio and on the Internet. When news coverage is overdone and too much brouhaha is made about any event, analysts refer to it as noise or fuss. Fuss makes waves, but only fundamentals have sustained effects on economies and markets.

At the end of this chapter, in the section on the two 'F' words of investing: fuss and fundamentals, I discuss approaches I have found useful to help interpret news when monitoring events to decide whether media activity amounts to fuss or to fundamental change.

When markets are distracted by fuss, prices can fall steeply for brief periods until the focus moves back to fundamentals. These are times when mispricing can be rife and well-informed, alert investors are ready to pounce on buying opportunities.

Reward

Improved earnings and price to earnings relationships of shares

In *Portfolio 2001* I use price to earnings ratios for current and future years to suggest potential rewards because they are universally used yardsticks. Comparing price earnings references from different publications can get confusing because newspapers quote historic earnings and markets are influenced by expectations of future earnings.

To avoid confusion, when you refer to price to earnings ratios, you need to identify them as trailing for last year's earnings or the last twelve months' earnings (abbreviated as TTM), current for this year's forecast or forward for next year and other years ahead. To avoid confusion it helps to mention an actual year – saying for example estimated 1999 earnings, or actual 1998 earnings. Price to earnings ratios are simplistic and widely criticized as a measure of value because they do not always reflect the actual performance of a business. For example, devious managers can boost earnings per share without really improving business performance and acquisitions, which result in earnings being taken in retrospectively to the beginning of a financial year, inflate earnings per share artificially.

The weaknesses of the measure as an analytical tool go much deeper and investors who do financial and performance evaluations will look at a range of measures. The thesis of this book is to invest on the strength of the growth story and in this context price earnings as a measure works well.

The *Financial Times* Lex columns have developed more refined measures of value based on a range of price to earnings relationships and have constructed a Lex P/E programme which suggests fair value after looking at additional parameters. The FT Lex calculator can be accessed free on `www.ft.com` where you can input information on a company and get free computerized calculations.

The price to earnings relationship of a market is reached by adding up the prices of all the shares that make up an index and also indicates whether valuations in the market as a whole are generally high or low. If all shares in an index traded at a P/E ratio of 20 times 1999 estimated earnings the price to earnings ratio of the market would also be 20.

The top reward: earnings rise and the price to earnings multiple rises

The $64,000 question Intel example quoted above illustrates that a well-timed purchase can lead to exceptional rewards when earnings grow and the market remains strong and values a company at higher earnings multiples in anticipation of improved earnings.

The long-term investing horizon demanded by equity investing bridges the ups and downs of investment performance, the exuberance and depression of markets and the pricing anomalies which would otherwise make holding shares too high-risk to contemplate. If earnings rise consistently, eventually higher value will be reflected in the share price and this expectation underpins long-term growth investing.

Dividends and share splits

Dividends paid regularly to shareholders have traditionally been expected as a necessary ingredient for an acceptable rewards package. It is only over the last few decades that growth investors have been satisfied with capital appreciation and no dividend payments. This has come about as leading growth shares have brought rich rewards following exceptional price rises and repeated share splits that have encouraged ever-rising market prices. In line with this modern trend I have not introduced dividends into commentary on growth investing and have not quoted dividend statistics in *Portfolio 2001*. In taking this approach I am not claiming that dividends are irrelevant. Some investors will want to see a tangible benefit, even if it is small, from shares they have paid for and may only sell many years ahead.

Timing an investment: the business cycle

Since the crises of 1998 and 1999, politicians, economists and investors are more alert to their exposure to global events, and investors can look forward to the already excellent transparency and frequency of forecast revisions improving.

Traditionally, investors have looked at the business cycle first, to take a view on business and stock market prospects, but over the last decades the patterns of the business cycle have changed.

In the US until the 1990s, the business cycle doggedly followed a boom to bust pattern, with the ups and downs of business cycles being reflected by the bull and bear markets of the stock exchanges.

The top of the cycle is boom time when the monetary authorities try to slow down growth and inflation by raising interest rates. This leads to falling bond and share prices and tighter money. In the business world, a recession or slump follows with business failures and, in the ensuing gloom, property values and inflation fall. At the bottom of the cycle, in the financial markets, interest rates fall, bond prices start to rise, a recovery begins, sentiment improves and equity investors start to buy shares to be in on the recovery. In the business world, money conditions ease, property values rise, bond and share prices rise, and inflation starts to rise again as the recovery moves to a strong upswing. Rising inflation eventually triggers a sell signal to equity investors who recognize that the top of the cycle has been reached and expect a switch to high interest rates and a move towards recession.

At the start of the twenty-first century we are in uncharted waters with the business cycle. Since the early 1990s the US economy has been in a phase of sustained growth with low inflation and there are indications that boom and bust cycles have been moderated. Three positive developments support this view: the monetary authorities have become proactive and anticipate inflationary pressures with modest interest rate corrections; there is now global cooperation in working for sustained growth in the global economy; and the flow of computerized economic information provides timely and meaningful data on which monetary authorities can react quickly and – as economic management has been largely depoliticized – independently.

Much of the credit for achieving the sustained growth cycle in the United States has been given to the chairman of the American Federal Reserve, Alan Greenspan, who has been seen as the architect of a Goldilocks economy where inflation is low, moderate growth is sustained, labour demands are contained and everything is 'not too hot, not too cold, but just right'.

Until the problems in South East Asia and Japan from 1997 onward, and in Russia which imploded in 1998, the global growth story was seen by many investors as unassailable.

The uncharted waters of the new global economy

In this changing economic climate, the respective advantages of investing in Innovators and Profit Harvesters are more relevant. Innovators do things that can change their earnings dramatically and this gives them a second string to their bows while Profit Harvesters must have a strong global economy to perform well.

When the flow of funds into markets is strong and large inflows of money need to find a home, money managers often target Innovators because of their potential to grow earnings even in weak economies. The effect of this can be that their prices spike and they can only be bought at prices which allow very little scope for reward. This buying pressure often explains the price volatility of shares.

An individual investor is at an advantage strategizing to buy or hold a share. You do not have to invest other people's funds in the way money managers do, and you can and should wait until the share is at a price that you find rational.

As late as 1997 there were few free accessible current information sources a private investor could tap to support an independent and well-formed approach to global issues. However, information is now widely available and access to the day by day analysis of leading economists has been democratized.

The transparency of accessible information on global and national economies is looked at in detail in Part Two.

■

A short monitoring checklist

Monitoring is a vital part of the investing process. By pointing to opportunities it enables you to make money, and by anticipating adversity it prevents you from losing it. The minimum commitment you should make when you monitor a portfolio is to:

1. Diarize the scheduled dates for results, announcements and company meetings, anticipate and study every report of a company you invest in, or consider, and check that revenues and profits are growing, margins are being expanded or maintained and cash flow remains positive and strong – and if not, why not? There may be acceptable reasons.

2. Satisfy yourself that the growth story is still intact and refresh your earnings forecast to keep it reliable after all company and news reports. Support this information base by regular visits to the web sites of companies you are interested in and, if you can spare the time, those of their competitors, to keep yourself informed on what is happening in the industry.

3. Follow news on a company and the sector it operates in, movements in the share prices of your investments and the sector and general market news. When movements are pronounced, try and establish why. It could be that valuations in the market are changing generally, or shares you own are moving contrary to the market, and you should try and understand the underlying reasons for these changes.

4. Keep well informed on both the global economy and your national economy and on currencies that affect you.

5. Adopt a live-wire attitude – be ready to take advantage of all situations including selling opportunities; and be ready to pounce when you see buying opportunities.

How long is a monitoring ball of string?

Getting information is mechanical, but using it makes money. Most of the data you need to monitor will be prepared for you daily at no cost by the Internet financial web sites which I described as the slaves that liberate us. If I write a long boring work list, it will make monitoring a chore instead of a meaningful and even fascinating challenge, so instead I pose the question: How long should your monitoring ball of string be? I leave you to answer it after you have read Part Two, where you will find your road maps to the World Wide Web and other investor resources on the information highways. You will find the topography of web sites covered from Amazon.com, the Internet book shop that has all the books you might ever need, to the World Bank web site for all the global economic data you thought you would never need until you bought this book.

Bulls and bears can make money on stock exchanges

'Bulls can make money . . . and bears can make money . . . but pigs just can't make money.' I received these pearls of wisdom while working in the dealing room of a hedge fund manager – not prone to getting it wrong and losing money. He made the pronouncement as he closed out a trade with an uncomfortable loss, which only the day before was making him a quick killing. Markets turn against even the smartest of us with little warning when we get too greedy and we mistakenly think we are running with the bulls or hunting with the bears when the truth is we are only flying with the pigs.

The serious bull case has been compelling for most of the 1990s and, as we are in uncharted waters, it could go on longer than any pundits might reckon. However, share prices and stock market indexes cannot and will not keep going up in straight lines for ever. Investors who stake their funds on a can't-go-wrong market will eventually find they have forsaken the bulls and the bears and joined the pigs.

Most analysts are down-to-earth bean counters and their forecasts are based on sensibly constructed earnings forecasts. They are your friends, whether you are a bull or a bear.

If you are a pig your only friends will be the capitalist zealots who delude themselves, and others, that the sky is always the limit, business cycles have ended for ever, valuations don't matter and the only thing that counts is supply and demand. Some zealots even claim that the strength of technology heralds the dawn of a new Jerusalem golden age capitalist global economy. They have their feet firmly planted in the heavens. Investors have to manage their affairs objectively.

Followers of Warren Buffett also have to manage their assets

Warren Buffett's concept of identifying big investment opportunities and seemingly being able to keep on delivering double digit earnings growth year after year, has captured the imagination of private investors. He will doubtless manage his interests with characteristic brilliance and success, and he may even sell some of his holdings if he can do better with the money, but he will not change tack and start short selling the market or panic and sell shares because the market looks hostile. This would be the antithesis of his strategy of holding growth shares for long-term value, without fretting about the share price day by day.

But what about the Buffetteers – the name I have given to the gallant legion of private investors who have adopted what they think is a foolproof Buffett system of getting rich quick? I worry about them because they just don't and won't believe that any share they own and 'Warren' also owns will ever really come down in value for more than a month or two. There are a lot of Buffetteers, and their wealth and influence is significant. Forrestor Research estimated in 1997 that there were three million users of the Internet for investing purposes in the US. By the end of 1998, the press suggested there were five million. It is a fair guess that at least a million of them are Buffetteers, and if they keep buying the shares they believe in, even if market sentiment changes, some shares could be supported at artificially high prices.

There are now millions of other get-rich-quick investors and day traders working the markets using the Internet and discount traders. Some are skilled operators, running like mini hedge funds. Others, like Buffetteers, think nothing can go wrong and chase speculative opportunities Buffett would not invest in. They are another dangerous tribe of the zealots, and the effect they are having on markets is a new dynamic which can encourage unrealistic pricing.

Investors who feel that the thing to do is what Warren Buffet does will probably win the day. These investors are the shareholders in his company, Berkshire Hathaway, a Millennial Niche prospect in *Portfolio 2001*.

The Sorophiles follow themselves

Bears are always prowling for opportunities to profit from lofty and artificial share prices which they expect will come back down to earth, and weighty money takes short positions when markets look overvalued. America's other legendary investor, George Soros, is the icon of those who take their own readings of markets, and go short or long in accordance with their own conclusions. Soros never publishes what he is doing and, unlike Warren Buffett, does not need to change his calling card if he switches strategy from bullish to bearish. He is Soros backwards and forwards and aims to makes money when markets go up and when they go down.

Among hedge funds, institutional investors and the very rich there are a lot of Sorophiles who recognize when markets look too high and they set their sights on profits that can be made from taking short positions. Then if the market over-corrects and shares get cheap, they come back and take long positions. They do not delude themselves by calling George Soros 'George' and waiting to see what he does. If markets over-correct and compelling buying opportunities appear, they strike.

Well-informed private investors can all benefit from market volatility if they know what they want, recognize the opportunities and act decisively. Short selling strategy is not a subject that fits in *Portfolio 2001*, but selling at the right time to protect an investment certainly is.

To buy or not to buy? To sell or not to sell?

Apart from the fact that Warren Buffett would not be a short seller, there may be surprisingly little difference in his buying strategy and the buying strategy of the Sorophiles. *In Buffettology*, a book published in 1997, Warren Buffett's one-time daughter-in-law Mary Buffett explains his investing strategy with an analogy to a baseball player 'waiting for a perfect pitch'.

The last few paragraphs of her book strike the message home:

Warren [Buffett] so subscribes to this theory of waiting for the perfect pitch that in 1971, when the market was really high, he folded up his investment fund, telling his investors that the strategy he had been using was no longer applicable to the market with which they were dealing. Instead of going forward with another strategy, one he was not comfortable with, he closed up shop and returned the money to his investors.

For two more years the market stayed high and many people made tons of money on what was a wild ride. But Warren just sat there on the side lines waiting. Then one day it happened. The market bombed and stocks sank like bricks, and who was waiting at that pit of fear but Warren 'loaded for bear'. And as he has said, suddenly Wall Street was giving things away and his business perspective investing strategy told him to start winging his money bat at what were some unbelievable pitches.

I opened this chapter by quoting Warren Buffett's encapsulation of a growth investing strategy and I have yet to read more useful information for investors. However, there is much more to learn about Buffett's skills and wisdom than the lines I quoted, or Mary Buffett's pitch that he is really a contrarian. Buffett has a value system, knows when shares should be bought and is not frightened to buy when others are actively selling, or sell when others are actively buying. She quotes him as saying, '. . . when the whole world is seeing gold under every rock you let sound business perspective judgement dictate your buying decision, and not the mad enthusiasm of the crowd.'

In 1991 after the Savings and Loan banking crisis in the US, Wells Fargo bank lost over 50 per cent of its value in under six months. Buffett bought $60 million of its shares realizing that Wall Street had underestimated the prospects, and by 1997 they had appreciated by 300 per cent. His investments in Capital City, Coca-Cola and American Express produced similar spectacular profits. Buffett will buy when there is blood on the streets, and will not buy when market prices are manic because the prices would not be rational. He also buys under normal conditions and made a $1 billion investment in Coca-Cola in 1988 when the stock was faltering, but at a price by no means cheap based on its price to earnings ratio at the time.

The message is to invest only at rational prices when an opportunity is compelling. If you cannot wait for a perfect pitch, at least wait for a very good one. There is no escaping the danger of volatility in the global economic system until several of the uncertainties at the turn of the century are resolved. We may think they have been but then find that they were only patched up. There is so much money in the financial system that when the news is good markets are likely to be chased up, and if there is bad news they are vulnerable to collapse.

The two f words of investing – fuss and fundamentals

Fuss

Portfolio 2001 is about research that targets great companies which we can expect to grow earnings one year, two years and ten years down the line. We should not be unnerved and sell our shares because of excessive media comment over the events of the day, even if it encourages buying or selling hysteria.

As investors, we have to look first at news, not commentary, and only then review how the news has been interpreted. It is a privilege to live in a free world and a free society, and part of the privilege demands that the media can comb and pan and filter and drain and strain all news items until even cyberspace chokes with opinions and analysis.

All writers craft language to get a certain pitch across. The quotation from Mary Buffett above mentions investors who misguidedly bought shares in the early 1970s and it closes her book with a home run. However, it is now way out of line with the facts: if investors had bought shares in America's top growth companies in the early 1970s they would be showing astronomical profits. $10,000 invested in Merck then would be worth over $550,000 now.

Most commentators' opinions follow committed attitudes entrenched over the years and even independent investment bankers and economists are inclined to follow a party line. Transparency of information gives us the opportunity to look at the actual reports behind the news. Then, afterwards, we can study opinions and interpretations by journalists and commentators and see what we can learn from them.

Much of the information which makes the financial headlines is not intended for private investors. When analysts at investment banks publish that they are shaving a few cents off an earnings forecast, they do it for the guidance of their major institutional clients, but their reports have disproportionate short-term effects on share prices, at times creating welcome buying opportunities for serious long-term investors:

Private investors have been attracted to Merck because their earnings per share look like this:

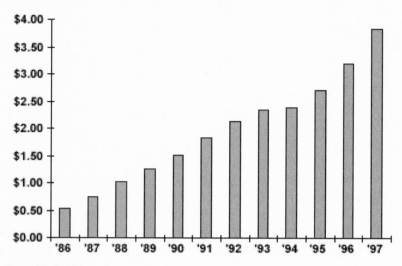

Source: Merck 1997 annual report

As long as the growth story is in place, weakness in earnings for a few quarters will not encourage a long-term private investor to sell his shares.

Share prices on Wall Street often respond more to surprise deviations from analysts' forecasts than they do to actual results. We used to say that fuss only makes waves, but it can also be a friend. Learn how to live with it and use it to your advantage.

Fundamentals
The flow of funds into equity markets is so deliberate and entrenched that a change in the passion for shares is not likely until there are better alternatives. In the capitalist economy, however, risk is in the system.

If markets fall because fundamentals have changed, losses can be dramatic. We can discount the effects of the small f-word 'fuss', and at times even use it to advantage, but we should be scared witless by the big f-word 'fundamentals'.

If the fundamentals turn hostile, equity markets will slash the premium out of growth shares. Fundamental changes can do such damage to the value of our assets that we are obliged to be on the lookout for danger, and dare not be too smart, dismissing all unwelcome news as fuss. Though the crisis of 1998, following Russia's default, affected US and European markets for only a few months, it can take years for markets to recover after severe losses.

If you smell the bear essentials sell the risk

Rising interest rates are expected to slow economic growth and make fixed income investments more competitive with equities. Following the analogy that when you can see a bandwagon coming you have missed it, if you are on a bandwagon that lurches off course to career down a mountain, you certainly do not want to stay on it. Even if you have been enjoying the most wonderful party, you don't want to stay around to be part of the wreckage.

The big f-word 'fundamentals' that could start a severe bear market are:

1. A sharp fall in the pace of growth of the global economy, and expectations of sustained weakness. A global recession could follow and the result would be that companies make lower profits and stock exchanges tumble across the board.

2. The flow of funds can move away from a market, or equity markets generally, following currency volatilities, better alternative investing opportunities, disasters in other equity markets, politics, politicians, wars, civil disorders, environmental disasters, mishaps, punitive interest rate rises, or unexpected events.

3. Sustained steep interest rate rises.

Never mess with the big f-word 'fundamentals' if it threatens real reversals, and never say 'no, no, no' to selling shares when markets switch decisively from bull to bear and you can still protect your assets.

The selling season arrives when changed conditions have undermined the growth story and you no longer believe that the shares you own are the best place for your money. Not everyone can be resolute if they see the market price of their assets fall rapidly in value by 20 or even 30 per cent or more – even if they expect them to rise in future.

If fundamental change is threatened, the answer may be to sell, or not to sell, or may be to sell and consider pouncing back on the next buying opportunity.

The new economy has not made markets crash proof. This

book goes to press in July 1999 – by the time you read it careful investors may be sitting on their money ready to ride out a storm. Nothing changes the inherent risk of share investment – the only real change is that we all have more information to use to support our decisions.

There will always be a time for buying and a time for selling and when the risk/reward relationship is high-Risk and low-reward it is the opposite of what it should be. There are times when the only rational response is to sell.

> *To every thing there is a season, and a time to every purpose under the heaven . . . a time to plant, and a time to pluck up that which is planted*
>
> Ecclesiastes 1:2

PART TWO

IN THE DRIVER'S SEAT ON THE INFORMATION HIGHWAYS

5

GETTING
ON
LINE

Getting started

This part of *Portfolio 2001* is called 'In the driver's seat' to bring home the message that when you have a computer and a connection to the Internet you can really start 'motoring' on the information superhighways. To use your time to best advantage, you should be properly equipped and have some guidance on how and where to find information.

Internet users often start off without sufficient advice on what equipment to buy, without 'driving' lessons, and without a road map. To help you make the most of the Internet opportunity I will show you where to go to find the information you need, offer some suggestions on equipment to get started, buying a new computer if you have to, and I will provide you with a road map with well-marked destinations.

Getting on line

The basic equipment and service requirements to access information on the Internet are minimal. You only need:

1. *Use of a telephone line* while you are connected with the Internet.

2. *Hardware* comprising *a computer with a modem* (the device that enables it to connect with the phone line).

3. Internet software which includes the *browser* software through which you can find and access information from other computers all over the world. When you use the Internet, anti-virus software is essential. Anti-virus programmes have regular updates that zap new computer viruses and virus programmes are usually supplied as a package which includes a subscription for updates. New computers will almost certainly have browsers and a virus protection programme installed. You will also need the software to communicate with your Internet access provider who will provide it for you, if it was not pre-installed in your computer.

4: *An Internet access provider* who connects you through your telephone line, giving access to the Internet superhighway and web sites all over the world – all for the cost of a small subscription (or even free) plus the cost of a local call while you are on line.

Buying new equipment or using old equipment

Using the Internet is straightforward and your computer hardware set-up need only match the use to which it will be put. It does not have to be the best specification on offer at the time. Shoppers who visit their local store to buy daily provisions and pick up the newspapers often manage perfectly well with an old car that gets them there and back, while an executive who uses a car to move around the country, or a parent ferrying a family round all day, will want the very best vehicle they can afford. It is the same with using the information superhighways. If you use the Internet only for prices and news, any computer that gets you on line will probably do the job. Once you start with stock analysis programmes, you will want to go for the best specification you can afford.

Buying computer hardware with good service

Experienced computer users will know exactly what they want to buy and will shop around to find the keenest bargain advertised in computer magazines and on the Internet. The computer industry is efficient at direct selling and the overwhelming success of companies like Dell www.dell.com and Gateway www.Gateway.com, who only sell their computers direct to customers using the Internet extensively, must be testament to the quality of their products and their good levels of service.

Novices and those of us who are 'technologically disadvantaged' are likely to be in need of help with information technology, and buying direct may have some disadvantages compared to buying from a retail outlet that can give personal service. For us, an important part of the buying process must be finding a local computer dealer who will make the effort to help us understand what we need when we are buying and, after the purchase, will be available with a high level of after sales support. This must include warranty service at our homes or offices for at least a year.

You will find that in many cases you cannot rely on buying a well-known computer brand name as a meaningful assurance of sufficient after sales support. The trading pattern in the industry tends to be that service is the responsibility of the firm that sold you the computer.

The computer hardware market is fiercely competitive and every deal is a bargain, but, even with the highest of high tech promotions, in the real world *2+2 always equals 4*. Bargain prices are often reached at the cost of good after sales service and even warranty service is shaved down to the bare bones.

I bought a well-specified leading brand and on day one after delivery, when I phoned to report that the computer I had just paid over £1,000 for had major faults, I found myself speaking on a premium rate phone number costing me 57p (almost $1) a minute. Problems with the computer persisted and I wasted hours and hours of working time because the high specification PC came from a dealer who gave poor service: my bargain purchase turned out to be a costly and painful experience.

I would gladly have paid more at the outset for a good level of service and been much better off.

Buying software
Software should present no problems as the Internet is a user friendly computer environment accessed with a browser software programme (discussed in Chapter 11, see page 270). Netscape and Microsoft Explorer Browsers are both excellent and easy to use, and with the rivalry between the two companies, at this stage you will get a browser free. The free browser contributes to the cheapness of Internet-ready computer packages.

Internet access providers

Internet access is another fiercely competitive business. The large number of providers gives the illusion that there is a lot to choose between them, but there are essentially only two choices for an Internet user. The first is whether to use the information networks like America On Line (AOL) or msn.com (Microsoft's Network), who give access to the Internet *plus* a range of value added services in their own networks. The alternative choice is to use an access provider who only provides access to the Internet and does not offer other value added products. An e-mail facility comes free with all Internet access packages. Internet access is being introduced free by several major groups and will be the obvious choice for most people.

Many investors will want to have access to Microsoft's excellent investors' programme **www.moneycentral.com** Part of this programme is accessible free on the Internet and part is accessible only to subscribers.

Making a good choice of an access provider is easy because most services offer a free trial for a month and, even after service arrangements are committed, most contracts can be cancelled on a month's notice. While you are trying out services, it helps to keep your options open by not telling too many people your e-mail address. Changing an address is always a nuisance and may encourage you to stay locked in with a trial supplier, when you could possibly do better by moving elsewhere.

I started using the Internet with Compuserve (now part of America On Line) in 1995 and had good service, but their subscription at the time included only a limited amount of free Internet access time, so I switched to BT Internet in 1997 when they offered unlimited Internet access for £10 per month plus VAT. I have found them excellent – particularly as they run a 24-hour help line accessible in the UK at local call charges, with an ever helpful team available to talk to. When I had problems because of my bad hardware purchase, BT Internet support kept me going.

Your Internet access provider is reached for the cost of a local phone call and their contract with telecom operators globally gets you free access to the web sites you will use on the Internet anywhere in the world.

Search engines

Chapter 9 is a comprehensive Webliography for investors. It

highlights the best sites for all investor information needs, plus other information resources which you may find useful.

Once you are on line to the Internet you have the world's information resources at your fingertips, and you can find whatever you want using electronic indexes called 'search engines'. Yahoo, one of the most successful Internet businesses, started as a search engine and www.yahoo.com is excellent.

You will find an enquiry box for your query on the home page of the search engine you use, and tips on how to phrase the query. It takes a bit of experience and at times some skill to pinpoint search enquiries and get your answers promptly. Often you have to rephrase, but with some persistence the search engines will find what you are looking for.

Whatever deficiencies there are in the Internet system, finding needles in haystacks is one of its incredible capabilities.

A road map for the information highways

Chapter 7 is on finding Information, Chapter 8 on using information and Chapter 9 is the Webliography. This compendium resource lists the necessary and popular web sites all investors need to research and monitor investments and follow the global economy. Whether you plan to start using the Internet to find out the share price of Yahoo Inc or read what the International Monetary Fund is doing about a national debt crisis, by referring to the Webliography you can have the information in minutes.

The *Wall Street Journal* www.wsj.com has a section which reviews, comments on and rates investor web sites, and is maintained to the high standards of their publication. www.portfolio2001.com will keep the Webliography up to date and help investors with their information enquiries.

6

FINDING

INFORMATION

Choose from several sources of information

Prices twenty minutes old, company overviews and graphics are published free by several Internet information providers. Microsoft's www.moneycentral.com, in characteristic Microsoft form, has set out to be the top investor information site and is well on the way to getting there, but currently it only supplies data on US and Canadian companies and ADRs.

The financial publisher Bloomberg's Internet presence is on www.bloomberg.com. Bloomberg is a master at presenting financial information, but again, at the time of writing, prices are only accessible for US and Canadian companies and ADRs, supported by excellent news and comment on world markets.

It would be a hard call, probably best decided in the end by a heads or tails decision, to say who the best information supplier on US companies is. Microsoft won the honours in a recent *Barrons* survey and Bill Gates does not usually give up leadership. However, Michael Bloomberg is a master of financial publishing and is improving his service day by day, and Reuters have several sites on the net which they may still pull together and surprise everyone with the best package.

The price data that follows is from Yahoo They are omnipresent on the Internet, have honed in on supplying information on financial markets globally, and their presentation is excellent and straightforward:

- www.finance.yahoo.quote.com covers the US and Canada.

- www.finance.yahoo.co.uk covers the UK, Ireland, France, Germany, Sweden, Italy and Norway. It also has links with all Yahoo financial web sites world wide.

- www.yahoo.jp is for Japan. The text is in Japanese with no English explanations.

Quotes, market data and overviews

The following is an example of a detailed Yahoo quote and accompanying graphic on Lucent. On www.finance.yahoo.com a menu of different presentations is offered for quotes for US and Canadian companies (including ADRs), ranging from a brief one line statement of the most recent trades to a full analysis of the trades, supported by a choice of graphic presentations.

Yahoo chart of Lucent technologies share price with 200 day (lower line) and 50 day (upper line) moving averages.

[IN THE GRAPHICS ON THE NET, THE THREE LINES ARE IN DIFFERENT COLOURS]

Wed Aug 5 7:30am ET – US Markets open in 2 hours.

LUCENT TECH (NYSE:LU)
More Info: News, SEC, Msgs, Profile, Research, Insider

Last Trade	Change		Prev Cls	Volume	Div Date
Aug 4 · 87	-4 (-4.40%)		91	10,199,500	Sep 1
Day's Range	Bid	Ask	Open	Avg Vol	Ex-Div
87 – 92 ⅞	N/A	N/A	92 ¼	4,704,954	Jul 29
52-week Range	Earn Shr	P/E	Mkt Cap	Div/Shr	Yield
36 3/16 – 108 ½	0.84	103.57	114.1B	0.16	0.18

Quotes delayed 15 minutes for Nasdaq, 20 minutes otherwise.

Like other US web sites with financial information, Yahoo gives a comprehensive picture of a company with a quote. The headline on the Yahoo quote above lists further data brought by the click of a mouse: News, SEC Msgs, Profile, Research, Insider.

Yahoo's News is fairly comprehensive and supported by an archive of recently published news items. 'SEC' reports when filings have been made by US companies and viewers can go to the SEC EDGAR web site and examine the filing directly. The 'Profile' from Market Guide gives a comprehensive fundamental and technical overview, and the Research is Yahoo's analysis of consensus earnings estimates and also reports when Insiders trade the shares.

Here is an example of a headline Market Guide www.marketguide.com profile for GE, accessed from a Yahoo report:

Business Summary

GE consists of 14 divisions which include aircraft engines, appliances, capital services, lighting, medical systems, NBC, plastics, Power Systems, electrical distribution and control. Total revenues for the nine months ended 9/30/98, rose 12% to $71.83 billion. Net income rose 13% to $6.63 billion. Revenues reflect increased revenues from Aircraft Engines, NBC and Transportation. Earnings also reflect higher operating margins from Aircraft Engines and Medical Systems.

More from Market Guide: Highlights – Performance – Ratio Comparisons

Statistics at a Glance – GE Last Updated: Jan 12, 1999

Price and Volume	Per-Share Data		Management Effectiveness	
Price and Volume (updated Jan 12, 1999)	Book Value (mrq)	$11.37	Return on Assets (ttm)	2.89%
52-Week Low $69.00	Earnings (ttm)	$2.66	Return on Equity (ttm)	25.55%
Recent Price $97.75	Sales (ttm)	$29.11	**Financial Strength**	
52-Week $104.875	Cash (mrq)	$1.76	Current Ratio	N/A
Beta 1.13	**Valuation Ratios**		Long-Term Debt/	1.54
Equity (mrq)				
Daily Volume 4.60M (3-month avg)	Price/Book (mrq)	8.60	Total Cash (mrq)	$5.77B
Share-Related Items	Price/Earnings (ttm)	36.80	**Short Interest**	
Market $319.4B Capitalization	Price/Sales (ttm)	3.36	Shares Short as of Dec 8, 1998	14.8M
Shares 3.27B Outstanding	**Income Statements**		Short Ratio	3.63
Float 3.20B	After-Tax Income (ttm)	$8.97B	**Stock Performance**	
Dividend Information	Sales (ttm)	$98.5B		
Annual $1.40 Dividend (indicated)	**Profitability**			
Dividend Yield 1.43%	Profit Margin (ttm)	9.1%		

See the Profile FAQ for a description of each item above; **M** = millions; **B** = billions; **mrq** = most-recent quarter (Sep 30, 1998); **ttm** = trailing twelve months through Sep 30, 1998

Global prices

Bridge Information Services www.bridge.com give global prices and charts free and run multi currency portfolios. Datastream www.datastream.com and the *Financial Times* www.ft.com give end of the day global prices.

Real time prices

Stock exchanges require a fee from publishers to redistribute live prices until the information is in the public domain and, with share prices, this is usually when the information is twenty minutes old.

If you are a client of an on line broker you will usually get real time prices free as part of the service. In the US the stage has been reached where free live quotes are increasingly also being offered packaged with other services, and *Wall Street Journal* subscribers have access to free real time stock quotes on the US exchanges with some small restrictions.

Web sites which provide real time quotes in the US and selected other markets for a charge include www.quote,com, www.nasdaq.com, www.interquote.com and www.pcquote.com. In the UK, real time quotes can be obtained for a fee from www.esi.com and www.marketeye.com. Some information vendors including www.woqats.com cover the US and several other major European markets with live fee based quotes.

UK and Ireland

www.finance.yahoo.co.uk publishes prices and news for the UK, Ireland, France, Germany, Sweden, Italy and Norway. They link with the financial publishers Hemmington Scott www.hemscott.co.uk and their well-arranged database of information on UK and European companies. Hemmington Scott now also publish prices and news on an expanding universe of European companies and their Research Menu provides company data for UK companies under this wide and useful list: Summary Detail, 5 Yr Summary P&L with Balance Sheet, Daily Share Price, Brokers' Consensus, Advisers, Directors, Major Shareholders, Registrars, Contact Details and Key Dates.

Company web sites

Company web sites often have links to share prices and some even publish brokers' research. Company sites give the picture of the company as a business and have current news and announcements, and archive material often including annual accounts. Preferences will vary on which information provider for prices and news is more convenient, but visiting company web sites should remain on all investors' agendas.

Subscribing to the *Journal* – the 'new media'

It costs $59 a year if you subscribe on line, and less if you are a print subscriber, for the *Wall Street Journal*, and you can subscribe on a monthly basis. For a small sum of money you can use the *Journal* as your primary research resource for a *Portfolio 2001* strategy and for investing generally. You can also use the *Journal* as your core monitoring resource.

The *Wall Street Journal* on line is 'new media' at work and our link with the central nervous system of the financial world. With its sister publication *Barrons* on line, which comes free with the *Journal*, it is the investment world's premier comprehensive financial resource publishing stock quotes, global stock market news and indexes plus:

1. News and extensive responsible commentary published as it happens, not in the next edition or the next day, on all global financial matters.

2. A Briefing Books resource on companies with extensive information, stock quotes, and interactive graphics on all companies traded in US and Canada and on ADRs. Information on other important companies traded on stock exchanges elsewhere in the world is also available but not in the same depth. The graphics programme includes all companies traded on UK stock exchanges and I expect that Euroland companies will follow soon.

3. A Personal Journal resource within their Briefing Books menu selects news and commentary according to the reader's preferences and prepares running reports on 'favourites' and 'news'.

4. Access to extensive databases of current and past financial information and archives of publications.
5. A review of investment, financial and economic web sites analysing the information and rating the service.
6. Share portfolios with current prices and news maintained through the Personal Journal.

Portfolio reports

The *Journal* has a facility for subscribers to run five portfolios. I have divided the *Portfolio 2001* shares into separate portfolios with Life Sciences, IT and Telecoms, Banks and Finance, Millennial Niches and Global Profit Harvesters. These reports are updated daily and tell me what each share and the market have done for the day. Together the portfolios give an indication of how the sectors are moving. The following is a sample *Journal* report on the portfolio with Life Science companies:

Share	price/change	number $ +-	value
Abbott Laboratories	40 3/4 + 1/8 00	-125.00	4,075.00
Baxter International Inc.	58 7/16 - 9/16	100 543.75	5,843.75
Glaxo Wellcome Plc	59 1/2 - 7/8	100 -150.00	5,950.00
Johnson & Johnson	75 5/8 - 1	100 -137.50	7,562.50
Merck & Co., Inc.	123 13/16 - 2 5/8 100	768.75	12,381.25
Monsanto Co.	56 1/4 - 3/4	100 -75.00	5,625.00
Pfizer Inc.	94 3/8 - 3 13/16	100 -1,662.50	9,437.50

Global Portfolio reports

Portfolio reports are widely available for national markets. Bridge Information Systems `www.bridge.com` have now enhanced their value considerably with global multi currency reports as a free service. This is an example of shares I am following in their portfolio:

Delayed data posted 9 Jan 1999,15:22

Symbol	Last Sale	%Chg	Chg	Bid	Ask	Volume	Currency
de:BMW	732.00	0.6878	5.00	720.00	730.00	18,874	EUR
us:LU	115 1/4	-1.0730	-1 1/4	0	0	6,523,900	USD
us:PFE	122 1/4	-1.8565	-2 5/16	0	0	3,787,700	USD
gb:AHT	145.00	0.0000	0.00	143.00	147.00	128,428	GBP
de:ADS	92.65	2.9444	2.65	92.00	93.00	102,807	EUR
us:MTC	45 3/8	-1.3587	-0 5/8	0	0	4,583,200	USD
us:MRK	153 13/16	0.9848	1 1/2	0	0	3,085,400	USD

In this list prices are quoted conveniently in euro, dollars and pounds.

Monitoring investments using Internet publishers

Once you have set up an information retrieval arrangement on line, and the information comes reliably, which it will, you will probably stay with the service. The earnings wheel of the Internet world turns on how many times a day a web page is accessed. Even if you pay nothing, you are a valuable client and you get valuable services, including portfolios and news screening and delivery by e-mail or web site access as you prefer.

There is a danger when using new media that news will be screened by pre-set electronic programmes and you will end up with electronic blinkers and miss out on information which you should know about. With this in mind, I set my selections for news screening with the *Journal* to cover a wider universe of news and comment than the word 'favourite' suggests. I have since developed a rhythm for scrolling through my 'favourites' from the *Journal* on line, and in a few minutes I get a feel for the day's news without missing more than I would have missed reading through a hard copy of the newspaper. The following page is an extract from my *Journal* 'favourites' daily report which points me to subjects I should be following and may have missed:

Jul. 10 (1998)

Asia Stocks: South Korean Labor Unrest Continues to Hurt Region

US Stocks: Stocks Rally to Post Gains Amid Summer Doldrums

Europe Stocks: European Stocks Decline After Early US Weakness

Foreign Exchange: Dollar Declines vs. Mark On Optimism About Russia

Americas Stocks: Profit-Taking Hits Argentina; Canadian Shares Extend Slide

Commodities: Corn, Wheat Futures Fall On Bearish USDA Data

Leader: Once a Monopoly, Televisa Faces Up To Competition, Cuts Bloated Costs

Americas Stocks: Stocks End Down In the Americas

Europe Stocks: European Markets Drop, Tracking Wall Street

Heard on the Street: Analysts See Cable Stocks Getting Set to Surge Again

Review & Outlook: Mickey Mouse in France

Review & Outlook: Middle Class Immigrants

Heard in Asia: KFC Malaysia Faces Struggle To Revive Stock After Report

Leader: For Many Workers, Measuring Up Has Become a Matter of Money

Washington Wire: Washington Wire

Commodities: Hog, Pork-Belly Futures Fall By Limits on Record Output

US Stocks: Blue-Chip Stocks Slide Amid Earnings Warnings

Foreign Exchange: Dollar Tops Other Currencies In Rally Driven by Technicals

News sorted for me electronically by the *Journal* follows my portfolio selections set up in their computer. It brings the day's news on each company and then brings other news under the headings Europe and the Economy.

The *Financial Times*

The *Financial Times* is London's financial publication covering global markets and is also accessible on line. It is still free on www.ft.com, but not yet as developed a resource as the *Journal.*

The *Financial Times's* extensive database can be accessed for share prices on world companies, company background briefings, prices on a global universe of shares, and for archive material. The *FT* also provides a portfolio service, intended to cover world shares but presently only the UK is available. Unfortunately, at present, the *FT* service lacks graphics, and until it offers them its Internet service is markedly inferior.

For decades I have been an appreciative reader of the *FT* and start the day reading it, transplanting their famous slogan 'No *FT*, No Comment' into 'No *FT*, No Breakfast'.

The Wall Street Research Net

This most comprehensive umbrella site for company research, still confined to US Companies and ADRs, has links with an exceptional range of free and fee charging services covering company-specific and general economic research. The following headline pages on Pfizer PFE, taken from its index pages, detail the databases on companies it links with. When there is a fee for the site a $ sign follows:

Quotes:
Current Quote
Option Quote
Historical Price Download ($)

Research, Reports & Summaries:
Company Profile ($)
Annual Financial Statements ($)
Quarterly Financial Statements ($)
Research Reports ($)

*Quick*Source: Description & Stats
*Quick*Source: Fundamentals,
Ratios & Earning
Industry Comparison
Zack's Annual Income Statement
Zack's Wall Street Recommendations
Reuters Inc.Link
Inc.Link Financials
Disclosure Key Annual Financial Ratios
CorpTech Reports
MarketGuide Report
Silicon Investor Company Profile
Yahoo! Company Profile

Earnings Estimates:
Zack's Earnings Estimates
Inc.Link Earnings Estimates
I/B/E/S Earnings Estimates
Stock Smart Earnings Estimates ($)
News Center:
Transium Business Journal Search
WSRN NewsSearch
NewsAlert
Yahoo! News
DLJ Direct Company News
Company Links:
Home Page
SEC Filings (PFIZER INC)
SEC Filings (Edgar-Online)
SEC Filings (Who Where)
Dividend Reinvestment & Direct Stock
Purchase
Search the Internet for Additional
Links
Wall Street Journal Briefing Book ($)
Value Added Links:
Clinical Laboratory News
Clinical Chemistry Links

Thomson's TipSheet

Graphs/Charts:
Bollinger's Equity Trader
WSRN/BASELINE Price Chart
*Quick*Source: Fundamental Data Charts
60 Month Price & Volume Chart
BigCharts
StockMaster Chart (6 Month)
Stock Graph (100 days)
Telescan Chart (2 Year)
Intraday Chart

Discussion:
Chat (Biotech & Medical)

National Center for Health Statistics
RxList – Drug Index
Food & Drug Administration
National Clearing House for Drug &
Alcohol Info
National Center for Health Statistics
Links
Medscape
World Health Organization
National Center for Biotechnology
Organizations
US Indust Outlook – Drugs

Wall Street Research Net's *Quick*Source Description and Stats and Fundamentals, Ratios & Earning reports and the Industry Comparison reports are amongst the most useful and well-presented short reports available. The following is the Descriptions and Stats report on Pfizer:

PFIZER INC

235 E 42ND ST	Ticker	PFE
NEW YORK, NY 10017	Exchange	NYSE
Phone: (212) 573-2323	Fiscal Yr Month:	DEC
Fax: (212) 573-7851 CEO: William C. Steere, Jr. Primary SIC:		2834

Research-based health care company which discovers, develops, manufactures and sells technology-intensive products in the following business segments: health care, consumer health care and animal health.

Stock Price Data as of close 09/10/98:

Latest Close:	94.38	Current Dividend Rate:	.76
52 Week High:	121.75	Yield:	.8%
52 Week Low:	56.25	Beta:	1.08
5 Year High:	121.75	Liquidity Ratio:	230467.4
5 Year Low:	13.13	Market Value (000):	132146423

Current Statistics & Growth:

Latest 12 Mos. EPS Change:	18.1%	Total Return Last 12 Months:	58.2%
5-Yr Revenue Growth Rate:	12.56%	Total Return Last 3 Years:	261.0%
5-Yr EPS Growth Rate:	22.91%	Total Return Last 5 Years:	554.3%
5-Yr Dividend Growth Rate:	11.19%		
No. Institutions Holding Shares:	2005	Shares Held by Institutions:	57.4%

The Internet for companies outside the US

Investors in the US need no introduction to the Internet or to investing with the backing of the information resources available. Major global companies are likely to have ADRs and in the next chapter on using information J. P. Morgan's great site on ADRs is highlighted as a benchmark among information services globally.

Country-specific sites in the Webliography include sources for prices, trading, news and corporate financial information on countries including Germany, France, the Netherlands, Switzerland and Japan.

The World Wide Web is a moving target. When you are looking for information on markets outside the US, start with the Webliography, and then make enquiries through search engines and umbrella sites to see if there is anything new.

Analysis on funds – www.trustnet.co.uk:

Trustnet, a UK based umbrella site, provides information on managed funds and unit trusts including free daily comparative performance data on 600 UK investment trusts and closed ended offshore and US funds. The site has a link with www.lipper.com for benchmark analysis of all major US funds.

Financial services with a UK bias – www.find.co.uk

Find is a UK financial information net directory which spans the financial services industry with live links to the sites it lists and provides a one-stop resource for information on fund management companies, unit trusts, investment trusts, personal equity plans, offshore investments and futures and options.

It also links with full lists of stockbrokers and portfolio managers, independent financial advisers and specialist dealing services. Find has been judged the best directory for UK financial services by the *Financial Times*.

IBES

IBES on www.ibes.com are one of the world's leading earnings forecast publishers and have fee-based services that report on any changes to forecasts as they happen. They also report on an ongoing basis on portfolios on global equities. The following is a sample report. Prices are all in pounds.

Company Name	Period	Ending#	#Ests'	High (BPN[1])	Mean (BPN[1])	Low (BPN[1])
ADIDAS-SALOMON AG (IAS)	FY1	12/98	30	449.506	387.629	344.153
BMW	FY1	12/98	36	3209.753	2750.730	2335.323
HONDA MOTOR CO LTD	FY1	3/98	11	65.739	61.679	54.897
ING GROUP N.V.	FY1	12/97	3	80.297	78.595	77.013
NOVARTIS	FY1	12/98	25	4306.929	3985.188	3748.307
ROCHE GS	FY1	12/98	27	25116.643	21676.729	19274.570
SAP AG	FY1	12/98	31	492.701	417.830	344.153
SWISS BANK CORPORATION R	FY1	12/98	24	1492.500	1139.971	949.656
TAKEDA CHEMICAL INDUSTRIES	FY1	3/98	13	33.304	30.147	27.906

[1]BPN is Pence

Company filings with the US government: Edgar sites

The statutory reports which US companies file, including the regular filings under the headings of 10Q (quarterly) and 10K (annually), call for financial disclosure and comment on the company's trading situation and prospects.

The US Securities and Exchange site with this information is `www.sec.gov.edgar.htm` and is an open site which can be accessed for this public information. In addition there are added value sites which are fee based and serve investors who need instant information on filings, analysis of filings and seek alerts and assisted retrieval. These are:
`www.edgar-online.com`
`www.disclosure.com`
`www.freeedgar.com` (which I find excellent)

EDGAR is an acronym for electronic gathering and retrieval and brings to your fingertips the full filings made to the Securities and Exchange Commission by US companies and foreign companies trading as ADRs.

New York Shares and American Depository Receipts

J. P. Morgan's web site on American Depository Receipts (ADRs) `www.adr.com` is a gateway for everyone everywhere on global companies and is fully discussed in the following chapter on using information.

7

USING
INFORMATION

Buying into the dream

Only a few years ago investors followed well-established valuation
criteria and it was possible to get to grips with subjects concerning
share valuations efficiently. One valuation rule was to relate the
earnings multiple a share was trading at to the share's earnings
growth rate and never pay more than the growth rate; pay the
growth rate only in exceptional circumstances and invest generally
at an earnings multiple lower than the growth rate. Accordingly a
share that was growing earnings at 25 per cent a year was unlikely
to trade at a multiple as high as 25 times earnings and trading above
it would have been seen by seasoned investors as hazardous.
Nowadays if you want to buy the big blue chips you will have to
pay not only the earnings growth rate but multiples of the growth
rate. When you buy such richly valued shares you take on board the
risk that if earnings growth slows, or markets retreat, your losses
will be severe.

What has changed to make shares so much more expensive by
comparison? The overhead answer is that we are buying into a new
global economy which is more efficient and more productive with
bigger markets and stronger prospects for future earnings growth
potential than the old economy. Some analysts also speak of a new
economic paradigm that explains America's economic miracle of
the 1990s and they claim that the competitive nature of the global
economy results in low inflation which in turn means that interest
rates will stay low and growth will continue to be strong. New

paradigm proponents do not yet include any leading mainstream economists.

Another answer to the valuation question is that following a global move from fixed income investing to equities, demand for shares in top companies exceeds supply. Whatever reason or reasons we find most persuasive, at high market levels investors are buying into a dream; the vision that globally we are entering an era of exceptional economic growth and corporate profitability. The opportunity has been likened to the chance that immigrants to America had over the century to share in the great American dream.

It is challenging for investors to come to terms with the new global economy and to make decisions based on whether the promise of growth and sustained prosperity is strong enough to justify the prices for shares they want to buy. The alternatives to facing up to the challenge are either to walk away from investing in the world's top companies for the time being or to invest recklessly. Investors who storm in thinking nothing can go wrong with big blue-chip names, without understanding the dynamics driving markets, will never make money by being adept at using information. When it comes to managing their investments in challenging times they will find they have nothing to contribute and they may not recognize signs that point to selling early enough or end up dumping investments in weak markets when they should hold on to them.

It is convenient to follow how information can be used to make money under six headings on the lines of the research agenda:

1) Top down research aimed at getting generally well informed on markets, investing sectors, and identifying prospects
2) Bottom up research on investing prospects, studying fundamental information on prospect companies in detail, deciding on the most favoured for a buying list and setting rational price ranges
3) Making and monitoring 'what if?' forecasts
4) Timing purchases supported by technical studies of market performance, often conveniently presented in charts
5) Monitoring. Monitoring embraces developments affecting existing holdings, including buying or selling opportunities, which may be indicated and buying opportunities for new prospects
7) Accessing efficient and economic broking and advisory relationships

Top down research: getting well informed

After a long boom market which has resulted in dramatic rises in share prices, investors have to keep asking whether rising share prices are sustainable and reviewing why equities now are regarded as being worth more than they were when traditional valuation metrics ruled. Supply and demand factors drive markets but eventually the validity of new valuation parameters for the new economy will depend on both strength in the US and world's developed economies and a revival of growth in emerging markets. The World Bank President James D. Wolfensohn, in recent speeches and discussion papers quoted in Chapter 15, is unequivocal on the 'essential interdependence' between the developed and the developing world and he warns that economically rich and poor nations 'will succeed or suffer together'.

Statistics and economic data available in the US has helped the chairman of the Federal Reserve Alan Greenspan and his team of economists to successfully fine tune monetary policy through one of the longest periods of sustained economic growth on record. The collections of data published by the US Government can be accessed through **www.census.gov.cgi.bin/briefroom**. Data on both US economic statistics and other world markets is also republished and commented on in the financial press and in several investor web sites listed in the Webliography following.

The key global economic forecasts are made by the World Bank, the International Monetary Fund and the OECD and their reports, particularly the most recent, are valuable material for investors to use:

The World Bank	**www.worldbank.org**
The International Monetary Fund :	**www.imf.org**
The OECD	**www.oecd.org**

Tapping into information from global investment banks

The most accessible information on the economic background comes from major global investment banks who research the economic spectrum including the global macro issues. Morgan Stanley Dean Witter's daily reports from their global economics team are available free on www.ms.com. Every few weeks they also update a global strategy review. Their information includes analysis and opinions from some of the world's leading economists and market strategists.

Deutsche Bank Morgan Grenfell's Chief Economist Dr Ed Yardeni's web site www.yardeni.com is a unique resource covering the US and global economies. Part of the site is only for client subscribers but comprehensive open information on the site includes an extensive collection of charts which he uses to explain what is actually happening economically world wide. Investors with economics training will instantly recognize the value of the range of information presented and, those who have not yet been educated as economists have a chance to start learning fast. Scrolling through Yardeni's charts on markets, the US economy and world economies can best be described as an education in itself.

Yardeni's site is focused on the new economy and technology. As one of the strategists who anticipated the progress and the effects of the new economy, and one of the first to call the Dow Jones index as over 10,000 by the year 2000 – which he did in 1995 – he is well positioned to explain current issues. His charts are annotated with useful explanations and supported by archives of essays and discussion papers on the key investing themes we have to consider including inflation and deflation, the new economy and the new paradigm. The following chart is from his collection on The New Economy:

– THE NEW ECONOMY –

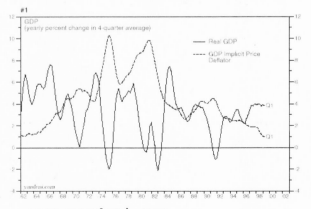

In the Old Economy, booms led to inflation, causing the Fed to tighten which eventually triggered a bust. In the New Economy, global competition keeps a lid on inflation. Competitive companies cut their costs, boost their productivity, and innovate. By offering consumers better goods and services at reasonable prices, they sell more units, especially as wages rise faster than prices. Low inflation leads to stronger

Chart www.yardeni.com

Time spent reviewing Yardeni's site will give investors insight and knowledge they will be able to use profitably in future. The focus is on the new economy, but historic data is widely used and the following chart illustrates that, contrary to the belief many speculators cherish that America's growth story was dreamed up in the cyber heavens, its economic achievements followed a century of solid industrial growth:

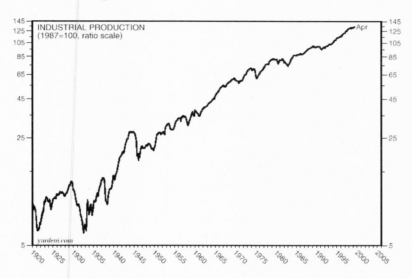

Chart **www.yardeni.com**

Yardeni also reports updated data on top down and bottom up forecasts for the S&P index and the multiple of earnings at which it currently trades and at which it has traded in the past. This is vital information both when investments are made and while they are being monitored.

Publications

The *Wall Street Journal* and the *Financial Times* are benchmarks for sober, well-presented information. *The Financial Times* Lex column may be the most respected financial editorial comment in the world and it is recognized as influencing the thinking of professional and private investors alike. Other excellent publications are more in a set mould.

America's *Business Week* <u>www.businessweek.com</u> has emerged as a leading publication on investing with an aggressive and new economy bias. Britain's *Economist,* <u>www.economist.com</u> has superb credentials characterized by a conservative and even cynical approach to the new economy. The *Economist's* view of the new paradigm is that it 'verges on claptrap', while *Business Week* claims that it heralds nothing less than 'a new kind of math'.

Several newspapers accessible on line cover information for investors. They include the *New York Times,* the *Washington Post,* the *International Herald Tribune* and the *Los Angeles Times* in the US and the *Independent, Telegraph* and *Guardian/Observer* in the UK. The *Independent* has the distinction of hosting at times as a columnist Gavin Davies, Goldman Sachs' International Economics Director, and his contributions often bring contentious economic issues into focus while others are floundering.

The *Investors Business Daily* <u>www.investors.com</u> which describes itself as 'written for people who want to succeed', has a strong bias towards the new economy. It is also the resource to use to tap into William O'Neil's strategies, with content weighted towards using charts, finding opportunities and stock picking.

To get a grip on economic issues and learn about investing as you gain skills and confidence, structured investor education may be the best choice before you risk money. The *Wall Street Journal* and the *Investors Business Daily* both offer training and in the Webliography following several other resources are listed.

Top down research on the investing climate is indispensable as we all must start the investing process by deciding how much of our resources we can allocate to equities at any time, according to our resources and investing strategies. Asset allocation is not only the first example of using information but it may be the most crucial, bearing in mind that markets are still likely to be volatile.

Bottom up research

The companies reviewed in the following chapters have been researched with a strong focus on their growth potential and the reports will be helpful for top down and bottom up research. Investing decisions have to be made in real time and the reports will have to be updated for bottom up research. When it comes to timing an investment technical factors will at times also take centre stage. Chapter 8 on researching financial data and Chapter 9, the Webliography, provide a guide to web resources that analyse performance and financial results, including resources with financial data on spread sheets for investors interested in running their own numbers.

'What if?' forecasts

Portfolio 2001 reports include 'what if' forecasts which generally start in line with market prices and assume that markets will continue strong. At the time the reports were written, and as this book goes to press, markets were high but the assumptions were reasonable with indications for global economic growth and strong markets. These same assumptions may not be well supported when you research, or when you invest, or when you monitor your investments. The two little words 'what if' are like '0 + 1' in the digital code – they tell the whole story. The well-known computing expression of 'garbage in garbage out' is apt here. If subsequently circumstances change, the assumptions for a 'what if' analysis could become garbage, and all conclusions reached following the assumption will also be at risk.

As major economic directions become entrenched and generally do not change overnight, it is realistic to make forecasts. However, when subsequent information challenges our underlying assumptions, we must use the information to re-examine the assumptions and respond to the changes. Whether these changes mean the investing case is weaker or stronger, using information and responding to changes will always go hand in hand.

So 'what if' we ignore important changes? We will not be managing risk and will probably lose our money.

Timing investing

Technical information on market trends and the price patterns in target investments are useful information to support fundamental research, particularly when timing the purchases of shares.

Technical information is time sensitive and convenient way of quickly finding technical indicators is to look at charts.

The Internet is magic for graphics. It is easy to draw charts picturing the performance of shares and excellent free material is available from many web sites. Some specialized charting services are for paid subscribers only.

Web sites that provide charts usually make it possible for you to customize a chart with information in time frames you select, and enable you to introduce comparisons with the performance of other companies and market indices such as the FT 100 or the S&P 500. Usually, they also enable the viewer to introduce technical measures like moving averages and a wide range of other indicators.

Best of all, charts and technical analysis have been demystified on the Internet, and in the Webliography following several sites are listed that explain the information available in charts and the meaning of various technical indicators.

CNN have an Investment Challenge site on www.sandbox.net for aspiring investors which unambiguously demystifies the whole field of cyber investing and explains the jargon. Using sandbox.net without opening your cheque book, you can get hands-on cyber-investing experience running a 'live' phantom portfolio with a 'real' phantom on line broker.

Charts and technical analysis

Charts which give a picture of events that have actually happened are efficient research tools because, as the saying has it, one picture is worth ten thousand words. Information in charts can be examined against various indicators some of which relate only to the past and are called lagging indicators, while others are used to predict future market action and are called leading indicators.

All investors can use charts to complete a picture they are building from fundamentals. Using charts as a convenient way of gathering information does not necessarily mean an investor is adopting 'technical' analysis as an investment strategy. Technical analysis is a strategy where decisions are based on share price and market movements which can be seen in charts or extracted from analysis of market performance. Technical investors may look only at charts and make investing decisions on what they see in them, measured against a range of technical indicators.

Some critics of technical analysis say that, as an investing strategy, technical analysis has no more reliability than fortune telling, while adherents believe that the stock market moves in broad patterns that can be identified by careful charting plus a knowledge of past performance. Because technical analysis has a large following, there is often a nagging fear that technical analysts who all follow the same theory or interpretation have the potential to make self-fulfilling prophecies.

Graphics and technical research

In a single chapter it will not be possible to include more than a few broadly introductory remarks on technical data. An attempt to do more would risk proving, to our mutual detriment, the well-known saying that a little knowledge is a dangerous thing. The Webliography includes comprehensive references to printed and on line sources for more information. On line chart providers also back up their information with explanations of chart patterns, technical indicators, and technical analysis jargon.

While technical analysis as an investment strategy has its critics, there is no question about the convenience of charts or their value as an information source. A skilled researcher will look at a chart and get a quick, comprehensive and often insightful picture of factors affecting a share's behaviour on the market – information that could take hours to absorb without graphic material. While technical analysis has to be learned, information in charts can be straightforward to grasp and understand using common sense. Contrary to what many people think, there are no secrets about charts, revealed only to a chosen few.

A chartist expresses an opinion on a share or a market in much the same way as a Fine Arts professor explains and interprets paintings. If there was an infallible and certain technical indicator we would all know about it and by now everyone would be very rich.

Some charts also discipline investing

William O'Neil is the author of the bestselling book *How to Make Money in Stocks* and Chairman of the financial newspaper *Investors Business Daily* www.investors.com and the US Investment Advisors William O'Neil & Co. He explains charts as recording and representing pure facts on stock prices that have actually occurred as a result of daily supply and demand in the largest auction market place in the world, the stock exchange. His research and opinions follow the premise that charts reflect 'facts on markets' which are more reliable than personal opinions and academic theories, and he has one of the most successful investing track records of the last few decades.

In the 1980s O'Neil introduced 'Datagraphs', which combined charts with fundamental analysis detailing on a single page over a hundred fundamental and technical indicators for professional investors. Datagraphs have been adopted by many of the world's leading institutional investors as an analytical and research benchmark.

The Datagraph format is now available on the Internet as a subscription service through www.dailygraphs.com. By reviewing the information in Datagraphs, Dailygraphs and similar agendas, investors will find that they can start following a professional research and monitoring discipline which should highlight risk and reward situations in time to act on the information.

Dailygraphs and other web sites that publish charts also explain technical analysis and the main features and chart patterns they concentrate on. The *Wall Street Journal* www.wsj.com in its Briefing Book menu includes interactive charts from www.bigcharts.com which offer an extensive menu of technical indicators that can be introduced in charts. There are several other excellent chart suppliers with helpful supporting material ranging from short glossaries to full training courses.

Microsoft's www.moneycentral.com has automatic stock analysis programmes that illustrate technical features, a glossary of technical terms and a well-arranged summary of the main technical analysis subjects.

Price patterns – bases

We usually think of shares as either going up or down, but move-ments sideways are among the important price and volume patterns to observe. One situation is where on fundamentals, or where because the market is positive, we expect a share to be going up but instead it moves stubbornly sideways. Abby Joseph Cohen, Goldman Sachs's highly respected equity market strategist, has explained this situation as being like a climb up a series of staircases which necessitates crossing level landings before accessing the next flight of stairs.

When share prices flatten out, it often indicates that supply and demand are in balance, and analysts may recognize this period as the share building a base at a new price level.

A well-established base can be a solid foundation for a share price rise when the supply and demand factors change. Investors feel reassured buying a share from a firm price base because it is like building a house on a good foundation.

The following chart of Microsoft reflects a base built for half a year from July 1997 to January 1998, followed by a significant rise in the share price on higher volumes:

MICROSOFT – OCTOBER 1996 TO AUGUST 1998

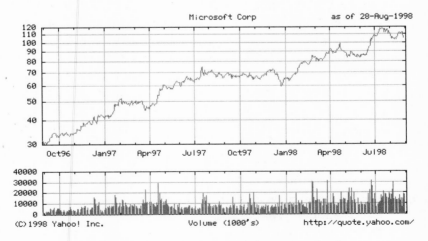

Price rises do not follow all consolidations and sideways move-ments, but when both volume and prices rise after a consolidation it is usually seen as a very bullish indicator.

Jagged price patterns

Share prices seldom move up or down in straight lines and, even when rising or falling steeply, appear as saw tooth patterns on charts. Below is an example of a saw-tooth pattern while markets were falling steeply in July 1998.

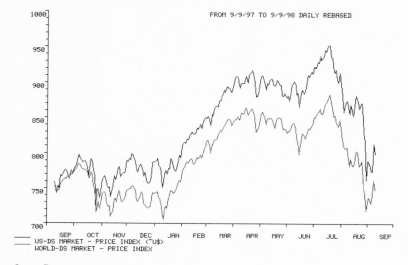

FROM 9/9/97 TO 9/9/98 DAILY REBASED

_____ US-DS MARKET - PRICE INDEX (~U$)
_____ WORLD-DS MARKET - PRICE INDEX

Source: Datastream

Support was fragile as markets fell, arresting the decline only momentarily while pressure built up for the next push downwards. This suggested to analysts that a more ominous phenomenon was taking place than just another short-term sell-off or correction.

Support and resistance

Shares and markets continuously hit price ceilings known as support points and price floors known as resistance points. Generally, whenever a price is reached where supply exceeds demand resistance is experienced, and when demand exceeds supply support is found again.

Shares and markets also tend to trade in ranges between their support and resistance points, and charts display these significant patterns which investors need to recognize. When shares fall below their resistance level, what had been the floor for the share price often becomes the ceiling and vice versa. The above illustration is from Reuters' excellent site www.equis.com. There is nothing mysterious about support and resistance — it is classic supply and demand.

Volume, accumulation and distribution

One of the most bullish signs for investors is when a share is being bought by institutions, which is described as the share being *accumulated.* One thousand private investors each buying a hundred shares will account for 100,000 shares; but if only a hundred pension funds each buy 10,000 shares it will account for a million shares. When institutions are buying a share, demand and volume rise, and if the share price rises with the increased volumes, it suggests that the share is being accumulated by large buyers and demand exceeds supply. If volume starts falling, institutional buying may be tailing off and the price may get capped at established resistance points. Then, if institutions start selling, a downward price movement is likely to follow. When institutions are actively selling a share, it is being *distributed* and this is usually bearish.

Accumulation and distribution can often be recognized in share price graphs. Generally institutions cannot build up a position in a stock over a single day or in a short time frame, and they stagger their purchases not to chase the market up. Investors who recognize accumulation can at times piggyback on institutional buying and score quick gains in the value of their shares.

Comparisons – moving averages, trends and market indexes

Averages point to the direction of markets and shares by smoothing out the volatility experienced in trading sessions. Most graphics available on the Internet now give the viewer the option of introducing average comparisons into the graph. Averages for 200 days and fifty days are popular measures. When a share is above a moving average line, it is leading the average up and this is seen as positive. However, when it is below the line, it is starting to pull the average down and this is negative.

Fifty day (that is, ten weeks at five working days per week), moving averages are frequently used to give a more current picture of the share price or market trend than 200 day averages.

Comparing a share with a market index shows whether the share is simply moving with the market or whether it is outper-forming or underperforming. It also will show whether a share which is rising or falling is doing so on its own merits, or doing so in movement with the market. Trends are important to investors as shares that are falling are likely to fall until a new support-level has been established, and buying them before then is not indicated. Shares that are in rising trends enjoy market support and probably reflect better opportunities.

New highs and new lows

Shares that reach new highs are the market leaders and are often the best investing opportunities – particularly if they are going to break out of historic trading ranges and continue making new highs. Investors often also look at new lows to 'bottom fish' or find bargains. However, bottom fishers should be cautious – they may be concentrating on failures rather than on future success stories.

Managing investments for high reward and low risk is effectively achieved at times by cutting losses to protect assets and running with profits when you have invested in winners.

Relative strength

Several charts on web sites include 'relative strength' indicators which quantify how the share is comparing on markets compared to other shares or past performance. Unfortunately they do not always analyse the same data and they give different relative strength pictures. The benchmark relative strength indicator which reflects the performance of the share compared to the market as a whole is provided in `www.dailygraphs.com`. Other information publishers use different relative strength parameters which will be defined in the glossary with the site. Relative strength should be a potent indicator of the strength of a share on the market and the investor support it is commanding.

Monitoring earnings

The main focus for picking investments and monitoring must be on earnings, as when earnings results are published, changes in investing strategy may be indicated. Companies usually hold analysts' briefings after results announcements and private investors have been at a disadvantage because they are not invited to attend. Fortunately, leading companies like Microsoft set a new trend and now give all interested investors the opportunity to follow analysts' meetings through conference calls or audio visual presentations on the Internet. The financial press are usually invited to company briefings after results announcements and their published reports inform private investors on the discussions at the briefings.

To put a value on shares, investors relate actual or expected earnings to the price of the share. A new market dynamic is now becoming increasingly prevalent where investors value shares on how results stack up compared to analysts forecasts. Shares may have performed well in the real world, but if the results announcements are even slightly below estimates share prices can drop abruptly.

Pricing anomalies can be used to advantage by investors if they were caused by short-term market players speculating in anticipation of results announcements. Results above or below analysts' expectations that mean a lot to speculators can mean little or nothing to long-term investors. In the long run. For investors, market prices affected by divergences between earnings expectations and earnings announcements are only meaningful if they signal fundamental change.

Investors guided by earnings and earnings prospects must position themselves to recognize changes that are fundamental or significant and they can ignore those caused by fuss and market frenzy. Over-reaction to analysts' expectations can also result in buying opportunities for well-informed and serious investors.

Earnings are the tangible reward for investors and the most rewarding opportunities are bound to follow strong, sustainable earnings growth. When analysts raise or lower their earnings forecasts they often upgrade or downgrade their ratings on the company.

Information on rating changes can be difficult to access. IBES on `www.ibes.com` offer a subscription service which keeps investors up to date as changes in forecasts are made. Yahoo report on rating changes made in the US daily and have an archive on individual companies. The following is a report in June 1999 on rating changes for Charles Schwab, the on line broker:

Jun-99 Bear Stearns Started - Buy *13-Apr-99* CIBC Oppenheimer Upgrade Hold to Strong Buy *19-Oct-98* Mrgn Stnly Dn Wttr Downgrade Outperform to Neutral *16-Oct-98* Deutsche Bank Downgrade Buy to Hold *22-Apr-98* Morgan Stanley Upgrade Neutral to Outperform.

There will be times when it is important to know the reason for the changes. The report should be accessible to your broker, may be obtainable from multex on `www.multex.com` and will probably be discussed on `www.portfolio2001.com`.

J. P. Morgan's web site on American Depositary Receipts `www.adr.com` brings together the spectrum of opportunities for investment research and risk management including fundamental, background and current technical information. It will be useful for investors to examine prospects and investments on this site and discover the armory of accessible information that can be used for for research and monitoring.

ADRs bring the world to your fingertips

J. P. Morgan's free web site on ADRs traded in the US `www.adr.com` is the information age at work for investors. It sets a new benchmark for financial information on the Internet and demystifies ADRs, which account for 10 per cent of sales on Wall Street. It also introduces a global research standard for non-US companies. Except for 3i, all companies in *Portfolio 2001* are either US companies or foreign companies traded as ADRs which can be researched using adr.com.

The web page pictured below is from `www.adr.com`

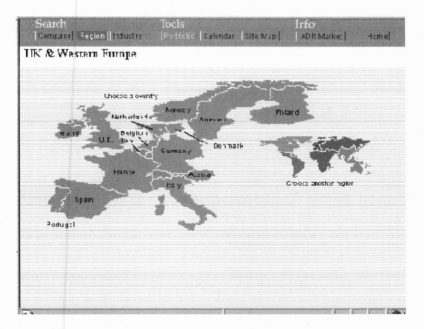

Click your mouse on the country of the ADR you want, and you will have access to a database with company specific, industry groups and market performances.

For a quick world overview of what is currently happening in markets, adr.com highlights the best and worst performing global markets:

World Overview

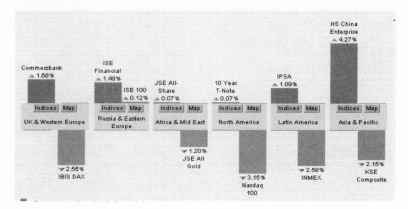

To 'drill down' for more details on the markets you are following, click your mouse on regional 'indices' for the day, or for one month, 6 months or 12 months, and the data appears.

I drew this one-day report on the UK and Western Europe in January 1999 (not surprisingly the 13th).

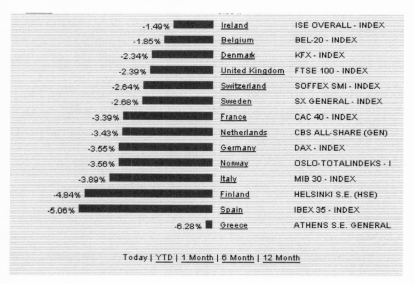

www.adr.com brings transparency to companies outside the US

US companies are transparent but European companies are still too often opaque, and www.adr.com can be an indispensable resourse when researching even well-known international companies outside the US. For example, the Swedish mobile telecoms giant Ericsson can be better researched on `www.adr.com` than any other site I have found. The general description given of Ericsson under the 'quick view' heading introduces the company:

Company Description

Ericsson is a world-leading supplier of equipment for telecommunications systems and related terminals. The company produces advanced systems and products for wired and mobile telecommunications in both public and private networks, for delivery to customers in more than 130 countries. Ericsson had 100,774 employees at year-end 1997. Ericsson has operations in virtually the entire telecommunications field. The company is divided into three business areas: Mobile Systems – Cellular systems, mobile voice and data communication systems, as well as personal pager systems; Infocom Systems – Multimedia communications solutions for transmission of voice, data and images to network operators, service providers and enterprises; Mobile Phones and Terminals – Mobile telephones and terminals as well as other end-user equipment for telecommunications systems. The business areas share a common core technology and strategy. They cooperate closely with one another and provide each other with products and services.

Price reporting, graphics, earnings forecasts and financial analysis are uniform and comprehensive for all companies covered, and interactive graphics enable comparison with other companies and indexes.

Research using `www.adr.com`

I started to research Ericsson using adr.com when the price fell steeply towards the end of 1998, to find out why. The first enquiry was to examine Ericsson compared to the S&P index in the US and the leading US telecoms share Lucent Technologies:

Chart www.adr.com: top line Lucent, middle Ericsson and bottom S&P Index relative

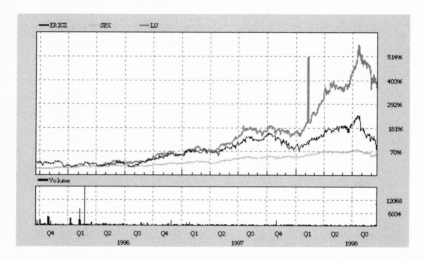

Right index top % gain; bottom index Ericsson volume ('000s)

Then I compared Ericsson with its Finnish rival Nokia, who dominate the mobile phones handset industry, and called up this company description:

Nokia is a leading global company focused on the key growth areas of wireline and wireless telecommunications. A pioneer in mobile telephony, Nokia is the world's leading developer of digital handsets and wireless data, the world's second largest manufacturer of all mobile phones, and one of the two leading suppliers of GSM-based cellular networks. Nokia is also a significant supplier of advanced transmission systems and access networks, multimedia equipment, satellite and cable receivers, and other telecom-related products.

Comparing Nokia and Ericsson over three years I found their price performance consistent except for the last three months when Ericsson fared much worse than Nokia.

Using www.adr.com I was able to review current and archived news on the prospect companies, which included news on the telecommunications sector. I drew further graphics comparing share price performances of Ericsson and Nokia, both as ADRs and as securities on their domestic markets. Then I compared detailed financial results and earnings using the current earnings forecasts available for both companies. When I had marshalled the information I set out to find I reviewed it using charts with comparisons to a range of market indexes and I introduced comparisons with other companies in the telecommunications sector to see which were performing best.

It was clear from the financial data and the charts at the time that Nokia was moving ahead of Ericsson and other competitors. I selected Nokia at the time as the telephone manufacturer for *Portfolio 2001* and the decision proved to be correct. Ericsson are a great company and have gained some lost ground in 1999 but Nokia continued to perform better as illustrated in this chart drawn in June 1999.

Chart www.adr.com: top line Nokia, lower line Ericsson

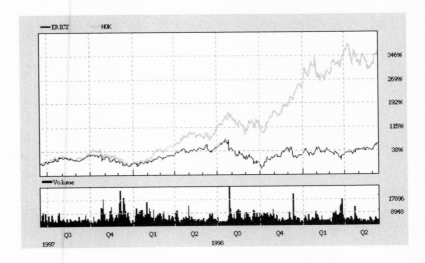

The research report on Nokia in *Portfolio 2001* was based on information from its own web site and from `www.adr.com`. You too can easily update information, monitor, and conduct further research using the extensive database of adr.com.

On line brokers and discount brokers

On line investing introduces several benefits to investors and it is both more efficient and considerably cheaper than conventional services.

A few years ago, when I started working on *Portfolio 2001* and I prepared an outline of the book, On Line Broking was one of the big section headings. Now, including comment on on line broking would be as useful as listing information on the departure times of fast trains from Euston Station in London to Birmingham. Or the cost of discount air tickets to New York.

On line broking has happened in the US and its success is detailed in the report on Charles Schwab the discount broker in the section on Millennial Niches. Investors can trade world stocks as ADRs using discount brokers, and in this chapter the research gateway for global investors www.adr.com has already been introduced. In the Webliography, web sites that list the names and addresses of on line brokers in the US and elsewhere are included.

On line broking is of course cheaper, but there used to be a weakness to dealing with discount brokers when they gave no research back-up. This has now changed, and is changing, as research information available on the Internet mushrooms and leading brokers make arrangements with investment banks to use their research.

As this book goes to press the world's biggest brokerage Merrill Lynch has announced that it is taking the plunge and going on line.

The year 2000 and the millenium bug Y2K

Y2K and the millennium bug are journalese used to describe the risk that some computers may not recognize the code for the year 2000. As this book goes to press in summer 1999, some analysts maintain that this could wreak havoc on systems from our local cash card dispensers to Russian nuclear warheads. Many investors who expect that global economic growth is gathering pace again and want to invest more in equities are being held back by fears of disruption and market anxiety related to Y2K.

Y2K will become an issue that affects equity markets if serious disruptions are threatened even if they never occur. There has also been a long running debate on whether the costs of preparing for Y2K compliance would become an economic burden which on its own could encourage a recession. Dr Yardeni runs a continuous update on the Y2K problem on his site `www.yardeni.com`. Generally leading economists do not expect any major disruptions and Yardeni is the most respected commentator who still has serious anxieties on the subject.

Portfolio 2001

`www.portfolio2001.com` will publish company-specific updates on the prospects in the *Portfolio*. The web site will also keep readers abreast of new research sites and draw attention to developments in the global and major world economies.

8

FINANCIAL

INFORMATION

Studying financial accounts will always be the first priority for many investors, and in previous sections on using information I have not covered this subject. This was no oversight or omission and there is a good reason why the subject has not yet been addressed. I left the best for last.

Interactive graphics, neural networks, meta charts and a galaxy of brilliant technological resources have transformed accessible financial information for investors beyond description. However, impressive as visual on line resources are, making investing decisions calls for attention to the financial numbers, and bean counting remains an essential investing discipline. The greatest strength of on line investor information is that everything in the public domain on a company's finances can be on your computer screen within minutes, if it is – like *Portfolio 2001* prospects – a US company or a non-US company traded as an ADR in the US. And, the information you work with will be up to date.

For companies not traded in the US it may at times still be more difficult to get comprehensive information, but access to information is improving all the time.

Financial analysis

Computers are brilliant number crunchers and, when powerful software resources link them to large information databases, they work fast and efficiently. Financial information suppliers on the Internet count the beans for you and, with the software applications they use and the databases they access, they have brought new dimensions to performance analysis.

I used basic information from Market Guide `www.marketguide.com` for historic data presented in many of the following company reports. Similar excellent information is available from several other publishers and Wall Street Research Net `www.wsrn.com` have links with a wide range of financial analytical reports.

Company accounts and reports

Most companies have web sites that include recent company accounts and reports with archives that can be accessed on line. The various Edgar services, listed in the Webliography, access the regular statutory reports filed by companies with the Securities and Exchange Commission in the US. Some Edgar services which have to be paid for include sophisticated analytical programmes which provide instant information on all aspects of performance from filings within hours after the SEC receives the documents.

Information available as Excel spread sheets

Technology companies including Texas Instrument and Intel include Excel spread sheets of their accounts, enabling investors to keep and update financial models manipulate the data and run their own models. Microsoft have gone the full distance and include a 'what if' analysis programme where you can input any variations to their financial accounts on line and draw a revised report based on your assumptions. Wall Street Research Net `www.wsrn.com` access a service which offers spread sheet data on all companes.

Measuring value

Information on earnings multiples, relationships of price to company sales and book value and to other measures can all be drawn off the Internet, based on calculations at the time related to current prices.

It would be going beyond the scope of this book to include little packages of wisdom on the spectrum of financial analysis and valuation.

Portfolio 2001 has been written for investors who will make investing decisions in real time and the Webliography shows you where to get the information.

'What if' forecasts

For almost all the companies reviewed in this book, a 'what if' earnings forecast suggests potential earnings per share a few years ahead. With the earnings forecast and a guess at the earnings multiple at which the share might trade, a price is targeted a few years ahead. 'What if' forecasting is based on both previous financial performance and expectations. Microsoft's financial web site **www.moneycentral.com** has a research wizard function which you can use to get a second opinion on the 'What if' forecasts in *Portfolio 2001*.

If you had used the Moneycentral research wizard in January 1999, you would have found far more optimistic outcomes than in these pages.

Computers processing numbers will not debate, doubt or discuss any information they are fed. It is important to keep in mind that financial information analysed on the Internet will vary from excellent to good to bad to hopeless and even illegal. The Microsoft research wizard will accurately prepare a forecast based on the price earning of say pharmaceutical shares as a sector on a certain day. It will not, however, make a decision on whether these valuations may or may not be sustainable. Hence, when a market is very strong, a computer generated forecast will probably assume it will stay that way. Conversely, if the market is very weak, the forecast will be jaundiced on prospects.

Must you understand financial accounts to invest?

The investing strategy followed in *Portfolio 2001* is based on identifying companies which are likely to grow earnings year after year, and the prospect companies are well-established industry leaders. The focus is on the strength of the growth story, but investors who have doubts about their competence to invest because of a lack of knowledge on financial accounts must ensure that they use brokers and advisers who have the knowledge to give them comfort.

Cash flows

Because a company's liquidity is its life blood and can be as important as its profitability, Investors should examine cash flows to reassure themselves on the financial strength of their investment or prospect.

Cash flow statements must be produced by companies with their annual accounts and usually follow the balance sheet and and income statements. A useful introduction to understanding cash flows can be obtained from the Individual Investor on line University web site:

`www.iionline.com/investor_university/state.asp`

9
_

INVESTORS'
WEBLIOGRAPHY

Using the webliography

1. Internet addresses all correctly start with http:// but as most browsers insert this code automatically we list addresses as www. If difficulty is experienced retry with http:// before www.
2. At the time of going to press the web addresses listed were correct but the World Wide Web is an evolving resource and addresses may change. If the listed address does not connect you with the site, run a search through a search engine to locate the current web site address.
3. The web sites listed are intended to put the reader in the driver's seat on the information highways and not as a listing of all investors web sites.

Primary Research Resources

Global

Wall Street Journal & Barrons **www.wsj.com**
Briefing books with background information on all US listed companies and ADRs.
Quotes and Interactive graphics for US & UK stocks. Global news and
commentary. Financial Web Site reviews, databases and searchable archive. Personal
Journal with e-mails $ portfolios

Bridge Information Systems **www.bridge.com**
Global quotes, excellent charts and news. Multi currency portfolios

Financial Times **www.ft.com**
Background data on global stock exchange listed companies. Company, country,
industry and market news and analysis. Pound sterling portfolios and e-mail news
alerts. Global archive. No graphics.

Bloomberg **www.bloomberg.com**
Live news and commentary on financial markets and global equities. Reports in real
time market indices with live graphic of Dow. Interactive charts supported by analysis
of reported earnings and forecasts. Magazine subscription brings additional information.

J.P. Morgan's adr.com **www.adr.com**
Benchmark resource for global investors with news on global markets and
industries, graphic presentation of global indexes, global company specific news and
analysis, interactive graphics and earnings forecasts.

Yahoo Finance **http://quote.yahoo.com**
Quotes service with news and background information keeps improving on companies
and markets with interactive graphics in the US. Yahoo country sites include the US
and Canada, UK and Ireland **http://finance.uk.yahoo.com**
and sites for Australia & NZ, Canada, China, Denmark, France, Germany, Italy,
Japan, Korea, Norway, Spain and Sweden.

Dr. Yardeni's economics site **www.yardeni.com**
US and Global macro economics resource : extensive charts, comment & archive.

Morgan Stanley Dean Witter **www.ms.com**
Daily global macro economics commentary & regular global strategy reviews.

Global from US perspective

Investors Business Daily **www.investors.com**
Dynamic modern approach to investing, economics, charts and technology.

Microsoft's Moneycentral **www.moneycentral.com**
Comprehensive company stock quotes and research, news and excellent interactive
graphics with on line analysis plus Jim Jubak's savvy stock picking which includes a
top 50 global companies portfolio;

Multex Brokers Research Library **www.multex.com**
Research site with daily commentary selling brokers research.

Individual Investor on line **www.iionline.com**
Quotes, news, research, stock picking and commentary well presented for private global investors by credible analysts and publisher.

CBS Market Watch **www.cbsmarketwatch.com**

CNNFN **www.cnnfn.com**
Two US TV Station investor sites with live news, quotes, graphics, commentary and growing range of investor services.

Portfolio2001.com **www.portfolio2001.com**
News on companies in portfolio, analysis of results, links to web sites and 'bear essentials' commentary on market risks as a reality check.

National financial web sites

UK
www.adr.com and the following

Hemmington Scott - UK Equities **www.hemscott.co.uk**
UK's Top financial publisher's Companies Direct Menu gives quotes and graphics for all UK companies with five year financial summaries, quotes, news, company time tables and news, brokers estimates and details of directors and major shareholders. Site is also gateway to Hemscott Company Refs, a benchmark report on UK companies.

Market Eye **www.marketeye.co.uk**
Quotes, graphics and fundamental data on UK listed companies and UK Stock Exchange. Site is presented by Primark a leading global information provider. Additional information and services for subscribers at different levels.

Yahoo UK & Ireland **http://finance.yahoo.co.uk**
Stock quotes and comprehensive data on UK companies and markets. Profiles on UK companies link with Hemscott UK equities direct.

Updata **www.updata.co.uk**
Comprehensive site on UK investing with market prices and graphics. Site promotes Updata analytical software.

ESI - electronic stock information **www.esi.com**
Extensive range of menus includes some free data and extensive resources for subscribers.

BBC **www.bbc.co.uk**
News site with updated commentary on companies, markets and economics.

IG Index **www.igindex.co.uk**
Financial gambling transactions not subject to taxation.

Europe
www.adr.com and the following:

Hemmington Scott – Europe– **www.hemscott.co.uk**
International Equities Direct Menu provides background and financial information on all European listed companies.

Finininfo – France **www.finminfo.fr**
Comprehensive resource with quotes, graphics, earnings estimates, news and analysis.

La Tribune – France **www.latribune.fr**
Leading French financial newspaper with extensive on line resources and French, European and global financial news and commentary.

Les Echos – France **www.lesechos.fr**
Rising French financial newspaper with focus on multimedia in Europe and French, European and global financial news and commentary.

Bank 24 – Germany **www.bank24.de**
Comprehensive resource with quotes, graphics, earnings estimates, news and analysis.

Handelsblatt – Germany **www.handelsblatt.de**
Germany's financial newspaper with extensive on line resources and German, European and global financial news and commentary.

German news in English

www.mathematik.uni-ulm.de/de-news/thisyear/thismonth/today.html#2

Swissquote – Switzerland **www.swissquote.com**
Comprehensive resource with quotes, graphics, earnings estimates, news and analysis.

Swiss Internet Investor – Switzerland

www.swissinternetinvestor.com
Extensive investor resource with Swiss focus and general market commentary.

Amsterdam Stock Exchange Netherlands **www.aex.nl**
Wide ranging information with prices on Dutch Companies and market

---

Yahoo Italy **http://it/finance.yahoo.com**

Yahoo Europe sites **http://finance.yahoo.com**
Similar format Yahoo sites linked with quotes, company data and market news cover Denmark, France, Germany, Norway Spain and Sweden.

Japan
www.adr.com and the following

| Nikkei net. | www.nikkei.co.jp |

| Yahoo | www.quote.yahoo.co.jp |

Emerging markets
www.adr.com and the following

| Russia To-day | www.russiatoday.com |

| Worldly Investor | www.worldlyinvestor.com |

| Global Investor | www.global-investor.com |

| Latin America | www.patagon.com |

| Brazil Bovespa | www.bovespa.com |

| Business Day - South Africa | www.businessday.co.za |

Financial neswpaper site with extensive data resources and customer services

Woza - South Africa www.woza.co.za
Lively informative comment on equities, markets and the new South Africa

Yahoo Australia and NZ, Korea, China http://finance.yahoo.com

United States
With quotes, news, graphics equities, funds and portfolios

| Microsoft Moneycentral | www.moneycentral.com | part free |

| Wall Street Research Net | www.wsrn.com | part free |

| Wall Street City | www.wallstreetcity.com | part free |

| Yahoo | www.yahoo.com | free |

| CBS | www.cbsmarketwatch.com | free |

| CNN | www.cnnfn.com | free |

| MSNBC | www.msnbc.com | free |

| Nasdaq: includes UK quotes | www.nasdaq.com | free |

| Reuters | www.moneynet.com | part free |

| Quicken | www.quicken.com | part free |

Daily Graphs	`www.dailygraphs.com`	subscription
J. P. Morgan adr site	`www.adr.com`	free
America on Line	`www.aol.com`	part free
S&P Personal Wealth	`www.personalwealth.com`	subscription
Dow Jones Business	`www.dowjones.com`	

Earnings estimates

Global

Wall Street Journal Briefing Books	`www.wsj.com`
Adr.com	`www.adr.com`
The Earnings Directory Subscription based service covers universe of global shares	`www.barra.com`
IBES Subscription based service covers US equities and leading global equities with facility for ongoing e-mail updates following any changes in earnings	`www.ibes.com`

UK and Europe

Hemmington Scott `www.hemscott.co.uk`
Free service linked to UK equities direct gives analysts' estimates and commentary on estimate revisions.

United States

S&P Index forecasts top down and bottom up `www.yardeni.com`

Revisions in current brokers research and analysts' upgrades and downgrades
`www.nordby.com`

Earnings estimates near announcements
`www.earningswhispers.com`
Revisions on Portfolio 2001 companies `www.portfolio2001.com`

Brokers & Stock Exchanges

Global

Investor links - Exchanges `www.investorlinks.com`
Linked list with All stock exchanges, commodities and futures exchanges.

United States

Investor links - Brokerages tab `www.investorlinks.com`
All brokers from advisory to discount, on line, deep and deep deep discount

Investor links - all world exchanges `www.investorlinks.com`

UK

Complete listing of Brokers `www.find.co.uk`
Advisory, execution only, on line and discount brokers

Economics and Statistics

Economists

Morgan Stanley `www.ms.com`

Dr. Yardeni `www.yardeni.com`

Princeton Economics `www.princetoneconomics.com`

Dr. Nouriel Roubini:
Asia Crisis Chronology
`www.stern.nyu.edu/~nroubini/asia`

Prof Paul Krugman `web.mit.edu/krugman`

Merrill-Lynch `www.merrill-lynch.com` free

Dismal Scientist `www.dismal.com` free

Warren Buffett `www.berkshire-hathaway.com`

International Monetary Fund `www.imf.org`

World Bank `www.worldbank.org`

OECD `www.oecd.org`

World Trade Organization `www.wto.org`

UK Treasury `www.hm-treasury.gov.uk`

Economic Report of the US President `www.gpo.ucop.edu`

The Levy Institute `www.levyinstitute.org`

Statistics

CIA World Fact Book `www.cia.gov`

US Economics and Statistics `www.census.gov`

United Kingdom & World Statistics `www.ons.gov.uk`
UK site links with European and global official statistical sites

Financial & Fundamental analysis

Edgar - US Company SEC filings `www.edgar-online.com`

Marketguide `www.marketguide.com`

The Street.com `www.thestreet.com`

Zacks Investment Research `www.zacks.com`

Wallstreetcity `www.wallstreetcity.com`

Hemmingtonscott `www.hemmingtonscott.co.uk`

Dailygraphs.com `www.dailygraphs.com`

Technical analysis and graphics

Technical analysis from A-Z `www.equis.com/free/taaz`

Clearstation `www.clearstation.com`

Dailygraphs.com `www.dailygraphs.com`

Omega Research `www.omegaresearch.com`

Updata Software `www.updata.co.uk`

Mutual Funds

US - S&P Personal Wealth `www.personalwealth.com`

US & Global `www.morningstarnet.com.`

Micropal `www.micropal.com`

UK - Trustnet `www.trustnet.co.uk`

Technology & life sciences

Technology

Michael Murphy's Newsletter www.ctsl.com
Highly respected California Technology Stock advisory letter

Durlacher www.durlacher.com

UK Broker with a focus on Technology
Intellectual capital www.intellectualcapital.com

Computer Information Centre www.compinfo.co.uk

International Data Corporation www.idc.com

Techguide www.techguide.com

What is www.whatis.com

C/Net computer network www.cnet.com

CIO www.cio.com

Upside Today www.upside.com

Redherring on line www.redherring.com

ZD Net www.zdnet.com

Silicon Investor www.techstocks.com

Semi Conductor Industry Association www.semichips.org

Life Sciences

Bio on Line www.bio.com

Biospace www.biospace.com

Science Magazine www.science.com

Nature Magazine www.nature.com

US Govt Healthfinder www.healthfinder.gov

Foxnews www.foxnews.com/nav/stage.health.sml

Reutershealth www.reuterhealth.com

National Centre for Biotechnology www.ncbi.nlm.nih/gov/

Human Genome Resources
`www.ncbi.nlm.nih.gov/genome/guide/`

US Food & Drug Administration `www.fda.gov`

Magazines

The Economist `www.economist.com`

Business Week `www.businessweek.com`

Forbes `www.forbes.com`

Fortune `www.fortune.com`

Individual Investor On Line `www.iionline.com`

The Motley Fool `www.motleyfool.com`

WSJ Personal Investing `www.smartmoney.com`

Financial booksellers on line

Global Investor - UK and US `www.global-investor.com`

Amazon (For US titles) `www.amazon.com`

For UK titles and faster delivery in Europe `www.amazon.co.uk`

Barnes & Noble `www.barnesandnoble.com`

Bol.com `www.bol.com`

Individual Investor on Line `www.iionline.com`

Portfolio 2001

`www.Portfolio 2001.com` will maintain listings of several classes of investments not directly related to equities including fixed income securities, futures and derivatives and will research investor training resources and investor web site links.

PART THREE

Research

—

10

INVESTING IN THE LIFE SCIENCES INNOVATORS

The biological sciences revolution

A century ago, if a share picker set out to select the best opportunities for the twentieth century, he – and without any doubt it would have been a 'he' – would have focused on the physical sciences and picked investing opportunities following them. Railroads, steel, mines, manufacturers and electric power generators would have been top of the list. He may have been on the lookout for an opening in the business of that clever Mr Benz and his nifty single cylinder horseless carriage, but probably he would not have heard or spared a thought for Mr Ciba and Mr Giegy, or the dapper Mr Hoffman and his beautiful wife Adele La Roche who, along with Mr Merck, Mr Eli Lily and others, were beavering away quietly and unnoticed in small pharmacies in Switzerland and Germany. The manufacture of packaged medications for a wider market than pharmacy customers was a new industry in Europe at the turn of the century and there were no signs there that it would ever amount to much.

However the booming patent medicines business in the United States at the end of the nineteenth century ushered in the beginnings of mass marketing and big budget advertising, and became a major pillar for the growth and profitability of the newspaper industry. By 1895, *Scientific American* reported that some drug advertisers were spending a million dollars a year on advertising, and the maker of Carter's Little Liver Pills 'cannot spend the money he is making . . . judicious advertising has made it possible'. Even Coca-Cola was introduced at the time as a nerve tonic. It was the real thing – Coca stood for *co*caine and *ca*ffeine, which latter ingredient it still has today. The drug industry certainly started on sound commercial foundations – profitability and good marketing.

As we leave a century dominated by the physical sciences and look ahead to the twenty-first century, if we ask a share picker for her top selections she – and probably it will be a 'she' – will certainly have industries related to the biological sciences on top of her list. The British Health and Sciences Foresight Panel, in 1996, concluded that a 'biological sciences revolution is under way the impact of which will be greater than the industrial or atomic revolutions'.

After a 300 per cent growth in the world's population and a 30 per cent increase in life expectancy to the credit of science and medicine in the twentieth century, it is a humbling thought that new science promises to eclipse these achievements in the next century. A scientific process has started which will profoundly change the way we live, and the future milestones which have been suggested by scientists and futurologists include:

2010   New advances in genetics enable doctors to combine gene therapy with immunotherapy to create more effective cancer treatments and enable the use of animal organs in transplant surgery to save human lives.

2015   The genetic roots of all diseases are identified.

2022   Foetuses conceived *in vitro* mature to term in extra-uterine incubators and are 'born' without ever having been inside a human womb.

2025   Computers connected directly to the brain are able to recognize and respond to thoughts, obviating the need for manual input of data and commands.

2030   Following on the development of artificial lungs, kidneys and livers, doctors will make artificial legs and fully functional artificial eyes.

2030   Human hibernation will be used for the first time in long-distance space travel.

2500   From an average of 78 years, human life spans will have been extended to 140 years.

The source for the above predictions is a special edition of *Time* magazine, in Winter 1997/1998, entitled 'The New Age of Discovery'. I added the use of animal organs in transplantation surgery for the year 2010.

The new era of lifestyle drugs

At the close of the twentieth century, the $300 billion pharmaceutical industry is most focused on the impact of Viagra, not for its effects on once impotent men, but because of the earnings potential of lifestyle drugs and the money that pharmaceutical companies can make on them.

Viagra has changed the lives of men with clinically diagnosed impotence, and the lives of their partners. Weight-loss drugs expected to come on to the market will change the lives of the seriously obese. Other drugs in the pipeline will control everything from minor problems like baldness to painful diseases like arthritis, debilitating diseases like Alzheimer's, and incapacities like incontinence. Eventually, drugs will attack the diseases of ageing, including osteoporosis, heart disease and some forms of cancer. As the baby boomers age, they will have opportunities to live longer and feel younger, and the pharmaceutical industry stands to be the financial beneficiary.

Lifestyle drugs are the major new dynamic in the industry. Within six months of introducing Viagra, Pfizer's market value increased by an incredible $30 billion. Pfizer now trades in the range of 50 times expected earning for the current year, with a price to earnings valuation at the top of the big league in line with Microsoft – almost double the rating accorded to many of its blue chip competitors.

In spite of all the attention the lifestyle drugs attract, the pharmaceutical industry's big business has been, and will continue to be, fighting serious disease, and the new direction in medicine is disease prevention. Merck's Fosamex and Eli Lily's Evista are for the treatment of osteoporosis, a weakening of the bones that affects 18 million post-menopausal women in the United States alone. Evista may also block cancer-causing oestrogen in the breast while increasing bone mass, and clinical indications are that the drug may prevent breast cancer in high-risk women. If so, there are an additional 30 million potential customers. Estimates for Evista sales for osteoporosis should exceed $1 billion a year by the end of the year 2000, and could be a multiple of two or three times that if the drug is approved for preventative cancer medication. Alerted to such earnings potentials, the pharmaceutical industry is looking at other preventive maintenance regimes over a range of diseases.

A priority for many researchers is to discover a new psychotropic drug to challenge the top blockbuster drug, the anti-depressant Prozac, introduced in the late 1980s. Prozac targets the brain chemical serotonin and is prescribed for conditions ranging from behavioural difficulties to eating disorders. Annual sales for Prozac and its derivatives in 1998 exceeded $6 billion.

Merck has been investigating a new class of drugs that block the action of a brain chemical called Substance P, which they expect could be used to treat depression and schizophrenia and Pfizer, in partnership with Neurogen Corp., is in early clinical trials with a drug that is aimed at GABA, a brain chemical involved in anxiety. If successful, the compound could have the benefits of Roche's one-time blockbuster tranquilliser drug Valium without its addictive and other harmful side effects.

Multi billion-dollar blockbuster drugs call for multi billion-dollar research-and-development budgets and potentially spiralling research costs have encouraged a wave of mergers in the industry so that research and development budgets can be shared.

Drug discovery and bringing new drugs to the market will never be undertakings that happen quickly. Even when drugs are out of the laboratory and can be tested on humans, making sure they are safe takes a long time. Until very recently it took five to fifteen years to develop a new drug, but, with advances achieved by molecular biologists in understanding how cells work, it is possible now for drugmakers to work more swiftly. New screening technologies test thousands of drug candidates in hours and scientists can identify the specific receptors on many cells that attract disease-causing agents.

Genetic engineering

The cloning by British scientists of Dolly the sheep in 1997, (see page 167) with several other animals cloned since, raises the prospects of cloning human beings and many people fear that scientists are starting to play God. However, whatever fears or hopes people have with cloning, the big story in modern medicine is genetic engineering.

Genetic research requires gigantic financial commitment. The costs of the scientific and computational work in genetics and genomics research currently in progress matches the public investments that space travel and exploration attracted to launch man into space. There is a difference, however, in where the money comes from. Space travel was funded by the US as a national project. Medical science is funded by private businesses and investments in genetic engineering could change the way disease is treated and the way we live our lives.

At one level genetic research plays an important role in identifying causes of illness. At another, genetic medicine approaches biological structures, functions and malfunctions as being determined by the genetic material present in every living cell. It aims to manipulate the genetic information – with the object of eliminating the disease by targeting its cause instead of its symptoms. Presently only a third of human diseases are treated causatively and cured by medical or surgical intervention. The other two-thirds, including major causes of death, are still only treated symptomatically.

The study of genetics started with the principles of heredity expounded by Gregor Mendel in 1861. Since then, biologists have been progressively gaining a better understanding of genes, the organizational units of heredity. In 1943, Oswald Avery recognized that genes are made of deoxyribonucleic acid (DNA). In 1953, James Watson and Francis Crick described the now famous double-helix structure of the DNA molecule.

Each of the 100 trillion cells in the human body (except blood cells) contains the entire human genome – all the genetic information necessary to build a human being. This information is encoded in 6 billion base pairs, sub-units of DNA. Inside the cell nucleus, six feet of DNA are packaged into 23 pairs of chromosomes (one chromosome in each pair coming from each parent). Each of the 46 human chromosomes contains the DNA for thousands of individual genes, the units of heredity. Each gene in turn is a segment of double-stranded DNA that holds the recipe for making a specific molecule, usually a protein. Proteins, made up of amino acids, are the body's workhorses, the essential components of all organs and chemical activities. Their function depends on their shapes, which are determined by the 50,000 to 100,000 genes in the cell nucleus.

Genetic engineering is the synthesis, alteration, replacement or repair of genetic material by artificial rather than natural means.

A breakthrough, as important to science as the discovery of the wheel was to physics, occurred in 1970. Arber, Smith and Nathan discovered restriction enzymes with which DNA molecules can be 'cut' out of one molecule in sections and inserted into another, which then produces proteins coded by the inserted genes. Genetic engineering was 'born' three years later, in 1973, when Stanley Cohen and Herbert Boyer succeeded in introducing a genetically engineered DNA molecule, which they had produced in a test tube, into a bacterium which then transmitted the modified molecule to its daughter cells. By inserting 'new' genes, it had become possible to use bacteria and cell cultures, which reproduce at incredible speed, as minute chemical factories. Cohen and Bower went on to establish the pioneer genetic engineering company Genentech, now in the Roche group. The rest of the story as it unfolds over the next century might resemble science fiction.

Gene therapy

Modern medicine has cleared several watershed hurdles over the last two centuries starting with public health, sanitation and disinfectants which arrested the rampant spread of infection and disease. Then anaesthesia made it possible to effect cures with surgery, and vaccines and antibiotics made it possible to prevent and treat many diseases spread by microbes.

The dramatic changes expected in medicine in the twenty-first century will follow a conceptual revolution which started in earnest a half century ago when molecular biologists realized that many medical complications could be diseases of DNA, the master molecule that encodes the genetic script of life. In the wake of these discoveries, the goal of medicine is shifting from treating symptoms to preventing and eliminating disease through genetic intervention, and to early diagnosis by genetic probes.

Genes produce proteins, and defective genes cause disease when they cause cells to deliver the wrong amount or the wrong kind of protein. When the gene defect results in a non-functioning protein, scientists can try to replace that function by introducing a corrected version of the protein into the body, or they can try to mimic the function of the missing protein with a synthetic molecule. The experimental technology of gene therapy could revolutionize medicine in the next century, if selected genes delivered into a patient's cells can relieve a symptom or cure a disease. Potentially, some coronary diseases, various cancers, Alzheimer's disease and many other conditions, even including the ageing process itself, are candidates for gene therapy treatment.

To understand genetic malfunctions in various diseases, molecular biologists have been probing inside the cell itself and coding its genetic material. By blocking or stimulating the production of defective proteins at the source, rather than dealing with them after they are circulating in the body and causing damage, new drugs and genetic treatments to prevent disease are being developed.

While gene therapy is still at an experimental stage, there are cases where it has already been effective. The most publicized was in 1990, when a young American girl Ashanti da Silva was treated. She was born with severe combined immunodeficiency (SCID), after inheriting a defective gene from each parent, which rendered her immune system ineffective and made her vulnerable to all infections.

In a well-publicized gene therapy experimental treatment, white blood cells were removed from her, normal copies of the defective gene were then mixed with the cells removed, and the treated cells were returned to her bloodstream. After four similar treatments over four months her condition was improved sufficiently for her to lead a normal life with only occasional follow-up treatments.

After the first human gene therapy tests were conducted nearly ten years ago, there were high hopes that gene therapy would soon help to ameliorate or cure diseases ranging from cystic fibrosis to cancer. However, the expectations were ahead of the science and later experiments have generally ended in disappointment. New genes have often proved to be ineffective, have caused harmful side effects, and are frequently destroyed by the immune system before they can do any good.

More questions remain unanswered than have been answered on the effects and risks of introducing genes, which may get into cells other than those targeted, with adverse effects. However, as more genes are identified which malfunction in specific diseases, and techniques for delivering gene therapy are developed and refined, gene therapy is expected to become mainstream and profoundly effect diagnosis, treatments and cures in future.

Switching genes on and off

A typical example of an early experimental treatment that passed a new milestone was reported in the January 1999 edition of the US publication *Science* on work done at the University of Pennsylvania being commercialized by the biotechnology firm Ariad Pharmaceuticals Inc. Successful animal experiments were conducted on a method they devised to deliver a gene that produces the natural protein erythroprotein (EPO). After a single injection, the gene stays in the body and can produce the protein for up to a year, while current treatments typically require protein injections several times a week.

In the new experimental technique, the gene is injected but remains dormant until an oral drug is administered which switches it on. This oral drug allows fine control of how much protein is produced. So far experiments have been on animals, but if the new technique works in people, it will be an overwhelmingly important breakthrough in a large therapeutic area. Annual sales of EPO by Johnson & Johnson and the biotechnology company Amgen are already above $3 billion a year. The new technology has the potential to lead to a new type of gene therapy that would replace with a simple pill the existing injectable treatments not only for anaemia, but also for other diseases including possibly diabetes or cancer.

Other researchers and companies are working on much the same lines. Merck & Co is developing similar gene-delivery methods and has conducted similar animal experiments with several other proteins, including leptin for regulating body weight. Merck won't disclose the other therapeutic proteins it is testing, or further details, pending publication of its results in a major scientific journal.

Genomics

In the thirty years following the consolidation of the chemical elements of the periodic table, chemistry was transformed from alchemy to modern science. Now a parallel has been drawn between this and present-day genomic research, but on a profoundly greater scale. The discovery of specific genes causing specific diseases means nothing less than that scientists can work towards eventually eliminating disease.

Several web sites are published by organizations involved in the Human Genome Project, a concerted global scientific effort aimed at mapping the human genetic code. The US Department of Health site `http://www.nhgri.nih.gov` is one and it gives this outline of the project, which is quoted and paraphrased below:

From Maps to Medicines:
About the Human Genome Research Project

The Human Genome Project is an effort to understand the hereditary instructions that make each of us unique. The goal of this effort is to find the location of the 100,000 or so human genes and to read the entire genetic script, all 3 billion bits of information, by the year 2005.

Inside the nucleus of nearly every cell in the body, a complex set of genetic instructions, known as the human genome, is contained on 23 pairs of chromosomes. Chromosomes are mostly made of long chains of a chemical called DNA – deoxyribonucleic acid.

Even before it is complete, the Human Genome Project promises to transform both biology and medicine. Our genes orchestrate the development of a single-celled egg into a fully formed adult. Genes influence not only what we look like but what diseases we may eventually get. Understanding the complete set of genes, known as the human genome, will shed light on the mysteries of how a baby develops. It also promises to usher in an era of molecular medicine, with precise new approaches to the diagnosis, treatment, and prevention of disease. In short, the international Human Genome Project, which involves hundreds of scientists worldwide, is an investigation of ourselves. Launched in 1990, the project is supported in the United States by the National Institutes of Health and the Department of Energy.

Hereditary instructions are written in a four-letter code, with each letter corresponding to one of the chemical constituents of DNA: A, G, C, T. Each band on this electrophoresis gel represents one of the letters. Our genes are made of DNA, a long, threadlike molecule coiled inside our cells.

If the DNA language becomes garbled or a word is misspelled, the cell may make the wrong protein, or too much or too little of the right one, mistakes that often result in disease. In some cases, such as sickle cell anaemia, just a single misplaced letter is sufficient to cause the disease.

Once the molecular basis of a disease is revealed, scientists have a far better chance of defeating it. Errors in our genes are responsible for an estimated 3,000 to 4,000 clearly hereditary diseases, including Huntington's disease, cystic fibrosis, muscular dystrophy, and many others and altered genes are now known to play a part in cancer, heart disease, diabetes, and many other common diseases.

The Human Genome Project will develop tools to identify the genes involved in both rare and common diseases over the next 15 or 20 years. Such discoveries will lead to detection and treatment of disease and new approaches to prevention. One approach is to design highly targeted drugs that act on the cause, not merely the symptoms, of disease. Another is to correct or replace the altered gene through gene therapy. Gene discovery can also lead to predictive tests that can tell a person's likelihood of getting a disease long before symptoms appear. In some cases, preventive actions can then be undertaken that may avert the disease entirely or else detect it at its earliest stages, when treatment is more likely to be successful.

But finding disease genes can be harder than looking for the proverbial needle in a haystack. This is especially true when the disease is poorly understood at the start of the gene search, as was the case for cystic fibrosis. The problem lies in the vast size of the human genome, which consists of 3 billion chemical bases. If printed out, the entire human genome would fill 1,000 one-thousand page telephone books. Somewhere in that mass of letters lurks the suspect gene – but where? Without clues to guide them, scientists have had to scour all the chromosomes, a practice that until recently could take up to 10 years. Not surprisingly, only about two dozen disease genes have been found this way.

The Human Genome Project is designed to speed this process by providing new tools and techniques that will enable scientists to find genes quickly and efficiently. The first of these tools are maps of each chromosome. One type of map, called a genetic map, consists of thousands of landmarks – short, distinctive pieces of DNA – more or less evenly spaced to enable researchers to pinpoint the location of a gene between any two markers. Another important step is to create what are called physical maps of each chromosome, a process that is also well under way. Physical maps consist of overlapping pieces of DNA spanning an entire chromosome.

Once these maps are complete, investigators can localize a gene to a particular region of a chromosome by using a genetic map and then can simply go to the freezer, where the DNA for the physical map is stored, and pick out that piece to study, rather than searching through the chromosomes all over again.

The ultimate goal of the Genome Project is to decode, letter by letter, the exact sequence of all 3 billion nucleotide bases that make up the human genome. It will be a daunting task. Before plunging into massive sequencing, researchers from numerous fields – biology, physics, engineering, and computer science, to name a few, are developing automated technologies to reduce the time and cost of sequencing. Once the human genome sequence is completed, attention can shift from the job of finding genes, which will then simply be a matter of scanning a computer database, to understanding them.

In its first 5 years the Human Genome Project has already had a profound effect. The pace of gene discovery has nearly quadrupled. The gene involved in cystic fibrosis, the most common lethal hereditary disease among Caucasians, was identified in 1989 and a diagnostic test is available to identify gene carriers among high-risk families. In early 1994, scientists discovered two genes involved in a hereditary form of colon cancer. An estimated 1 million Americans carry misspelled copies of these genes, which give them a 70 to 80 per cent likelihood of developing colon cancer. Now that the genes are known a simple blood test to detect those high-risk individuals is being developed. The test will open the door to preventive strategies that promise to greatly reduce deaths from this disease.

The above lengthy extract of information on the Human Genome Project has been included because the project itself is at the epicentre of the modern pharmaceutical industry.

Another approach to dealing with defective protein production is known as antisense. Glaxo Wellcome are working on the p53 gene which normally has a role in the proliferation of cells, but at times a mutation in the gene results instead in the formation of tumours. To arrest the release of the deadly protein that causes the tumours, Glaxo scientists are exploiting antisense technologies that target a single stranded bit of genetic material which carries the genetic message to the cellular machinery producing the protein. The drug they are developing will bind to the genetic material, make it change what it was doing, and halt production of the deadly protein.

The importance of molecular biology to medicine and the drug industry was recognized a half a century ago, but, as with gene therapy, initial high expectations for rapid cures were not forthcoming. What has been achieved is a body of accumulated knowledge which has enabled scientists to delve into cells to change the way they function or malfunction, the way they reproduce themselves, and even the way they can be cloned.

Cloning and pharming – using animals

The first animals to be cloned in the 1960s were frogs. John Gurdon, now at Cambridge University, took a frog's egg, destroyed the nucleus, and transplanted a nucleus from another frog. By December 1997, developed mammals were being cloned, and Dolly, the world's most famous sheep, cloned from a single mammary cell of her six-year-old mother, was named by *Science* magazine as the scientific achievement of 1997. Dolly was cloned from a cell of a six-year-old animal and, having successfully used an old animal's genes to make an embryo, scientists will seek new insights into the ageing process. As an animal grows older, it accumulates tiny genetic errors or mutations and these can now also be studied in detail by seeing their effect on the development of sheep embryos.

By December 1997, the scientists in Scotland who had cloned Dolly announced they had cloned identical lambs carrying a human gene for a protein treatment for haemophilia. These ewes will produce milk yielding a blood clotting agent for haemophiliacs. Behind these developments were a UK commercial firm PPL Therapeutics Limited, and the UK government-sponsored Roslin Research Institute, which had already been experimenting with 'altered' sheep to produce human proteins for the treatment of emphysema and cystic fibrosis.

PPL Therapeutics is progressing trials with alpha-1-antitrypsin (AAT), a drug now secreted in the milk of a flock of transgenic sheep, that can possibly be administered to patients with cystic fibrosis, using an aerosol that delivers the drug into the lungs where it is needed. In cystic fibrosis repeat infections damage the lung tissues and AAT acts to block the human body's own enzyme, elastase, that causes this damage.

PPL claims that the cloning process will allow scientists to produce identical copies of transgenic sheep that secrete high levels of pharmaceuticals in their milk. Other cloned animals are opening new markets for nutraceuticals which could include, for instance, infant milk formula with improved nutritional content; preserving endangered species; achieving consistent carcass size for meat production; and transgenic organs for use in transplant surgery. Cloning could make the production of many other drugs more cost efficient than by other means.

PPL's next candidate pharmaceuticals are protein C, for the treatment of deep vein thrombosis, and fibrinogen, for use as a tissue sealant. Two transgenic sheep lines expressing protein C and fibrinogen in their milk have already been established. Protein C is not yet commercially available by any other manufacturing process, and has a different, local action compared with other anticoagulants. Also in development at PPL is bioactive factor IX, a clotting factor that is deficient in haemophilia B patients.

Other companies are following hot on the heels of PPL with recombinant proteins derived from transgenic animals. For instance, Genzyme Transgenics (USA) has its blood-clotting agent, antithrombin III, derived from the blood plasma of transgenic goats, and also has a transgenic goat carrying BR96, an antibody being developed by Bristol-Myers Squibb as a potential cancer therapy.

Pharming (Netherlands) is also involved in transgenic animal proteins, and has already produced samples of human lactoferrin from the milk of a transgenic cow. In terms of biological activity, the transgenic animal protein was indistinguishable from lactoferrin produced normally in humans. Lactoferrin has potential uses in the treatment and prevention of gastrointestinal infections in people with low immunological resistance, including AIDS patients, premature infants and cancer patients undergoing radio- or immunotherapy. Pharming has also developed human serum albumin and lysozyme in transgenic animals, and is collaborating with another US company, AutoImmune in the production of human collagen. Collagen has potential for the treatment of rheumatoid arthritis, and several other applications.

Scientists claim that cloning will uniquely advance scientific knowledge in ways that will improve the quality of human life, and research on cloning will provide an increased opportunity to discover and understand how genes work, how cells differentiate and age and how cells multiply in controlled ways and in uncontrolled ways, as they do in cancer. Agriculturally, cloning also has several potential applications including the genetic improvement of livestock, removal of the protein in milk that causes allergies, and other changes in milk and meat composition.

There are serious moral issues concerning cloning. There is the danger that once it has been possible to clone a developed mammal like a sheep it will be possible to clone a human being, and such cloning could easily be abused. The moral issues of cloning are not discussed in this book – not because I do not have serious concerns, but because they cannot be properly addressed in a few pages of a book on investing opportunities.

Transplant surgery and disarming the immune system

In December 1967, following a dramatic four-hour pioneering operation, Professor Christian Barnard, then a relatively unknown young cardiac surgeon in Cape Town, gave an electrical stimulus to start the first transplanted heart in a human being. As it responded and started to beat, Barnard is reported to have gasped 'Christ, it's going to work.' History was made and the first human heart transplantion operation had been a success. However, the trans-planted heart did not survive for long and the recipient of the organ, Louis Washkansky died eighteen days later. The human immune system treats any foreign substance as an invader which might destroy it, and responds by trying to destroy the invader. The response of Louis Washkansky's immune system could not be sufficiently controlled and so it rejected the heart that worked perfectly mechanically.

Before transplantation could become a cure, the mechanical component of transplantation had to be complemented by immunosuppressant drugs, which control the immune system's rejection response. By disarming it and preventing it from recognizing and acting against the foreign antigens of the donor organ these drugs would make transplant surgery viable.

The discovery of the immunosuppressant Cyclosporin A by Sandoz Research Laboratories (now part of Novartis) in the early 1970s transformed transplantation from an experimental technique to an effective means of treating kidney, pancreas, liver and heart failure. By the early 1990s, over 300,000 organ transplants had been performed, and one-year success rates with Cyclosporin range from 70 per cent for pancreas and liver transplants to 80-90 per cent for kidney and heart grafts.

The success of Cyclosporin A and other immunosuppressants has now led to effective controls on organ rejection, but while the organ waiting list grows longer each year, the number of donors remains fairly static.

In November 1997, `http://www.dhs.gov` shows that

the US United Network for Organ Sharing national patient waiting list for transplants contained over 50,000 registrations. At the same time there were 37,859 registrations for a kidney transplant; 9,323 for a liver transplant; 3,869 for a heart transplant; 2,588 for a lung transplant; 356 for a pancreas transplant; 76 for a pancreas islet cell; 1,596 for a kidney-pancreas transplant; 94 for an intestine transplant and 233 for a heart-lung transplant – in all 55,994 patients waiting for available organs.

Patients can be listed with more than one centre so the number in the list can be greater than the number of patients. However, there were only 19,410 solid organ transplants performed in the US in 1996, indicating a likely shortfall of some 20,000-plus for solid organs in the United States alone. In addition there were about 12,000 bone marrow transplants in the year.

Research is now being directed to prevent thousands of people from dying unnecessarily each year and thousands more from suffering deteriorating health and compromised quality of life while they wait for an organ transplant. One way of increasing the availability of organs will be to control the immune system's destruction response, making possible the transplantation of animal organs and tissues, known as xenotransplantation. A route to making xenotransplantation work now being developed is pharming animals' organs for transplantation, and genetically humanizing the animal's organs to lessen chances of rejection by the human immune system. A subsidiary of Portfolio 2001 company Baxter is already experimenting with transplanting hearts from pigs into baboons.

Managing the immune system and genetic material

At the other end of the spectrum, a benefit of increased understanding of the immune system will be when ways can be found to stimulate it to eliminate invaders such as cancer at early stages. This will contrast with present treatments of cancer which overwhelm it with force by cutting it out surgically, bombarding it with radiation or poisoning it with chemotherapy. Unfortunately, some cancer cells often manage to survive the onslaughts and cancer is still the second largest killer in the western world after coronary disease.

The term 'cancer' covers more than 200 separate diseases, each with its own cause, prognosis and potential treatment. Most cancers begin with an abnormal cell that multiplies, forming a tumour that invades and destroys nearby healthy tissue. These abnormal cells can also break away from the tumour, spread through the bloodstream and lymphatic system and form metastases and secondary tumours in other parts of the body.

As the cancer cells accumulate, they stimulate the growth of the blood vessels that supply them with nutrients and oxygen. Eventually, the cancerous growth exceeds the ability of the body to supply it with blood and, in time, healthy tissue begins to suffer. This results in extreme weight loss, a decrease in muscle mass and profound weakness often accompanied by severe pain. The classification of cancer is based upon the type of cell and tissue involved, and often too much damage has been done by the time a diagnosis of cancer has been confirmed and treatment commences. In the future, diagnosis may be possible earlier and preventative treatment might even start as soon as a person knows the genetic risks they are exposed to.

Dr Francis Collins, the director of the Center for Human Genome Research at the US National Institute of Health has suggested that in time we will start our adult lives with a genetic blue print and be aware of any genetic risks we are exposed to. In her opinion:

It is reasonably likely that by the year 2010, when you reach your 18th birthday you will be able to have your own report card for your individual risks for future diseases based on the genes you have inherited. I suspect many people will be interested in this information particularly if it is focused on diseases where alterations in lifestyle and medical surveillance can reduce that risk to a more manageable level. In addition to being able to predict risk for disease quite early, two other consequences of gene discovery are important. One will be the ability to move detection of actual disease to earlier stages, particularly for cancer. At the moment, by the time you have a positive mammogram for breast cancer, you have had the tumour a long time and the chance that the cancer has spread is substantial. If we could come up with molecular probes that highlighted the first few cells when they moved down the pathway toward cancer, then the probability of treating that disease would become drastically better.

Also, there is growing confidence . . . that the time is coming when there will be magic bullets to treat cancer the way we now treat many infectious diseases with vaccines and antibiotics. Our understanding of oncogenes and tumour suppressors and of the detailed steps that carry a cell from being normal to being malignant is going to allow us to develop drugs that will make our current chemotherapy poisons as obsolete as arsenic is now for treating infectious illnesses. And I think that time is coming potentially within the next 20 to 25 years.

Biotechnology

Many biotechnological applications are old and traditional, and were well used for generations without any understanding of how they worked. Traditional applications include fermentation with yeast to produce beer, cheese, and yes, back to the new millennium celebrations in case you fear they have been forgotten, champagne. Here is an elegant example of how biotechnology has progressed. Traditional biotechnology used yeast to ferment beer as we still do, but, using techniques of genetic engineering, modern biotechnology has genetically modified a species of yeast to brew better beer.

In the 1980s and 1990s, promising new biotechnological and scientific discoveries spawned a separate 'Biotech' sector for investors, alongside the pharmaceutical sector. 'Biotech' for investors is not based on a textbook definition of biotechnology, but includes all innovative enterprises commercializing new scientific discoveries and applications. There are now over 1,500 biotechnology companies worldwide, of which over 500 are quoted on stock exchanges, and over half of them are directed to medical therapeutic and diagnostic applications.

In the ten years prior to 1994, an average of three biotechnological drugs were approved a year. In 1995 twenty were approved and in 1996 and 1997, thirty were approved. With more drugs now out of the laboratory and on the market, the biotechnology sector is maturing with new companies making the transition from being an R&D project to a *de facto* pharmaceuticals manufacturer.

Major pharmaceutical companies often take stakes early in promising biotech companies, or make arrangements to market the products when they have been developed. Once they have a vested interest, they support the new biotech companies financially and often make agreed progressive milestone payments as the technology gets validated. In this way pharmaceutical companies can spread the high costs and risk of drug innovation with entrepreneurial scientists and venture capitalists.

For private investors, the only low-risk route into biotechnology is by investing in major pharmaceutical companies which have both their own research programmes and associations with biotechnology ventures and other research associations. For example Novartis, in its large portfolio of cutting-edge investments, owns the fledgling American company Genetic Therapy Industries, which developed the pioneer gene therapy treatment used for treating Ashanti da Silva, mentioned earlier, and they control the major independently listed American biotech company Chiron. Like other large pharmaceutical companies, they also support a wide range of associations in new scientific discovery programmes with biotech companies and academic institutions.

The first time I met with a biotech company to discuss funding, and they spoke about seed capital as 'burn off' money, I was shocked. I soon learned that seed capital for biotech is 'burn off' fuel for the years before commercialization is achieved, and the speed at which it is used is the 'burn rate'. This highlights the difference for investors between the labels 'pharmaceutical' and 'biotech'. Pharmaceutical companies are exceptionally rich and well capitalized and develop new drugs using their own money, ploughing billions of dollars into research and development every year, year after year. In the US, the research-based pharmaceutical companies spend as much as 20 per cent of their revenues on research and development, compared to an average industry spend of 4 per cent. The top ten pharmaceutical companies in the US alone invest going on for $20 billion a year in R&D. Biotech companies raise money from investors which they burn off. If they are successful the rewards can be spectacular. If their projects fail there will be no rewards at all.

The regulatory approvals process

The supply of drugs is rigidly controlled throughout the world by regulatory authorities and the leading organization is the US

Food and Drug Administration (FDA), which you can find at www.fda.gov The FDA sets the standards and other countries usually follow similar procedures. In Europe, the drug industry is regulated by the European Medicines Evaluation Agency, an independent agent of the European community based in London. On their web site www.eudra.org/emea.html they publish extensive data on drugs approved and being evaluated.

The Federal Drug Administration approval process starts with the applicant filing an Investigational New Drug Application (IND) which contains all the preclinical studies conducted on the drug with the chemistry and manufacturing data available. These will include safety and toxicology studies using the drug in animals, and efficacy results from animal experiments. The FDA examines the application and responds with queries. When it is satisfied testing can start, a test protocol is agreed and Phase I studies, the first of three studies with humans, can commence.

Phase I studies are designed on a small scale to demonstrate that the drug is safe for human use, and examine the pharma-cokinetic and pharmacological effects of the drug and its mechanism, and seek to gain early confirmation of effectiveness. Pharmacokinetics examine the effects on the body of a drug, specifically examining issues such as how quickly the drug is absorbed into the blood and how different dosages affect the absorption; how the drug is distributed into organs or tissues of the body; how the body metabolizes the drug, whether what the drug is changed into by the body is still active; how long it takes the body to metabolize half the drug (the drug's half life); and how long it takes for the drug to clear the body and be excreted.

Pharmacology looks at such issues as how the drug works, its safety, whether it affects one organ or area of the body more than another, and what common adverse experiences are associated with its use.

Phase Ia trials can include examining healthy volunteers without need for the drug, to see how the body reacts to a single dose of the drug in a monitored situation. The trial progresses to the next dosing level with a different group of volunteers who may be patients with the condition for which the drug has been designed. Phase Ib trials examine how the body reacts to multiple doses of the drug over a period of time ranging from a few days to a few weeks. Before a drug reaches Phase I studies it will probably have been in the laboratory and in animal tests for five to ten years. The average length of time that a product is in Phase I testing is about one year.

Once a drug has gone successfully through Phase I, and has been proven safe to test further on humans, Phase II studies examine the efficacy of the drug. Phase II testing is conducted with a relatively small number of patients suffering from the condition for which the drug is indicated as a treatment. Based on the data obtained in Phase I, several doses, hypothesized to be efficacious, are given to the patient. A placebo is also tested to obtain a baseline value for the comparison of drug effectiveness. Phase II testing takes a minimum of three to six months and often runs for two to three years.

Phase III testing, the last step before the drug can be approved, is efficacy testing in a large number of patients who are representative of the population as a whole. As well as establishing the efficacy of the drug independently, the study usually also compares the efficacy of the candidate drug compared to other approved drugs. Phase III testing takes on average 24 months, and often the regulatory authorities require a longer period.

When a drug has completed all three stages of testing, the applicant company files a New Drug Application (NDA) with the FDA. When the FDA has examined all the data presented, it can approve the NDA for the drug to be marketed and sold, or it can schedule a hearing to bring experts together to comment on the clinical data. At times, an additional study is called for to clarify scientific data or to show more proof of efficacy, including comparisons of the drug to existing medications.

After a drug is approved, Phase IV studies are at times conducted for post-marketing surveillance on the drug's risks, benefits and optimal use. Many promising drugs fail in Phase II or even late Phase III trials. In September 1997, Raymond Gilmartin, the chairman of the US pharmaceutical giant Merck, put the gestation period from discovery of a new compound to marketing it at an average fifteen years, and the average cost of getting it to the market as $400 million.

Innovation and pricing power

Following scientific advances and new patented drugs, the pharmaceutical manufacturing industry enjoyed increased global demand for its products and spectacular profit growth globally for over twenty years from the 1970s. However, in the early 1990s its fortunes reversed when public and private health care providers in the developed world turned their attention to the ever rising health care cost burden. The pendulum swung overnight from pharmaceuticals being a sellers' market to a buyers' market.

The most publicized cost containment initiative was in the United States in 1992, after President Clinton was elected to office. An early campaign on health care reform was launched and an unwelcome spotlight was fixed on the pharmaceutical industry. Other countries followed a similar line and threatened a mixture of supply side price cuts and demand side curbs. In response, share prices of pharmaceutical companies globally fell dramatically. Within a few years, they recovered even more dramatically when the wide-ranging Clinton reforms failed to materialize. However, though President Clinton's sweeping reforms did not materialize, they left a legacy. Containment of health care costs is, and must remain, on the priority agendas of health care providers worldwide.

Synergy, mergers and acquisitions

The pharmaceutical industry's response to containing costs was generally vigorous and frequently structural. To save costs by gaining economies of scale and increased efficiencies, $150 million of global mergers and acquisitions were consummated between 1992 and 1995. In 1994 alone 28 corporate transactions in the industry involved $38 billion, and in 1995, thirty-six deals involved $35 billion. It was a quiet year in 1997, but in 1998 there was a spate of new global mergers in the industry as the emerging global pharmaceutical empires consolidated research and development and marketing costs.

The merger of the German Group Hoeshst Marion Rousel and France's Rhone-Poulenc SA, closing in July 1999, was the most recent and largest transaction. The merged business will be called Aventis SA.

In 1998 estimated worldwide prescription drug sales grew about 3 per cent to $302 billion and the world's top twenty drug companies accounted for 57.3 per cent of sales, according to industry analysts IMS, who track drug sales. The percentage share of the top ten increased fractionally to 36.1 per cent from 35.4 percent. At the end of 1998 the top twenty pharmaceutical companies ranked by global pharmaceutical sales were:

Rank		1998 Sales (Bln £)	% gobal sales	% global yr-on-yr
1	Novartis	10.6	4.2	5
1	Merck	10.6	4.2	8
1	Glaxo Wellcome	10.5	4.2	1
4	Pfizer	9.9	3.9	21
5	Bristol-Myers Squibb	9.8	3.9	11
6	Johnson & Johnson	9.0	3.6	8
7	American Home Products	7.8	3.1	1
8	Roche Holding	7.6	3.0	6
9	Eli Lilly	7.4	2.9	17
10	SmithKline Beecham	7.3	2.9	6
11	Astra	6.9	2.8	16
12	Abbott Laboratories	6.4	2.5	8
13	Hoechst MR	6.2	2.5	2
14	Schering Plough	6.2	2.5	14
15	Warner-Lambert	6.0	2.4	37
16	Bayer	5.2	2.1	1
17	Rhone Poulenc Rorer	4.6	1.8	7
18	Pharmacia & Upjohn	4.5	1.8	8
19	Zeneca	3.7	1.5	6
	Leading 20 companies	143.9	57.3	9

Size matters in the drug industry in view of the costs of research and development and the formidable strength of the leading players. In 1999 Aventis is expected to be the world's number one drug maker ahead of AstraZeneca who, with Novartis AG, are expected to be ahead of Merck & Co. ranked number one in 1997 and neck and neck with Glaxo Wellcome.

In three separate agreements in December 1998, six European companies announced that they were joining forces to spread the costs of research and marketing and boost drug development. Through these transactions they have bought time and structured themselves to be in a better position to compete with US companies who have been gaining ground through the introduction of new drugs. Eventually new products of the merged units will be marketed from stronger commercial bases.

When the Swiss-controlled groups Ciba and Sandoz merged in the new $36 billion company Novartis in 1996, it was hailed as one of the most visionary corporate transactions ever. It was followed by the $40 billion merger of the UK group Zeneca and the Swedish group Astra, which completed in 1999.

Corporate deals are newsworthy and visible and can be very rewarding for shareholders, but the fundamental attraction of strong pharmaceutical companies is that they are profitable with the business they have, and their entrenched positions support predictable and growing earnings streams. When new therapies are developed and patented, they can be marketed at rewarding prices, and pharmaceutical companies have amassed their wealth from successful patented drugs. Glaxo's fortunes, which raised it to be at one time the most profitable company in the United Kingdom, were built on the acid inhibiting drug Zantac for control of gastro-intestinal acid and treatment of ulcers, the first proprietary drug to chalk up sales of over $1 billion a year.

Once a drug goes off patent, any other manufacturer is free to copy it under patent law and the product becomes commoditized. The 'generic' copy has to be approved by the regulatory authorities, and it takes time and is costly for a generic drug to wind its way through the regulatory approvals system. Once it does, profit margins for similar products are bound to be eroded. Innovation and investment in R&D are therefore core to the profitability of the Pharmaceutical and Life Science industries, and necessary to counter the effects of relentless pressure on containing costs by health care providers.

The attractions of pharmaceuticals as investments

Pharmaceutical companies attract as investments for several reasons. Demand for their products is not cyclical: even if economic conditions tighten, people will still prioritize medical treatment. Investors therefore buy into these companies as defensive holdings, but pharmaceuticals are unique because they are both defensive investments and growth investments. In addition to this tempting combination, there are also opportunities for super profits from breakthrough new biotechnology discoveries and techniques such as gene therapy, animal pharming and xenotransplantation.

The profits of pharmaceutical companies are underpinned by a prescription drug market which records sales of above $300 billion annually. Drug sales are set to keep growing, even though health care providers will look for every opportunity to rein in costs. Pharmaceutical companies expect health care providers to recognize the cost savings of more effective drug therapies and the increased quality of life they often bring. The following table lists the main drug classes sold in the world's six largest prescription drug markets:

September 96 to September 97: Retail Pharmacy Purchases in $ Billion

	US	Japan	Germany	France	Italy	UK
Cardiovascular	12166	7906	3779	3762	2009	1450
Alimentary/ Metabolism	19711	7190	2409	2162	1363	1438
Anti infectives	6673	5191	1232	1658	1214	464
Musculo-skeletal	2476	3070	688	660	494	443
Genito-urinary	4199	886	909	795	431	421
Others	10136	13679	2761	1842	1578	1001
Total	65990	43441	14917	14128	8753	7526
% Change	15	0	1	2	7	8

The new blockbusters

With several important approvals expected for new drugs, and the ageing baby boomers driving demand for prescription drugs, the US top pharmaceutical companies and the global companies active in the US markets are likely to record sales growth of over 10 per cent a year into the next century. Industry growth in the US is expected to exceed 12 per cent.

In 1997, the legislative restrictions on advertizing prescription drugs to the public in the United States were relaxed, and brands have become increasingly important as drugmakers take their sales messages directly to patients. The pharmaceutical industry research firm IMS forecast that consumer advertising for pharmaceuticals would grow to $1 billion in 1998, almost double the amount spent in 1997.

The pressure from health care providers is expected to cap price increases on prescription drugs at under 3 per cent a year, and drugmakers are aware of the need to succeed in winning major approvals for proprietary breakthrough products to support their margins. On their side is the emergence of the super blockbuster drug. Blockbusters can now sell billions of dollars in a year but need not address critical medical conditions. Pfizer's Viagra, introduced in 1998, had the most successful drug launch ever, but it treats a medical condition which is not life threatening. Viagra is a lifestyle drug with estimated sales potential between $5 billion and $10 billion a year. Other blockbusters include Warner-Lambert and Pfizer's Lipitor cholestrol reducer, launched in 1987 with estimated sales potential above $5 billion; Eli Lily's Zyprexa for schizophrenia with sales potential above $3 billion and their Evista for osteoporosis with sales over $2 billion; Warner-Lambert's drug Rezulin for adult onset diabetes and SmithKline's similar drug Aventia with sales projected above $2 billion. 1999 has seen the launch of two new drugs for the treatment of pain: Searle and Pfizer together will be marketing Celebrex, and Merck will be marketing a similar drug Vioxx, each with sales potential of above $2 billion a year. BioChem Pharma's hepatitis B drug Lamivudine was launched in 1998 by Glaxo Wellcome in China and also has the potential for sales above $2 billion when it is more widely available.

Drug companies have identified targets with large patient populations that include 60 million obese people, 360 million sufferers from hepatitis infections, 120 million affected by incontinence problems, 25 million with depression and 25 million migraine sufferers. Also, as the ageing population grows, all the age-related diseases become target areas for blockbuster drugs, from Alzheimer's treatments to everyday cardiovascular maintenance medicines.

The *Portfolio 2001* Life Science companies

Selecting Life Science companies for *Portfolio 2001* was challenging, with the sector's vast potential for innovation in prospect companies. Selecting prospects was made even more difficult because the historically high valuations at which drug companies are trading limit the scope for low-risk high-reward investing. If markets reverse or companies encounter setbacks, investments in the best blue chips could turn negative rapidly, so the *Portfolio 2001* companies included will only offer insulation from this risk for long-term investors who intend to stay the course and harvest benefits over the years.

At the time of writing this chapter in January 1999, the pecking order for the top pharmaceutical drugs slots were Merck & Co, Glaxo Wellcome and Novartis each with 4.2%, and Pfizer catching up fast with 3.44%. The top players all command a position in a research portfolio, though some of the companies present similar investing opportunities. Between them almost $20 billion is invested in Research and Development every year.

Johnson & Johnson is a rather different opportunity. It is the world's largest health care company, with a third of its business supplying consumer products. This makes it a blend of a committed Innovator and a Profit Harvester.

The reasons that led to including the prospect companies in *Portfolio 2001* are in the individual research reports, but an explanation must be made why top companies like Roche, Warner-Lambert and Eli Lily were not included. The short answer is that there is only space in this book for ten Life Science slots, and for a research portfolio the intention was to introduce a range of opportunities.

Some prospects may at first sight appear to be less compelling stories than those of unambiguously successful names not included. Baxter has not had the best earnings track record and is a relatively higher risk opportunity, but is included as the world's leading blood technology and critical care company. It has contributed breakthrough technology for blood banks, blood transfusion and transplant surgery, and is likely to contribute breakthrough technologies again in areas including animal organs for human transplants.

Medtronic is another niche company in the medical devices sector but, unlike Baxter, its earnings performance has been stunning. It is the world's leading manufacturer of implantable electronic devices including pacemakers, and is now introducing implantable devices to relieve Parkinson's and other neurological diseases. Implantable devices for neurological disorders could be as exciting an opportunity for the beginning of the new century as pacemakers have been at the end of this century.

The US company Abbott Pharmaceuticals has been included because it has a strong franchise in hospital products including anaesthesia, and is a partner in the US with the Japanese company Takeda, which has an impressive line-up of drugs that are being introduced globally. The British group SmithKline Beecham is launching major new drugs that should raise its potential strongly.

One company reviewed briefly, Monsanto, does not meet the requirements of *Portfolio 2001* at present, but an outline review is included because of its unique position in agribiotech, including genetic seed modification.

The individual company reports which follow spell out the growth stories of the prospects and by visiting their web sites investors can start to build a picture of the exceptional opportunities and profitability which innovation in Life Sciences yields.

What can go wrong with Life Science investments?

In addition to the range of risks that face all commercial undertakings, Life Science companies are expensive shares and trade at high multiples of earnings. Share prices may not factor in loss of business in the future with patent expiries; risks related to failures of products before and after approval; wasted development costs which can run to hundreds of millions of dollars if drugs fail in the late stages of testing; competition from improved new products; and patent and other litigation. There is also the ever-present pressure from health care providers to contain costs. When investing in Life Science companies, as with all growth companies, you will be paying for profit growth expectations which cannot be assured. You will often read a disclaimer on the following lines:

This report and other written reports and oral statements made from to time may contain so-called 'forward-looking statements', all of which are subject to risks and uncertainties. One can identify these foward-looking statements by their use of words such as 'expects', 'plans', 'estimates', 'forecasts', 'projects' and other words of similar meaning. One can also identify them by the fact that they do not relate strictly to historical or current facts

These statements are based on current expectations, forecasts and assumptions that are subject to risks and uncertainties which could cause actual outcomes and results to differ materially from these statements. Risks and uncertainties include general industry and market conditions; general domestic and international economic conditions, such as interest rate and currency exchange rate fluctuations; technologies advances and patents attained by competitors; challenges inherent in new product development, including obtaining regulatory approvals; domestic and foreign healthcare reforms; trends toward managed care and healthcare cost containment, and governmental laws and regulations affecting domestic and foreign operations.

The statements are likely to address growth strategy, financial results, product approvals and development programmes. One must carefully consider any such statement and should understand that many factors could cause actual results to differ from the Company's forward-looking statements. These include inaccurate assumptions and a broad variety of risks and uncertainties, including some that are known and some that are not. No forward-looking statement can be guaranteed and actual future results may vary materially.

The Company does not assume the obligation to update any forward-looking statement. One should carefully evaluate such statements in light of factors described in the Company's filings with the Securities and Exchange Commission, especially on Forms 10-K, 10-Q and 8-K . . .

Low risk investing in Life Sciences will never be no risk.

MERCK

Share Graph 1997–1998 Merck & Co Inc.
Primary Market – NYSE

Price January 1999 $75
Market Value January 1999 $183 billion

SECTOR Health Care INDUSTRY Major Drugs
Top Line MRK Bottom Line S&P 500 Index Relative: Triangle
Marks Split
Left Scale: Top $ Price, Bottom Volume in Thousands

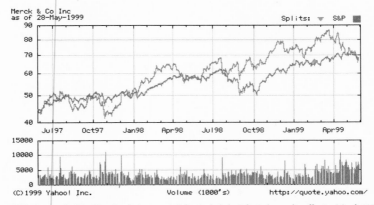

Note: This chart tracks Merck's price during a period that included a 2 for 1 share split, effective March 1999.

PRICE PERFORMANCE Year 1998 %	MRK		An investment made in January 1994 grew 367 % by January 1999		
PRICE HISTORY	1998	1997	1996	1995	Notes
High Price	80.87	54.00	42.12	31.31	
Low Price	50.69	27.00	21.06	15.65	
High P/E	37.58	28.39	26.94	25.46	
Low P/E	23.55	20.83	18.07	13.77	

Chmn/Pres/CEO Raymond Gilmartin, www.merck.com
59,300 employees
Merck & Co., Inc. PO Box 100, One Merck Drive, Whitehouse Station, NJ 08889
Phone: (908) 423-1000 Fax: (908) 735-1253

Global Franchise: Prescription drugs, cardiovascular leadership, vaccines and pharmaceutical benefits management.

America's number one supplier of prescription medicines, Merck has the leading world franchise supplying prescription drugs for cardiovascular medicine, the biggest pharmaceutical sector globally. Leading Merck cardiovascular drugs include Vasotec for hypertension and heart failure and Zocor and Mevacor for cholesterol lowering. The sector accounts for over 50% of Merck's drug sales. Other important franchises are anti-ulcerants and digestive palliatives, including their own product Pepcid, the largest selling over-the-counter product of its kind in the US. Merck co-marketed Prilosec, the world's best selling drug; in the US in a joint venture with Astra which is now being dissolved. Important market share is also held in antibiotics, vaccines and opthalmologicals. In 1995, Merck introduced Fosamex for the treatment and prevention of osteoporosis, Crixivan for the treatment of HIV and Proscar for the treatment of benign prostate growth. In 1998, Singulair was introduced for the treatment of asthma. In 1999, Vioxx, a major new type of drug for the treatment of extreme pain, including arthritic pain, is being introduced following regulatory approval in May 1999. Merck-Medco LLC, a division of the group, is a pharmaceutical benefits manager supplying over 50 million people and trading effectively as a wholesaler and retailer of drugs. It is the largest operation of its kind which makes Merck one of the world's largest ethical drug retailers. Over 40% of revenues come from Medco. Combined annual revenues exceed $25 billion with over 70% of sales in the US, 18% in Europe and 9% in the Asia Pacific region.

■■■■
Setting a rational price

Portfolio 2001 WORKSHEET FOR TARGETING SHARE PRICES OF MERCK & CO IN 1999, 2000, 2001 & 2002 BASED ON FORECASTS MADE IN JANUARY 1999 EPS FISCAL 1998 $2.15

Growth	Year	Estimated EPS	P/E	Share Price Target	+10%	-10%	Notes
15 %	1999	$2.47	24	$59	$65	$53	
15 %	2000	$2.84	24	$68	$75	$61	
15%	2001	$3.26	24	$68	$75	$61	
15%	2002	£3.74	24	$90	$100	$81	

This 'what if' forecast suggests potential earnings and share prices based on current indications. Forecasts must be revised continuously in the light of all company results and industry, market and economic news. Forecasts can be misleading and can not be treated as investment advice or used to motivate investments. See page 69.

Earnings per share growth expectations

Merck's clockwork-like pattern of strong earnings per share growth encourages investor expectations that growth will be ahead of the 12% expected across the drug industry. However, Merck is facing the biggest challenges in its 107-year history. Between 2000 and 2005, it will see patents expire on a range of major drugs that represent about $4 billion in US sales. Competitive generic versions of the drug will be offered at lower prices and Merck must assure a sequence of new drug approvals over the next few years in substantial growth areas to sustain its high growth rate. Chairman Raymond Gilmartin has assured investors that expected revenues from drugs in the development pipeline and sales from recently introduced products will keep company growth at the top range for the industry over the coming years. Major growth products will include new treatments for asthma, osteoporosis, migraines, arthritis and depression. However, there are questions on when the revenues will kick in and if they will be enough to replace margin and volume losses when patent protections lapse on blockbuster products.

Supporting its leading products as investment attractions, Merck has exceptional cash generation of more than $2.5 billion a year. In the short term this sum has been boosted by joint venture unwinding arrangements with Astra who merged with Zeneca, bringing an expected additional $1.5 billion into Merck's coffers over the next few years, to compensate for lost product revenues.

Merck have used financial muscle well in the past to license in product where necessary to maintain growth or fill gaps in therapeutic areas. They licensed in Prilosec, Mevacor and Pepcid to maintain market share, and revenue and profit growth and future earnings can be boosted if they use their tremendous financial strength to acquire another drug company. While it is known that chairman Gilmartin is against such a move, many analysts expect he will reconsider the prospect if necessary.

A titan in research, Merck is thought to have a stronger pipeline than most analysts recognize. Other companies often start to promote drugs in earlier stages of development, but Merck does not show its cards unless it has to. Beyond the thrust for innovative new products and increased earnings, Merck is beefing up its marketing strengths and an entrenched share buy back programme improves earnings per share performance. An additional $5 billion was committed to share buy backs at the end of 1998.

A sustainable 15% earnings per share growth should be a rational albeit slightly optimistic expectation for Merck on current information.

Earnings multiple expectations

The attractions of holding leading pharmaceutical shares are being recognized by increasing numbers of institutional and private investors and forward earnings multiples of more than double the annual earnings growth rate of these shares are now commonplace. To target share prices with a high-reward low-risk focus for Merck, as patent expiries pose a serious threat to earnings, a multiple of 30 times earnings in line with current market valuations in the sector would be ambitious because it would be double the already ambitious earnings per share growth rate of 15. A multiple that values the company radically below its price on the market reflects unrealistic comparisons with peers is also unlikely to be helpful. Against this background 24 times earnings is a compromise which seems rational in January 1999.

There is potential for the earnings multiple of 24 to be either too high or too low. If Merck starts to lose market share and profits suffer with patent expiries, investors may fear a rerun of Glaxo's debacle when Zantac went off patent and earnings collapsed. On the other hand, if major new drugs are announced, Merck's share price could follow the pattern for Pfizer after Viagra was announced and Merck could even trade at 50 times current earnings, or more.

Based on historic valuation norms, earnings multiples would have been far lower, but the flow of funds into markets and into blue chip shares cannot be ignored. Nor can the exceptional strengths of one of the world's greatest blue chip investments. Quarterly dividends were increased by 25% at the end of 1998 and Merck increasingly appeals to a widening range of investors.

Past performance indicators

Growth Rates %		MRK	S&P 500	Industry	Sector	Notes
Earnings per share 5 year		12.04	20.56	12.80	13.34	
1998 last reported vs 1997		16.43	12.25	14.92	14.11	
Sales 5 year 1994-1998		19.59	15.83	11.95	15.10	
Profitability Ratios						
Gross Margin 1998	%	48.31	49.16	65.51	65.90	
5 year average	%	58.96	48.83	69.83	66.01	
Net Profit Margin 1998	%	19.88	10.85	18.46	14.82	
5 year average	%	19.95	10.21	16.22	12.86	
5 Year Returns on:						
Assets	%	15.49	8.26	14.58	11.46	
Investment	%	20.46	13.03	22.09	17.51	
Equity	%	31.32	21.49	32.80	26.75	

The growth story

Merck success goes back to its origins as a pioneer drug company and an industry leader over the century. In 1995, Roy Vagelos, who as chairman and CEO steered the company through almost two decades of exceptional achievement reached retiring age and Raymond V. Gilmartin was appointed as chairman and CEO. Gilmartin's strong managerial skills and clear focus have kept Merck's financial operations and marketing achievements on a true course. However, it is not yet clear whether the drug discovery machine is working as well as it should be.

In its core cardiovascular sector Merck is facing patent expiries on major drugs including Vasotec and Mevacor and strong competition which, from the turn of the century, threaten volume and margin losses. Uncharacteristically, Merck is playing catchup instead of setting the pace, and in April 1998 the valuation of Pfizer on the New York Stock Exchange exceeded Merck for the first time, following the launch of several of Pfizer's new drugs including Viagra for male impotence.

Merck-Medco LLC

Merck-Medco LLC is a pharmaceutical benefits manager, a new and unique kind of business that emerged in the US over the last decade, as the buying strength of health care providers and insurers compounded. Pharmaceutical benefits managers set themselves up as middlemen in the drug supply chain by leveraging the buying power of several health care payers into single buying contracts. The combined volumes enabled them to strike deals at lowest prices with pharmaceutical companies and brought appreciable savings to their clients. Benefits managers are essentially a kind of wholesaler, but as they also deliver prescriptions directly to patients using postal and similar door to door delivery services, they are also a kind of retailer.

After Merck's 1993 $11 billion investment to acquire Medco, it vertically integrated operations and Merck-Medco LLC now services pharmaceutical benefits for 50 million people in America – over twice the number on the books when Merck made the acquisition. However, Merck-Medco LLC operates in a different commercial environment to drug discovery and trades high volume on tight margins. Over 40% of group revenues come from Merck-Medco LLC which only produces about 3% of Merck's operating profits. Considering this unfavourable comparison, Merck has been most successful in maintaining a net margin of 20% overall, in the top range for the drug industry. While profit margin is paramount, as it affects what the company earns, Medco means more than margin to Merck. With Medco it almost owns a share of the drug market and, when its drugs come off patent and prices inevitably drop, the risk of losing market share to generic competition can and will be reduced.

Core drugs and new drugs

Heart disease is the leading killer in the industrialized world and cardiovascular disease is among the top three diseases in terms of health care spending in every country worldwide. The United States spends more to treat cardiovascular disorders – over $100 billion a year – than it does on any other medical condition.

Merck's Mevacor and Zocor together hold more than a 40% share worldwide of the cholesterol-lowering market which continues to grow at a rate of more than 20% a year in major markets, with some of Merck's drugs still growing at above 30%.

Since 1995, Merck has launched 14 medicines and vaccines that accounted for over 21% of revenues according to a recent company report. Five of the 14 products were launched in 1998, including Singulair for asthma, Maxalt for migraines, Aggrastat for cardiovascular disorders, Propecia for male pattern hair loss and Cosopt for glaucoma.

New drugs, including the oral medication Singulair for asthma, have been exceptionally successful, while others, like Propecia, have been slow starters. Recent new products are at the very early stages of their product life cycles and generally have not yet been comprehensively launched worldwide. In 1999, Merck has continued to roll out these products in key markets in Europe and globally, and has started to market the potential blockbuster painkiller Vioxx in the US.

Portfolio of top drugs

Of the world's ten top drugs in 1997, Merck marketed number one Astra's Prilosec (co-marketed in a joint venure with Astra in the US), number three Zocor and number ten Vasotec. Zocor is Merck's top drug with sales exceeding $3.5 billion and Vasotec is Merck's number two with sales exceeding $2.5 billion. Mevacor (again for cholesterol reduction) is Merck's number three with sales exceeding $1.25 billion and Pepcid was number four with sales of $1.1 billion. Recently introduced new therapies include Fosamex for the treatment and prevention of osteoporosis, which affects post menopausal women and has reached sales exceeding $500 million, and Proscar for the treatment of benign prostate growth which affects men in latter years, also with sales now approaching $500 million. A sister drug Propecia is being marketed as a treatment for baldness but it is early to forecast the success it will have, though early indications are not impressive.

Singulair, an oral treatment for asthma launched in 1998 with potential sales above the $500 million range has been successful from the outset and reached sales of $800 million in that year. Vioxx, Merck's Cox-2 blocker arthritis drug, which has fewer side effects and greater efficacy than existing arthritis and painkilling drugs, has the potential of exceeding $1 billion a year, but faces competition from a similar drug, Celebra, discovered by Monsanto's Searle Pharmaceuticals, which is being marketed with Pfizer.

Crixivan, a protease inhibitor for the treatment of HIV infection in adults, introduced in 1996, has been cleared for marketing in more than 60 countries and has sales of over $500 million a year.

Joint ventures

Traditionally Merck chose to work in joint ventures with qualified partners in areas where it was not dominant to give access to new products and markets. Johnson & Johnson still market Merck's Pepcid, the most successful over-the-counter medicine in the US and other Merck over-the-counter products. Other Merck joint venture arrangements have been affected by mergers and re-alignments in the industry and strategically Merck is concentrating now on its own research and commercial resources.

It is common in the industry for major drug companies to build research alliances with academic institutions and emerging biotechnology companies. These associations are in the nature of working arrangements, rather than structured joint ventures, and Merck has among the most impressive body of these associations assembled.

Research and development

Research spending increased by 12% to $1.9 billion in 1988 to support the flow of new drugs and $2.1 billion, about 14% more, will be spent in 1999.

Present priority areas for development are arthritis and pain relief, fungal infections, bacteria resistant to present therapies (the so called superbugs), vaccines, cancer, depression, neuropsychosis and ageing. When blockbuster drugs like Vasotec go off patent in 2000, and Mevacor goes off patent in 2001, Merck's earnings growth will stall if substantial market share has not been secured with new product. All signs are in the right direction, but so far, except for Vioxx and Singulair, the new potential blockbusters are not yet identifiable.

Assurances from management that losses through patent expiries will be replaced by new drugs are meaningful but could prove to be wrong.

Competitive advantage

Merck's focus on cardiovascular drugs and core sectors of drugs for humans has positioned it increasingly in growth sectors as longer life expectancy for an increasingly ageing population in the US increases the consumption of medicines. A global focus has also established it in world markets as a preferred supplier in the key sectors it dominates in the US.

Merck-Medco buffers erosion of sales by promoting Merck's products and keeping the group well informed on changes in buying preferences as they happen in the market place. However, while Medco will doubtless promote Merck's drugs wherever possible, it will not be able to block competition from innovative new drugs if physicians prescribe them in future in preference to Merck's drugs. Merck has therefore beefed up its sales force.

Driving revenue growth from a solid base

In December 1998, Merck's president of Human Health for the Americas, David Anstice, announced that the company had embarked on expanding its sales force by 700 people. This was partly to support the expected launch of Vioxx, but 100 of the new team will work in the cardiovascular area, with a particular focus on Zocor, Merck's cholesterol-lowering drug which has been losing market share to Lipitor, a product co-marketed by Warner-Lambert Co. and Pfizer Inc.

Merck claims that Zocor is holding its own well against the new competition; in the third quarter of 1998 the drug still led product sales, bringing in $990 million, a 15% increase from a year earlier.

Merck's long-term goal is to achieve earnings per share growth within the top quartile of its peer group, which Gilmartin defined as twelve large-cap multinational pharmaceutical companies including Pfizer, Eli Lily & Co. and Glaxo Wellcome plc. He claims that, 'The key to achieving this growth goal is to drive revenue growth.' In the short term, Gilmartin is driving revenue growth by increasing the promotional support for its major in-line products and investing in the launch of its new products world-wide. The company will fund the investment behind these two growth drivers partly by re-allocating productivity savings in manufacturing and administration, but the main funding will doubtless be from revenues and will affect earnings adversely before it improves them.

Innovation

Success over the years has been built on developing drugs or buying in innovative drugs for unmet medical needs, and the focus for future growth remains the same. Unlike some other pharmaceutical companies who build strategies to create value with corporate transactions, Merck is not on the acquisition or merger trails. At the time of a merger frenzy in the industry early in 1998, Gilmartin was asked if he was in any corporate discussions and replied that he did not have time for distractions.

In 1998 Merck also withdrew from several joint ventures with other pharmaceutical companies. Concentration moved back to the route which brought success in the past – successful innovation.

What can go wrong?

Apart from the risks that face all drug companies, and the risks of equity markets weakening generally, Merck may not be able to replace sales on drugs which lose patent protection at the turn of the century fast enough to sustain earnings growth, and this could have a severe effect on the valuation of its shares on the market.

Investors in the pharmaceutical sector should monitor the industry, the companies in which they are invested and their competitors. Details of Merck's actual product sales can only be found in published comment by leading analysts because, unlike Pfizer, Merck does not publish full details on sales. Leading analysts buy market information from specialist research organizations, and comment on all changes in sales mix and important changes in Merck sales get circulated to the financial community and the everyday press in this way. Leading brokers will have access to all important research published and investors can access this information through their brokers.

Monitoring

www.merck.com in an interesting information resource for an

overview of operations, but investors will need to follow commentary on Merck in the financial press particularly as it relates to competitors and to loss of market share following patent losses over the next few years. Chapter 9, the Webliography, lists several informative web sites for the pharmaceutical industry which could also be usefully followed. Following the news on the web sites of competitors, particularly the new merged industry leaders, should also be informative and useful.

PFIZER

Share Graph 1997–1998 Pfizer Inc.
Primary Market – NYSE – PFE

Price January 1999 $122
Market Value January 1999 $158.6 billion

SECTOR Health Care INDUSTRY Major Drugs
Top Line PFIZER Bottom Line S&P 500 Index Relative: Triangle
Marks Split
Left Scale: Top $ Price, Bottom Volume in Thousands
Chart not rebased for three-for-one share split in 1999.

PRICE PERFORMANCE	PFE		An investment made in January 1994 grew 726% by January 1999		
PRICE HISTORY	1998	1997	1996	1995	Notes
High Price	42.98	80.00	45.63	33.44	
Low Price	23.68	40.31	30.13	18.63	
High P/E	29.08	47.11	30.46	27.10	
Low P/E	16.02	23.74	20.11	15.09	

Chmn/CEO William C. Steere Jr., www.pfizer.com
49,200 employees
235 East 42nd Street, New York, NY 10017
Phone: (212) 573-2323 Fax: (212) 573-7851

Global Franchise: Pharmaceutical drugs for hypertension, depression, infections, impotence and other diseases.

In April 1998, Pfizer overtook Merck to become the US pharmaceutical company with the highest market value. The share price surge followed the launch of Viagra, the first oral drug for male impotence, and it is possible that Viagra could become the best selling drug ever introduced. However, Viagra is still a wild card and it may or may not live up to expectations when competitive products are on the market. Pfizer was on track to become the world's top drug company, even without Viagra. Its other new blockbuster drugs include Norvasc for hypertension and angina, already a $2 billion product; Zoloft, an antidepressant; Procardia XL for hypertension; Lipitor for elevated cholesterol; Aracept for the treatment of Alzheimer's; and Zeldox, for schizophrenia. Drugs in the pipeline will further strengthen franchises in cardiovascular, central nervous system and anti-infective medicine, and include important treatments for cancer, pain relief, and osteoporosis. With G. D. Searle, a subsidiary of the Monsanto group, Pfizer are co-promoting and co-marketing a new breakthrough arthritis and pain relief drug called Celebra, which will be on the market early in 1999. Lipitor for cholesterol reduction co-marketed with Warner-Lambert was, until Viagra, the highest selling new drug in the US on launch. Pharmaceuticals contribute 85% of Pfizer's annual revenues of $11.3 billion and 96% of profits of $3 billion. Of revenues, 52% are from the US, 25% from Europe, 14% from Asia Pacific and 9% from the rest of the world.

Setting a rational price

Portfolio 2001 WORKSHEET FOR TARGETING SHARE PRICES OF PFIZER IN 1999, 2000, 2001 & 2002
BASED ON FORECASTS MADE IN JANUARY 1999
EPS FISCAL : FISCAL 1998 $0.85

Growth	Year	Estimated EPS	P/E	Share Price Target	+10%	-10%	Notes
22.5 %	1999	$0.85	45	$38	$42	$34	
22.5 %	2000	$1.04	42.5	$47	$52	$46	Lower P/E
22.5 %	2001	$1.27	40	$51	$56	$46	Lower P/E
22.5 %	2002	$1.55	37.5	$58	$65	$52	Lower P/E

This 'what if' forecast suggests potential earnings and share prices based on current indications. Forecasts must be revised continuously in the light of all company results and industry, market and economic news. Forecasts can be misleading and can not be treated as investment advice or used to motivate investments. See page 69.

Earnings per share growth expectations

It would be easier to consider a rational value for Pfizer without Viagra than with Viagra because expectations are so high. For *Portfolio 2001* earnings have been forecast to grow at 22.5% a year to the year 2002, based on the successful new drugs on the market, the major new drug launches planned and the initial success of Viagra. If Viagra becomes the most successful drug ever, and if Pfizer manages to keep the drug selling retail at $10 per pill, it could make Pfizer the most profitable company ever, but this potential cannot be introduced now. Quarterly results may not always conform to long term expectations, but on past performance and management indications, Pfizer is on track to grow earnings at 25% a year plus. Plans to achieve higher earnings growth year after year have a nasty habit of hitting unexpected obstacles and the annual earnings per share growth rate used in the *Portfolio 2001* worksheet has been set at 22.5% to allow for modest setbacks.

Earnings multiple expectations

The combination of Pfizer's exceptional earnings growth potential and current strong equity markets are likely to result in Pfizer shares trading at a market multiple of between 40 and 50 times current earnings, corresponding to about 50% and 100% above the expected earnings per share growth rate. It would be cautious and comforting to set price targets at 37.5 or even 30 times earnings, but doing so would ignore both the potential in the drug pipeline discussed in the next section and the realities of supply and demand on the stock market. The multiple of 45 times expected earnings used in the worksheet to target share prices is a compromise on high but very attainable expectations and caution on high market valuations. However, it will not help rational decision making to smother future investing opportunities with a blanket fear because shares are already highly valued. High valuation does not mean overvaluation, and a strong case can be made with Pfizer that the rational value will be high as long as equity markets remain strong.

For 2000, 2001 and 2002 the price earnings multiple has been scaled down to 42.5, 40 and 37.5 to draw attention to two situations. Firstly, competitors will probably launch alternative products to Viagra on the market, or have drugs well advanced in the approval process, and secondly, information in the public domain concerns only drugs being launched in the next year or two. It is early to make guesses on what will follow after then. On current indications, high expectations are rational but, until more tangible information is available, it is sensible to trim long-range expectations. Without this explanation, scaled down figures might give the wrong impression to readers that a well-documented forecast was being fine tuned on the basis of known information.

Pfizer's shares have made great annual leaps over latter years and traded in wide price ranges responding to market volatility. The following chart indicates that buying opportunities could appear again and be recognized by alert investors:

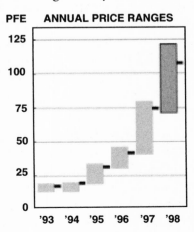

PFE   ANNUAL PRICE RANGES

Past performance indicators

Growth Rates %		PFE	S&P 500	Industry	Sector	Notes
Earnings per share 5 year		15.90	20.56	12.80	13.34	
1998 last reported vs 1997		NM	12.25	14.92	14.11	
Sales 5 year 1994-1998		11.58	15.83	11.95	15.10	
Profitability Ratios						
Gross Margin 1998	%	83.33	49.16	69.51	65.90	
5 year average	%	79.43	48.83	65.90	66.01	
Net Profit Margin 1998	%	16.75	10.85	18.46	14.82	
5 year average	%	15.12	10.21	16.22	12.86	
5 Year Returns on:						
Assets	%	12.29	8.26	14.58	11.46	
Investment	%	20.19	13.03	22.09	17.51	
Equity	%	27.70	21.49	32.80	26.75	

NM=not meaningful

The growth story

Investment in leading edge science and leading in investing
Pfizer is thought to have the strongest drug pipeline in the industry, with 50 major drugs in development, including potential blockbusters that could be approved within the next five years. It also sets the pace for investment in Research and Development and has been a leading company in the use of the most recent advances in microbiology, combinatorial chemistry and robotic systems to achieve a new pace for the drug discovery process.

Existing billion-dollar franchises include Norvasc for hypertension, Zoloft for depression, the antibiotic Zithromax, and Viagra. New drugs, well advanced in the pipeline, are being developed to treat the diseases which have up to now been the most intractable, and include therapies for chronic heart disease, schizophrenia and lethal cancers of the colon, breast and pancreas. Pfizer currently has four promising tumour-killers in human testing, and two more will go into trials every year for the foreseeable future as they intensify efforts to make cancer a manageable disease, much like diabetes.

Strategy and growth steered by William Steere

William Steere, Pfizer's chairman and CEO is a lifelong Pfizer executive with a scientific training, who climbed the company ladder through sales and marketing. In the eight years that he has led the company he has launched an epic assault on the high ground of new drug discovery, with the support of Research and Development investment reaching $2.2 billion in 1998. This amounted to 16% of Pfizer's total revenue, while Merck at the same time, spent only 10%. Since he has been in charge, Pfizer's Research and Development spend and earnings have tripled, sales have doubled and the stock price at its peak had grown 800% – the best performance in the drug industry worldwide. In 1999 R&D expenditure will reach $2.8 billion.

Steere targeted research with military precision and commitment. The extensive body of genetic information now available make it possible to target genetic flaws for drug discovery, and robotic systems screen tens of thousands of chemicals in hours or days, rather then the month it would have taken only a few years ago. Drug discovery has become much less hit and miss than before, and Pfizer has scored the greatest number of hits.

Steere recognized that unless the best opportunities are first identified as research targets, scientific research can become a financial bottomless pit that yields nothing of commercial value. He led the charge on the marketing front as effectively as he led on the scientific front. Pfizer's marketing resources and its laboratories work together as a team, determining research priorities in the light of commercial opportunities.

Before major resources are committed, new drug opportunities have to be run through Pfizer's CRAM programme, an abbreviation for Central Research Assists Marketing. Inevitably, scientists dominate teams developing drugs, but the team captains are from marketing. This is a unique Pfizer strategy and ensures that if the potential financial outcomes from the drug are not convincing, the project will not go ahead, even if it might result in a great contribution to science.

The drug industry in the US has been advertising and promoting to consumers since consumer advertising of drugs was first allowed in 1997. Pfizer has built its consumer image well, but its marketing strength to the medical profession has been the first priority. Before a drug is prescribed by the physicians, they must be persuaded it is the best treatment available. Steere's 5,500-plus army of field sales representatives to the profession is the largest sales force in the pharmaceutical industry.

Meaningful reporting

Like their operating results, Pfizer's reports to investors on performance and sales set the benchmark for others to follow. Pfizer maintained strong revenue, earnings and earnings per share growth in 1998, when the impact of the strong US dollar and weak global markets affected the profitability of other drug companies. In 1998, Pfizer's increased revenues followed a 21% increase in world sales of pharmaceuticals, with price increases contributing only 1.5 percentage points to revenue growth.

The reports in the following tables give a general overview of 1997 and 1998 revenues across the company's operating divisions.

■■■

Pfizer Inc segment/product revenues full year 1998 $m

				Quarter-to-Date					
		Worldwide			US		International		
	1998	1997	% Change	1998	1997	% Change	1998	1997	% Change
TOTAL REVENUES	13,544	11,055	23	8,218	6,089	35	5,326	4,966	7
PHARMACEUTICALS	11,788	9,239	28	7,381	5,249	41	4,407	3,990	10
CARDIOVASCULAR DISEASES	4,186	3,806	10	2,249	2,103	7	1,937	1,703	14
NORVASC	2,575	2,217	16	1,206	993	21	1,369	1,224	12
PROCARDIA XL	714	822	(13)	714	822	(13)	0	0	–
CARDURA	688	626	10	322	278	16	366	348	5
INFECTIOUS DISEASES	2,823	2,483	14	1,522	1,115	36	1,301	1,368	(5)
DIFLUCAN	916	881	4	440	397	11	476	484	(2)
ZITHROMAX	1,041	821	27	775	554	40	266	267	0
TROVAN	160	0	–	155	0	–	5	0	–
UNASYN	327	346	(5)	141	150	(5)	186	196	(5)
SULPERAZON	133	139	(4)	0	0	–	133	139	(4)
CENTRAL NERVOUS SYSTEM DISORDERS	1,924	1,553	24	1,497	1,233	21	427	320	33
ZOLOFT	1,836	1,507	22	1,484	1,220	22	352	287	23

DIABETES	273	234	17	239	195	23	34	39	(13)
GLUCOTROL XL	226	175	29	217	165	31	9	10	(15)
ARTHRITIS/ INFLAMMATION	225	269	(16)	12	15	(21)	213	254	(16)
FELDENE	204	241	(15)	12	15	(21)	192	226	(15)
ALLERGY	422	273	55	417	267	56	5	6	(12)
ZYRTEC/REACTINE	416	265	57	411	259	58	5	6	(12)
VIAGRA	788	0	–	656	0	–	132	0	–
ALLIANCE REVENUE	867	316	175	780	303	158	87	13	562
ANIMAL HEALTH	1,314	1,329	(1)	558	541	3	756	788	(4)
CONSUMER HEALTH CARE	442	487	(9)	279	299	(7)	163	188	(13)

What can go wrong?

Apart from the risks that face all drug companies, and the risks of equity markets weakening generally, Pfizer faces the risk that Viagra may not be as successful as anticipated and competition may come sooner than expected.

If there is ever any let down in Viagra sales, the headlines will scream from the world's top financial newspapers to village rags across the planet that 'Viagra cannot keep it up.' And if sales do not stay up, Pfizer's share price will be vulnerable to correction.

Competition to Viagra will also affect market expectations for Pfizer, and will be seen within a few years. Leading contenders include Icos – www.icos.com – a US biotechnology company in which Bill Gates is a major shareholder. Its competitive product is already in Phase 3 trials in the US. Takeda and Abbott together are also seeking approval for a drug, Uprima (apomorphine), which they say does the job, and Schering Plough have applied to market Vasomex in the US and are already marketing it in Mexico. Vasomex has a solid performance record.

Upjohn Pharmaceuticals, now part of Pharmacia and Upjohn, raised investor expectations with Prostoglandin, the first medication for erectile dysfunction, in the early 1990s, but the drug was a let down. It was successful physically but requires a sensitive local injection. Upjohn is now working with a new drug delivery company, Powderject PLC, which is developing a novel technology for painless transdermal drug delivery. Prostaglandin is one of the first candidate drugs they are working on.

Monitoring

www.pfizer.com is one of the most informative company web sites, and their reports give the most comprehensive details of the affairs of the company. Investors who are well informed and monitor Pfizer for buying opportunities will probably be well rewarded for their efforts. Investors should keep informed on industry developments and competitive product introductions.

JOHNSON & JOHNSON

Share Graph 1997–1998 Johnson & Johnson
Primary Market – NYSE – JNJ

Price January 1999 $78.50
Market Value January 1999 $105 billion

SECTOR Health Care INDUSTRY Major Drugs
Top Line S&P 500 Index Relative Bottom Line JNJ Share Price:
Left Scale: Top $ Price, Bottom Volume in Thousands

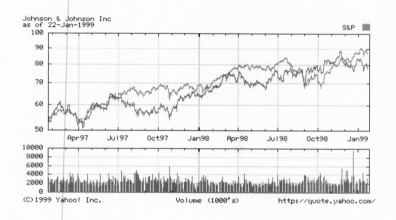

PRICE PERFORMANCE	JNJ		An investment made in January 1994 grew 310% by January 1999		
PRICE HISTORY	1998	1997	1996	1995	Notes
High Price	89.75	67.31	54.00	46.19	
Low Price	63.38	48.36	41.56	26.81	
High P/E	40.26	27.92	25.42	29.61	
Low P/E	28.43	20.17	19.57	17.19	

Chmn/CEO Ralph Larsen, www.jnj.com
90,000 employees
One Johnson & Johnson Plaza, New Brunswick, NJ 08933
Phone: (732) 524-0400 Fax: (732) 214-0332

Global Franchise: Pharmaceuticals, consumer health products and professional medical and surgical devices

Johnson & Johnson is the world's largest and most diversified health care product maker.

The famous Johnson & Johnson bandage franchise goes back to the 1880s and the early days of surgery, when one of the founder Johnson brothers attended a public lecture given by Sir Joseph Lister and learned that germs were major causes of infection in the operating room contributing to the high post-surgical mortality rates being experienced. In 1885, the Johnson brothers developed the world's first sterile ready-to-use surgical dressings which brought a dramatic reduction in post-operative infection – and led to J&J establishing itself as the world's leading surgical bandage suppliers. J&J now has three divisions – Pharmaceuticals (34%), Consumer (28.7%) and Professional which includes medical, diagnostic and surgical devices (37.3%). Owning several top global household brands has helped make J&J become the world's largest supplier of over-the-counter pharmaceuticals, the world's leading supplier of contact lenses, and a leading supplier of equipment for cardiology and minimally invasive surgery. J&J is also the world's sixth largest pharmaceutical company and the third largest medical diagnostics company. About 50% of $23.7 billion annual revenues are earned outside the US. The group has over 180 operating companies and sales in more than 175 countries.

Setting a rational price

Portfolio 2001 WORKSHEET FOR TARGETING SHARE PRICES OF JOHNSON & JOHNSON IN 1999, 2000, 2001 & 2002
BASED ON FORECASTS MADE IN JANUARY 1999
EPS FISCAL 1987 TO DECEMBER $2.41: FISCAL 1998 $2.69(E)

Growth	Year	Estimated EPS	P/E	Share Price Target	+10%	-10%	Notes
12.5 %	1999	$3.00	25	$75	$83	$66	
13 %	2000	$3.39	25	$85	$94	$76	
13 %	2001	$3.83	25	$96	$107	$86	
13 %	2002	$4.32	25	$108	$10	$97	

This 'what if' forecast suggests potential earnings and share prices based on current indications. Forecasts must be revised continuously in the light of all company results and industry, market and economic news. Forecasts can be misleading and cannot be treated as investment advice or used to motivate investments. See page 69.

Earnings per share growth expectations

Management have set an earnings growth target of 12–14% and the *Portfolio 2001* forecast follows this indication and analysts who review the company.

Earnings multiple expectations

In conditions at the beginning of 1999, with low interest rates in the US and Europe and strong demand for pharmaceutical shares, stretching an earnings multiple to twice the expected rate of growth appears to be rational for a top life sciences company like J&J. As long as earnings growth is sustained at current levels, whether organic or by acquisition, J&J is an attractive investment prospect for institutions and private investors. With an improving global economy and some success with major new products, J&J could be well upgraded by demand on the market.

Past performance indications

Growth Rates %		J&J	S&P 500	Industry	Sector	Notes
Earnings per share 5 year		10.85	17.63	12.94	15.71	
1998 last reported vs 1997		4.54	14.87	11.89	15.13	
Sales 5 year 1994-1998		10.85	17.63	12.94	15.71	
Profitability Ratios						
Gross Margin 1998	%	68.31	49.88	70.35	67.34	
5 year average	%	67.50	48.79	69.89	66.82	
Net Profit Margin 1998	%	12.93	10.91	17.74	14.87	
5 year average	%	13.28	10.45	17.48	14.14	
5 Year Returns on:						
Assets	%	14.54	8.36	15.40	12.42	
Investment	%	19.71	13.24	23.15	18.81	
Equity	%	28.49	21.72	34.69	28.73	

The growth story

1998 results

J&J is a supertanker. On course it produces predictable growth at acceptable levels and to its credit J&J count 66 consecutive years of sales increases, 37 consecutive years of net income increases (excluding one-time charges), 55 continuous years of dividend payments and 37 consecutive years of dividend increases. J&J performed satisfactorily in 1998 with operating earnings per share up 10.78%.

	1998	1997
Sales	$23.657 bln	$22.629 bln
¹Net income	$ 3.059bln	$ 3.303 bln
Average shares (diluted)	1.3716 bln	1.369 bln
Reported eps (diluted)	2.23	2.41
Operating eps	$2.67	

¹Excluding special charges

Special charges in 1998 arose from writing off associated research and development arising from J&J's largest ever acquisition Dupey, plus a further one-time group restructuring of $700 million charge intended to generate annual savings of $250m to $300m from the year 2000.

The global pharmaceutical industry had a difficult year in 1998, with weaker demand in emerging markets and weakening currencies globally that eroded eventual dollar earnings. J&J did well to achieve growth of over 10% but had the benefit of earnings from the major business Dupey which they acquired that year, and which contributed 12% of the revenues of J&J's orthopaedic business.

Johnson & Johnson's reported sales for the first quarter ending March 1999 were $6.6 billion with net earnings of $1.1 billion, increases of 14.8% and 11.7% respectively over 1998 first-quarter results. The results were 2.5% higher than analysts' consensus forecasts and followed broad-based strength across group businesses and markets. Pharmaceutical sales of $2.5 billion for the quarter increased 18.4% over the same period in 1998, including 23.3% growth in domestic sales. The growth reflects the strong performance of the erythroprotein Procrit and other leading drugs. Sales of $2.4 billion in the Professional segment represented an increase of 18.6% over the first quarter of 1998. The 1998 acquisition of DePuy, Inc., a leading orthopaedic products manufacturer, contributed to the strong sales growth in the Professional segment.

In addition, strong performance was achieved by Ethicon Endo-Surgery's laparoscopy and wound closure products, LifeScan's blood glucose monitoring systems, Ethicon's Mitek suture anchors and Gynecare's women's health products.

Worldwide Consumer segment sales for the first quarter of 1999 were $1.7 billion, an increase of 5.4% versus the same period a year ago. Domestic sales were up 10.4% while international sales gains in local currency of 5.0% were almost entirely offset by a negative currency impact of 4.7%. During the quarter, J&J launched its Neutrogena line of cosmetics, and also launched Benecol in the United Kingdom as both a margarine spread and a cream-cheese style product.

Pharmaceutical prospects

The pharmaceutical division accounts for about a third of sales and produces about 60% of profits, and strong margins earned in pharmaceuticals are behind the 14% net profit achieved.

The J&J group sells about a hundred drugs generally not under the Johnson & Johnson name and brand. Pharmaceuticals are marketed under the brands of the group companies that own them, including Janssen Pharmaceutical, McNeil Pharmaceutical and Ortho Pharmaceutical. Well-known brands include Propulsid (cisapride) for gastrointestinal problems; Sporanox antifungal; Risperdal antipsychotic for schizophrenia; Hismanal anti-histamine; Floxin antibacterial; Ultram analgesic; Nizoral anti-fungal; Retin-A acne treatment; Orthum Novum oral con-traceptive; Orthoclone OKT3, for kidney, liver and heart trans-plant rejection; and the flagship erythroprotein Procrit/Eprex for chemotherapy support and anaemia.

Procrit has sales approaching $1.5 billion, and both Risperdal for schizophrenia and oral contraceptives have sales of over $600 million. Patent expiries will occur in respectively, 2004, 2005 and 2002.

The pharmaceutical pipeline is robust rather than strong. Thirty-four approval applications were lodged with the FDA in the US, 23 of which were in Phase III trials, including Ergoset, an important new diabetes treatment which encountered setbacks.

Important new drugs, on which announcements are expected in 1999 include Reminyl for Alzheimer's sufferers and Pariet for treatment of ulcers and gastric disorders. Pariet is a proton pump inhibitor, a similar drug to Astra Merck's Prilosec, the world' best selling drug, and is a potential blockbuster. J&J recently won approval to market Regranex, a new treatment for diabetic ulcers on the feet and legs which plague over 1 million patients in the US – and a similar number again worldwide. A second application for which regulatory approval is being sought will allow treatment of pressure sores and ulcers which affect four times as many patients.

Erythroproteins and Amgen

J&J markets an erythroprotein licensed from the US biotechnology company Amgen as Procrit in the US and Eprex in Europe. It is the company's largest drug and has annual sales growth above 30%. Erythroproteins are used mainly to treat anaemia, to counter blood cell loss in chemotherapy, and following surgery with high blood loss. Areas of conflict with Amgen are discussed at the end of this report in the section 'What can go wrong?'

Professional prospects

Professional sales, accounting for 35% of total group sales, grew 15% in 1998, including the Dupey business acquired. Without Dupey, sales in the professional sector would have fallen as a result of J&J's losing important market share in their coronary stent supply business.

Stents are small metal scaffoldings implanted to keep coronary arteries open following minimally invasive cardiac angioplasty procedures which open blocked arteries by inflating a balloon inserted in the artery. Inserting stents at the end of the procedure extends the benefits of the angioplasty, and frequently this avoids the need for open heart surgery to keep the arteries clear.

J&J dominated the coronary stent market since these small devices were first introduced in the mid 1990s. After acquiring a leading competitor, Cordis Corporation, in 1995, J&J controlled over 50% of the world market for stents and almost the entire US market. However, technically improved stents have been intro-duced by Boston Scientific, Medtronic and Guidant, and J&J has lost dominant market share since late 1997.

Professional product lines also include contact lenses, where J&J is the world's largest suppliers, blood glucose monitoring systems; special purpose minimally invasive surgical devices; endoscopic instruments; surgical implants; artificial limbs; hip replacements;

cardiovascular monitoring and vascular access products; intravenous catheters and shunts; instruments, needles and sutures; wound closure devices and general hospital and first aid products.

Well-known brands include the Dupey line of prosthetic orthopaedic appliances; Acuvue disposable contact lenses; Prolene sutures; Endopath trocars; One Touch Profile blood glucose monitors; Cidex disinfecting solution; Protectiv IV catheters; Barrier packs and gowns; PFC modular knee systems; Delta-Lite casting systema and Palmaz-Schatz balloon-expandable stents.

J&J is not likely to win back its commanding share of the stent market, particularly since Medtronic has entered the field aggesssively. J&J's strength in its professional business is that it has all the resources necessary to find new opportunities and introduce innovative new techniques globally.

Major disease areas have been targeted for professional products that will provide innovative and improved treatments for diseases with large patient populations. They include new treatments for malignant and benign prostate gland conditions, monitoring glucose for diabetics and alternative out patient treatments that replace surgical hysterectomies for women.

J&J professional products are marketed as the Versapoint bipolar electrosurgery system, Indigo LaserOptic treatment system for enlarged prostate glands, TheraSeed Palladium-103 implants for the treatment of prostate cancer, *Take* Meter compact blood glucose monitoring system, Ultracision Harmonic Scalpel, the Mammotome Breast Biopsy system and Band-Aid brand antibiotic adhesive bandage.

The consumer division

J&J hold top brand major consumer franchises in skin and hair care, sanitary protection, wound care, oral care and over-the-counter pharmaceuticals with leading brand names including: Band-Aid; Johnson's baby powder, shampoo, lotion and oil; Neutrogena shampoo, soap and lotions; Tylenol (acetaminophen) and Motrin (ibuprofen) analgesics; Stayfree tampons and sanitary protection products; Reach toothbrushes; over-the-counter medicines including Imodium anti-diarrhoeal products; Mylanta antacid products; Monstat for vaginal yeast infections; Pepcid gastric acid treatments and children's Motrin.

Global consumer sales rose 7% overall in 1998, 10% in the US and 5% internationally, but profits have stalled. J&J needs a new big story to energize this division's earnings – and it may have it with a food additive, Benecol, on which it acquired global marketing rights in 1997. Benecol is a food ingredient for margarine that reduces cholesterol by inhibiting its absorption, and J&J expects to launch Benecol additives in 1999 in the US, Europe and in other markets.

A strategy for planned diversification

In the 1920s, J&J's businesses started to internationalize and since then it has been organized into operationally autonomous divisions or subsidiaries. If there is one principle that governs group thinking, it is that no single product should account for more than 5% of sales, and strength can come from diversity if the management structure recognizes that disparate and individual businesses need innovative management regimes.

The Ortho division which began with one birth control product in the 1930s, became the Ortho Pharmaceutical Corporation and is a major world supplier of oral contraceptives. The disposable surgical packs and gowns business evolved into Surgikos, Inc., now Johnson & Johnson Medical Inc., and the sanitary napkin line led to today's Personal Products Company.

In 1941, a separate division was formed for J&J's suture business which in 1949 became Ethicon, Inc., and in 1992, Ethicon Endo-Surgery was formed to manufacture and market endoscopic products and mechanical wound closure devices. In 1959, McNeil Laboratories, Inc., a producer of prescription pharmaceuticals, was acquired. In 1977, McNeil split into two companies, McNeil Pharmaceutical and McNeil Consumer Products, best known for the Tylenol brand of pain-relieving products. In 1993, Ortho-McNeil Pharmaceutical was formed incorporating the business units McNeil Pharmaceutical and Ortho Pharmaceutical.

In 1981, J&J acquired Frontier Contact Lens which was the foundation of Vistakon, now the world's leading contact lens company, and in 1986, LifeScan, Inc., which provides home blood glucose monitoring systems for diabetics, was acquired.

Ortho Biotech, formed in 1990, was the first biotechnology company developed and operated as a subsidiary of a major pharmaceutical manufacturer. The 1994 acquisition of Clinical

Diagnostics from Kodak, now Johnson & Johnson Clinical Diagnostics, expanded J&J's existing diagnostic businesses, including Ortho Diagnostic Systems, Inc., LifeScan and Advanced Care Products.

In 1989, Johnson & Johnson – Merck Consumer Pharmaceuticals Co., a 50/50 joint venture between J&J and Merck was formed to develop and market a broad range of non-prescription products. In 1995, it launched Merck's Pepcid AC over-the-counter, the first OTC advancement for heartburn since the introduction of antacids over a century back.

Johnson & Johnson's skin care business was expanded with the 1993 acquisition of RoC, SA, of France and the addition in 1994 of Neutrogena Corporation, two manufacturers of high quality skin and hair care products. In 1989 J&J's consumer businesses, with the exception of sanitary protection products, were consolidated to form Johnson & Johnson Consumer Products, Inc., and in the same year, Surgikos Inc. and Johnson & Johnson Patient Care were combined to form Johnson & Johnson Medical.

The growth of the managed health care market in the US led to the formation in 1994 of Johnson & Johnson Health Care Systems Inc., which includes the former Johnson & Johnson Hospital Services and Johnson & Johnson Advanced Behavioral Technologies and handles contracting and accounts management with managed care organizations, hospitals, physician networks, government and employers.

J&J's international growth has been both organic and through acquisitions which include Janssen Pharmaceuticals of Belgium, purchased in 1961, which is itself now a major global pharmaceutical company. In 1974, the Dr Carl Hahn Company in Germany, a manufacturer of sanitary protection products for women, was bought, followed in 1986 by the Penaten Group, Germany's leading baby toiletries company.

J&J has branches or affiliates in over 50 countries and the group is now expanding into new markets in mainland China and Eastern Europe. Janssen Pharmaceuticals was an early entrant to the Chinese market in 1985 with a pharmaceutical joint venture and by 1990 Johnson & Johnson Shanghai was producing Band-Aid brand adhesive bandages, followed the next year by the formation of Johnson & Johnson China Ltd. An administrative office was opened in Moscow in 1990, and offices have since been opened in Hungary, Poland, and the former Yugoslavia.

Marketing strength has been achieved with and in spite of the group's diversity The vastness of product spread makes it difficult to focus on individual opportunities, but no one product has the potential to be a 'killer' – in the good or evil sense.

Platforms for growth

Ralph Larsen, J&J's CEO, outlined a strategy of platforms for growth to shareholders in April 1998, and cited the following and other new growth opportunities:

- Wound healing – Ortho-McNeil Pharmaceutical recently introduced Regranex Gel, the first wound healing agent for the topical treatment of lower extremity diabetic skin ulcers, and Ethicon has licensed a wound closure product, called Dermabond, that acts as a glue to close small wounds quickly and painlessly. Dermabond could have application in as many as 10 million procedures annually.

- Diabetes – LifeScan, is the world's leading maker of blood glucose testing products and plans to launch an innovative new test strip, enabling diabetics to obtain accurate blood glucose readings without a meter. The product, called Smartstrip, will first be introduced in key markets outside the United States.

- Nutraceuticals – McNeil Consumer Products has seen sales for its Lactaid product line, for people with lactose intolerance, grow significantly over the past two years, and earlier this year obtained worldwide marketing rights to Benecol, a leading European margarine product containing a dietary ingredient patented for use in reducing cholesterol. McNeil Specialty Products also recently gained FDA clearance to market its no-calorie sweetener, sucralose, in 15 different food and beverage categories.

- Circulatory diseases – Cordis, which pioneered the use of coronary stents, is developing Nitinol's shape-memory metals to make crush-resistant stents for blood vessels and the heart; collaborating with IsoStent to create stents that deliver low dose radiation to reduce plaque in arteries; and working on its own to develop polymer-coated stents embedded with plaque-fighting pharmaceuticals.

• Women's health – Johnson & Johnson broadened its presence in women's health with the acquisition of Biopsys, which produces products for minimally invasive breast biopsies, and Gynecare, which markets minimally invasive medical devices for treating uterine disorders. Gynecare products include Versapoint for the removal of uterine fibroids, and the Thermachoice uterine balloon therapy system for treating excessive menstrual bleeding, a simple outpatient alternative procedure to hysterectomy that serves the needs of many patients.

Competitive advantage
With an unmatched global presence in the health care industry, an annual R&D spend of more than $2 billion for innovation, and the financial and managerial resources to in license product and acquire new companies successfully, J&J can ride out storms like a supertanker and still keep on course for sales growth, profit growth and earnings per share growth.

What can go wrong?

The drug pipeline and innovations must deliver profits. In the fiercely competitive and rapidly advancing world of pharm-aceuticals and medical devices, promising new products are the crucial driver of profit growth. For all its supertanker size, J&J is not a focused investing opportunity. It is a hybrid pharmaceuticals, professional medical supplies and consumer marketing company. Because of the disproportionate contribution to profits from the pharmaceuticals operations, significant group profit growth will be dependent on blockbuster or near blockbuster new drugs or massive technological breakthroughs in the professional sector.

Erythroprotein growth and competition from Amgen
J&J experienced a setback early in 1999 when an arbitration

determined that Nesp, a new erythroprotein compound developed by Amgen, did not fall within the scope of a marketing agreement with Amgen, who, with J&J, currently split the lion's share of a $3.5 billion erythroprotein market. The new compound could lead to more effective competition from Amgen in future.

The financial effect of the Nesp arbitration ruling is probably not severe as the new compound is still in the development stage and only offers improvements in frequency of dosing. J&J claims that it has developments of its own on similar lines in hand, and does not see exposure to serious losses. Investors will need more information before they are convinced.

Supertanker safety

The robust performance of J&J's shares is testimony to the advantages of investing in a life sciences supertanker. However, the Nesp setback followed a series of setbacks for J&J, including loss of market share with stents, the threat to Tylenol from a powerful new class of prescription painkillers which Merck and Monsanto Co will have on the market in 1999, and major setbacks with diabetes drugs in development.

If J&J fails to bring major new drugs to the market that keep up pharmaceutical profit growth, it will have to license in product or acquire key biotech companies that can deliver the growth instead. Otherwise it will risk profit slowdowns that could damage the company's high standing with investors.

Benecol may not be enough for the consumer division

Benecol has been a huge success in Finland where it was discovered and first marketed, and optimism on the prospects for J&J's consumer division has been encouraged by claims of exciting prospects for the cholesterol lowering food additive. J&J expects the product will take off in the US and European countries where increasingly health-conscious consumers are as concerned as Americans about elevated cholesterol levels. However, it soon ran into unexpected competition from Unilever who, by the end of 1998, secured permission to market its own cholesterol lowering margarine in Europe. According to clinical trials, both J&J and Unilever's margarines are derived from sterols and are proven to reduce levels of LDL-cholesterol, or so-called 'bad' cholesterol, by up to 13% with minimum daily use. However, Benecol will prove to be less of a bonanza than first expected if competition in the market place commoditizes the product and suppliers lose pricing power. The field has become even more crowded now with the Swiss company Novartis also taking an interest.

Monitoring

Portfolio 2001 reports review the investment growth for all prospects over an arbitrary five-year period from 1994 to 1999. In the Life Sciences sector, Pfizer was number one with 726% growth – an exceptional performance boosted appreciably by a single drug Viagra and the exceptional marketing opportunity it opened. Medtronic, the leading medical implants company was next with 697% growth, following expectations that electronic implants will be as successful in the treatment for neurological diseases as pacemakers have been with cardiac diseases. In the same five-year time frame, the J&J supertanker produced an impressive 310% investment growth.

The last five years have been exceptionally profitable for the life sciences industry and J&J has performed well in a buoyant market – slower than the most successful companies, but well in line with the sector. One view of J&J is that its size and wide product portfolio make it really more a cyclical Global Profit Harvester than an Innovator, and hence its fortunes will inevitably be more affected by macro economic conditions than by innovative strengths. If J&J comes to be perceived by the market as a cyclical investment, it will be less highly rated than if it is identified as a dynamic life sciences investment.

Investors monitoring J&J will need to follow company and industry reports and satisfy themselves that dynamic innovative growth is being achieved and that the supertanker is not in any danger of going off course. The web site www.jnj.com is an informative reference point on products, news and company thinking, and is a good starting point.

ABBOTT LABORATORIES

Share Graph 1997–1998 Abbott Laboratories
Primary Market – NYSE – ABT

Price January 1999 $42.62
Market Value January 1999 $72.376 billion

SECTOR Health Care INDUSTRY Major Drugs
Top Line ABT Share price Bottom Line S&P 500 Index Relative:
Triangle marks split
Left Scale: Top $ Price ABT, Bottom Volume in Thousands

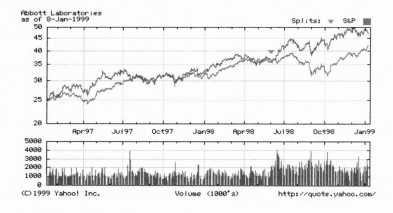

PRICE PERFORMANCE	ABT		An investment made in January 1994 grew 258% by January 1999		
PRICE HISTORY	1998	1997	1996	1995	Notes
High Price	50.06	34.88	28.69	22.38	
Low Price	32.53	24.88	19.06	15.31	
High P/E	33.07	26.01	24.09	21.29	
Low P/E	21.49	18.55	16.01	14.57	

Chmn D. L. Burnham, www.abbott.com
54,400 employees
100 Abbott Park Road, Abbott Park, IL 60064
Phone: (847) 937-6100 Fax: (847) 937-1511

Global Franchise: Pharmaceuticals, diagnostics, anaesthetics, hospital and nutritional products

Founded by Dr Abbott in the 1880s, Abbott Laboratories is a diversified global health care company with franchises in pharmaceuticals, diagnostics, nutritionals, and hospital products which include anaesthetics, systems for blood banks and laboratories, intravenous and irrigation fluids, drug delivery systems, and critical care products. Abbott is a worldwide leader in the supply of diagnostic products, therapeutic and disease monitoring tests and instruments. In pharmaceuticals it manufactures the antibiotic zithromycin and several other important drugs. An equally owned joint venture, formed in 1996 with Japan's Takeda Chemical Company, TAP Pharmaceuticals, markets several of Takeda's drugs in the US and contributes significant profits through major new drug franchises, presently for gastro-intestinal and prostate cancer applications. Abbott's nutritional products include the leading infant formula in the US and the world's leading adult nutritional supplement. Other Abbott products serve the chemical and agricultural industries. Over 54,000 people are employed and products are marketed in more than 130 countries. Sales are $12.5 billion with 30% coming from outside the US.

Setting a rational price

Portfolio 2001 WORKSHEET FOR TARGETING SHARE PRICES OF ABT IN
1999, 2000, 2001 & 2002
BASED ON FORECASTS MADE IN JANUARY 1999
EPS FISCAL 1987 TO DECEMBER 1998 $1.51

Growth	Year	Estimated EPS	P/E	Share Price Target	+10%	-10%	Notes
14%	1999	$1.72	25	$43	$48	$39	
14%	2000	$1.96	25	$49	$54	$44	
14%	2001	$2.23	25	$55	$62	$50	
10%	2002	$2.45	22.5	$55	$62	$50	Prilosec off patent

This 'what if' forecast suggests potential earnings and share prices based on current indications. Forecasts must be revised continuously in the light of all company results and industry, market and economic news. Forecasts can be misleading and cannot be treated as investment advice or used to motivate investments. See page 69.

Earnings per share growth expectations

Investors can be well reassured by Abbott's earnings track record which reflects consistent growth for over a quarter of a century.

With the strong earnings growth being achieved now by TAP Pharmaceuticals, which accrue half to Abbott, 14% earnings per share growth which it is targeting appears to be realistic.

Earnings multiple expectations

A multiple of 25 times earnings positions Abbott in the lower range of expectations for leading pharmaceutical companies, and reflects the current pricing of shares on the market.

Past performance indicators

Growth Rates %		ABT	S&P 500	Industry	Sector	Notes
Earnings per share 5 year		8.64	15.83	11.95	15.10	
1998 last reported vs 1997		12.57	12.25	14.92	14.11	
Sales 5 year 1994-1998		8.64	15.83	11.95	15.10	
Profitability Ratios						
Gross Margin 1998	%	57.51	49.16	69.51	65.90	
5 year average	%	56.97	48.83	69.83	66.01	
Net Profit Margin 1998	%	18.54	10.85	18.46	14.82	
5 year average	%	16.96	10.21	16.22	12.86	
5 Year Returns on:						
Assets	%	18.61	8.26	14.58	11.46	
Investment	%	31.15	13.03	22.09	17.51	
Equity	%	40.52	21.49	32.80	26.75	

The growth story

The Abbott prescription for shareholder wealth

Abbott describes itself as a company that manages its assets carefully, always weighing long-term investment against short-term gains, with four growth strategies – internal research and development, market expansion, collaborations and targeted acquisitions. Abbott delivers what shareholders want – earnings per share growth – year after year, as illustrated in this twenty-five-year chart to 1997:

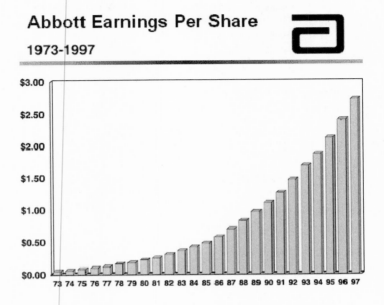

Abbott Earnings Per Share
1973-1997

Results for 1998 followed the established growth pattern:

Abbott Laboratories	1998	1997
Sales	$12,477,845,000	$11,883,462,000
Net income	2,333,231,000	2,094,462,000
Avg shrs (basic)	1,522,702,000	1,539,746,000
Avg shrs (diluted)	1,545,658,000	1,561,462,000
Shr earns (basic) Net income	1.53	1.36
Shr earns (diluted) Net income	1.51	1.34

Abbott has built a marketing niche globally as a major pharmaceutical company with strong hospital, diagnostics, anaesthesia and laboratory portfolios. The growth story has been strengthened over recent years as it has:

- expanded into new therapeutic areas including diabetes and AIDS.

- augmented research in traditional areas including antibiotics.

- built a urology franchise with pharmaceutical and diagnostic products to manage prostate disease. Its product Hytrin is effective in treating benign prostate gland enlargement and Takeda's Lupron is marketed for prostate cancers.

- established TAP Pharmaceuticals in equal partnership with Japan's Takeda Chemical Industries to market various Takedas' pharmaceuticals in the US. TAP Pharmaceuticals has become a major contributor to group profits.

Diagnostics

Abbott introduced and commercialized many of the blood tests which are now part of everyday clinical practice and it has strong positions in clinical and home diagnostics, ranging from laboratory tests for major diseases to rapid pregnancy tests. Home monitoring and diagnostics markets are expected to grow significantly as they support outpatient treatments for an increasingly ageing population.

Competitive advantage

Abbott's hospital portfolio gives it access to hospitals worldwide to introduce other products which it supplies from others or develops itself. Abbott's partners are leading companies whose products fit strategically with their worldwide pharmaceutical business. One of their goals is to be the leading healthcare company in the HIV arena, and a worldwide strategic alliance concluded in May 1999 with Triangle Pharmaceuticals gives them access to segments of antivirals and pharmaceutical interventions that round off their existing HIV portfolio. Abbott already have significant exposure with pharmaceutical and diagnostic HIV products. Under the terms of the agreement, Abbott agreed to purchase approximately 6.57 million shares of Triangle's Common Stock, and to provide funding.

Another strategic alliance announced in 1999 is with SangStat Pharmaceuticals who have introduced the first generic competitor to Novartis's cylosporine used in transplant medicine. Approximately 140,000 transplant patients in the United States and

250,000 worldwide require daily immunosuppressive therapy for life from the time of transplant surgery, and the majority of these individuals take cyclosporine. Cyclosporine products account for approximately $1.35 billion in sales globally and more than $500 million in sales in the United States. The partnership is a continuation of an initial agreement for Abbott to supply bulk cyclosporine to SangStat.

The alliance broadens Abbott's presence in the $2.5 billion worldwide transplantation arena and they will leverage their existing transplantation healthcare expertise in renal care, therapeutics, drug monitoring and marketing to hospitals. As part of the agreement, Abbott are making an equity investment in SangStat, providing finance and making milestone payments. With a research and development spend of $1.3 billion, Abbott also responds to market opportunities with products developed in house.

What can go wrong?

The wide hospital and pharmacuetical franchises, with the support of other sales areas, insulate the group from setbacks with any product. Abbott can be expected to perform well in most market conditions.

Monitoring

www.abbott.com is informative on group activities and www.takeda.jp reports on Takeda's products and marketing plans. Investors should monitor Takeda for new drugs that may be marketed with Abbott, particularly as Takeda have announced dramatic new discoveries.

MEDTRONIC

Share Graph 1997–1998 Medtronic Inc.
Primary Market – NYSE – MDT

Price January 1999 $71.889
Market Value January $31.5 billion

SECTOR Health Care INDUSTRY Medical Equipment and Supplies
Top Line Medtronic Share price Bottom Line S&P 500 Index
Relative: Triangle Marks Split
Left Scale: Top $ Price, Bottom Volume in Thousands

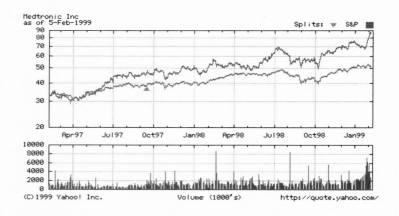

PRICE PERFORMANCE	MDT		An investment made in January 1994 grew 697% by January 1999		
PRICE HISTORY	1998	1997	1996	1995	Notes
High Price	76.75	52.75	34.94	30.00	
Low Price	45.44	28.81	22.25	13.09	
High P/E	79.78	48.31	39.48	47.02	
Low P/E	47.23	26.39	25.14	20.52	

Global Franchise: Implantable stimulation devices

Founder Earl Bakken with his brother-in-law Palmer Hermundslie started Medtronic as a medical equipment repair shop in the 1950s. By 1960, Bakken had invented and was selling the first cardiac pacemaker implant. Since then, more than 2 million Medtronic pacemakers have been implanted and Medtronic has become the world's leading medical technology company specializing in implantable and interventional therapies. Medtronic now has three divisions.

The cardiac rhythm management division includes implantable defibrillators and pacemakers, and pacing products are the group's core business, accounting for 64% of fiscal 1998 sales. Under this heading the company supplies pacing products for bradycardia (slow heart) and for tachycardia (fast heart). This division also supplies the world's smallest and lightest device, the Micro Jewel II implantable defibrillator.

Medtronic's cardiac surgery division caters for the needs of surgeons with pumps, oxygenators and prosthetic heart valves which have been implanted in nearly 130,000 patients over the last fifteen years. This division embraces a wide range of of minimally invasive surgical apparatus, including blood vessel supporting stents, balloon catheters and a variety of instruments.

Neurological products are the newest and fastest growing division. These include pulsing and drug-delivery devices that are used for managing chronic pain and alleviating uncontrolled tremors via direct brain electrical stimulation.

Medtronic is headquartered in Minneapolis, Minnesota and employs nearly 14,000 people worldwide. Its products and services are used in treating over 1.5 million people each year in more than 120 countries. Annual revenues are $3 billion.

Setting a rational price

Portfolio 2001 WORKSHEET FOR TARGETING SHARE PRICES OF MEDTRONIC
MDT IN 1999, 2000, 2001 & 2002
BASED ON FORECASTS MADE IN JANUARY 1999
FISCAL 1987 $1.25 1999 $1.65(E)

Growth	Year	Estimated EPS	P/E	Share Price Target	+10%	-10%	Notes
Consensus	1999	$1.86	45	$74	$82	$67	
20%	2000	$2.19	45	$89	$99	$80	
20%	2001	$2.37	45	$107	$118	$96	
20%	2002	$2.84	45	$128	$142	$115	

This 'what if' forecast suggests potential earnings and share prices based on current indications. Forecasts must be revised continuously in the light of all company results and industry, market and economic news. Forecasts can be misleading and cannot be treated as investment advice or used to motivate investments. See page 69.

Earnings per share growth expectations

Analysts have been able to make earnings growth forecasts for Medtronic on known business potential, but currently more is expected and less is known about the company's potential than before. Medtronic has been on the acquisitions trail and the effect of several acquisitions cannot yet be factored in; nor can growth in implantable neurological devices, expected to be the main growth platform in future, as sufficient data on products and potential is not yet available.

Management's track record encourages high expectations and analysts follow company briefings, but forecasts lack substance. The *Portfolio 2001* 20% earnings growth expectation follows analysts' consensus and the forecast has a particularly short sell-by date.

Earnings multiple expectations

Medtronic technology helps people to live longer with appreciably less pain and more peace of mind. Its financial achievements have also materially improved the lives of long-term investors who have been rewarded with a 10-year total return of 21 times each invested dollar. This compares with an average of barely four times each invested dollar for the same period from peer companies in the medical device sector.

The word 'rational' fits poorly with forecasting what investors will pay for Medtronic shares. The company has a unique position as leader in implantable cardiac devices and is the only visible contender in the market for neurological implants, an area where investors are expecting high growth. The *Portfolio 2001* forecast stretches to 45 times earnings to set target share prices, over twice the earnings growth rate and this multiple brings share price targets near to current market levels. There is no logic involved except that investors will pay a high price for Medtronic. The following chart shows three Life Science companies reviewed in *Portfolio 2001*. Medtronic was trading at a price earnings relationship of over 70 times earnings, Baxter was trading at a multiple of over sixty times earnings and pharmaceutical bellwether Merck was trading in the low thirties.

P/E Ratio Comparison

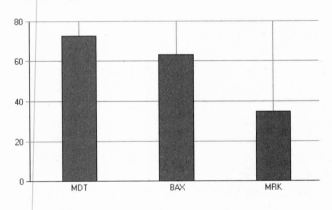

Source: www.quicken.com

Investors in Medtronic have one of the most credible management track records to back, and management have announced that they expect revenues to grow from $3 billion in 1998 to $5 billion in 2001.

Medtronic's share price rises, year after year, can give the impression of guaranteeing investors high rewards but this cannot be the case, tempting as it is to think that it might be.

Past performance indicators

A series of acquisitions, with related growth and write downs, minimizes the value of past financial performance indicators. However, strong earnings per share growth, high profit margins and high returns on assets, investments and equity have been maintained consistently:

Growth Rates %		MDT	S&P	Industry	Sector	Notes
Earnings per share 5 year		16.67	20.56	11.52	13.34	
1998 last reported vs 1997		-18.05	12.25	-10.56	14.11	
Sales 5 year 1994-1998		16.67	20.56	11.52	20.56	
Profitability Ratios						
Gross Margin 1998	%	72.61	49.16	59.09	65.90	
5 year average	%	72.00	48.83	57.26	66.01	
Net Profit Margin 1998	%	16.97	10.85	6.73	14.82	
5 year average	%	18.52	10.21	9.15	12.86	
5 Year Returns on:						
Assets	%	18.09	8.26	8.92	11.46	
Investment	%	23.53	13.03	12.89	17.51	
Equity	%	25.98	21.49	18.16	26.75	

The growth story

As a major industry force that has capitalized on the success of innovations in medical devices for the human heart and the cardiovascular system, Medtronic has entrenched itself further in recognized growth segments through acquisitions. Major acquisitions completed over the last quarter of 1998 included the Sofamor Danek Group and Arterial Vascular Engineering, following smaller acquisitions including Physio-Control International, Midas Rex and Abecor Cardiovascular. Together, the acquisitions should lead to a year of exceptional growth, but, until a company financial report integrating the acquisitions is published, little tangible information is available to support expectations.

Shortly before Medtronic reported its fiscal second-quarter 1999 results in mid-November, it announced plans to buy Sofamor Danek Group Inc. (SDG) in a $3.6 billion stock swap. Two weeks later, it agreed to buy a leading stent company Arterial Vascular Engineering Inc. (AVEI) for $3.7 billion. These companies now have to be looked at as part of the broader Medtronic. They were important industry consolidations within Medtronic's operational framework that strengthened platforms for growth in implantable neural devices and cardiac surgery respectively.

Stents

The multibillion dollar stent market is an area of rapid growth and technological improvement and change. Johnson & Johnson first dominated the market but were challenged by new technology products from Boston Scientific, Guidant and Arterial Vascular.

The Arterial Vascular deal with Medtronic was concluded as a pooling of interests and resulted in the establishment of a new organization known as Medtronic Vascular, structured to provide 'best-in-class' products for physicians worldwide. Medtronic effectively merged three strong product lines (AVE, Medtronic Vascular and the former USCI Division of C R Bard) into one, with market leading products in every category and an advanced line of stents, catheters and related products.

Supporting the group's established positions in cardiac rhythm management and cardiac surgery, Medtronic set out to gain, and have gained a leadership position in the interventional vascular and stent arena.

Sofamor Danek

Sofamor Danek develops and markets spinal implant devices which are used in the surgical treatment of spinal conditions such as degenerative diseases, deformities and trauma, and are used for the relief of neurological diseases. Implantable neurological devices are a natural growth area for Medtronic for three reasons. Firstly, like implantable cardiac devices they serve an ageing population and are a key multibillion dollar growth market. Secondly, Medtronic is industry leader with implantable devices and has the resources to develop products and market them. Thirdly, as an industry consolidator it can absorb businesses with new technologies that arise, and maintain product leadership.

Neurological implants and products

Neurological products include neurostimulation systems, drug delivery systems, neurosurgical implant devices, surgical access products, and diagnostic and therapeutic systems for chronic pain and neurologic, urologic and gastrointestinal disorders.

Essential tremor is the most common movement disorder in the United States, affecting at least one million people. In 1997, Medtronic introduced the first new treatments in more than thirty years for patients with movement disorders including essential tremor, tremor associated with Parkinson's disease and the major symptoms of advanced Parkinson's disease. Medtronic's Activa tremor control therapy, which uses specialized leads connected to an implanted device to block tremor-causing brain signals, received market clearance from the US Food and Drug Administration (FDA) in fiscal 1998. When turned on by a hand-held magnet, the implanted Activa system stops the involuntary shaking of limbs or other parts of the body almost instantly, allowing patients to resume normal life activities.

During 1998, Activa therapies were approved in Europe for the most disabling symptoms of advanced Parkinson's disease. In these situations leads are implanted slightly deeper in other areas of the brain such as the sub-thalamic nucleus or globus pallidus. Activa Parkinson's therapy controls major symptoms of Parkinson's disease, including rigidity, immobility, postural instability and involuntary abnormal movements. Medtronic neurological developments include various acute pain management techniques, including spinal cord stimulation to treat angina pain.

Medtronic is leveraging its neurostimulation know-how to develop therapies for incontinence. InterStim continence control therapy, the first implantable treatment to use electrical stimulation of the sacral nerves to manage urinary urge incontinence, received market clearance from the FDA during fiscal 1998. This new treatment option can improve the quality of life for many of the 13 million US patients, mainly women aged 30–59, who suffer from the debilitating and confining effects of incontinence. Therapies for faecal incontinence, urinary urgency/frequency, and urinary retention are already marketed in Europe, and clinical trials continue in the United States. At the same time new treatments are also being developed for sleep apnoea and epilepsy.

An area of growth in neural medicine that has been targeted outside Medtronic is stroke therapy. In 1997, an estimated 700,000 Americans suffered strokes – about 402,000 of those were first-time strokes, and that number is expected to increase steadily, surpassing 1 million in 2050. This signifies a 167% increase in stroke incidence among men and a 140% increase among women. Stroke is the leading cause of long-term disability and the third-leading cause of death – after heart disease and cancer – for persons over the age of 45 in the United States. Microcatheters, guidewires, neurological balloon angioplasty catheters, stents and cerebro-vascular aneurysm clips, which fall in the scope of the Sofamor Danek and Medtronic product range, have been recognized as likely devices that will play a critical role in improving outcomes in stroke therapy.

Investors expect that Medtronic will bring the technology they have developed with implantable cardiac devices to neurological diseases, and as therapies are marketed, more information on which to forecast growth will be known.

Implantable pacemakers
Of total sales of $2.6 billion in 1998, pacing products accounted for $1.6 billion of Medtronic's revenue, representing about 38% of the global market. Since product approvals Medtronic has achieved for a dual chamber implantable cardiac device and other product refinements, sales of pacing devices have been forecast to reach $2 billion by the year 2000.

Competitive advantage
Technological and financial barriers to competition in implantable devices are formidable, and Guidant and Medtronic together compete for 90% of the market for cardiac devices. The stent business is subject to much wider competition and the success of the Arterial Vascular acquisition will, in the long run, depend on the group's ability to keep ahead in product leadership and development.

What can go wrong?

Rapid technological growth areas are prone to their own family of risks. Products in development can fail to gain approval, or may have to be recalled once on the market, at great cost.

With products serving a prosperous ageing generation of baby boomers, the US, Europe and Japan are the key countries with patient populations in Medtronic's sights, and it will not depend on growth in emerging markets for some years. However, currency fluctuations can, as they have done in the past, affect earnings.

If Medtronic disappoints markets at any stage, a steep downgrading of valuations will be inevitable.

Monitoring

Medtronic is a company which only a trained professional can monitor in terms of its technological developments. Investors are backing management and a growth story. The market rating for the share will follow the growth story and the achievements of management. Investors should follow `www.medtronic.com` and look closely at financial results achieved.

BAXTER

Share Graph 1997–1998 Baxter International Inc.
Primary Market – NYSE

Price January 1999 $69.75
Market Value January 1999 $19.9 billion

SECTOR Health Care INDUSTRY Medical Equipment and
Supplies
Top Line S&P 500 Index Relative Bottom Line Bax Share Price
Left Scale: Top $ Price BAX, Bottom Volume in Thousands

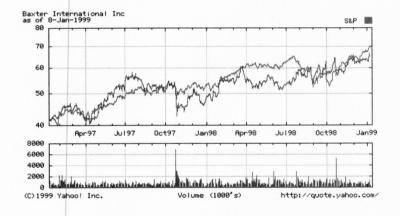

PRICE PERFORMANCE	BAX		An investment made in January 1994 grew 262% by January 1999		
PRICE HISTORY	1998	1997	1996	1995	Notes
High Price	66.00	60.25	48.13	44.75	
Low Price	48.50	39.88	39.75	26.75	
High P/E	60.61	56.63	23.18	34.00	
Low P/E	44.54	37.48	19.15	20.33	

Pres/CEO Jansen Kraemer Jr., **www.baxter.com**
41,000 employees
One Baxter Parkway, Deerfield, IL 60015
Phone: (847) 948 2000 Fax: (847) 948 3948

Global Franchise: Technologies to the blood and circulatory system

Since it was founded in 1931, Baxter has contributed to dramatic medical and scientific life-saving breakthroughs, many of which we take for granted today including open heart surgery, intravenous medicine, kidney dialysis, heart-valve replacement, blood banks and blood-component therapy. Baxter products are supplied to hospitals, laboratories, blood banks, dialysis centres, nursing homes, doctors' offices, and for home use under medical supervision. Blood therapy products collect, separate and store blood, renal products cleanse blood and therapeutic products supply proteins derived from blood. The product range with over 1,000 cardiovascular products includes tissue heart valves, blood transfusion systems, hospital and home dialysis systems, and heart surgery equipment. Baxter products support blood pumping through the body and intravenous (IV) products infuse drugs and other solutions into the blood. New products at the cutting edge of science include an electronic implantable pump designed to keep the blood circulating in people with end-stage heart disease, and a blood sealant or surgical glue. Baxter is also the world's leading manufacturer of plastic blood collection containers and related transfusion products.

In 1996, Baxter spun off its health care products and cost management business to shareholders as Allegiance Corporation, to focus on its core technologies and global expansion. Products are manufactured in 25 countries and sold in approximately 100. More than half annual sales of $6 billion are outside the United States.

Setting a rational price

Portfolio 2001 WORKSHEET FOR TARGETING SHARE PRICES OF BAXTER INTERNATIONAL BAX 1999, 2000, 2001 & 2002 BASED ON FORECASTS MADE IN JANUARY 1999 EPS FISCAL 1987 TO DECEMBER $2.54

Growth	Year	Estimated EPS	P/E	Share Price Target	+10%	-10%	Notes
12.5%	1999	$2.85	22.5	$64	$71	$56	
12.5%	2000	$3.20	22.5	$72	$80	$65	
12.5%	2001	$3.60	22.5	$81	$90	$73	
12.5%	2002	$4.05	22.5	$91	$101	$81	

This 'what if' forecast suggests potential earnings and share prices based on current indications. Forecasts must be revised continuously in the light of all company results and industry, market and economic news. Forecasts can be misleading and cannot be treated as investment advice or used to motivate investments. See page 69.

Earnings per share growth expectations
Management have indicated that they expect to achieve earnings growth in the low teens and 12.5% growth is accepted by analysts as being attainable.

Earnings multiple expectations
The multiple of 22.5 times earnings to target share prices is consistent with market valuations in January 1999. The medical equipment sector is regarded as having strong growth potential and in strong markets high valuations appear sustainable.

Past performance indicators
In 1985, Baxter spun off its chemicals business as Allegiance Chemicals. Comparisons that go back prior to the spin-off therefore present distorted information.

Growth Rates %		BAX	S&P 500	Industry	Sector	Notes
Earnings per share 5 year		NM				Spin-off
1998 last reported vs 1997		6.04	11.09	-16.04	6.69	
Sales 5 year 1994-1998		NM				Spin-off
Profitability Ratios						
Gross Margin 1998	%	45.54	49.16	59.09	65.90	
5 year average	%	NM				
Net Profit Margin 1998	%	4.46	10.85	6.73	14.82	
5 year average	%	NM				
5 Year Returns on:						
Assets	%	3.33	8.26	8.92	11.46	
Investment	%	4.53	13.03	12.89	17.51	
Equity	%	9.29	21.49	18.16	26.75	

NM = not meaningful

The growth story

The high technology opportunity

High technology is triggering rapid productivity advances through-out the economy, but few industries stand to benefit more than medical products, devices and instrumentation companies. More than 700,000 open heart surgeries are performed in the US each year, and the market for cardiovascular and renal products and services is expected to continue to grow, due to the large ageing population, the progressive nature of the diseases they suffer from and enhanced opportunities for treatment in developing econ-omies and emerging nations.

Baxter is a leading high technology global medical products and services company with exceptionally strong growth potential. It focuses on critical therapies for life-threatening conditions, with products and services in blood therapies (biopharmaceuticals and blood collection, separation and storage devices), cardiovascular medicine, medication delivery and renal therapy which are used by health care providers and critically ill patients in more than 110 countries.

Growth strategy

Baxter operations include servicing therapies used in transfusion medicine and dialysis, and producing therapeutic proteins used to treat haemophilia, immune deficiencies and other blood related disorders. One of Baxter's core strategies has been to expand rapidly outside the United States and it has established a strong global presence, with more than half of its sales coming from non-US markets. The largest international market is Europe, representing more than half the company's sales outside the United States. The fastest-growing region is the Pacific Rim, where revenues are expected to grow five-fold within a decade.

In 1998, Baxter received an important approval from the US Food and Drug Administration to manufacture Recombinate rAHF, its genetically engineered clotting factor for people with haemophilia, at its new manufacturing facility in Thousand Oaks, California. The approval enables Baxter to increase its global supply of the much-needed medical therapy by up to 40%.

Baxter became the first company to receive FDA approval to market its fibrin sealant in 1998. Tisseel fibrin sealant replicates the natural blood clotting process to stop bleeding in surgical procedures involving cardiopulmonary bypass, repair of the spleen and colostomy closure. Also in 1998, Baxter launched in the United States its Novacor heart-assist system, which is a device that keeps patients who suffer from heart failure alive until a donor heart is available. Both of these products are also available in Europe. Additionally, in the United States and Canada, Baxter introduced a more advanced version of its Colleague electronic infusion pump, which allows medical clinicians to administer multiple intravenous medications and fluids to their patients, using only a single pump.

Baxter's Renal Therapy Services continued to expand rapidly outside the United States, and generated more than $100 million in sales in 1998. This unit operates dialysis clinics in partnership with leading local physicians and hospitals, to increase access to treatment, improve patient outcomes and reduce clinics' operating costs.

Transplantation and Xenotransplantation

Baxter is the world's leading supplier of tissue and mechanical heart valves. Its Novacor electronic left-ventricular assist system (LVAS) has been approved in Europe as both a bridge to transplant, and as a long-term alternative to transplant. In the United States, the LVAS has been approved as a bridge to transplant.

Working with the Mayo Clinic, Baxter is currently experimenting with transplanting pig organs into baboons. The goal of the research is to provide an additional source of organs for people whose kidneys, hearts or livers are failing because there aren't enough human organs available to transplant into all the patients who need them. CEO Jansen Kraemer has suggested that Baxter may be able to begin human clinical trials with these animal organs within a year to eighteen months.

Artificial blood

Despite Baxter having abandoned its artificial blood product, HemAssist, Kraemer has indicated that the company is continuing research into a recombinant artificial blood product produced by its Somatogen unit. However, he did not say how long it might take to bring a so-called 'second-generation' Somatogen product to human clinical trials.

Competitive advantage

Baxter's leading position and the depth of its knowledge, particularly in the blood technology industry, give it an edge in researching, developing and marketing in an industry sector with high barriers to entry. A global marketing strategy has also led to the successful opening of new markets in the developing world.

What can go wrong?

Past mishaps and potential claims

Baxter is a hybrid biotechnology and medical devices company and it could be argued that on track record it should not be included as a *Portfolio 2001* low-risk high-reward opportunity. Intensive care procedures and biotechnology research are intrinsically high risk, but Baxter attracts as a prospect because of its focus and industry dominance in areas which are core to the progress of surgery, renal care and life support. However, while it may resemble a major pharmaceutical company which sponsors biotechnological opportunities with risks cushioned by other profitable operations, with Baxter the risks are more direct. Baxter has faced periods when profits have been elusive and failures have threatened progress. Continuous litigation and claims have also drained resources, and even in 1998 $300 million was paid in settlement of accrued claims.

Present indications are favourable and Standard & Poor's recently affirmed its single-A corporate credit and senior unsecured note and debenture ratings and A-1 commercial paper rating on Baxter. At the same time the ratings were removed from CreditWatch, where they were placed in September 1998.

S&P found that recent governmental approvals which greatly increased Baxter's blood-based product manufacturing capacity offset continued concerns regarding potential for earnings softness from businesses in Japan and Latin America. Additionally, management had reiterated its intention to reduce debt levels quickly.

The investment-grade ratings reflect Baxter's solid positions in four speciality medical product markets, and strong cash flow generation. However, in the industry Baxter services, the risk is always present of a major product problem which could cause delivery delays, profit losses or claims.

Controversial areas of development
Xenotransplantation technology is being developed by Baxter's Nextran subsidiary which is working towards transplants with pig hearts, kidneys, livers and potentially other organs for humans, and clinical trials are advanced that use transgenic pig livers as an extracorporeal (outside the body) perfusion device for transplant patients suffering from acute liver failure.

Transplantation of animal organs would meet an urgent need and open a new era for transplant medicine, and Baxter is one of the few companies in the world actively engaged in making it happen. However, while xenotransplantation has the potential to be a dramatically important life-saving technology, and an equally important commercial opportunity, it is also a subject that could lead to a public controversy and progress could be halted by public opinion. If this were to happen, investments made by Baxter could be costly commercial failures.

Monitoring

Baxter is an opportunity for well-informed investors with sufficient knowledge to research and monitor the company and the sector. Lay investors can only focus on whether management are delivering in accordance with expectations.

www.baxter.com presents what the company is doing and expects to achieve, and the regular 10Q and 10K reports to the SEC give full details of touchy areas including competition, claims and litigation.

The financial press cover news on Baxter, with sufficient information for investors to keep informed on financial performance and important developments.

MONSANTO

Share Graph 1997–1998 Monsanto Co.
Primary Market – NYSE – MTC

Price January 1999 $39
Market Value January 1999 $25.9 billion

SECTOR Basic Materials INDUSTRY Chemical Manufacturing
Top Line S&P 500 Index Relative: Bottom Line MONSANTO
Left Scale: Top $ Price MTC, Bottom Volume in Thousands

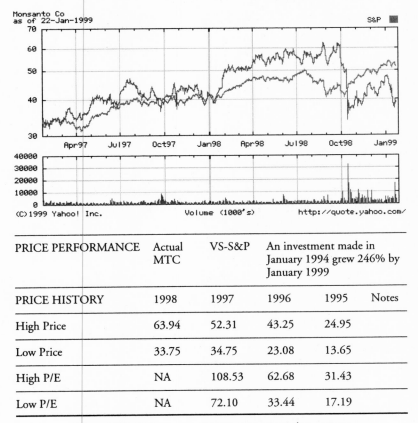

Monsanto Co
as of 22-Jan-1999   S&P ■

(C)1999 Yahoo! Inc.   Volume (1000's)   http://quote.yahoo.com/

PRICE PERFORMANCE	Actual MTC	VS-S&P	An investment made in January 1994 grew 246% by January 1999		
PRICE HISTORY	1998	1997	1996	1995	Notes
High Price	63.94	52.31	43.25	24.95	
Low Price	33.75	34.75	23.08	13.65	
High P/E	NA	108.53	62.68	31.43	
Low P/E	NA	72.10	33.44	17.19	

Chmn/CEO R.B. Shapiro, www.monsanto.com
21,900 employees
800 North Lindbergh Blvd., St Louis, MO 63167
Phone: (314) 694-1000 Fax: (314) 694-7625 800

Global Franchise: Genetically modified seeds, agricultural biotechnology, pharmaceuticals and Nutrasweet

Monsanto was incorporated in 1932 under Delaware law and is the successor to a Missouri corporation Monsanto Chemical works organized in 1901. In 1997, Monsanto spun off its conventional chemicals business to shareholders who received one share in a new company, Solutia (SOI), for every Monsanto share held. Monsanto is now commercializing genetic science and genetic engineering in the seed industry, and its name could be read as an acronym for 'Modified Organisms, Nutrasweet & Tomatoes Company'. Monsanto is the world leader in commercializing genetically engineered seeds, including the well-known one with a 'pg' gene introduced that delays ripening of tomatoes to give them a longer in-store shelf life, and the seed modified to include a bacterium, bacillus thuringiensis, which produces a protein in the plant toxic to pests feeding on it. Monsanto also genetically modifies seeds to make them resistant to its chemical herbicide Roundup, the world's largest selling agrichemical product. There are an estimated 50 million acres of agriculture worldwide affected by Monsanto technology.

G. D. Searle, Monsanto's innovative pharmaceutical subsidiary, produced the first oral contraceptive, and researches and develops pharmaceuticals focusing on key therapeutic areas including cardiovascular disease, arthritis, and cancer. Its new drug Celebrex, first of a new class of painkillers, was approved for sale in the US early in 1999.

Monsanto's third division, nutrition and consumer products, is best known for Nutrasweet, the world's leading brand of artificial sweeteners.

Agrochemicals and seeds are now well over 50% of Monsanto's business. Annual sales are $4 billion with 80% of income generated in the US.

Setting a rational price

Monsanto, under present conditions, does not fit any of the criteria for low-risk high-reward investing, and it is impossible to set a rational price. It is a concept stock identified with plant biotechnology and is currently highly speculative at any valuation. The company is also burdened with high debts, incurred in buying companies with secure technology to corner market share, and is being affected by public action against genetically modified foods.

Information on Monsanto is included in *Portfolio 2001* because the likelihood is that, either by raising fresh capital or through a merger or other corporate transaction, Monsanto will become a leading life sciences investment target again. It has the world's leading franchise in genetically modified seeds, and an important pharmaceuticals subsidiary G. D. Searle. The message of this report is to keep an eye on Monsanto for when it appears as a more stable prospect.

Monsanto is on the trail of researching major new product lines, launching major marketing initiatives and acquiring, selling and spinning off businesses. With these transactions, exceptional costs and charges against income on acquisitions, and at times exceptional revenues, arise. Management need pages of comment to explain financial reports and present their information in several formats, including conventional income statements, operating income statements and economic value tables. There is no short cut to understanding Monsanto other than to work through current announcements in detail and review them as presented in www.monsanto.com

The growth story

Determined to become the leader in agribusiness, Monsanto gave up short-term earnings and concentrated on ongoing investment and expansion in agricultural biotechnology. Over the three years 1996 to 1998, $6 billion was invested to consolidate their position. The motivation was a one-time opportunity to dominate acreage with their seeds and herbicides and secure the market long-term position.

The economic logic of genetically modified seeds is compelling. Plants that can protect themselves from insect pests, viruses and other attacks are bound to increase agricultural yields and, if less chemicals are used in food production, it saves costs and yields food that is healthier. Many pressure groups oppose genetically modified crops, but increasingly they are being seen as not only economically beneficial but also beneficial to the global ecology.

In 1998, millions of acres of US and other farmlands were planted with seeds of genetically altered cotton, corn and soybeans and, for the first time, genetically engineered crops comprised a significant portion of American agriculture. More than three-quarters of the cotton in Alabama was genetically engineered to kill insects. Elsewhere, farmers planted 8 million acres using genetically engineered soybeans, 3.5 million acres using modified corn and 10,000 acres of altered potatoes.

Monsanto's agri-biotech pipeline has 51 products under development, including disease-resistant plants and vitamin-fortified, low-fat oils, in addition to its existing herbicide-tolerant and insect-resistant crops.

Unfortunately, there are several risks in Monsanto's structure. The first is the expiration of patents on its flagship product, the herbicide Roundup which accounts for nearly 60% operating profit. The second is that it is over-borrowed and the third is that profits are elusive. Cumulatively, Monsanto's problems mask one of the most important growth stories in Life Sciences. Monsanto is the most significant company in commercial plant biotech.

G. D. Searle

Lost in the maze of problems is also the potential of the group's pharmaceutical company G. D. Searle. It has launched a new pain-killer, Celebrex, ahead of a competitive product from Merck in 1999. Celebrex is in a class of drugs known as Cox 2 blockers that treat severe pain and inflammation from diseases like arthritis, without harming the stomach lining as other agents do, and it is likely to become a blockbuster drug with sales of over $1 billion. Pfizer has paid Monsanto more than $200 million for marketing rights to Celebrex, and Yamanouchi made an upfront payment of $75 million for the right to co-market certain Searle products in Japan.

In the next five years, G.D. Searle plans to launch as many as 10 drugs.

Financial restructuring

Monsanto's debts of $6 billion are likely to be reduced through a secondary offering in 1999, and it is likely assets may be sold to build cash reserves. When a new corporate structure is in place, and revenues from Celebrex and other new drugs in the pipeline start supporting improved earnings from agri-biotech, Monsanto could become a stable investing prospect again.

Competitive advantage

Monsanto dominates in the biotechnology field of genetic seed modification through ventures in seed development, patent libraries, technology, and effective sales forces in the market place. Following a $1 billion purchase of Holden's Foundation Seeds in 1997, Monsanto increased its share of the corn seed market in the US to 40%. Then in May 1998, it invested a further $4.2 billion in cash and stock for two seed and biotechnology companies, De Kalb Genetics Corp and Delta Pine, to gain ownership of key genetic engineering technology. DeKalb Genetics controlled 11% of the lucrative North American corn-seed market and held strategically important patents for genetically modifying seeds. One is the patent for genetically engineering a corn plant to make an insecticide that is harmless to humans and US farmers planted about 12 million acres with this seed in the spring of 1998.

What can come right?

www.monsanto.com presents a development pipeline which could change the way the world's agricultural industry works.

Monitoring

Monitoring for the opportunity to invest will call for an understanding of company plans, opposition to genetically modified crops and Monsanto's complicated financial structure.

In many ways Monsanto is a mirror image of Novartis in the field of agri-biotech. Novartis has the cash to do what Monsanto is doing, but lacks the aggression. Novartis's progress in marketing genetically modified seeds, as reported in www.novartis.com, should be an interesting information source when monitoring Monsanto. Public resistance to genetically modified foods should also be monitored as it could delay progress in the industry.

SMITHKLINE BEECHAM

Share Graph 1997–1998 SmithKline Beecham PLC – ADR
Primary Market – London SKB – ADR SBH

Price January 1999 $67.81
Market Value January 1999 $75.2 billion

SECTOR Health Care INDUSTRY Major Drugs
Top Line SBH ABR $ Price: Bottom Line S&P 500 Index Relative:
Triangle Marks Split
Left Scale: Top $ Price, Bottom Volume in Thousands

PRICE PERFORMANCE	SBH		An investment made in January 1994 grew 415% by January 1999		
PRICE HISTORY	1998	1997	1996	1995	Notes
High Price	71.88	53.63	34.69	27.14	
Low Price	48.06	32.56	24.31	17.28	
High P/E	NA	43.16	26.88	50.75	
Low P/E	NA	26.21	20.04	32.31	

CEO Jan Leschly, Chmn Sir Peter Walters, **www.sb.com**
52,900 employees
New Horizons Court, Brentford, Middlesex, TW8 9EP
Phone: (681) 975-2000 US Shareholder Services: (800) 882-3359

Global Franchise: Prescription drugs, vaccines and over-the-counter medicines

Britain's SmithKline Beecham (SBH) is one of the world's leading healthcare companies. It discovers, develops, manufactures and markets pharmaceuticals, vaccines, over-the-counter (OTC) medicines and health-related consumer products. SBH is the eleventh largest pharmaceutical company in the world marketing over 400 branded products. These include Augmentin a leading antibiotic, Seroxat/Paxil a leading anti-depressant and several household name products including Aquafresh, one of the world's leading lines of toothpastes and toothbrushes; and NicoDerm CQ and Nicorette smoking cessation. SBH patches and gum have over 90% of the over-the-counter smoking cessation market. Engerix-B, a hepatitis B vaccine is the number one vaccine worldwide. SBH undertakes pioneering research and development, including cutting-edge biomedical research and molecular diagnostics programmes. New major drugs which will be introduced in 1999 and 2000 include Avandia for adult onset diabetes, Idoxefene for osteoporosis, and a vaccine against Lyme disease LYMErix. Operations in over 160 countries produce annual sales approaching $9 billion. About 50% of revenues are earned in North America.

Setting a rational price

Portfolio 2001 WORKSHEET FOR TARGETING SHARE PRICES OF SMITHKLINE
BEECHAM IN 1999, 2000, 2001 & 2002
BASED ON FORECASTS MADE IN JANUARY 1999
EPS FISCAL 1998 TO DECEMBER $1.69
1 ADR = 5 SHARES

Growth	Year	Estimated EPS ADR	P/E	Share Price Target	+10%	-10%	Notes
15%	1999	$1.96	40	$78	$87	$70	
15%	2000	$2.30	37.5	$86	$96	$86	
15%	2001	$2.64	35	$92	$102	$83	
15%	2002	$3.03	32.5	$98	$109	$88	

This 'what if' forecast suggests potential earnings and share prices based on current indications. Forecasts must be revised continuously in the light of all company results and industry, market and economic news. Forecasts can be misleading and cannot be treated as investment advice or used to motivate investments. See page 69.

Earnings per share growth expectations

Significant new drug approvals include Avandia for the treatment of adult onset diabetes with sales potential of over $1 billion a year. With Avandia SBH should meet management's growth targets and support earnings per share growth of 15% from 1999 with upside scope as other new drugs gain momentum.

Earnings multiple expectations

Pharmaceutical shares are trading at multiples of two and three times their earnings growth rate and the forecast of 40 times current earnings reflects the current market price of the share and its high rating on the market. In the *Portfolio 2001* forecast earnings per share growth is constant at 15% but the multiple used to forecast share prices is scaled down 2.5 points a year and falls to 32.5 by 200 to anticipate lower valuations of pharmaceutical shares generally.

Past performance indicators

Growth Rates %		SBH	S&P 500	Industry	Sector	Notes
Earnings per share 5 year		16.29	21.00	12.83	13.21	
1998 last reported vs 1997		NM	12.79	11.60	14.88	
Sales 5 year 1994-1998		8.35	16.49	11.91	14.86	
Profitability Ratios						
Gross Margin 1998	%	70.14	49.51	69.92	66.36	
5 year average	%	64.93	49.15	70.09	66.36	
Net Profit Margin 1998	%	15.45	10.85	17.49	14.46	
5 year average	%	11.97	10.27	16.16	12.80	
5 Year Returns on:						
Assets	%	11.73	8.47	14.43	8.47	
Investment	%	21.91	13.28	21.86	13.28	
Equity	%	33.72	21.60	32.45	21.60	

NM = not meaningful

The growth story

Building on a strong base

SmithKline is recognized as having stable and growing earnings underpinned by strong positions in antibiotics, vaccines, central nervous system drugs and over-the-counter medicines. In consumer health care leading products include Tums for digestive relief, Tagamet for acidity, Panadol for pain relief, the Nicorette and Nicodern smoking cessation products and Aquafresh dental products.

For almost a decade SmithKline has been engaged in genetic and molecular research and new drugs developed within their group resources are now reaching the market regularly. The vaccine LYMErix for Lyme disease was launched in January 1999 and addresses a target market of over 60 million Americans who live in endemically infected areas and significant numbers in Europe and elsewhere.

Several drugs in the portfolio are reporting successful growth. They include Famvir for genital herpes, Requip for Parkinson's, Hycamtin for ovarian and lung cancer, Coreg a beta-blocker for the treatment of congestive heart failure. Well-established drugs include the antibiotic Augmentin and the anti-depressant Paxil continue to grow market share, and growth in vaccines has been particularly strong. With the introduction of a new paedriatic vaccine, Infantrix, further strong growth is expected.

Merrill Lynch upgraded SmithKline to a key focus stock in January 1999.

Avandia

Markets focus now on blockbuster drugs and Avandia has the potential for sales of over $1 billion annually. Adult onset diabetes, known as Type 2 diabetes, presents a growing target market as demographics swing towards larger numbers of ageing people. Avandia enhances the body's sensitivity to diminishing insulin production and is a strong candidate drug for treatment of patients among the the 14 million diagnosed Type 2 diabetes sufferers in the US and Europe.

A competitive drug Rezulin, marketed by Warner-Lambert, reached sales of $750 million in 1998, its first year 1998. However Rezulin has from the outset had problems with liver toxicity while Avantia has throughout its trials shown no toxicity.

Takeda's Actos, a competitive drug for adult onset diabetes already on the market in Japan and several European countries, will also be launched in the US in 1999 by Takeda and Eli Lily. Analysts expect that Avandia could reach 15% of patients in the US and Europe by 2002 and if these targets are met annual drug sales of the drug will pass $1.5 billion a year. Avandia has been approved by the FDA and is being marketed in the US.

Drugs in Phase III trials
SmithKline's pipeline has several important new drugs in various stages of development. Drugs in Phase III which are likely to reach the market over the next few years include Idoxefene for the prevention of osteoporosis and breast cancer, a new quinoline antibiotic for chronic infections, Ariflo for chronic obstructive pulmonary disease and an antibody for the treatment of non-Hodgkin's lymphoma.

Effects on earnings of new drugs
SmithKline have indicated that they see scope for improvement in their margin on drugs which is expected to be about 25% in 1999. Several competitors earn 30% margins and the combination of higher margins and higher revenues brings the potential of earnings growth extending from 15% forecast currently to 20% within a few years. Among product driven pharmaceutical growth stocks which are favoured investment targets SmithKline will be an increasingly attractive candidate if margin and product growth is achieved.

Patent expiries and litigation
1999 pharmaceutical sales are forecast to reach slightly over $5 billion. Two major drugs, the antibiotic Augmentin and the anti-depressant Seroxat/Paxil reached sales of $1 billion and $1.4 billion respectively in 1998. Augmentin loses Patent protection in 2001 and Paxil patents have been challenged in pending litigation. Success with new products will be essential to counter the effects of Augmentin going off patent and any upset the litigation on Paxil might have on earnings growth prospects.

What can go wrong?

Expectations are already running high for Avandia, yet the drug still has to prove itself on the market against competitors. Valuations in the pharmaceutical industry are at all-time highs and, while at the beginning of 1999 there is nothing on the horizon to suggest that investor sentiment to the major drug companies will change, markets could weaken generally.

SmithKline earns almost 50% of its revenues in the US and is well insulated from emerging market weaknesses. The group has divested its interests in a pharmaceuticals benefits manager and in clinical laboratory operations to concentrate on its core business as a pharmaceutical manufacturer.

Monitoring

www.sb.com presents group operations comprehensively, and the progress of Avandia and other drugs will be well followed in leading financial publications.

GLAXO

Share Graph 1997–1998 Glaxo plc – ADR
Primary Market – London GLXO – ADR NYSE GLX

Price January 1999 $69.50
Market Value January 1999 $124.3 billion

SECTOR Health Care INDUSTRY Major Drugs
Top Line GLX ADR Bottom Line S&P 500 Index Relative
Left Scale: Top $ Price, Bottom Volume in Thousands

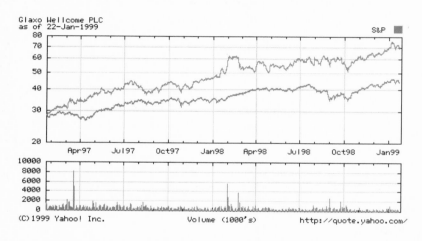

PRICE PERFORMANCE	GLX ADR		An investment made in January 1994 grew 303% by January 1999		
PRICE HISTORY	1998	1997	1996	1995	Notes
High Price	69.69	48.50	34.38	28.38	
Low Price	47.13	29.88	22.38	18.75	
High P/E	NA	57.03	38.80	101.24	
Low P/E	NA	35.13	25.26	66.90	

Chmn Sir Richard Sykes, www.glaxowellcome.co.uk
52,500 employees
Glaxo Wellcome House, Berkeley Avenue, Greenford, Middlesex, UB6 0NN
Phone: (212) 308-5186 Fax: (212) 308-5263

Global Franchise: Anti-viral, respiratory and other prescription drugs

Britain's Glaxo Wellcome plc was formed in 1995 as a result of the merger of Glaxo and Wellcome, both of which were major global pharmaceutical companies. Glaxo Inc. was established in the US in 1977. The group maintains the largest private Research and Development resource in the pharmaceutical industry and is one of the leading global pharmaceutical companies measured by revenues. In its research role, Glaxo has built franchises in the technologies of modern drug discovery using combinatorial chemistry and bio informatics, and is the industry leader in HIV research and therapies. Glaxo's global fortune was built on its ulcer drug, Zantac, the world's first 'blockbuster' drug with sales exceeding $1 billion. Until Zantac went off patent in 1996/7, it accounted for 45% of revenues. Two therapeutic categories – respiratory and anti-virals – now exceed Zantac sales, and the central nervous system (CNS) sector is growing rapidly following the introduction of two major new drugs, Imigran for migraine and Lamictal for epilepsy. With the merger, Wellcome introduced its anti-virals franchise including Retrovir, the first effective anti-viral drug for AIDS sufferers, and Zovirax for the treatment for herpes, mouth sores, cold sore blisters and other common infections. Antibiotics and oncology drugs continue to account for 16% of sales. Annual sales are £8 billion, with 42% coming from the US and 34% from Europe.

Setting a rational price

Portfolio 2001 WORKSHEET FOR TARGETING SHARE PRICES OF GLAXO WELLCOME ADR IN 1999, 2000, 2001 & 2002
BASED ON FORECASTS MADE IN JANUARY 1999
EPS/ADR FISCAL 1998 TO DECEMBER $1.65
1 ADR = 2 SHARES

Growth	Year	Estimated EPS	P/E	Share Price Target	+10%	-10%	Notes
15%	1999	$1.89	30	$56	$63	$51	
15%	2000	$2.17	30	$65	$72	$59	
15%	2001	$2.50	30	$75	$83	$67	
15%	2002	$2.87	30	$86	$96	$72	

This 'what if' forecast suggests potential earnings and share prices based on current indications. Forecasts must be revised continuously in the light of all company results and industry, market and economic news. Forecasts can be misleading and cannot be treated as investment advice or used to motivate investments. See page 69.

Earnings per share growth expectations

The *Portfolio 2001* forecast suggests an ambitious 15% growth starting in 1999. Pitching expectations in the mid-teens takes into account major new drugs that have been approved to be marketed in 1999. It also takes into account that comparisons for 1999 earnings will be made with 1998 earnings that reflected negative growth. Glaxo has had several years to catch up for losses following the loss of patent protection on Zantac, and should deliver substantial earnings growth from 1999 if management have been effective.

In 1998, Glaxo Wellcome's portfolio of medicines grew by 13% with Zantac accounting for only 9%. Seven major products (Flixotide, Serevent, Flixonase, Zyban, Valtrex, Wellbutrin and Lamictal) and HIV and migraine products were growing at double-digit rates. Management forecast that the existing portfolio and new products will deliver double-digit sales and earnings at constant exchange rate terms in 1999.

Earnings multiple expectations

Thirty times earnings suggested as the multiple of earnings in the forecast to target share prices is double the earnings per share growth rate of 15% forecast, and is in line with current market multiples. Glaxo's exceptionally rich development pipeline could lead to even higher valuations as new products are successfully introduced.

Previous performance indicators

Growth Rates %		ADR/GLX	S&P 500	Industry	Sector	Notes
Earnings per share 5 year		10.11	15.83	11.95	15.10	
1998 last reported vs 1997		-3.99	12.25	14.92	14.11	
Sales 5 year 1994-1998		10.11	15.83	11.95	15.10	
Profitability Ratios						
Gross Margin 1998	%	80.89	48.83	69.83	66.01	
5 year average	%					
Net Profit Margin 1998	%	23.40	10.85	18.46	14.82	
5 year average	%	21.54	10.21	16.22	12.86	
5 Year Returns on:						
Assets	%	16.34	8.26	14.58	11.46	
Investment	%	30.30	13.03	22.09	17.51	
Equity	%	52.38	21.49	32.80	26.75	

The loss of patent protection on Zantac arrested Glaxo's growth as expected in 1997 and 1998. However high margins and high returns on assets, investments and equities were achieved, reflecting the strength of the merged Glaxo-Wellcome group.

The growth story

1997: The first year with Zantac off patent

Glaxo's blockbuster drug Zantac came of patent at the end of 1996 and, while in 1997 Zantac sales volumes remained high, competition from generic manufacturers forced profit margins down. When patent protection was lost and Zantac became a non-prescription, over-the-counter pharmaceutical, Glaxo contracted for it to be marketed by Warner-Lambert in the US and Europe. The effects of the loss of earnings from Zantac were mitigated by two major initiatives undertaken by Glaxo in anticipation of the patent expiry:

1. The merger of Glaxo and Wellcome in 1995 that brought cost-saving synergies.
2. The initiation in the early 1990s of a large scale Research and Development investment programme, targeted at discovering innovative new pharmaceuticals which would replace lost revenues and discover innovative new products.

In a performance update covering ten months to 31 October 1998, Glaxo management confirmed that overall sales were still on a plateau, and in fact the reported sales of £6,462 million fell by 4% in sterling terms, after adjusting for currency fluctuations. However, excluding both Zantac and Zovirax, which had also come off patent, sales growth was up 11% in sterling and 16% if measured at a constant exchange rate, a measure Glaxo call CER.

In 1998, Glaxo's new largest therapeutic area, respiratory products, was growing positively, as were anti-viral products, though HIV therapeutics experienced some slowing. Across the product portfolio, growth prospects were seen as good and, while growth in migraine products was below expectations, the CNS portfolio still performed positively.

Management highlighted that the respiratory franchise is now

17% of group sales and is growing at 24%, the HIV portfolio is still the market leader and is growing at 18%, and CNS is a continuing success story growing at 36%. Within the portfolio seven major products are growing at double digit rates and five key new products are to be launched by the end of 1999.

Two new HIV products are being introduced in 1999 and are expected to revive the anti-viral franchise dramatically.

Though trading profit was less than that produced in the same period in 1997, the chairman, Sir Richard Sykes, found the results satisfactory and summed up the position as follows:

> Glaxo Wellcome is now delivering growth in total sales in CER terms. This is an improved performance compared to the half-year, when sales declined 1% on the same basis, and confirms that the impact of the US Zantac patent expiry is behind us . . . these results keep us on track to deliver our sales and earnings targets for 1998. The current growth of our broad portfolio of products, together with the contribution expected from the five new products we plan to launch by the end of 1999, give us confidence in the strength of our business and in our future prospects.

Behind the Glaxo Wellcome merger

Sales of Zantac, on which Glaxo's empire was built, peaked in 1995 at £2.255 billion, and accounted for over 40% of sales revenues, fell to £1.931 billion in 1996 and were below £1.5 billion in 1997, with considerably lower contributions to profits.

The merger of Glaxo and Wellcome in 1995 was conceived to protect both firms from the effects of loss of patent protections pending on their lead products, Glaxo's Zantac and Wellcome's Zovirax.

The merger was a well-conceived corporate transaction efficiently implemented, and £1.5 billion was written off in the 1995 accounts as a provision for restructuring costs. Since then the group has been harvesting the synergy benefits of two organizations with one set of overheads, and the results of the savings are visible in the group's strong positive cash flow. In 1996, 1997 and 1998 free cash flow continued in the $750 million a year range, and this financial strength cushioned Glaxo from wider fallout following losses of margin on sales of Zantac and Zovirax.

It seems that 1999 will be the year that answers definitively whether Glaxo will lift off its earnings plateau with sustained rising profits, or tumble into the abyss and become another statistic in the chronicle of one-time successful growth companies. The answer will depend on whether the drug discovery investment will pay off and management can deliver new therapeutic products that can be marketed successfully.

The road to discovering new drugs

Glaxo has kept its identity as a company that discovers and markets innovative new prescription drugs, and when drugs move from prescription to over-the-counter sales, Glaxo licenses them out, as it did with Zantac to Warner-Lambert. By positioning itself as a drugs company, Glaxo maintains high profit margins which are not diluted in the competitive arena of consumer products. Its trading report to October 1998 reflected some trimming of margins, as had to be expected after Zantac went off patent, but gross profit only fell a few percentage points, in spite of the complete change in the product mix:

	FIRST HALF 1998 %	SECOND HALF 1998 %	FIRST HALF 1997 %
COST OF SALES	19.7	18.9	18.1
GROSS PROFIT	80.3	81.1	81.9
TRADING PROFIT	32.00	32.00	38.5
SELLING, GENERAL & ADMINISTRATION	34.3	35.6	30.6
RESEARCH & DEVELOP	13.3	15.2	13.6
OTHER INCOME	(0.5)	(9.7)	(8.8)

Glaxo's substantial investments in new research facilities have involved its own research programmes and an extensive range of partnerships with emerging biotechnology companies. Following these initiatives, it now has one of the deepest pipelines of any drug company in the world, and expects to introduce three significant new medicines a year from the year 2000. Its Therapeutic Area Overview, published in January 1999, detailing the development pipeline, is included at the end of this report – See page 261.

Compared to the achievements of Pfizer, who in the early 1990s also boosted efforts directed at discovering and marketing new drugs, Glaxo management have underachieved, but making judgements would be hasty as Glaxo's development pipeline is overwhelmingly impressive.

Glaxo's first research focus is directed at the anti-viral, respiratory and central nervous system segments, but they have a wide spectrum of other projects. They include: migraine; chronic pain; Alzheimer's; asthma; breast, lung, and prostate cancers; eczema and psoriasis; hypertension and coronary heart disease; influenza; hepatitis B; bacterial infections; fungal infections; diabetes; rheumatoid arthritis; irritable bowel syndrome; sleeping disorders; osteoporosis; gastric ulcers; tuberculosis; epilepsy; depression; herpes; and erectile dysfunction.

www.glaxowellcome.co.uk is consistently informative on the development pipeline and the company's general strategies.

Modern drug discovery

Between 1995 and 1997, Glaxo claims to have achieved a ten-fold increase in the number of compounds it makes available for assay, and predicts this will increase a further ten-fold over the next two years. Screening compounds has grown even faster, some 100-fold between 1995 and 1997, and screening is also expected to grow ten-fold over the next two years.

The number of drugs in Phase III clinical trials rose to 130 in 1997, from 110 in 1996, with 170 forecast for 1998/1999.

Among Glaxo's important new drugs are Epivir and Abacavir. Epivir, an anti-viral drug used in combination therapy with other drugs for the treatment of Aids patients, has sales approaching $500 million a year. It is manufactured by Biochem Pharma and licensed to Glaxo who own 16% of Biochem Pharma. Abacavir is a protease inhibitor, which was introduced in 1998, and will extend the Aids franchise into a class of drugs widely used in combination with other therapies in the treatment of Aids patients. While there are other well-established protease inhibitors, particularly from Merck, Roche and Agouron, Glaxo's strong marketing channels will support Abacavir, Epivir and Retrovir together as a combination therapy. Analysts estimate Abacavir sales potential at near $1 million.

Lamivudine is a novel oral anti-viral treatment for hepatitis B, which was developed using a modification of Epivir, and Glaxo expects it will bring significant benefits to the majority of hepatitis B patients. New treatments are urgently required for hepatitis B, a potentially fatal liver disease, which is the ninth leading cause of death worldwide. There are 350 million people who are long-term carriers of the hepatitis B virus, and about one-third of these individuals are expected to develop serious progressive liver disease. Lamivudine could serve a major unmet medical need, with potential sales well above $1 billion a year, and be approved for certain markets in 1998. Lamivudine has been approved in China and is being introduced there in 1999, before marketing elsewhere in the world commences.

The innovative migraine drug, Imigran, was introduced in 1994, and sales reached almost $1 billion in 1997. However, sales growth has been challenged by other drugs on the market and new competitive drugs launched by Merck and Pfizer.

Serevent and Flixotide are both asthma drugs, and have achieved strong sales growth – this category is on course for sales of over $1 billion a year. Competition is increasing in the asthma inhaler market and, in 1998, Merck introduced Singulair, an oral drug for the treatment of asthma, which has been highly acclaimed and very successful.

Other interesting products in the pipeline include Zanamivr, an influenza vaccine, and Zyban which assists in giving up smoking.

Strong earnings growth was not expected in 1999, but it should be the year when Glaxo growth is back in double digits.

Competitive advantages

Operationally Glaxo is exceptionally well resourced as a drug discovering and a drug marketing enterprise. It is working on the 'third generation' of pharmaceutical research and development which they define as reflecting what is happening in both medicine and the market place, and in science and technology. The first generation, which started about 100 years ago, was based on chemistry and serendipity, while the second, from the 1950s onwards, has been based on biology and empiricism. Now researchers also use genetics, computers, robots and miniaturization to move to a more predictive phase.

What can go wrong?

Glaxo faces the same risks as all pharmaceutical companies: cost containment initiatives, competition, and the failure of drugs at advanced stages of trials. Also, its pipeline may not yield enought new drugs to replace profits from older products, sufficient to lift earnings off their plateau fast enough. Earnings per share growth could also be held back if launching new products and opening new markets calls for more investments in sales and marketing infrastructure.

Glaxo's share price is subject to a 'corporate' variable which could affect investors favourably or unfavourably. In January 1998, Glaxo announced a merger with SmithKline Beecham, but it was called off within a few weeks when management of the two companies could not agree on a structure for the merged group. The proposed merger was a reminder that, with its strong positive cash flow, Glaxo is likely to seek another merger in the industry to repeat the successful Wellcome cost rationalization formula.

Glaxo's share price may be higher than its performance warrants for two reasons. The first is that investors put a value on the merger potential and speculation drives the price up regardless of underlying performance. The second is that Glaxo is a share that British investors class as a national blue chip, and when allocating funds to pharmaceutical holdings, Glaxo is on top of many institutional and private lists.

In their published lists of favoured shares for 1999, NatWest Bank, HSBC and several other leading British financial organizations included Glaxo among their top choices, motivated by 'stable cash flow and growth sectors that can withstand the pressures of continued price erosions and low nominal growth'.

By including Glaxo in *Portfolio 2001*, I obviously endorse high expectations, but if the drug development pipeline does not deliver to expectations we are all going to be very disappointed. Investors should be in no doubt that, in spite of all its positive cash flow, cash in the bank, merger potential and well-deserved blue chip status, an investment in Glaxo is an investment in a drug delivery pipeline with all the attendant risks.

Monitoring

The key question for investors is whether management are delivering on promises. Only successful new drug introductions will bring Glaxo back to its former glory. News on Glaxo is well covered in the British, US and European press and `www.glaxowellco.uk` is informative.

Therapeutic area overview: January 1999

The following document, published by Glaxo in January 1999, outlines its drug development portfolio. The content of the portfolio will change over time as new compounds progress from research to development and from development to the market and, owing to the nature of the drug development process, it is not unusual for some compounds, especially those in early stages of investigation, to be terminated as they progress through development.

			Estimated filing dates	
Compound/Type	Indication	Phase	MAA	NDA
Gastrointestinal, metabolic & rheumatology				
Gastrointestinal disease Lotronex (alosetron)	irritable bowel syndrome (IBS)	III	2000	1999
Metabolic disease GW328713 microsomal transfer protein inhibitor	mixed hyperlipidaemia	I		
264W94 bile acid transport (BAT) inhibitor	hyper-cholesterolaemia	II		
GI262570 peroxisome proliferation activated receptor gamma agonist	non-insulin dependent diabetes mellitus (NIDDM)	II	2001	2001
GI198745 5-alpha reductase inhibitor	alopecia benign prostatic hyperplasia	II III	2002 2000	2002 2000

Romozin (Europe) insulin action inhancer	non-insulin dependent diabetes mellitus (NIDDM)	Filed	re-filed	N/A

HIV & opportunistic infections

GW420867 non-nucleoside reverse transcriptase inhibitor	HIV infections (adult & paediatric)	II	2001	2001
1263W94 CMV-DNA synthesis inhibitor	treatment of congenital CMV disease	II		
Malarone electron transport system inhibitor	malaria prophylaxis	Filed	Filed	Filed
	malaria treatment	Filed	Approved	Filed
Triple combination Epivir/Retrovir/Ziagen	HIV infections (adult & paediatric)	III	TBD	TBD
Epivir reverse transcriptase inhibitor	once daily dosing	III	TBD	TBD
Ziagen (abacavir) reverse transcriptase inhibitor	HIV infections (adult & paediatric)	Filed	Filed	Approved
Agenerase (amprenavir) protease inhibitor	HIV infections (adult & paediatric)	Filed	Filed	Filed
Mepron/Wellvone anti-protozoal	Pneumocystis carinii pneumonia prophylaxis	Filed	Approved	Approved

Hospital & critical care
Oncology & emesis

GR205171 plus ondansetron NK$_1$ antagonist	chemotherapy induced emesis	II	1999	2000
	post operative nausea and vomiting	II	2000	2000
eniluracil (776C85) chemotoxic agent enhancer	refractory breast tumours	II	1999	TBD
	advanced pancreatic cancer	III	1999	N/A
	colorectal cancer	III	2000	2000
506U78 prodrug of guanine arabinoside	chronic lymphocytic	II	2000	2000
	acute lympho-blastic leukaemia	II	2002	2002
	aggressive non-Hodgkin's lymphoma	I	2002	2002

Panorex monoclonal antibody	colon cancer (Dukes-C)	III	2000	2001
	rectal cancer; colon cancer (Dukes-B$_2$)	III		

Cardiovascular

Pritor (telmisartan) angiotensin II antagonist	hypertension	Filed	Approved	N/A
telmisartan + lacidipine angiotensin II antagonist plus calcium channel blocker	hypertension	I	2002	N/A

Stroke

GV150526 glycine antagonist	ischaemic and haemorrhaegic stroke	III	2000	2000

Infectious diseases & hepatitis

PowderJect technology DNA vaccines & delivery technology	hepatitis B and other indications	I		
GV143253 injectable trinem antibiotic	methicillin- resistant, staph aureus/ epidermis hospital infections	Preclinical		
GW419458 herpes simplex virus (HSV) vaccine	genital herpes treatment and prophylaxis	I	2002	2002
Relenza (zanamivir) neuraminidase inhibitor	influenza treatment	Filed	Filed	Filed
	influenza prophylaxis	III/Filed	Filed	1999
Raxar (grepafloxacin) quinoline antibiotic	sinusitis	III	1999	1999
	urinary tract infections	III	1999	N/A
Valtrex/Zelitrex nucleoside analogue	line extensions inc. prevention of HSV transmission CMV	III	2000	2000
	prevention in transplant patients	III	1998	N/A
Zeffix (lamivudine) reverse transcriptase inhibitor	hepatitis B (Far East and Japan)	Filed	Approved	N/A
	hepatitis B (West)	Filed	Filed	Approved
Wellferon alpha-interferon n1	hepatitis C	Filed	Filed	Filed

Neurology & psychiatry

GW275919 indanylidene	back pain	I	2002	2002
GW273293 sodium channel inhibitor	epilepsy and bipolar disorder	I		
GV196771 glycine antagonist	chronic pain	I	2002	2002
1555U88 noradrenaline reuptake inhibitor	attention deficit/hyperactivity disorder (ADHD)	II	2001	2002
	smoking cessation	II	2001	2001
4030W92 sodium channel inhibitor	chronic pain	II	2003	2003
Lamictal sodium channel inhibitor	bipolar disorder – acute mania/rapid cycling	III	TBD	2000
	bipolar disorder – depression	III	TBD	2000
Zyban noradrenaline reuptake inhibitor	smoking cessation	III	1999	Approved

Respiratory disease

GW328267 adenosine A₂ agonist	asthma	Preclinical		
GW215864 hydrolysable steroid	asthma	I		
GW250495 hydrolysable steroid	asthma	I		
GR213487 gene therapy	cystic fibrosis	II		
Flixonase intranasal corticosteroid	sinusitis	III	2000	N/A
Flixotide/Flovent inhaled corticosteroid	chronic obstructive pulmonary disease (COPD)	III/Filed	Filed	2001
	nebules for chronic asthma	II	2001	2001

CFC-free propellants (GR106642)

Flixonase/Flonase intranasal corticosteroid	rhinitis	II	2000	2000
Flixotide/Flovent inhaled corticosteroid	asthma/COPD	III	Approved	2000
Ventolin beta$_2$ agonist	asthma/COPD	Filed	Approved	Filed
Serevent beta$_2$ agonist	asthma/COPD	III	2000	2001
Seretide beta$_2$ agonist/inhaled corticosteroid	asthma	III	1999	2000

Devices

Diskus/Accuhaler (dry powder inhaler)				
Flixotide/Flovent inhaled corticosteroid	asthma/COPD	Filed	Approved	Filed
Ventolin beta$_2$ agonist	asthma/COPD	Filed	Approved	Filed
Becotide inhaled corticosteroid	asthma	Filed	Filed	N/A
Seretide beta$_2$ agonist/inhaled corticosteroid	COPD asthma	III Filed	2001 Approved	2001 1999
Surehaler (breath operated inhaler) Ventolin, Flixotide/Flovent, Serevent, Seretide	asthma	III	1999-2000	2000-2001
Respiratory Powder Inhaler Device (RPID) Becotide, Ventolin	asthma	III	1999	N/A
MDI Dose Counter Ventolin, Flixotide/Flovent, Serevent, Seretide	asthma/COPD	III	2000	2001

Development phase overview

Phase I	Phase II	Phase III	Filed
GR328713	264W94	Lotronex	Romozin
506U78	GI262570	GI198745	Malarone
telmisartan +	GI98745	Triple combination	Ziagon
lacidipine	GW420867	Epivir (once daily)	Agenerase
PowderJect	1263W94	eniluracil	Relenza
GW419458	GR205171	Panorex	Zeffix
GW275919	eniluracil	GV150526	Wellferon
GW273293	506U78	Relenza	Flixotide/Flovent
GV196771	1555U88	Raxar	
GW215864	4030W92	Valtrex/Zelitrex	CFC-free propellants
GW250495	GR213487	Lamictal	(x1)
	Flixotide/Flovent	Zyban	
		Flixonase	Devices
	CFC-free propellants	Flixotide/Flovent	Diskus/Accuhaler
	(x1)		(x4)
		CFC-free propellants	
		(x3)	

Devices
Diskus/Accuhaler (x1)
Surehaler (x4)
RPID (x2)
MDI Dose Counter (x4)

NOVARTIS

Share Graph 1997–1998 Novartis ADR
Primary Market – Zurich

Price January 1999 $99
Market Value January 1999 $102 billion

SECTOR Health Care INDUSTRY Major Drugs
Top Line S&P 500 Index relative: Bottom line NVTSY ADR
Right Scale: ADR Price, Bottom Volume in Thousands

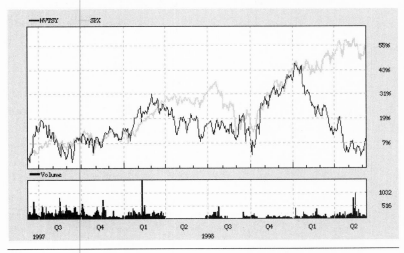

PRICE PERFORMANCE	ADR NVTSY		An investment made in January 1994 grew 58% by January 1999		
PRICE HISTORY	1998	1997	1996	1995	Notes
High Price	102.00	86.25	NA	NA	
Low Price	72.00	51.88	NA	NA	
High P/E	NA	31.69	NA	NA	
Low P/E	NA	10.06	NA	NA	

Chairman/CEO Daniel Vasella **www.novartis.com**
85,000 employees
CH-4002 Basel, Switzerland
Phone: (973) 522-6899 Fax: (973) 522-6833

Global Franchise: Drugs for human and animal health, agribusiness, transplant medicine, genetics & genomics

Novartis was formed in 1997 by the merger of two giant Swiss global pharmaceutical and chemical groups, Ciba Geigy and Sandoz. The merger created one of the world's top three pharmaceutical companies, with drugs for treatment of disorders of the central nervous system, organ transplantation, cardiovascular diseases, dermatological diseases, respiratory disorders, cancer and arthritis. Novartis is also a leader in agribusiness, contact lenses, veterinary drugs and nutritional supplements, and owns 49.5% of the shares in the listed American biotech company Chiron, with strong positions in cancer therapy and vaccine development. Novartis's highest value drug franchise is the immunosuppressant Neoral, with over CHF (Swiss francs) 2 billion sales, used mainly in transplant surgery. In the cardiovascular arena relatively new drugs account for sales of CHF2 billion. Other significant drugs are antibiotics including generic penicillin and cyclosporin, and drugs used in the treatment of arthritis, fungal infections, schizophrenia and epilepsy. Drugs in the pipeline include new treatments for specific cancers, Alzheimer's, asthma, malaria, and genetically engineered human skin for wound healing. Generics and over-the-counter medications account for almost 10% of group sales. The group has a widespread involvement in genetic medicine and research and has established an Institute for Functional Genomics.

In 1998, group sales were CHF31.7 billion, of which CHF17.5 billion were in health care, CHF8.4 billion in agribusiness and CHF5.8 billion in consumer health. The group annually invests more than CHF3.6 billion in R&D. Novartis employs about 85,000 people and operates in over 100 countries around the world.

■■■
Setting a rational price

Portfolio 2001 WORKSHEET FOR TARGETING SHARE PRICES OF NOVARTIS
ADR NVTSY IN 1999, 2000, 2001 & 2002
BASED ON FORECASTS MADE IN JUNE 1999
EPS FISCAL 1998 TO DECEMBER $3.60
20 ADRs EQUAL ONE SHARE

Growth	Year	Estimated EPS	P/E	Share Price Target	+10%	-10%	Notes
17.5%	1999	$3.33	25	$83	$93	$75	
15%	2000	$3.82	25	$96	$107	$86	
15%	2001	$4.39	25	$110	$122	$99	
15%	2002	$5.05	25	$126	$140	$113	

This 'what if' forecast suggests potential earnings and share prices based on current indications. Forecasts must be revised continuously in the light of all company results and industry, market and economic news. Forecasts can be misleading and cannot be treated as investment advice or used to motivate investments. See page 69.

Earnings per share growth expectations
In 1998, flat sales were a disappointment and the only encouragement to expect improved earnings per share growth for 1998 was a Novartis management statement that: 'Novartis is now reaping the major cost savings from merger synergies. For the full year, an increase in operating margin is expected. In addition, net financial income will reflect the impressive investment performance. As a result, a marked improvement of net income is foreseen. Full details will be published with the annual report on 16 March 1999 at the financial results press conference.'

Earnings per share for the merged companies grew 46% in 1997 and, with the indication that cost savings, synergy benefits and investment income will markedly affect 1998 results, earnings per share growth has been projected at 23%, half the 46% gained in 1997. The 1997 earnings per ADR of $2.60 have been estimated at $3.20 in line with the mean estimates of twelve analysts.

Earnings multiple expectations
With the support of cost savings flowing from the Ciba-Sandoz merger amounting to over $1 billion a year until 2001, with organic profit growth, Novartis should be one of the most highly valued life science shares. However, sales in 1998 have been flat and

while necessary foundation building has been undertaken within the group, performance has been disappointing. Until it improves Novartis is likely to attract modest valuations. Strong cash generation and a cash reserve of $7.5 billion will, however, encourage investor interest, and share prices have been targeted at 25 times earnings through to 2002.

Within a few years the Novartis group will probably change structurally and operationally. Mergers in the drug industry, like the merger of Ciba and Sandoz, are supported by such potent synergies that they are on all agendas, and Novartis will be no exception. Novartis is still sustained commercially by synergy benefits exceeding $1 billion a year from the Ciba/Sandoz merger with corresponding strong cash flows. But operationally it is burdened with a large pedestrian off patent drug portfolio at low margins, and declining revenues in agrochemicals. The drug development pipeline is all important.

The growth story

Strong earnings growth in 1997
The 1997 financial results in Novartis's first post-merger year, supported by synergies between the two groups, were exceptionally rewarding. In 1998 the results were disappointing.

Novartis results for the year to end December 1997 and 1998

	1997 CHF millions	Change %	1998 CHF millions	Change %
Sales	31 180	19	31 702	1.7
Operating income	6 783	38	7 356	8.4
Net Income	5 211	43	6 064	16.4
Earnings per share CHF	76	46	89	13.5
Dividends per share	25	25	29	16
Operating cash flow per share	68	N/A	86	25

Reported net income growth came from a margin improvement and net financial income that increased sharply by CHF421 million to CHF516 million in mid 1998.

Novartis improved its net profit from 16.7% in 1997 to 19.1% in 1998 and cash flow from operating activities grew 20% to CHF 5.9 billion.

Weak sales growth in 1998

Sales in 1998 were very disappointing and grew a mere 2% from CHF31,180 million in 1997 to CHF31,702 million in 1998. In local currency terms the growth was a pedestrian but slightly more respectable 5%. The details follow:

NOVARTIS GROUP	1998 CHF millions	1997 CHF millions	Change in CHF %	Change in local currencies %
Healthcare	17,535	16,987	3	7
Pharmaceuticals	14,501	14,112	3	6
Generics	1,529	1,452	5	13
CIBA Vision	1,505	1,423	6	9
Agribusiness	8,379	8,327	1	4
Crop Protection	6,021	6,088	-1	2
Seeds	1,457	1,346	8	12
Animal Health	901	893	1	5
Consumer Health (excluding divestments)	5,289	5,255	1	3
Nutrition	3,598	3,500	3	6
Self-Medication	1,691	1,755	-4	-2
Divested Consumer Health activities (Roland, Red Line)	499	611		
Total	31 702	31 180	2	5

Pharmaceuticals

Pharmaceuticals accounted for 46% of total sales, and 82% of health care sales, and grew at 6%. The leading product, the immunosupressant Sandimmun/Neoral, used with transplant surgery, achieved sales growth of 5% and passed CHF1.8 billion sales. A new class of anti-hypertensives, Diovan and Co-Diovan, together achieved sales above CHF409 million.

Generics, drugs without patent protection, were stable and CIBA Vision (+9%) topped a good year with improved fourth-quarter growth. Neither of these two operations are likely to contribute meaningfully to earnings growth in the near term.

Agribusiness

The genetically modified seed opportunity, as Monsanto has shown in the United States, is potentially a major growth industry with the potential to generate high growth and high margins, and Novartis has an important presence in chemicals for agriculture and in genetically modified seeds.

In 1997, Novartis invested $900 million to purchase Merck's agricultural chemicals business and has committed itself to growing its agribusiness by the development and marketing of seeds and chemicals which will increase agricultural yields.

In 1998, the Novartis seed business saw sales growth of 12%, with considerable expansion of corn sales in the US supported by a strong demand for the genetically-improved 'Bt' hybrids – seeds modified with bacillus thuriengus which repels insect pests.

While Novartis is a very visible presence in new developments in agribusiness, there are unfortunately no signs that it has any killer plan to gain telling market share and public opposition to genetic seed modification could negate the opportunity for several years.

1998: a year of building the base

Large and small corporations have cultural identities and Novartis is no exception. The merger in 1996 of the two Swiss giants Ciba and Sandoz, which 'gave birth' to Novartis, was inspired and managed by two American investment banks who stole a march on the Swiss banking establishment and put together Switzerland's biggest corporate transaction right under the noses of its traditional banking dynasties. The deal was hailed by the financial community as the most imaginative merger of equals that had ever taken place. Daniel Vasella, the CEO designate, was recognized as the business leader with the vision that made the transaction possible, and investors assumed that Vasella would run Novartis with the ambitious performance targets and reporting transparency of American peer companies.

To take a view on Novartis, it is important to recognize Vasella as a visionary business leader but definitely not a dreamer. The merger of Sandoz and Ciba was probably a commercial necessity because the Research and Development programmes of each unit were potential bottomless pits. Vasella's greatest vision was that he realized this and was able to persuade others that they could respond to the situation by building a more efficient structure by merging interests.

The shares in both Ciba and Sandoz soared when the merger was announced. After the complex process of national, international and shareholder approvals had run its course, when Novartis started as a free-standing business in 1997, it was the darling of the financial community and the outstanding results produced in 1997 were welcome and expected.

In 1998, it was a different story. Companies in the fast lane have to keep up with minimum speed limits and Novartis has been jogging along too slowly. Investment bankers cannot afford the luxury of waiting and have been losing patience because nothing exciting has come from Novartis for over a year.

Novartis has the financial resources to change its fortunes almost instantly by making a strategic acquisition or licensing in products, but Vasella has not followed this track. Instead, he has concentrated on building management, improving group businesses and securing foundations for future growth. As he goes about this methodically, Novartis's financial resources continue their powerful post-merger gains.

If I was working for a fund that had an investment in Novartis, and had to explain why the share price was uninspiring, I would share the frustrations of bankers and professional investors. However, looking at the company as a potential long-term investment still confirms expectations that Novartis will capitalize on its strengths as a leader in Research and Development in medicine and agribusiness with the backing of its formidable financial reserves.

While global companies all march to Wall Street's beat, Novartis is not an American company. In the best American traditions, management are committed to shareholder value and are exploiting the potential of biotechnology and modern techniques for drug discovery. However, they take a different view of timetables and priorities to counterparts in the US. The Swiss are bankers at heart, and while Monsanto's Bob Shapiro was prepared to borrow billions of dollars to corner market share in agricultural biotechnology, Daniel Vasella evidently prefers to build a massive cash war-chest to use when the right opportunity arises. Neither Vasella nor Shapiro are necessarily right or wrong, or better bankers or industrialists. Bob Shapiro's financial credentials could not be stronger. He is a director of Citigroup, the world's largest financial services organization. It is unlikely, however, that he would be as successful in business in Switzerland as he is in the US, or that Daniel Vasella would be seen as a visionary manager in Silicon Valley to the extent that he is in Switzerland.

Setting pharmaceuticals on course

Early in 1998, Vasella recruited Dr Gerry Karabelis from SmithKline Beecham to head Novartis's pharmaceuticals division. Karabelis pursues a marketing driven research focus and found that drugs discovered by Novartis had a higher attrition rate during development than the industry average. To improve the success rate of compounds that enter testing, and to limit costly setbacks at late stages of development, he organized teams headed by senior research executives to lead research projects. These teams keep research efforts commercially motivated, and act decisively if a project has to be stopped for commercial reasons, even when it has potentially important scientific potential.

Within the companies introduced from both the Ciba and Sandoz sides of the merger, the process of building on strengths, maintaining research talent and rationalizing is progressing.

In 1998, the operations of two important gene-therapy units in the US, Systemix Inc., based in Palo Alto, California, and Genetic Therapy Inc., based in Gaithersburg, Maryland, were successfully combined under a single management. They had both lacked critical mass, and by merging them operating costs were reduced and improved research potential was built. (Genetic Therapy Inc. provided the technology for the watershed treatment of Ashanti Da Silva mentioned on page 161)

Novartis and new science

Novartis is an acronym for 'new arts'. However, although Novartis performance reports have details of sales of chemicals to keep domestic pets free of fleas, infant formula and over-the-counter prescriptions, they do not give a picture of Novartis as a leading and bold pioneer in scientific research aimed at technologies for the future. They don't highlight the 'new arts', the new opportunities, the target growth areas for Novartis which include gene therapy, xenotransplantation and plant biotechnology.

Novartis has a focus on finding new cures for various cancers and dedicates substantial resources to wide-ranging scientific research on the causes of cancer. Cancer currently accounts for 25% of all deaths, but oncology drugs still represent less than 5% of drug sales. The cause of the discrepancy is that, unlike heart disease or diabetes, cancer is more often fatal than chronic. However, as new therapies extend patients' lives, outlays on cancer drugs will grow at possibly twice the rate of spending in the overall drug market. In 1996, worldwide sales of oncology drugs totalled under $5 billion. This could increase to $8 billion by 2000 and some analysts have suggested almost $20 billion by 2010. The reasons for high commercial expectations for cancer drugs are: the potential for a range of new therapies; an ageing population; and a policy of expedited cancer drug approvals in the US Food and Drug Administration.

New science opportunities are all some years away from commercialization, but Novartis's drug development pipeline is already well stocked. It includes new therapies for Parkinson's, Alzheimer's, schizophrenia, epilepsy, cardiac disease and several cancers.

Xenotransplantation

Novartis is developing leading edge technology for xenotransplantation – animal organs transplanted into humans – which could become a significant growth opportunity early in the next century. Pigs' hearts and livers for humans are a priority, and through an acquisition, Imutran, Novartis acquired the technology to cross two major hurdles, hyperacute rejection and acute vascular rejection. Concentration is now on how to avoid 'zoonosis', the transmission of animal diseases to man. Novartis is producing pigs that are free of known pathogens for man, and is conducting research on other post-operative complications which could clear the way to xenotransplantation by the early years of the next century. If xenotransplantation can be performed successfully, it will open a major new industry in medical science.

Chiron Corp

Novartis owns 49.5% of the important US biotech company Chiron Corp., which is itself seeking to increase revenue by 10% in 1999, while expanding earnings per share by 25%, as it advances several clinical trials and brings more products into the first phase of human trials.

Among Chiron's development projects are a new agent for coronary artery disease and an agent that promotes the growth of cartilage in the knees of arthritis patients. Chiron is also expanding its vaccine business.

Restructuring for profitable operations in 1998, Chiron sold its diagnostics business for $1.1 billion. Helped by this sale, earnings reached $359 million in 1998 from $52.8 million in 1997 and the price of Chiron shares rose substantially:

Top Line Chiron Corp Bottom Line 200 day moving average Right scale: Top $ Price, Bottom Volume in Thousands

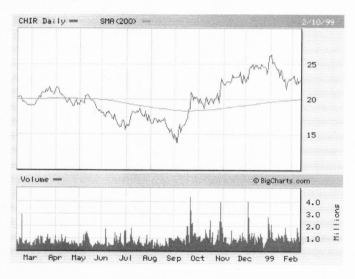

Source: www.wsj.com

In 1995, when Ciba-Geigy acquired control of Chiron, it transferred its $450 million diagnostics business to Chiron and, in effect, the diagnostics business was a legacy from that commercial deal. Diagnostics were not really a business for a leading edge biotechnology company as, while they are are steady sellers, they carry low margins. Diagnostics came to account for $541 million of Chiron's product sales in 1998, versus $124 million in combined sales for its two major therapeutic protein drugs, Betaseron (beta interferon, prescribed for multiple sclerosis) and Proleukin (interleukin-2, a treatment for kidney cancer).

In 1995, Chiron also acquired Johnson & Johnson's maker of ophthalmology products and added it to its own division, creating Chiron Vision. In January 1998, Chiron surprised Wall Street by selling Chiron Vision – with sales of some $200 million – to Bausch & Lomb, for $300 million. Novartis's strategy is to promote focused businesses and Chiron which it controls was no exception, even with the independent management structure retained in Chiron. Under Vasella's guidance, Chiron is again a well-focused biotechnology company, discovering and marketing new therapies, and in this role it is an increasingly important part of Novartis's commitment to discovering new medicines.

Competitive advantage

Daniel Vasella has developed a strategy to capture and hold a leadership position in all Novartis's businesses by building competitive strength 'founded on enhanced power in the market place with substantial sales forces in all major countries'.

In the next three years, he expects to launch 20 new pharmaceutical products and advance research on about 100 compounds identified as potential drug candidates. Backing the research is a CHF3.5 billion budget which has been committed to 'discover breakthrough technological advances that will truly change the paradigm of how diseases are understood and treated'.

To direct research funds more efficiently and accelerate the pace of dicovery, Vasella has established the Novartis Functional Genomics Institute. Company researchers use the Institute to foster close interaction with academic groups and external associates, which assist them to work on a large number of known genetic leads.

Following the importance of functional genomics and a strategy of leveraging scientific and financial resources in drug discovery through strategic alliances, in June 1998 Novartis announced an ambitious genetic research partnership with Rigel Inc., a fledgling biotechnology company in California.

Under a five-year $100 million genetic research partnership, the companies will use new technology developed at Stanford University licensed to Rigel to unravel the functions of genes in five diseases and investigate the role of key immune-system cells, with the aim of developing drugs for organ transplants, a market that Novartis has dominated for more than a decade.

Novartis Research Director Paul Herrling commented on the development: 'We are convinced that we can gain a competitive advantage by becoming the group that best understands the next step: gene function.' Novartis's genetic-research institute in La Jolla, California, will focus on the basic function of genes.

In the same way that the Human Genome Project brought robot-driven economies of scale to gene discovery, Rigel is attempting to apply large-scale, industrial methods to the study of gene function.

Progress is bound to be slow because functional genomics boils down to solving daunting biological puzzles; individual genes are links in bigger biochemical pathways that regulate everything from the production of hormones such as insulin to the transmission of signals across the brain.

Rigel unravels pathways from the ground up by testing the effects of millions of different microscopic probes in cells. They discovered that T-cells – white blood cells that are the shock troops of the body's immune system – switch on a previously unknown receptor as protection from the deadly chemical weapons which they themselves unleash to kill foreign bacteria or viruses. T-cells also cause rejection of transplanted organs. So by shutting down the protective receptor on T-cells near a transplant, it might be possible to develop drugs that protect the transplant without crippling the immune system, as does Novartis's blockbuster immunosuppressive medicine, cyclosporine A.

Financial and corporate opportunities

Novartis has focused on internal growth, getting products to market faster and exploiting them better. If and when acquisitions or mergers are considered to accelerate growth, Novartis will have the financial firepower. Its cash pile reached CHF10 billion francs by the end of 1998.

What can go wrong?

Neoral, Novartis's cornerstone product and largest selling drug, went off patent in 1998. There is generic competition from a biotechnology company, Sangstat Pharmaceuticals, now in a strategic alliance with Abbott. The impact of this will be felt by Novartis, but it expects to retain market share as it has developed new formulations of Neoral, a specialized drug not easily replaced. However, when any product comes off patent, generic competition eventually erodes margins and any decline in the sales of Neoral will certainly injure financial performance.

As much as new science is an opportunity for Novartis, it also introduces a wide range of risks, including adverse public opinion and hostility from many people to genetic crop modification.

In December 1998, France's highest administrative court upheld a decision to freeze authorization for Novartis to market gene-modified maize, pending a ruling from the European Court of Justice, notwithstanding the fact that French farmers had been authorized to grow genetically modified maize developed by Novartis in February 1998. Upholding a ban on a product that has been approved for sale throughout the European Union could even be in breach of EU laws, but consumer reactions to genetically modified seeds and foods could be damaging for years.

Monitoring

Greater transparency and reporting and timetables, in line with standards followed by major US companies, would improve the quality of investor information. Novartis has an ADR listing and ongoing reviews of news, reports and prices using www.adr.com and www.novartis.com will ensure investors keep their eye on the ball.

Biotechnology is prone to high risks, and investors in Novartis stand to be rewarded in the end by two very different engineering concepts – genetic engineering and financial engineering. Many investors will see Novartis as a prime candidate for an important corporate transaction or another industry merger which, with the wonders of financial alchemy, will bring instant high rewards to investors. Others will have faith in the new scientific opportunities of genetic medicine and genetic crop modification and expect these technologies to reward in time.

Whatever view investors take on Novartis, one question must stay on their monitoring agenda: what will happen when the merger synergies between Ciba and Sandoz have been used up? If at any time there is reason to doubt that a very profitable global operation will not be powering ahead by then, the question of whether Novartis is still an investment with potential for low-risk high-reward investing will need to be reviewed.

11

INVESTING IN TECHNOLOGY

Innovation

Although 'innovation quotient' is a popular buzz word of our times, the wealth creating power of innovation is not a new story. We can look back over a long time frame and see how wealth has followed invention. The transformation of life on our planet in the twentieth century followed the invention in the nineteenth century of the telegraph, telephone, electricity, the railways and the internal combustion engine. Then, in the second half of the twentieth century, after the transistor and microprocessor were invented, we entered the information age and an even stronger phase of economic growth and wealth creation.

History honours the inventors of telegraphy and telephony, Thomas Edison and Alexander Graham Bell, and credits them with starting the communications revolution that led to the information age. However, while Microsoft's Bill Gates has become the world's richest person and the most visible innovator of our times, controversy about Bill Gates and Microsoft and its alleged monopoly continues.

Bill Gates has a vision for the Internet. Everyone in the world should be in contact with everyone else by using only Microsoft communications. His competitors fear him and, prodded by them, the US Justice Department is conducting anti-trust proceedings, examining Microsoft's business practises and Microsoft and Intel's hold on the personal computer market, often called the Wintel Duopoly, discussed later this chapter.

Microsoft's position is so pervasive in computing and on the Internet that while this chapter is about Investing in Technology, the content is, of necessity, also about Microsoft. The subjects are, in the jargon of the day, networked.

The Internet and putting a value on 'dot com'

The Internet is now the focus growth area for information technology and communications companies, and those who can stake out dominate positions in Internet infrastructure, equipment and services are potentially the most rewarding technology investments. Another route to investing in Internet potential is to buy shares in companies that have figuratively staked out territory in cyberspace. America On Line (AOL), the world's biggest internet service provider, and Amazon.com, the world's biggest bookseller, are examples of such companies with turnovers in billions of dollars.

Amazon.com's billion dollar revenues turnover and America on Line's $2.5 billion revenues are commercially something very real investors can relate to, even if the valuation is astonishing compared to any measures recognized up to now by investors. Many other Internet start-ups have reached values of hundreds of millions of dollars as they hit the market on the back of only analysts projections.

Portfolio 2001 includes several major prospects that are well set to benefit from Internet marketing opportunities, including IBM, Sun Microcomputers, Microsoft, America On Line, the on line stock broker Charles Schwab, and clothing retailer The Gap who are supplementing their business on the Internet.

America On Line is discussed in the context of millennial investing niches but I do not understand how its market valuation is reached. The analysts whose research and opinions helped form the basis for *Portfolio 2001* forecasts have their feet firmly planted on the ground while analysts promoting Internet issues, have their feet firmly planted in cyberspace. Some investors have done well with Internet issues, though the chances for those who get carried away are that their experiences will end in tears.

Technology and putting a rational value on '0 plus 1'

All digitized data is coded as '0' or '1' and technology companies are the children of the digital age. What is '0 plus 1' worth? In bull markets, optimists will quickly answer by putting six or more noughts after each one, and millions and even billions of dollars get added to the market values of technology companies without promoters of the shares even stopping for breath.

Many investors will find it as unapproachable and impossible to value a technology company as they would to write a computer programme and, even for those who have a good grasp on the technology sector, putting a rational value on technology companies with exceptional growth is never going to be straightforward.

There are no reliable old or new yardsticks or formulae to use, as the valuation a technology company will command on equity markets comes from a package. Typically it will include breakthrough technology, potential market leadership and dominance, innovations securing high level profit growth, plus the financial muscle and marketing skills as resources without which no ventures can succeed.

Technology has produced some of the world's most rewarding investments over the last three decades. By 1999, the market value of five companies who have been writing the script for the digital age passed a trillion dollars. This is almost 50% more than America's big-three top automobile makers Ford, General Motors and Honda (Chrysler is now part of Daimler), plus America's second most valuable Company, GE, plus Boeing, the world's leading airliner manufacturer and space technology company, plus Citigroup, the world's largest banking and financial services empire.

THE 0+1 TEAM – MARKET VALUE $1.064 trillion ($1064 billion)
January 1999 market cap in $ billion

Microsoft	360
Intel	226
IBM	173
Cisco Systems	160
Lucent Technologies	145

THE B TEAM – MARKET VALUE $635 BILLION

GE	329
Citigroup	117
Ford	70
General Motors	54
Honda	32
Boeing	33

An even more startling example of the high values of technology companies was seen in January 1999 when the market value of Lucent Technologies spun off from the Telecoms Giant AT&T three years earlier and AT&T both reached about $150 billion. From the time of the spin off early in 1994 Lucent grew in market value 637% and AT&T grew 140%. Lucent was trading at a price to earnings ratio of about 100 and AT&T traded at about 23.

The best performing blue chip stocks over last 10 years bull market were:
1. DELL ($1000 in 1988 would be $1.0million in 1999)
2. CSCO ($1000 in 1988 would be $0.9million in 1999)
3. MSFT ($1000 in 1988 would be $30,000 in 1999)
4. INTC ($1000 in 1988 would be $18,000 in 1999)

Following a low-risk high-reward strategy, the buying prices of growth shares must be set with the backing of a reliable earnings forecast. If you buy shares which trade at rich price earnings relationships in the range of forty, fifty and even a hundred times forecast earnings, you will need to feel secure that your expectations are likely to be met because, if they are not, price reversals will be extreme and rapid.

Private investors knowledgeable about technology can often form a well-thought-out opinion on earnings prospects for a technology company and successfully value, pick and monitor technology shares. However, for those who are not as well informed, a better route into technology will be through a fund run by managers who know the prospect companies and understand the sector. Your input is then to study the track record of the fund manager before you invest, time your investment well, and monitor by tracking the fund's performance and the general economic changes that could affect it. If the general economy moves into a recession, some technology companies will enjoy some insulation from the effects of the downturn, but they will not escape the

adverse effects of weak consumer spending or falling equity
markets. The market will also be unforgiving if you time your
investment badly and invest when prices have run away with
themselves and are not rational.

The digital age

A chain of enabling discoveries made the digital revolution
possible, culminating in three watershed inventions in the second
half of the twentieth century: the transistor, the integrated circuit
or silicon chip, and the microprocessor.

Scientists at AT&T's Bell Laboratories (now part of Lucent
Technologies) invented transistors to improve telephony
switching. Bell Labs had established a research a team led by
William Shockley which worked for over ten years, trying various
semiconducting materials and different designs, to develop a
reliable power amplifier, and the result was the solid state
amplifying circuit, later named the transistor.

On 17 December 1947, two of the engineers in the team,
Walter Brattain and John Bardeen, first demonstrated a small
device built from a paper clip, a few pieces of gold foil, a razor
blade, a piece of plastic and a crystal of germanium. As they applied
a control current to the device, a signal current through it was
amplified nearly 450%. A week later, they wired it to a microphone
and speaker and it amplified voice signals. Five weeks later,
Shockley followed up on the first breakthrough with the invention
of the junction transistor. More complex electronically but easier to
make physically, it amplified and used the control current to switch
the main signal on and off very rapidly, and this design became the
basis for all modern transistors. By 1956, when the team were
awarded the Nobel Prize for Physics for their invention, transistors
were everyday commodities.

The first new consumer product to use a transistor was a
hearing aid, and every electronic device that used vacuum tubes was
rapidly made smaller, cheaper and more efficient with transistors.
In addition, a new world of transistorized electronic applications
opened, including mass market computers. A transistor is the basic
element of all integrated circuits and hence of computing.

Integrated circuits, often loosely called silicon chips, are miniaturized electronic circuits, mass produced on tiny wafers of semiconductor material, usually cured silicon. Robert Noyce, one of the co-founders of Intel, was a co-inventor of the integrated circuit.

Chips duplicate the functions of several transistors and other electronic components. The first contained only a few circuits, but manufacturing techniques were developed to print and etch multiple transistors and connections on to ever smaller wafers of silicon that now contain millions of circuits that store data. The individual transistors in the chips each cost millionths of a cent to manufacture.

In 1978, Intel went on to develop the silicon gate metal-oxide semiconductor (MOS) microprocessor chip as the central processing unit (CPU) or brain of a computer. It is a miniaturized integrated circuit, including transistors, capacitators, resistors and all the connections between them on a single fingertip-sized silicon chip. By following codes, the microprocessor accesses data, performs operations on it, and stores the processed data in a retrievable form.

The landmark inventions that led to the transistor and the microprocessor marked the beginning of a technology leap that ushered in the digital age and changed the way the world works. Transistors and microchips are used in almost every function we can think of on the planet – and beyond – to control the wireless phone revolution currently rampaging through the world, probes into outer space, avionics in airliners, programme switches in washing machines, pacemakers in hearts and even jingles on birthday cards. The silicon chip and the digital revolution are to the end of the twentieth century what the industrial revolution was to the end of the nineteenth century. The feared Y2K bug may disrupt our lives over the millennium date change if any chips do not recognize the code for the year 2000, because the world is now run by microprocessors, and a chain is only as strong as its weakest link.

The growth of the semiconductor industry from 1981, when IBM launched its personal computer with an Intel microprocessor, to the late 1990s, reflects a zero start and sales already in excess of $300 billion a year, with no sign of the growth slowing down.

Digital computing follows a binary number code where all information is reduced to the numbers '1' and '0', and transistorized circuits are built which recognize only two states of electric current, high and low, corresponding to the numbers '0' and '1' which function to open the circuit or close it. All text and numerical data, images and sound can now be digitized and stored in small silicon chips, processed and transmitted rapidly and easily anywhere in the world. With the ease of using information in digital code, applications for personal computer extended beyond number crunching and word processing, and computers also became the appliances that connect people to information and people to people.

Moore's law

Today's laptop computer, using a well-specified Pentium processor, can be bought off the shelf for under $2000 and carried around in a briefcase. Twenty-five years ago, the cost of a computer with the same capacity would have been in the millions of dollars, and special buildings would have been necessary to house it.

The phenomenal growth in computing power which ushered in the digital age resulted from the performance capacity of semiconductors doubling every eighteen months. When, in 1985, Intel's microprocessor was state of the art, it could perform 4 million instructions per second. The current Intel Pentium chip can perform over 200 million instructions per second. Intel's Gordon Moore forecast the capacity potential of semiconductors and, as one of Intel's founders, actually made it happen. His forecast is known as Moore's Law. It is a 'law' in technology idiom but not a scientific law. One effect of semiconductor capacity growth has been the rise in performance of personal computers and their fall in price. Another effect has been the ongoing transformation of industry, commerce, communications, science and society in the digital age.

Mainframes, personal computers and computing systems

IBM introduced its first commercial computer in 1952, and went on to build large mainframe computers, nicknamed big irons, which it leased to clients with technical support, consultancy services and maintenance contracts. These services earned IBM exceptionally high profits, and it came to dominate computing globally. By 1961, computers and related products accounted for three-quarters of IBM's income and positioned it as the world's leading computer company until the late 1980s.

The mainframe computer is a central computer performing heavy duty processing and multiple tasks. It serves terminals with individual users – typically departments in an organization who input data into the mainframe and access it for computed information. Mainframe computer manufacturers other than IBM used mainly the Unix platform which was developed by AT&T's Bell Laboratories.

In the 1970s when AT&T introduced the Unix computer for use in telephony, it was unable to enter the commercial computer market place because of anti-trust restrictions. One way of establishing its technology in the market place was to make Unix computers available to universities for nominal licence fees. This status paid off when students, who had learned on Unix, became employed and ran computing facilities and they specificed the Unix system, which they were familiar with for their employers. Among major users who adopted Unix was the US Federal Government. Unix remains entrenched in Government applications in the US.

Unix is also still the most commonly used operating system in the telecommunications industry, including the infrastructure that serves the Internet.

In the 1980s, both IBM and Sun Microsystems introduced versions of Unix for workstations and smaller computers. Unix computers are powerful, well-backed with software, can run multiple programmes simultaneously, and multiple users can access a main computer. However, they are complex to operate, and costly and unattractive for personal and small business use.

With today's personal computers (PCs) being more powerful than many of yesterday's 'big iron' mainframes, the boundaries between personal and business computing are no longer defined by the appliance itself. It is more meaningful to speak about computers as stand alone personal computers, professional workstations, centralized computing systems and distributed computing systems:

- *Stand alone computers.* The PC is an example of a computer designed originally for single user applications, including small business, executive and personal computing. It does not rely on external resources like central databases nor does it share computing resources with others.

- *Professional workstations*: A PC or a mainframe computer can be designed as a powerful stand alone computer with the processing capacity and display required for professionals like scientists, financial planners and engineers.

- *Centralized computing systems*: In these systems, programmes, data and processing capabilities are retained in a central control and many users can access the data at the same time. Stand alone computers can be used in different departments within organizations to access the central resource.

- *Distributed computing systems*: These are a network of personal computers which access information from a central server and from external computing resources such as central databases. These systems are often referred to as enterprise computing as they spread through the business enterprise.

The Internet

The Internet is at the epicentre of growth in communications and computing, and investors in technology have to understand the Internet. An *inter*net is any network of computers, and an *intra*net is an internal communications network where users can access information and transmit documents between themselves. The Internet, written with a capital 'I', is the standardized open communications channel and information resource, with well over a hundred million users, which the whole world can access.

The Internet is a massive global and growing universe of computer connectivity, and functions universally because it uses a standard open communications protocol known as TCP/IP (transmission control protocol/Internet protocol). The Internet can be used by all computers, in the same way as the world's telephone systems can be used by all voice telephones. It is well described as the world's telephony system extended to include communications with computers at the end of the exchange lines instead of voice telephones. We can all speak to each other through our computers on the Internet.

The Internet started in the cold war in the 1960s as a strategic United States defence project, developed to keep military and government lines of communication open in the event of disruption and even nuclear war. Designed as a network within the global telephone exchange networks, it built alternate connections and entry points and introduced a web of new connectivity links between exisiting telephone exchange networks.

The Internet is like a spider's web spanning the global telecommunications network. If part of the web were to be destroyed, as long as some of the strands remain, some connectivity would be preserved.

When the prototype network was developed in 1969, the engineers who created the Internet designed functionality around interface messaging processors which we now call routers . Routers distribute individual messages bundled together in a high speed data stream over telephone lines, and have been the domain of the *Portfolio 2001* company Cisco Systems.

When the cold war ended, the United States Defence Department had no motivation to continue funding the Internet infrastructure, and in 1991 the Internet was effectively 'privatized' and became an open resource. No Internet Inc. took over but a raft of new independent businesses established links into the Internet. They sell Internet access to people like us. These new businesses include local services, telephone companies like BT and AT&T, and networks within networks like America on Line and Microsoft net.

The Internet was first used extensively by academics to access information stored in other computers, in libraries and in scientific databases at other universities. Academics also used electronic mail long before it became popular as a quick, cheap and immediate means of widespread communication. The Internet Protocol TCP/IP makes it possible to send a complete computer file by e-mail with graphics, financial analysis, company accounts, spread sheets and whatever other information is in the file. This extra functionality upgraded e-mail to an essential business, academic, scientific, cultural and, of course, personal resource. A picture taken using a digital camera can be sent in full colour anywhere in the world, using e-mail, within seconds. I know a very clever grandmother who is a technophobe and still has difficulty setting up her video, but she soon figured out how to send e-mail pictures of her grandchildren round the world. A graphic presentation of how the Internet works can be seen on `www.whatis.com`.

The World Wide Web, cyberspace and browsers

The information links comprising the World Wide Web span the globe, are impervious to distance, race and language, and enable millions of people to share information, experiences and activities and transact business with each other.

Since the advent of the World Wide Web, the growth in Internet users has been breathtaking. There were under two million users in 1992 and there are an estimated 100 million plus users in the world now. America has 70 million, Britain over fifteen million (after growing at at over 90% in 1997 and 1998), and by the year 2000 there are likely to be over 200 million Internet users globally.

The World Wide Web was started independently in 1989 at a research institute in Switzerland, the European Laboratory for Particle Physics, to help scientists share information, and became part of the Internet in 1991. A few years later the Internet captured the imagination of the world by associating the World Wide Web with cyberspace.

The term cyberspace owes its origins to a science fiction writer, William Gibson, who defined it as 'a consensual hallucination . . . a graphic representation of data abstracted from the banks of every computer in the human system'. Marshall McLuhan, writing thirty years ago, forecast an interconnecting telecommunications web that would become 'the electronic extension of our central nervous system'.

Cyberspace is a concept, but the World Wide Web is a terra firma-based communications system. When I have information I want to publish to the world, I set up a World Wide Web site in much the same way as I could set up a bill board on the main road announcing what I have to sell. My computer, or a computer from a firm which runs World Wide Web sites for others, can be accessed by any other computer in the world through the Internet, to find out what I have to offer on my web site. And the cost to anyone of accessing any World Wide Web site across the globe is only the local call charge to their Internet access provider.

It took a few years from the time the World Wide Web became part of the Internet for it to be easy to access. The example of my billboard in cyberspace would not work unless anyone could search the World Wide Web and find me. To make this possible, as man has always done, we made tools to do the job. For Internet access the tool is a software browser, which searches for information in the global network. Once we have found each other the Internet communications protocol http:// (hyper text transport protocol) does the rest and gives us quick access to all the information on the web.

On **www.portfolio.2001.com**, the companies in the *Portfolio* are highlighted and you can click on the name of a company, and instantly find detailed research on the company chosen.

An investor researching a company can go to its web site. Then, at that web site, where other pages or other web sites sites are highlighted, the viewer clicks the highlighted reference he's interested in and connects to it. A company's 'home' pages will usually include its annual report. In the annual report the chairman may refer to a new scientific discovery, which is highlighted, and the viewer can click on it and examine the original report, possibly at a university in another country.

Browsers are application programmes and tools for searching out information on a network, and make it easy and user friendly to find and connect with World Wide Web sites and navigate between them on the Internet. The World Wide Web brings graphics, sound, and even international telephony at the cost of local calls. Video telephony on the Internet will eventually become commonplace, but expectations have been ahead of infrastructure. There is still not enough bandwidth capacity on existing copper telephone lines for phones and video to function well.

Browsers are now supplied free, since Microsoft started putting pressure on its competitor Netscape. A browser software programme comes with the software from the Internet access provider, and is installed with the operating system in new computers. Microsoft wants its browser part of the Windows operating system to be supplied with the computer, but the US anti-trust authorities have other ideas, and the dispute could rumble on for years.

The Internet has changed investing

On line broking is in its infancy outside the US, but there are now over six million on line brokerage accounts in the United States, and this number is set to grow to as much as half of the investing public over the next five years. Forrestor Research, which analyses and forecasts Internet usages, has cited three primary reasons for the rapid growth in on line investing: 'households are going on line at a faster pace than expected; more brokerages are moving towards offering on line trading; and more mutual funds will offer on line trading'.

I suggest there is a fourth reason. Investing on line is tuned in to the way the world is working now. Obtaining information is meaningful and using it sensible. People want to do things well, and to use the amazing resources which the Internet has opened for them. Reviewing the progress of information for investors on the Internet in 1996 and 1997, the *Wall Street Journal* on line editor Howard Gold, wrote, 'As the year 2000 approaches, I am convinced that, in investing, the next century will belong to the individual – and the Internet will deliver it into his or her hands.'

e-business

The World Wide Web has become a global business and shopping mall, where investing opportunities have brought even more astonishing returns than technology shares, even though growth in Internet commerce generally has been slower than first expected. The reluctance many people had to give their credit card numbers over the Internet was a barrier, until secure channels were agreed with credit card companies. Internet trade is now on course to soar, but it is hazardous to pick shares in this sector because earnings are generally not entrenched and cannot be predicted reliably. At the same time, market enthusiasm has established an Internet standard for valuing these shares which will frighten most investors.

A main focus for investors interested in the Internet can still be in companies supplying infrastructure and the services which make the the Internet work. This brings us back to Microsoft and Intel. Bill Gates has recognized the potential of the digital age and the World Wide Web where millions of transactions will be made every day over the Internet by millions of buyers and he plans to supply the operating systems for all this commerce. Beyond the market for Microsoft products he has value added services which will collect a small piece of the action from the transactions themselves. Intel sees the Internet as the application where its more powerful Pentium chips come into their own, and is encouraging use of the Internet for communications and media.

The PC and the Wintel duopoly

Microsoft Windows software and operating systems and Intel processors are supplied in over 80% of all computers sold, and have become the universal language of personal computing. This market dominance gives Microsoft and Intel overwhelming competitive advantage.

Windows programmes dominate the software market because they work well and are easy to use, so easy that we find we can start using our computers intuitively, and often only look at the manuals long after we switch on for the first time. Windows is easy to use because it works with point and click commands through a graphic user interface (GUI) in the computer screen. When the computer is switched on, we see icons identifying the programs available, select the programs we want with a mouse, click on them, and windows appear on the screen in which the computer asks us what we want to do and offers us a menu of choices. We point the mouse again to the choice on the screen, click it and the computer obeys our command. Before point and click computing it was far more difficult to work with computers, as instructions were given by complicated codes which had to be typed in.

Windows, by contrast, is magic, and it works so well that no one is ever too surprised that Microsoft has been so successful, and that Bill Gates is so rich. That is, until we realize that Bill Gates did not invent Windows, graphic user interfaces, the mouse, or point and click computing. The graphic user interface was invented by Bell Laboratories; icons were invented by Xerox; and Apple built the first computer with a graphic user interface, icons, windows, pull down menus and the pointing device we call a mouse. Bill Gates borrowed the ideas and marketed them.

Personal computing has grown spectacularly, spurred by ever more powerful computers, and Intel's contribution has been the computing power. The origins of the Wintel duopoly started with IBM's entry into the world of personal computing in the early 1980s. IBM, though it was the world name synonymous with computing, had been dismissive of the personal computer until Apple became a dazzling success. Then IBM recognized the imperative for a personal computer in its range and wanted it in a hurry. It found that it could get a product to the market quicker by contracting with two fledgling companies, Intel and Microsoft, who could rapidly design and provide a central processing unit and software.

The IBM personal computer, which came to be known simply as the PC, was launched in 1981, with an Intel microprocessor and Microsoft software, and rapidly gained market share. Point and click computing had not yet been developed, but MS-DOS (Microsoft disc operating system) was a more user friendly system than the disc operating system IBM had been using . With the Intel microprocessor, which was state of the art at the time, and IBM's name and resources behind the product, the IBM PC soon dominated the personal computer market.

Amazingly, after selling its systems to IBM, Microsoft were left free to licence MS-DOS to others, and Intel was free to sell the same microchip as IBM used to other manufacturers. Both addressed the potential of selling their wares to other manufactures vigorously, and the IBM PC was extensively cloned by other manufacturers.The letters PC came to stand for any computer running on Intel hardware and Microsoft software, and inevitably the IBM clones took the lion's share of the personal computer market. They were selling the same product as IBM, but could undercut its price and innovate quicker.

Under American copyright law, computer software and computer chips are protected, and as Microsoft and Intel controlled the operating system for PCs, other software writers needed their cooperation to write programmes. Cooperation came at a price. When it suited them, Microsoft wrote similar new programmes themselves, starting at an advantage because they had the codes for MS-DOS and Intel and, in addition, knew what software competitors were developing.

Microsoft also tightened its grip on its operating system's market dominance by insisting in software licensing arrangements that computer manufacturers would be penalized if they supplied any computers with systems from other software houses. Accusations followed that Microsoft was blocking other software manufacturers from competing with it, and in 1994 the US Justice Department reached an agreement with Microsoft which aimed to put a stop to these arrangements.

Microsoft launched Windows 2 in 1987, and this must have marked one of Bill Gates's toughest deals. At the time, he was working with IBM developing an alternative system to MS-DOS known as OS/2, which had no graphic interface. Windows 2, with all the resources of point and click computing, was announced on the same day that OS/2 was launched, and instantly eclipsed OS/2, dealing IBM a punishing blow.

Microsoft's competitors, who had written software for the OS/2 system, were also caught wrong footed, when Windows 2 was launched with Microsoft's word processing programme 'Word' and spread sheet 'Excel'. These programmes enabled Microsoft to take the market away from Word Perfect and Lotus who had dominated these high volume software applications.

Over 300 million computers with Windows software and Intel processors have been sold, and they are supported by the world's most extensive library of software ever written. This software resource is probably the most powerful sustainer of Wintel, and it entrenches the dominance of Microsoft and Intel.

The ruthless side of Bill Gates makes for provocative reading, but there is another side to the way he runs Microsoft which is core to the company's success story and far more important for investors. Microsoft is the product leader and its marketing is courageous, brilliant and effective. Microsoft deliver the right new products, and improved versions of old products, as soon as increased computing capacity makes it possible to introduce them, and it invests billions of dollars a year developing products and hundreds of millions of dollars getting them on to the market.

With the advent of Intel's high capacity 32 bit Pentium chip in 1996, the Wintel duopoly started an advance on the corporate market. Microsoft introduced Windows NT in 1996, when Intel's 32 bit Pentium chip matched the performance of the more expensive and less user friendly Unix workstations. Windows NT works as a network server in centralized and distributed computing systems, and as a stand alone computer resource for professionals who execute computer intensive tasks.

In 1996, NT sales grew 85%, and for the first time hardware sellers placed orders for more server units than for Unix. This trend has accelerated and 1997 and 1998 also saw a new mass market develop with the popularity of a PC selling at below $1000. While meeting the low price initially affected Intel and other micro-processor's markets, in the end the higher volumes paid off for both Intel and Microsoft.

Intel's next generation of 64 bit chips will be more powerful than the processors used generally in mainframes, and in the research reports which follow on Sun Microsystems, Intel and Microsoft, this subject is explored.

Browsers and the future of computing

The only time Bill Gates was caught wrong footed was in the early days of the Internet when he let the grass grow under his feet before recognizing the opportunity.

In 1994, Netscape launched a browser which they planned would give them ownership of a *de facto* Internet standard, the same way that Windows had become the standard for personal computing. This raised danger signals for Microsoft as a browser used to access the Internet and other networks could also be developed to work around Microsoft Windows. It might even work as a complete alternative operating system. If this were to happen, the future of computing would be at stake, and the competitive advantage of Microsoft's installed base of Windows software would become watered down.

Microsoft recognized the danger, made a 360-degree turn, and went after Internet opportunities aggressively. It introduced a Micrososft browser 'Internet Explorer', Internet access and content services and structured deals with every Internet service provider to give its browser away free. Netscape had been earning revenue by selling its Browser but had to follow suit and give its browser away. By 1997, Microsoft had launched their Explorer 4 browser which was equal to Netscape's best.

Network computers and Java software

Unable to break the Wintel hold on stand alone computers, competitors in the industry are trying to change the mould. Oracle, IBM, Netscape and Sun Micro have been promoting less powerful network computers and Java software as alternatives to Pentiums and Windows.

Sun Micro's Java & Jini software can create applications that will run on anything from mainframe computers to mobile phones and smart cards, and Java will run in computers whether their basic operating systems are Microsoft, Apple, IBM or Unix.

Java software on the Internet is introduced by the World Wide Web sites which use Java and, as users, without doing anything ourselves, we often get a download of a specific single use Java application on our computers when we contact a web site. The bits of Java software we get are called applets – tiny one time computer applications. With the applets, rather than our computer doing its own thing, using its own software, the server computer we have contacted does the work and our computer only runs the specific Java application received.

Java software use is growing fast in many applications and particularly on the Internet. You will find that you will need a browser that can respond to Java with many World Wide Web sites.

Microsoft and Intel's vision of the Internet for the future is that we will all have ever more powerful computers using the highest performance Intel chips and the most up to date Microsoft software for computing and multi media. The vision of Sun Microsystems and its allies is that we will only need a small network computer to process the Java applets we download for individual applications, and services with massive computing power and central databases will do the rest for us. Put another way, they are promoting a move away from stand alone computing, back to something between centralized and distributed computing. If they succeed, they will have broken the Wintel mould.

The case for simplified network computers follows two threads. One is that many buyers simply do not want to pay for powerful computers which they will not be using, other than for simple applications. The other argument is that in the business world it costs $2,000 to buy a computer and up to $12,000 a year to maintain it. Java enthusiasts claim that these costs can be cut by as much as $9,000 a year, by accessing a central computer from simplified workstations.

Who is going to win? Probably both sides. If you read the headlines you may get the wrong impression. Davids always get a better press than Goliaths, and the media can be relied on to fight the 'prosecution' case as the US anti-trust regulators and the rest of the industry take on Microsoft and Intel. To be well informed, you should follow both sides by logging on to Microsoft `http://www.microsoft.com` Microsoft know how to defend themselves and will be a formidable adversary to puncture, and, if the network computers do take off, Network computers that run on Microsoft are already available.

Technology is in a stage of rapid growth and rapid change and nothing is certain. Hand held devices that interact with a TV set, like remote control handsets, and sell for a few hundred dollars, can access the Internet and may yet prove to be the most popular Internet connector of all. Third generation mobile phones will certainly interact with the internet and their use will increase with this capacity.

Technology potential

Technology companies are fighting for their corners and the size of the market makes the battle worth the effort. Information technology sales are still growing at above 15% a year from a 1996 base of almost $500 billion a year, split up according to the Gartner Group into five sectors:

	1996$b	1992$b
Servers and mainframes	58.52	65.88
PCs and workstations	101.22	56.12
Packaged software	85.08	53.04
Data communications & equipment	20.02	11.00
Services	165.15	124.25
	$430.28	$310.69

Industry estimates are that a trillion dollars a year is in sight by 2003 or 2004 for the information technology industry. In 1997, worldwide sales of packaged software were $120 billion, and could have passed $130 billion by the end of 1998. Applications software which includes word processing, spread sheets and enterprise applications, is growing fastest. Industry analysts reported forecasting growth of almost 15% and targeted sales of over $60 billion in 1998.

Portfolio 2001 technology companies

Portfolio 2001 includes the key players in the information technology and telephony sector. Eight of the ten prospect companies are from the US and Canada.

Microsoft and Intel are of course top of the list. IBM is no less important with operations which spread from mainframe computing to mass market software, chip manufacture, computing services and consulting. Sun Microsystems manufactures and sells Unix mainframe computers and operaring systems, and owns the software languages Java and Jini. Sun is also buying Netscape with America On Line in a development which could have wide implications for the industry. Outside the US, the German Company SAP has secured a dominant position as an originator of software applications for banking and commercial computing, and has successfully expanded into the US. SAP is the world's leading supplier of enterprise computing software and is an opportunity to invest in software without the dramas of the US anti-trust dispute and other competitive issues that will concern investors in Microsoft.

The respected American futurologist and technology writer, George Gilder, has been quoted as saying that the growth in personal computing will not slow down until anyone in the world can walk up to a box, speak to it in any language, and get any computation or piece of data they want instantly.

His vision of the future is not fantasy. All information can be digitized and delivered anywhere in the world via telephone lines, cellular phones, and by satellite. The computer keyboard will eventually give way to voice commands and the technology for instant language translation is well advanced. Gilder's prediction introduces the overlap between computing and communications which is currently the dynamic growth area of the digital age.

Communications

Five companies in the communications industry are included in *Portfolio 2001*: Lucent Technologies, Texas Instrument, Cisco Systems, Motorola and Northern Telecom (Nortel).

Lucent Technologies has been mentioned earlier, as the home of Bell Laboratories operations of AT&T, which were spun off in 1996. Lucent has estimated the compound annual growth of the communications industries it is serving at above 14% a year. In its first reported accounts as an independent company in 1997, it boosted earnings per share by over 40%, with growth driven by unprecedented traffic on public and private telephone networks, demand for Internet infrastructure, the pressing need for new networks in the developing world and deregulation encouraging more service providers in the developed world.

It may take years before investors finally harvest the wealth of intellectual property that must have been sitting in the Bell Laboratories' packing cases that shifted to Lucent from AT&T. Here are some examples. Bell had developed 'Inferno' as an alternative software to Java, which Lucent has now formed into a separate venture to commercialize. Bell's research pipeline also led to Lucent being awarded nearly 800 patents in 1997, and to over 120 innovations being introduced by Lucent in the same year. Lucent has dominant and key positions in most areas of the sectors it services. It is the world's second largest manufacturer of digital signal processions used in mobile phones, and in 1999 it purchased Ascend Communications, a leading supplier of networking equipment. The acquistion of Ascend brings Lucent into the market territory dominated by Cisco Systems.

Cisco Systems has been engaged in the design and supply of routers from the inception of the Internet. It has a market share of over 50%, and its products are frequently the industry standard. Whatever debates progress about other aspects of the Internet, there is agreement on one subject: infrastructure has to grow as the number of users grows explosively.

Mobile telephony is the world's fastest growing technology market. Texas Instrument is one of America's pioneer semi-conductor companies, and is now the world's largest producers of digital signal processors, known as DSPs, which are used in mobile phones and other digital appliances.

According to Texas, in 1997 worldwide shipments of digital cell phones reached almost 90 million, up from less than 50 million in 1996, and 1997 marked the first time ever that cell phone volumes surpassed PC shipments. Sales of digital wireless phones certainly passed 120 million in 1998, and some researchers suggest even higher results. Within five years, digital cellular phone sales are expected to exceed 300 million. More than half of all the digital cell phones made today use one of Texas Instrument's digital signal processing solutions. New technologies will make it possible in the future to offer wireless phone users a wide range of advanced features, including Internet access.

Motorola pioneered wireless telephony and was the IBM of the industry until Nokia and Ericsson mounted an overwhelming challenge. Motorola is still a titan, with interests that span from pocket calculators and cheap analogue phones to making satellites and running the Iridium low earth orbiting satellite consortium which it masterminded. The fifth company reviewed is Canada's Northern Telecom (Nortel), Lucent's very worthy and often overlooked competitor. In 1998, Nortel acquired Bay Networks, which acquisition also brought them into the networking market as a major player.

The most dramatic growth in telecommunications at present is in wireless telephony, and the world's largest manufacturer of handsets, Nokia, and the world leader in wireless telephony services, Vodafone-Airtouch, are reviewed as Millennial Niche Opportunities.

MICROSOFT

Share Graph 1997–1998 Microsoft Corp.
Primary Market – NASDAQ – MSFT

Price January 1999 $86
Market Value January 1999 $431.2 billion

SECTOR Technology INDUSTRY Software & Programming
Top Line MSFT Bottom Line S&P 500 Index Relative
Left Scale: Top $ Price MSFT, Bottom Section Volume in
Thousands
Note graphic not rebased for 2 for 1 split in 1999

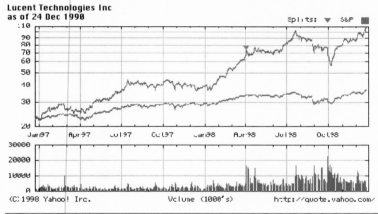

PRICE PERFORMANCE Year 1998	MSFT		An investment made in January 1984 grew 1285% by January 1999		
PRICE HISTORY	1998	1997	1996	1995	Notes
High Price	80.00	37.69	21.53	13.78	
Low Price	37.62	20.19	9.98	7.28	
High P/E	86.54	53.45	50.25	47.60	
Low P/E	37.37	30.77	23.30	25.15	

Chmn William H. Gates, www.microsoft.com
29,000 employees
Microsoft Corporation, One Microsoft Way, Redmont WA
Phone: (425) 882-8080 Fax (425) 936-7329

Global Franchise: Computer operating systems, software and Internet services and content

Microsoft was formed in 1975, and by 1981, the same year it was incorporated as a company, it was supplying the software operating system for IBM's personal computer, the ubiquitous PC. IBM PCs, and cloned PCs made by other companies with Intel processors and Microsoft software installed, have since sold in the hundreds of millions. Microsoft soon came to dominate the personal computer software industry with a market share of 90%. Microsoft stock went public in 1986 when it started introducing an unparalleled family of Windows software for personal and small office computing applications. These have come to include the world's best selling word processing and spread sheet programmes 'Word' and 'Excel'. Microsoft Windows 3 was launched in 1990, and Windows 95, Microsoft Office and Windows 98 have since followed. When Intel launched its Pentium 32 bit processors in 1995, the increase in computing capacity they provided was sufficient to service network computing and business applications and Microsoft introduced its second franchise, 'NT' programmes for network servers and enterprise computing in business applications. Since 1995, Microsoft has been building a third franchise on the Internet opportunity as a software, content and service provider, with its sights set on becoming a global digital nervous system for an 'information at your fingertips' society.

Annual revenues are approaching $18 billion, with about 47% coming from sales of installed operating platforms to computer manufacturers as original equipment, and about 43% coming from other software applications and tools, with media and other sources contributing about 5%. Sales in over 50 countries and over 30 languages account for about 58% of revenues. As of 30 June, 1998, Microsoft employed over 29,000 people, with 11,000 engaged in research and development; 13,000 in sales, marketing and support; and 3,950 in operations.

Accepting responsibility for an investing decision on Microsoft's present valuations is a daunting prospect and the following review discusses key issues which are likely to affect prospects.

Setting a rational price

Portfolio 2001 WORKSHEET FOR TARGETING SHARE PRICES OF MICROSOFT IN
1999, 2000, 2001 & 2002
BASED ON FORECASTS MADE IN JULY 1999
FISCAL YEAR TO JUNE 1999 EPS $0.84

Growth	Year	Estimated EPS	P/E	Share Price Target	+10%	-10%	Notes
80%	1999	$1.56	60	$94	$104	$85	
30%	2000	$2.02	60	$121	$134	$109	
30%	2001	$2.62	60	$157	$174	$141	
30%	2002	$3.40	60	$204	$226	$183	

This 'what if' forecast suggests potential earnings and share prices based on current
indications. Forecasts must be revised continuously in the light of all company results
and industry, market and economic news. Forecasts can be misleading and cannot be
treated as investment advice or used to motivate investments. See page 69.

Past performance indicators

Growth Rates %		MSFT	S&P 500	Industry	Sector	To 06/98
Earnings per share 5 year		33.46	20.43	35.45	37.31	
1998 last reported vs 1997		54.37#	12.34	51.12	25.07	
Sales 5 year 1994-1998		31.01	15.68	31.93	22.47	
Profitability Ratios						To 06/98
Gross Margin 1998	%	91.83	49.22	82.80	52.13	
5 year average	%	87.46	48.87	80.86	52.01	
Net Profit Margin 1998	%	36.00	10.90	22.27	11.19	
5 year average	%	27.17	10.17	18.93	10.75	
5 Year Returns on:						
Assets	%	25.23	8.22	18.55	12.88	
Investment	%	32.13	11.97	24.42	16.89	
Equity	%	34.32	21.46	28.37	20.83	

Microsoft is a unique company. Inside twenty-five years it has
become the world's most valuable company, with a market
capitalization of over $400 million. It is now most likely to become
the world's first trillion dollar company – and it could happen
within a few years. It is the world's most profitable company

earning gross margins of over 90% and a clear profit after tax that is usually above 30%, and even reached 40%, for the last quarter of 1998. It has $20 billion in the bank and no debt.

With all these virtues Microsoft should be a simple company to write about, but it is not. No list of glowing figures will resolve investors, concerns on whether Microsoft is potentially a bubble that grew too big too fast, whether its growth is sustainable and whether buying Microsoft shares now is an investment or only a speculation.

Microsoft's investor relations site on www.microsoft.com deservedly won an award in 1998 from *Investor Relations* magazine for the best company web sites for investors, and readers studying it will find the most transparent and comprehensive financial reporting possible. Microsoft also offers the support of on line analytical tools, and publishes reports of presentations which have been made by senior company management to institutional investors.

The question cynics must ask

Many potential investors have only one question about Microsoft's amazing profits, but being polite they seldom raise it. The question is whether it is possible to make so much money honestly. The answer is Yes, it is possible – unless the US courts decide otherwise.

Because of Microsoft's unique profitability and market position, this report includes more detail and discussion than other *Portfolio 2001* reports, and the four schedules included at the end contain most of the relevant numbers:

1. The analysis of Microsoft's growth from 1989 to 1987
2. The earnings statement for six months to end December 1998
3. The analysis of revenues by market and product
4. The listing of global operations

Finding the low-risk high-reward opportunity

Investors with a comprehensive knowledge of the computer industry and Microsoft products may find low-risk high-reward investing opportunities, but most investors will lack the information and knowledge to structure a research-led investing opportunity in the company. They will probably follow the market and base their investing decision on their faith in Bill Gates, the opinions of commentators in the securities industry, the financial press and credible newsletters.

For some years I have discussed an escape route from a difficult investing decision with friends who were keen to invest in Microsoft, but frightened of the soaring share price. A line-of-least-resistance strategy emerged of buying small parcels of shares with seriously long-term investing horizons. This recognized the high risks of buying richly valued shares, without closing the door to potentially great investing opportunities.

Forecasting using Microsoft's 'What if' financial model and other analytical tools

www.microsoft.com offers viewers a range of on line analysis tools including a 'What If' Excel on line programme. Using this programme, you can forecast Microsoft's current financial year against the most recent income statements, and introduce your own volume and percentage change assumptions to come up with revised numbers. Other analysis tools are also included on the site, and you can even call up alternative income statements in local languages, different currencies and prepared for different accounting conventions.

Time spent in getting to understand Microsoft could prove to be well invested. Over the years, there has been a pattern with a solid 100% between the tops and the bottoms of the share price range in a year.

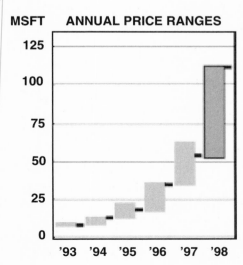

When price volatility follows general market jitters, informed investors may recognize buying opportunities. In 1999 and 2000, the forthcoming launches of Office 2000 and 'NT' are likely to affect sales materially and present buying opportunities based on fundamentals.

The challenge to Microsoft as a monopoly

Examining a range of well-thought-out numbers in spread sheets can be very useful, but with Microsoft the value of diligent research is watered down because future earnings could come under attack from an unpredictable event. The anti-trust proceedings initiated by the US Justice Department must be a cause for concern for investors. The macro challenge is whether Microsoft's exceptional profits have come from a monopoly which is going to be broken by the US courts and, as litigation is capricious and long-winded, it might take years to know the answer.

The approach taken for *Portfolio 2001* is that Microsoft will most probably continue to prosper, in spite of the anti-trust proceedings and maybe with its wings a bit clipped, because it provides exceptional value for money and innovation keeps it as the number one player. However, investors will be very unwise to assume that competitors who have pressed for the Justice Department investigations, or the US Justice Department itself, will eventually go away politely without causing any problems. A fine of a few million, tens of million or even hundreds of million dollars would hardly hurt Microsoft, but forcing it to run its business differently from the present successful formula could be severely damaging.

Java and other possible replacements for Microsoft

A second threat to Microsoft's prospects comes from Sun Microsystems' Java software, which potentially can be developed as a computer language that will simplify computing appliances. Some believe that Java, or other different approaches to computing, could make Microsoft redundant.

For personal computing, the case for a simpler, cheaper alternative to Windows is that users do not require all the vast resources of Windows programmes and will settle for less if they pay less. In the corporate and server markets, Sun dismisses the prospects for Microsoft Windows NT5 because the new programme will have forty million lines of code, and Sun's Scott McNeally has been quoted as saying 'There wasn't that much code on the planet a while back. And they're going to put that on every desktop and every server? I don't think so. The new version of NT is Solaris 93 [Sun's operating system].'

I find the fact that Microsoft will put '40 million lines of code' on every desktop is a compelling reason why Microsoft will succeed rather than it being a constraint. Yes, Java and Jini computer language (and there are others being developed) will make inroads – technology is dynamic and new innovations can change the landscape radically – but it takes time to change the way the world works.

Personal computing and, increasingly, the business world now work with Windows and Microsoft NT, and Microsoft invests billions of dollars a year to stay in front of the pack. As developments in the industry progress, experts and analysts may start to think otherwise on Microsoft's chances, and when they do www.portfolio2001.com will publish their revised opinions.

Earnings growth and price earnings expectations used for the Portfolio 2001 forecast

Portfolio 2001 'What If' forecasts follow past earnings and broad indications after studying a company, its peers and competitors, but have not been built with complete financial models. Microsoft has formidable pricing power and produces exceptional earnings, but is cautious about growth in 1999. It expects organizations to reduce their non-Y2K-related IT spending, and it is concerned about the uncertain international economic outlook. Microsoft's caution must be considered, but it usually proves to be misleading as it always talks down future exuberance about earnings prospects. It is very aware of the danger of a share price bubble developing on high expectations.

The *Portfolio 2001* forecast assumes earnings growth for the next three years of 30%, which is not ambitious in the light of past performance and growth prospects. With the forthcoming introductions of Office 2000 and Windows NT5, an earnings multiple of 60 times current earnings is used to target share prices. This is double the forecast earnings per share growth rate and will certainly prove to be ambitious if earnings growth slows below 20%, or monetary conditions in the US tighten and market multiples fall generally in response.

Investors who are not frightened off by the anti-trust proceedings, and industry competitors' plans to replace Microsoft, should focus on the growth story to reach a view on whether earnings growth will be sustainable.

The growth story

The PC success loop – a virtuous circle

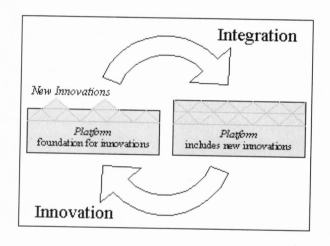

Source: **Microsoft.com** in 1997

This chart illustrates the cycles of innovation and integration which Microsoft follows and the virtuous circle which has established the Windows platform as one of the world's leading computing standards. There are two parts to the sequence. Innovation is the heart and soul, and the Microsoft platform is the body. The platform is the foundation for innovations, it digests new innovations and feeds them back into the platform.

The Windows PC family of applications was Microsoft Phase One and came to dominate the personal computing industry. Microsoft's Phase Two developed from the same platform when Intel's 32 bit Pentium chip enabled more powerful software applications for business computing and Windows NT was introduced to run servers for multiple workstations. Phase Two opened the corporate market and Microsoft's NT5 software, which will be a giant leap again, will open opportunities for Microsoft across the full spectrum of business and corporate computing.

Dramatic increases in earnings per share in 1998

For the fiscal year ending June 1997, Microsoft produced net revenues of $11.36 billion and net income of $3.45 billion, and 1998 revenues grew to $14.48 billion and resulted in net income of $4.49 billion. For the quarter ended 31 December 1998, Microsoft's net income rose to $1.98 billion, $0.73 a share, a staggering 74% increase over the corresponding quarter of 1997.

The growth came from increased PC shipments in the industry generally fuelling broad demand for products including Microsoft Windows NT Server and Windows NT Workstation, server applications, and Office 97. Demand was also spiked by Year 2000 concerns.

Significantly, corporate customers' support has been growing, and Microsoft Office, SQL Server and Exchange programmes all reached new highs with shipments of all server applications nearly doubling in 1998. Microsoft SQL Server 7.0 programmes were launched to over 45,000 customers in 53 countries around the world, and made a clean sweep of COMDEX industry awards at the beginning of 1999, with the 'Best Productivity Software' and 'Best of Show' awards. By the end of 1998, Microsoft was the second-largest database vendor, moving up from fifth-largest in the past two years. The SQL Server programme grew at nearly twice the rate of the next fastest competitor.

Microsoft Exchange Server programmes set a new record, shipping 4.5 million client access licences in the fourth quarter of 1998 and, over the calendar year 1998, Exchange outsold all competitors with 14.4 million 'seats' in total.

Microsoft Windows NT Server out-sold all other server operating systems, in terms of unit sales, for the second consecutive year, according to International Data Corp (IDC). Microsoft Windows NT Workstation licensed more than 25 million units, with over 3 million new users over the last quarter.

The last quarter of 1998 was also seasonally strong for Microsoft's consumer products and interactive media group, with a solid year end holiday quarter for games and gaming devices and the Encarta reference line. In online businesses, the MSN network of Internet services reached more than 40% of Internet users in the

United States, and membership to the MSN Hotmail Web-based e-mail service grew to exceed 30 million active accounts worldwide.

In July 1998, Microsoft began to consolidate its Internet services at a single portal site – msn.com – and total reach grew at a rate of nearly 60% during the year.

The full profits announcement made in January 1999, on the second six months of 1998, is with the schedules at the end of this report.

Moore's Law and the PC success loop

www.microsoft.com publishes details of presentations made at investor conferences by Microsoft management. In this section I quote from and paraphrase, somewhat impolitely without strictly identifying the quotes and the paraphrasing, a particularly informative presentation made by the chief financial officer, Greg Maffei, at a Merrill Lynch conference on 2 March 1988 http://www.microsoft.com/msft/speech/ maffeimerrill.htm

We are in a world where most things increase in price, but technology has broken that trend. In the 23 years since Microsoft was founded in 1975, the cost per MIP (millions of instructions per second) is the compelling one. Following Moore's Law, as we've all come to know it, (see page 312-313), the cost has fallen from $10,000 per MIP down to $7 per MIP. Looking forward to 2011, Intel's chairman Andy Grove has projected two cents per MIP. The enormous opportunities these technology leaps have created have resulted in faster and cheaper PCs, where what was seemingly the cutting edge as recently as 1993 now looks like a joke in terms of the hard drive size, processor speed etc.

Software is not considered under the Moore's Law concept, but in general it progresses on similar lines, and Microsoft has made improvements in software with comparable gains in the value of the services. 'What were three separate components in 1990 are now combined and two more components have been added, with better integration and more features and capabilities, and the price is less than half. Microsoft call this the PC success loop and have tried to ride it and also expand it – hardware advances, leading to price reductions, leading to increased volume, leading to software integration. To some degree, if Intel and the hardware guys are the supply side, we are the demand side of this equation.'

The result of these trends for Microsoft has been 22 consecutive years of increases in revenue and profit, and matching increases in market capitalization. This is both a great testimony to the effects of Moore's Law and to Microsoft 'riding it' reasonably well. It's also a little daunting looking forward, according to Mr Maffei and many analysts!

Schedules reflecting Microsoft's awesome revenue and profit growth are included at the end of this report.

Microsoft scalability in business applications

Microsoft's fastest growing opportunity in recent years has been selling its software applications to large business accounts. By 1998, Microsoft desktop applications passed $5 billion annual revenues following the release of Microsoft Office 97 the previous year. Office applications exceeded the PC growth rate, and Greg Maffei forecast it would continue to exceed the PC growth rate for the next few years with growth from a family of programmes called BackOffice. These are used to bring new software management applications into the systematic running of businesses.

One of the key strengths of Microsoft BackOffice is scalability from a common platform. Basic BackOffice Software programmes run small businesses like a dentist's office using a small business server, and major businesses like Boeing and General Electric run on versions of Microsoft BackOffice Enterprise Edition.

The Digital Nervous system

In the same way as the PC loop developed, integration between desktops and servers has brought the demand for easier and better management administration support across the spectrum of business applications. Responding to the new opportunity, Microsoft sees building an information system that utilizes microprocessor technologies to help run it as a core objective.

Bill Gates has posited a vision for how corporations can take advantage of Microsoft's programmes as a management tool into the twenty-first century, which Microsoft calls the Digital Nervous System. It's a combination of building the basic operations of a business around microprocessor technology, with the ability both to act on known transactions that have to occur, execute on planned events that are expected like price changes and, in addition, have a responsive mechanism for dealing with things that are a surprise in the market, like a change in the exchange rates or a change in market forces.

Microsoft's commercial goal is clear. It wants businesses to build a digital nervous system around Microsoft software to give them competitive advantage in the running of their own businesses, and, of course to ensconce even further Microsoft's competitive advantage. Microsoft's dominant position with personal computer software has been one of the strongest examples of competitive advantage ever. It is now well past the early stages of serving big business, and capturing a hold on this potential with the digital nervous system concept becomes Microsoft's real first prize.

Falling prices in the personal computer industry

Indications of Microsoft's prospects serving business computing are encouraging because the company is entering a market where it has the price advantage over competitors. However, the sustainability of Microsoft's legendary margins and pricing power in the PC industry is more difficult to understand, and glibly accept as secure, because its position is so dominant.

Holding the price of Windows steady has enabled Microsoft to maintain its legendary margins on the software that now runs 90% of the world's PCs. Sustained high prices fly in the face of experience in technology, where as product performance goes up, price comes down. In spite of sub-£1000 and even sub-$750 computers, Microsoft maintained its margins when everyone else in the technology business, from chip makers to disk drive and router makers, found prices had to fall as competition for market share intensified.

Microsoft does not publish the price at which it sells Windows for installation to computer makers, but industry analysts estimate that Windows 95 sold for about $45 a copy in quantity, the same price or slightly more than the price of its predecessor which combined Windows 3.1 and DOS software. Windows 98 is thought to be priced about the same as Windows 95, and upgrades retail at the same $90 as before.

Microsoft claims that Windows buyers do get far more for their money as the functions and features of Windows have increased exponentially. Windows 3.1 had three million lines of software code and Windows 95 has 11 million. Microsoft also claims that Windows software now includes the web browser and other additional programmes. However, improved performance has not kept hardware prices up. Competition drove down Intel's chip prices. The first Pentium processor in 1993, with a speed of 60 megahertz, contained 3.1 million transistors and was sold by Intel for $878 in quantities of 1,000. The Pentium II chip came out in 1997, running at 233 megahertz, and with 7.5 million transistors, and sold for less than half this. Lower specification Pentium prices have now fallen below $300.

Can Microsoft maintain its competitive advantage and still lock in its exceptionally high profits? Cynical observers believe Windows should be much cheaper in line with industry dynamics, and claim the price of Windows is only kept up through unfair monopolistic practices. On the other hand, users are inclined to accept that Microsoft Windows maintains its price because of what it is and what it does and, regardless of what Microsoft earns, the software is a bargain.

Bill Gates has no doubts that Microsoft will only stay on top if it has the best products and that if he fails to innovate successfully he will be replaced by competition. To keep ahead Microsoft spends upwards of $3 billion a year on Research and Development.

Interactive media and Windows CE

Microsoft's interactive media enterprise is a several hundred million dollar concern, including a package consumer software business with products like Microsoft Encarta and various games. Encarta is the number one selling encyclopedia and the Microsoft Flight Simulator is the most widely sold packaged software games product.

In the media businesses, Microsoft Network, Moneycentral, Microsoft Expedia, and CarPoint have exceptional growth and earnings potential and corporate value as owners of strategic territories in cyberspace.

What can go wrong?

Microsoft's growth story is convincing, but there are risks that have to be considered, with the US government proceedings first on the list.

Technology changes are the second risk. The expansion of the

Internet has probably been the biggest driver of growth in personal computing, while the PC has been the only practical tool to use for Internet access. This could change. Internet access could become the domain of mobile-phone-like instruments with smart cards, or hand-held devices like TV remote control switches.

Another risk could come from competitors' plans to introduce the simplified computers they call network devices or slim computers, which access central databases for computing. They have already been introduced and have not been successful up to now, but could succeed in future. Computer operating systems that do not use Microsoft may also be developed, using Java or another software code.

I expect there were evenings when Henry Ford was disturbed and anxious that Mr Chrysler's new Dodge would capture market share from him. However, Mr Gates has been different from other industrialists who get nasty surprises from competitors. Bill Gates is always wide awake and keeps ahead of the market and competitors. He ploughs billions of dollars into research each year, and is recognized as one of the century's most brilliant and effective marketers.

Microsoft's greatest weakness will be if it stops innovating and eases off on marketing. The chances of this happening? Slimmer than the chances for the slim computer as we know it today. In the jargon of the day, this would be Bill Gates screwing up. It's unlikely, but it could happen. Napoleon ruled the world until he attacked Russia and started an inexorable decline of his fortunes.

Monitoring

Monitoring Microsoft for news about the Justice Department, new programmes, computer sales volumes and chit chat requires no more than following the daily press. `www.microsoft.com` gives viewers the opportunity to listen to conference calls with institutional investors and presents comprehensive information as well as the state of the art enables. The site also gives a comprehensive picture of company resources. Competitive products, including the increasingly visible Linux open code software `www.linux.com`, should also be monitored.

Schedule 1: Analysis of Microsoft's growth: 1989 to 1998

Fiscal Year Ending	World-wide Hdcnt	Net Revenue	% Growth	Net Income	% Growth
6/30/89	4,037	$804m	36%	$171m	38%
6/30/90	5,635	$1,183m	47%	$279m	63%
6/30/91	8,226	$1,843m	56%	$463m	66%
6/30/92	11,542	$2,759m	50%	$708m	53%
6/30/93	14,430	$3,753m	36%	$953m	35%
6/30/94	15,017	$4,649m	24%	$1,146m	20%
6/30/95	17,801	$5,940m	28%	$1,450m	27%
6/30/96	20,561	$8,671m	46%	$2,195m	51%
6/30/97	22,276	$11.36b	31%	$3,450m	54%
6/30/98	27,320	$14.48b	28%	$4,490m	30%

Schedule 2: Earnings statement for six months to end December 1998

	Three months ended December 31		Six months ended December 31	
	1997	1998	1997	1998
Revenue	$3,585	$4,938	$6,715	$8,891
Operating expenses:				
Cost of revenue	313	433	566	740
Research and development	627	667	1,194	1,278
Acquired in-process technology	0	0	296	0
Sales and marketing	876	940	1,664	1,770
General and administrative	106	149	201	248
Other expenses	50	35	121	59
Total operating expenses	1,972	2,224	4,042	4,095
Operating income	1,613	2,714	2,673	4,796
Investment income	157	337	299	598
Gain on sale	0	0	0	160
Income before income taxes	1,770	3,051	2,972	5,554
Provision for income taxes	637	1,068	1,176	1,888
Net income	$1,133	$1,983	$1,796	$3,666
Earnings per share (1):				
Basic	$ 0.47	$ 0.79	$ 0.74	$ 1.47
Diluted	$ 0.42	$ 0.73	$ 0.67	$ 1.35

Schedule 3: Analysis of revenues by product and market

Product Groups	Three months ended December 31		Six months ended December 31	
Platforms	$1,546	$2,321	$2,944	$4,246
Applications and Tools	1,696	2,150	3,109	3,862
Interactive Media and Other	343	467	662	783
Total revenue	$3,585	$4,938	$6,715	$8,891

Channels				
South Pacific and Americas Region	$1,169	$1,571	$2,287	$3,013
Europe, Middle East, and Africa Region	876	1,198	1,560	2,037
Asia Region	328	373	673	680
OEM	1,212	1,796	2,195	3,161
Total revenue	$3,585	$4,938	$6,715	$8,891

Schedule 4: Listing of global operations

International revenues account for 56% of Microsoft's total revenues (as of fiscal year ending 6/30/97). Microsoft Corporation has subsidiary offices located in the following countries and regions:

Argentina	Guatemala	Philippines
Australia	Hong Kong	Poland
Austria	Hungary	Portugal
Belgium	India	Russia
Brazil	Indonesia	Saudi Arabia
Canada	Israel	Singapore
Caribbean	Italy	Slovakia
Chile	Japan	Slovenia
China	Jordan	South Africa
Colombia	Korea	Spain
Costa Rica	Malaysia	Sweden
Czech & Slovak Republics	Mexico	Switzerland
Denmark	Middle East (Dubai)	Taiwan
Ecuador	Morocco	Thailand
Egypt	Netherlands	Turkey
Finland	New Zealand	Uruguay
France	Norway	Venezuela
Germany	Panama	Vietnam
Greece	Peru	United Kingdom

INTEL

Share Graph 1997–1998 INTEL Corp.
Primary Market – NYSE – INTC

Price January 1999 $138
Market Value January 1999 $228.3 billion

SECTOR Technology INDUSTRY Semiconductors
Top Line INTEL Bottom Line S&P 500 Index Relative: Triangle
Marks Split
Left Scale: Top $ Price INTC, Bottom Volume in Thousands
Note: Graphic not rebased for two-for-one split in 1999.

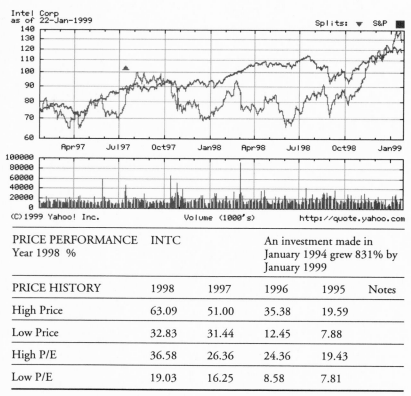

PRICE PERFORMANCE	INTC		An investment made in		
Year 1998 %			January 1994 grew 831% by		
			January 1999		

PRICE HISTORY	1998	1997	1996	1995	Notes
High Price	63.09	51.00	35.38	19.59	
Low Price	32.83	31.44	12.45	7.88	
High P/E	36.58	26.36	24.36	19.43	
Low P/E	19.03	16.25	8.58	7.81	

Chairman Andrew S. Grove, Pres/CEO Craig R. Barrett, **www.intel.com**
63,700 employees
2200 Mission College Blvd., Santa Clara, CA 95052
Phone: (408) 765-8080 Fax: (408) 765-9904

Global Franchise: 'Intel Inside' – king of microprocessors

'Moore's Law', the forecast made by Dr Gordon Moore shortly after Intel was founded in 1968, predicted that the power of a computer chip would double every eighteen months, while the costs fell. Intel research and development and manufacturing resources made the prediction happen, and in its wake the digital age was ushered in. With annual revenues now more than $25 billion, Intel is the King of the Microchips. Tangible success as the suppliers of microprocessors which are the 'brains' of computers was achieved in 1981, when IBM introduced their PC containing Intel microprocessors and Microsoft Windows software. 'Wintel', as the duo have since often been called, came to dominate the global desktop and mobile computer markets, and Intel has held a market share of between 85% and 90%. With the introduction in 1995 of Intel's powerful 32 bit Pentium processors and Microsoft's Windows NT software for network servers and high performance workstations, Intel built a second franchise in corporate computing. Globally recognized as the company which stretches the leading edge of computing technology and with its global brands 'Intel' and 'Pentium' established, Intel is the world's leading supplier of what it calls 'building blocks' for computer hardware manufacturers worldwide. State of the art manufacturing microchip plants in the US, Ireland, Israel, Malaysia and the Philippines set the benchmarks for semiconductor performance, manufacturing efficiency and productivity. Intel is also the world's largest manufacturer of computer chips used in all aspects of life today, from space probes to domestic washing machines. Sixty per cent of annual sales of $25 billion are outside the US.

Setting a rational price

Portfolio 2001 WORKSHEET FOR TARGETING SHARE PRICES OF INTEL IN 1999, 2000, 2001 & 2002 BASED ON FORECASTS MADE IN JANUARY 1999 EPS FISCAL 1998 TO DECEMBER: $1.73

Growth	Year	Estimated EPS	P/E	Share Price Target	+10%	-10%	Notes
Consensus	1999	$2.32	30	$70	$77	$63	98
20%	2000	$2.78	30	$83	$93	$75	
20%	2001	$3.33	30	$100	$111	$90	
20%	2002	$4.00	30	$120	$133	$108	

This 'what if' forecast suggests potential earnings and share prices based on current indications. Forecasts must be revised continuously in the light of all company results and industry, market and economic news. Forecasts can be misleading and cannot be treated as investment advice or used to motivate investments. See page 69.

1998 Profits set back and recovery
In the second quarter of 1998, Intel issued a profits warning. The profit dip, and how it was reversed by the end of the year, are discussed fully in this report.

Revenues in 1998 set a new annual record, and fourth quarter revenues were $7.6 billion, up 17% from fourth quarter 1997 revenues of $6.5 billion. Fourth quarter revenue was also up 13% from third quarter 1998 revenue. Record fourth quarter net income of $2.1 billion was up 18% from fourth quarter 1997 net income of $1.7 billion. Net income in the fourth quarter was up 32% from third quarter 1998 net income of $1.6 billion.

Record fourth quarter earnings per share of $1.19 increased 21% from $0.98 in the fourth quarter of 1997 and rose 34% from $0.89 in the third quarter of 1998.

Earnings per share growth expectations
Earnings per share growth of 20% is consistent with past performance, management indications and analysts' opinions.

Intel is poised to resume earnings per share growth in line with past performance and 30% growth could be achieved. For the purposes of forecasting growth has been set at 33% for 1999 in line with company indications and analysts' forecasts. From 2000 the forecast is based on growth of 20% which is likely to be exceeded.

Earnings multiple expectations

Because Intel has in the past had earnings disruptions, the share price is often less richly valued than other companies in the sector. In market conditions for January 1999, a multiple of 30 times earnings to reach a target price is rational for investors who can take on board the risks of the sector and individual companies.

Past performance indicators

Growth Rates %		INTC	S&P 500	Industry	Sector	Notes
Earnings per share 5 year		33.81	15.68	33.11	33.65	
1998 last reported vs 1997		(16.62)	12.34	(11.75)	25.07	
Sales 5 year 1994-1998		33.81	15.68	33.11	33.65	
Profitability Ratios						
Gross Margin 1998	%	53.75	49.22	49.20	52.13	
5 year average	%	56.55	48.87	51.68	52.01	
Net Profit Margin 1998	%	22.84	10.90	15.55	11.19	
5 year average	%	24.09	10.17	17.98	10.75	
5 Year Returns on:						
Assets	%	23.20	8.22	18.30	12.28	
Investment	%	29.44	12.97	23.12	16.89	
Equity	%	34.01	21.46	28.24	20.83	

The growth story

Twelve consecutive years of revenue growth

Intel achieved its twelfth consecutive year of revenue growth in 1998, in spite of the challenges of a turbulent market, and in the fourth quarter it achieved record revenue in the Americas, Europe and also in Asia-Pacific.

CEO Craig Barrett concluded the results annoucement in January 1999 with these comments:

> Intel enters 1999 with a first quarter roadmap offering new products in every segment of the computer market. This quarter we will launch Pentium III and Pentium III Xeon processors, the first products in the next generation of Intel Architecture micropro-

cessors. On the manufacturing front we will soon begin the transition to 0.18 micron, the next generation of process technology.

The investments of the last year in new product development and productivity improvement have strengthened the company and positioned it well for a market that will continue to be competitive and dynamic.

Investment, product development and marketing
Intel had a triumphal year in 1997, with record sales and earnings per share growth. The year even ended with chairman Andrew Grove featuring as *Time* magazine's man of the year. Then growth stalled in the first quarter of 1998 and Intel reported a 36% drop in earnings. After the setback, characteristically for the company, it invested in becoming better and more competitive and, by the end of 1998, it set new quarterly records for revenue, net income, earnings per share and microprocessor unit shipments.

Management restructuring
Andy Grove, the chairman, passed the role of CEO to Craig Barrett early in 1998. Until this appointment, the CEO had always been one of the 'gang of three' who started Intel.

Barrett joined Intel in 1974, nine years after it started, from Stanford University and left a tenured professorship to become a manufacturing technology development manager. Ten years after joining Intel he was named a vice president, and was promoted to senior vice president in 1987 and executive vice president in 1990. In 1992, he was elected to the board of directors and appointed chief operating officer in 1993.

He spearheaded refitting Intel's manufacturing to stave off a Japanese threat, and oversaw a multibillion-dollar capital expansion in the early 1990s. The huge commitment, undertaken on the assumption that personal-computer demand would soar, was executed with textbook precision and became a key strength that enabled Intel to dominate the world market for microprocessors. Barrett summed up his strategy: 'Put the capacity in place, and don't blink.' Intel is characteristically a company with a vision, a strategy and a commitment to stay the course and be the leader.

The first 30 years – 1965 to 1995
Few companies have matched Intel's phenomenal rise from when

it was started in 1968 by one of the inventors of the integrated circuit, the late Dr Robert Noyce, and by Dr Gordon Moore, now chairman Emeritus of Intel. They were joined shortly after the company started by another physicist, Dr Andrew Grove, now the chairman.

The fledgling company's mission was to develop memory storage for computing. By the late 1970s, Intel's research led to the development of the microprocessor, which ushered in the mass computing revolution and hastened the digital age. Intel legend is that as a start up company it developed the technology that 'turned the world on its ear and changed the way it works'.

Unlike Microsoft which has only known good times, Intel has had its share of bad times, and its overall success has followed three primary initiatives: first, the exponential growth in the computing capacity its microchips achieved, proving Moore's 'law' that semiconductor capacity would double every eighteen months at constant production costs; second, protecting its technology and intellectual rights against all invaders with conviction, aggression and determination; and third, marketing its products globally. Since 1987, Intel's revenues have increased more than ten-fold, and with gross profit margins that reached 60% it did its investors proud. Earnings per share jumped from 37 cents in 1987 to more than $5 in 1997.

Intel's gross margin expectation for 1999 is 57%, plus or minus a few points, compared to 54% for all of 1998. In the short term, Intel's gross margin percentage varies primarily with revenue levels and product mix.

The Intel story is well told in several books, including Andy Grove's *You Have to be Paranoid to Survive*. However, whatever happened in the past, Intel faces increasing competition and new market demands now, and as investors we may be fascinated by the past but must make our decisions on how we see the future.

The beginning of the end or the end of the beginning?

In 1997, long-running litigation sagas and bitter disputes were settled between Intel and two competitors, Advanced Micro Devices (AMD) and Cyrix (now part of National Semiconductor, NSM), who had both developed chips that competed with Intel in the PC market and could run Microsoft software. Competition followed the settlements and set the stage for microprocessor prices to fall. As they fell, the sub-$1000 PC, made possible partly because of the lower microprocessor prices, rapidly became the new growth sector in computer hardware. Analysts started questioning whether these low prices marked the beginning of the end for Intel's hitherto unassailable growth.

The 'beginning of the end' argument was that, regardless of anything else, Intel's big franchise was the high volume PC market and as microprocessor supply for this market now exceeded demand, inevitably microprocessors would become priced as commodities – following a pattern that has eroded profitability across most of the other silicone chip products.

The 'end of the beginning' argument for Intel was just as plausible. Yes, the mass PC market had become more competitive, and the 'Wintel' dominance of the PC market was being challenged, but the number of PCs installed worldwide was set to rise five-fold from 200 million in 1998 to more than one billion in the early years of the new century. Industry reports on the first quarter of 1998 showed Intel with 96.3% of the over-$1,200 PC market and 74.8% of the under-$1,200 segment.

As long as the industry grows, even if mass demand is spurred by availability of cheap products, Internet use is creating demand at such a high rate that the increased volume will call for both budget cost and high performance products. Intel's leadership over the years has come from both the new and ever more powerful chips it develops and the 'yesterday's' specification which it can sell cheaper.

Even though 1998 was a tough year, globally the demand for PCs grew at above 25% and Intel scored when Windows 98 was launched and Internet sales surged. The market for lower specification processors took off and so did the market for higher specification processors.

Industry analysts had expected that strong earnings growth would only resume after the introduction of Intel's 64 bit Merced chip for mainframe computing, after the turn of the century. They were wrong. The demand for powerful computing grew, and with it grew the demand for Intel's upmarket chips in the consumer market and in corporate computing. Intel proved again that it has the leading edge technology and manufacturing resources to make strategies for new beginnings.

A core technology for different markets

Intel's strategy developed in 1998 was to use one core technology as a foundation for developing a range of new generation products designed specifically for the needs of particular market segments, and to spread growth across the different sectors in the computing industry. To implement the strategy, four focused new operating groups were established. The Consumer Products group, the Business Platform group, the Small Business and Networking group, and the Digital Imaging and Video division. The new structure marked the change from the traditional strategy of designing ever-more powerful processors, aimed at the top end of the computer market segment, and migrating 'previous-generation' chips to the lower-end market segment.

Intel has been targeting the Unix mainframe and large corporate server markets, as a major market opportunity to service with leading technology. In 1997, Intel processors represented less than 20% of user spending on servers, and by the end of 2002 they are expected to represent over 55%. This rise in the importance of Intel processors in servers will be driven primarily by the launch, early in 2000, of the first processor (Merced) based on the 64 bit Intel IA-64 architecture.

Expectations are now that spending on Unix servers built on Intel-based architectures will largely displace Unix/RISC sales, rather than stopping NT. As a result, Unix on Intel is expected to increase from less than 15% of all Unix server spending to more than 40% by year-end 2002.

Business desktops and portable computers

Pentium and Pentium II chips already dominate the market for business desktops and portable computers, and the fastest versions are used in professional servers and workstations. Professional and enthusiast Performance PCs will remain under the Pentium II brand name and operate at speeds up to 600 mhz. The Pentium II Xeon is a new brand name for a line of processors designed specifically to meet the needs of mid-range and higher server and workstation business critical applications.

Basic personal computing

Sub-$1,000 computers now make up over a third of the retail desktop market in terms of units sold. Intel, which at one time had leaned towards leaving this market to AMD and Cyrix, moved aggressively into the entry level computer chip market, which it calls Basic Computing, with a new range of competitively priced Celeron chips running at 266 mhz and made the business payable, with the high volume compensating to some extent for the lower margins.

64 bit Intel architecture

By 2000, Intel will have introduced its 64 bit Alpha chip which will set new standards for server and Unix computing. Much as the Pentium and Windows NT opened a new franchise, the Alpha chip will do so again, bringing Intel's leadership into all levels of business computing.

Competitive advantage

Because Intel produces some 80 to 85% of the world's PC chips, economies of scale gives it an edge over all competitors. Product leadership underpins its strength. Intel can continue introducing new high-end technology in the PC market progressively, and, 'every time we do that, we raise the technology bar at the low-end.'

As the leader in 0.25 micron microprocessor production, Intel converted its entire microprocessor production to 0.25 micron technology by the beginning of the fourth quarter of 1998. The ability to ramp 0.25 micron process technology into full production enabled it to supply higher performance microprocessors at lower relative costs.

In January 1998, Intel announced it had created a chip-manufacturing process that will enable it to ship 600-megahertz microprocessors by the end of the year. It will begin shipping microprocessors based on its 0.18 micron manufacturing process – which allows the company to create chip circuits that are one five-hundreth the width of a human hair – in the third quarter of 1999, months and possibly years ahead of competitors.

The Research and Development spend in 1999 will be about $3 billion, up from $2.7 billion in 1998.

What can go wrong?

In the past, Intel's earnings growth momentum has been affected by economic downturns and latterly by increased competition. The new product strategy established in 1998 appears to have been effective in meeting competition and supplying different market needs, and only an extreme deterioration in global markets would be seriously damaging to prospects now.

Monitoring

`www.intel.com` is informative and an essential starting point. At times the scale of Intel's operations is such that inside a financial year projects cannot be brought to fruition and when monitoring an investment in Intel it is useful to remember this. It also helps to think of it as a highly tuned Ferrari on a racing track, not a fast BMW saloon on an autobahn. To investors who understand the company it has yielded opportunity after opportunity for low-risk high-reward investing.

Monitoring with a focus on finding buying opportunities should be rewarding.

IBM

Share Graph 1997–1998 International Business Machines Corp.
Primary Market – NYSE IBM

Price January 1999 $92
Market Value January 1999 $173 billion

SECTOR Technology INDUSTRY Computer Hardware
Top Line IBM Bottom Line S&P 500 Index Relative: Triangle
Marks Split
Left Scale: Top $ Price IBM, Bottom Volume in Thousands
Note: Graphic not rebased for two-for-one split in 1999.

PRICE PERFORMANCE	IBM		An investment made in		
Year 1998 %			January 1994 grew 570% by January 1999		

PRICE HISTORY	1998	1997	1996	1995	Notes
High Price	94.97	56.75	41.50	28.66	
Low Price	47.81	31.78	20.78	17.56	
High P/E	28.91	18.89	16.57	16.25	
Low P/E	14.55	10.58	8.30	9.96	

Chairman Louis V. Gerstner Jr., www.ibm.com
270,000 employees
One New Orchard Road, Armonk, NY 10504
Phone: (914) 499-1900 Fax: (914) 765-6021

Global Franchise: The business of information technology

With revenues double the combined revenues of Intel and Microsoft, IBM remains the 'big blue' of the information technology industry supported by global marketing and manufacturing operations. IBM's traditional 'big blue' franchise was built half a century ago with large mainframe computers, serving big blue chip corporate clients and public organizsations. For today's world, IBM's product range of hardware runs from high specification servers to sub-$1000 PCs. In 1986, extending its software franchise to this new arena, IBM acquired Lotus for its software applications in the developing networked world. Lotus was a software pioneer for the mass market, author of the first spread sheet and the popular communications programme Lotus Notes. IBM is uniquely powerful both in technology and as a marketing company with formidable financial resources. IBM revenues are generated by computer and communications hardware (41%), global services (37%), software (14%), global financing (3%) and other sources (2%). Operations are global with $81.5 billion revenue, 57% of which are from outside the US.

Setting a rational price

Portfolio 2001 WORKSHEET FOR TARGETING SHARE PRICES OF IBM IN 1999, 2000, 2001 & 2002
BASED ON FORECASTS MADE IN JANUARY 1999
EPS FISCAL 1998 TO DECEMBER $3.30

Growth	Year	Estimated EPS	P/E	Share Price Target	+10%	-10%	Notes
17.5%	1999	$3.88	26	$101	$112	$91	
17.5%	2000	$4.55	26	$118	$131	$106	
17.5%	2001	$5.35	26	$139	$154	$125	
17.5%	2002	$6.28	26	$163	$181	$146	

This 'what if' forecast suggests potential earnings and share prices based on current indications. Forecasts must be revised continuously in the light of all company results and industry, market and economic news. Forecasts can be misleading and cannot be treated as investment advice or used to motivate investments. See page 69.

Earnings per share growth expectations

In 1998, IBM proved that it can power earnings growth, even with the weakness in Asian economies that affected its export markets, regional businesses and hardware sales. Earnings per share growth of 9.2% for the year 1998 and 18.1% for the last quarter was achieved. The projected earnings growth of 15% for 1999 and 17.5% from 2000 is in line with revised expectations, following IBM's important growth in services and software, and the outlook for revival of growth in the global economy in 2000. The projected 17.5% earnings growth is a few per cent higher than analysts' consensus, and has been factored in to bring into the equation the group's importance as an Internet services and product supplier. In other companies in the sector, this Internet potential encourages considerably higher forward valuations.

Earnings multiple expectations

IBM's improved earnings growth for the year to December 1998, its blue chip credentials, an environment of low interest rates, and the strong technology equity market support a rational and conservative forecast for share prices at a multiple of 1.5 times the expected 17.5% earnings per share growth rate from 2000 – 26 times earnings per share. Relevant company, industry, market and economic news should encourage readers to revise forecasts as IBM is increasingly recognized as a prime investing priority for institutional and private investors globally.

Past performance indicators

Growth Rates %		IBM	S&P 500	Industry	Sector	Notes
Earnings per share 5 year		NM	20.71	40.92	37.42	
1998 last reported vs 1997		6.22	12.93	22.49	25.62	
Sales 5 year 1994-1998		4.00	16.02	23.11	34.08	
1998 last reported vs 1997		2.99	12.04	18.12	23.21	
5 yr P/E Comparison: high		32.91	41.61	52.61	41.60	
low		11.59	14.37	11.53	15.91	

Profitability Ratios						
Gross Margin 1998	%	38.10	49.12	31.65	52.36	
5 year average	%	2.54	10.19	4.28	11.00	
Net Profit Margin 1998	%	7.54	10.84	4.20	11.24	
5 year average	%	2.54	10.19	4.28	11.00	
5 Year Returns on:						
Assets	%	2.72	8.29	8.56	12.56	
Investment	%	4.44	13.04	14.32	17.33	
Equity	%	10.52	21.44	19.86	21.28	

■■■

The growth story

Drenched in the blue

Louis V. Gerstner, Jr., is the chairman and chief executive officer of IBM, and his introduction to the announcement of results for the year 1998 and the last quarter to December summarized the achievements of an exceptionally successful year:

> We had a good quarter that capped a year of significant progress for us. We showed particular strength in services and software – two areas of critical importance as our customers increasingly embrace e-business and network computing. In fact, nearly 60 per cent of our total gross profits now come from global services and software, and both businesses provide substantial recurring revenues. Our OEM business – the sale of our technology to other companies – also continued to grow strongly, benefiting from an expanding base of IBM technological leadership.

We achieved good earnings results in the quarter despite a number of challenges: continued weakness in Asia and Latin America, ongoing softness in memory chip prices, and pricing pressures and product transitions that adversely affected our server business. We have been able to deliver consistent financial results because of the breadth and diversity of our overall business portfolio, which is unmatched in our industry.

Total hardware sales declined 2% from the year-ago period to $11.3 billion. Overall, IBM services revenues were $7.1 billion, an increase of 20% compared with the fourth quarter of 1997. Services revenues grew by more than $1 billion compared with last year's fourth quarter, and the company's services unit signed more than $9 billion in new services contracts in the quarter.

Total software revenues were $4.1 billion, up 9% (8% in constant currency) year over year, with particular strength in database, transaction processing, and Tivoli systems management products. In addition, IBM had record shipments of more than five million Lotus Notes seats in the fourth quarter. The overall software gross profit margin rose more than 3 points to 75.2%.

IBM's total gross profit margin was 39% in the fourth quarter compared with 40.1% in the year-ago period and the expense-to-revenue ratio improved by 1.5 points year over year to 25.9%.

Full-year 1998 results

Net income for the 12 months ended December 31, 1998 was $6.3 billion, or a record $6.57 per diluted common share, compared with net income of $6.1 billion, or $6.01 per diluted common share, in the year-earlier period. Revenues for the year ended 31 December 1998 were a record $81.7 billion, an increase of 4% (6% at constant currency) from the previous year's $78.5 billion.

IBM generated $9.3 billion in cash from operations in 1998, and the company completed the year with $5.8 billion in cash.

Common share repurchases totalled $6.9 billion in 1998. The average number of shares outstanding in 1998 was 934.5 million compared with 983.3 million in 1997. There was a total of 915.9 million common shares outstanding at year-end 1998.

IBM before Gerstner

IBM's attraction to investors has turned a full circle since 1992, the year it sustained a $4.97 billion loss which led to the recruitment of Louis Gerstner as new CEO – with a brief to save the business.

IBM's history pre-Gerstner covers two distinct periods from when it was formed in 1911. The first was to the 1970s when it was well established as the world's dominant computing company and one of the world's largest and most profitable enterprises. Then, the second phase ran on into the 1980s as the company was hampered by a bureaucratic management regime unable to cope with a new computing environment which started when the upstart desktop computer industry started to set the pace of change. In this environment, IBM's dominance in the mainframe market became progressively less relevant.

In addition to its management woes, restrictions introduced by the US anti-trust authorities dampened entrepreneurial opportunities and, at the same time, management misjudgements led to blunder after blunder. In an increasingly competitive business climate, by 1992, IBM's loss of market share and competitive advantage culminated in the multibillion-dollar losses which ushered in the Gerstner era and the prospect that a break-up of IBM would be necessary to salvage value for shareholders.

Louis Gerstner came in as chief executive in 1993, from outside the industry. Though he came from the food company Nabisco, the description which newspapers like to use of him as a 'snack food salesman' is nonsense. He knew the real world of business in the computer age hands on from heading American Express's global credit card operations before joining Nabisco.

Gerstner soon scrapped the mooted break-up plans and initiated a programme to regenerate IBM by building on its strengths. A 'restructuring' which called for slashing operating expenses was inevitable to firm the foundations for a new growth strategy from a position of strength.

IBM strategy redefined

Gerstner's core strategy was redefining IBM as a serious player in the digital age. He recognized that the Internet would result in explosive growth in the pool of data available to computer users globally and, in this environment, that big mainframe computers, where IBM still held a strong foothold, would become the core resource for millions of personal computers globally accessing information from databases stored on them.

This 'networkcentric' computing environment would also lead to a rise in the sales of mainframe computers, which in turn would grow IBM's highly profitable software, semiconductor and service units.

Gerstner concentrated next on building software resources. In 1995, IBM acquired the software company Lotus for $3.5 billion, to position the group as a communications software supplier for both the business and personal mass computing markets. In 1996 Tivoli, a niche supplier of distributed software for networking and then Unison Software and Software Artistry, both of which complement Tivoli's network computing offerings, were acquired.

The following schedule of IBM's earnings for the first quarter of 1999 to 31 March show the significant growth in high margin services and softwares revenues which have encouraged investors:

| | Three Months Ended 31 March | | |
	1999	1998	Per cent Change
REVENUE			
Hardware	$8,584	£7,318	17.3%
Gross profit margin	27.2%	28.7%	
Global Services	$7,550	$6,341	19.1%
Gross profit margin	26.3%	27.0%	
Software	$2,920	$2,644	10.4%
Gross profit margin	81.0%	79.6%	
Global Financing	$705	$719	-1.9%
Gross profit margin	55.9%	47.1%	
Enterprise Investments/Other	$558	$596	-6.4%
Gross profit margin	32.6%	33.1%	
TOTAL REVENUE	$20,317	$17,618	15.3%
GROSS PROFIT	$7,258	$6,450	12.5%
Gross profit margin	35.7%	36.6%	

Commitment to marketing

Underlying all Gerstner's plans has been a commitment to marketing. IBM, once known for its arrogance in the marketing world, is now characterized by responsiveness to the market place and dynamic product development across the range of computer systems, software, networking systems, storage devices and microelectronics. Wherever there is an opportunity, IBM is a player.

Corporate computing

IBM remains a major global force in corporate computing. While the personal computer market snatches the headlines, corporate and public service computing pays much of the $800 billion spent annually on computing goods and services, and brings most of the profits earned by the industry. IBM still gets a healthy share of these revenues, but no longer defines itself as serving any particular market. It has redefined its role as creating the industry's most advanced information technologies, and helping customers apply those technologies to improve what they do and how they do it.

Over the last decade, PCs have evolved to become as powerful as the mainframes of a few years earlier. Predictably, mainframe users have been switching to networks of PCs, so IBM's response has been to develop the server computer market by modernizing its mainframe computers to make them less expensive; developing server computers running Windows NT; and capitalizing on the growth of Windows NT, SAP's R/3 and other leading software applications for enterprise computing.

Selling solutions

Traditionally, in the 'big blue' era, IBM only sold its own products. Gerstner, the marketing man, changed the focus to concentrate on selling solutions, rather than packages of hardware and software. IBM is no longer wedded to its own products, and where a better result can be achieved by integrating and consolidating products and services from other companies, it delivers what the market wants.

Lotus Tivoli and other software acquisitions

Total software revenues were $4.1 billion, up 9% (8% in constant currency) year over year, with particular strength in database, transaction processing, and Tivoli systems management products. In 1998, IBM's software revenues grew to $13.5 billion, closely trailing

Microsoft. When the company bought Lotus, industry cynics had 'no doubts' that the enterprising Lotus team would not survive as a unit in the IBM family, but they were proved wrong. There were 1.6 million Lotus Notes users when IBM bought the company. In the fourth quarter of 1998 alone, five million were supplied, and now there are over 24 million. Since acquiring Tivoli systems in 1996 for its software to manage distributed computing systems, IBM has made fourteen strategic acquisitions of software and services companies, and now a third of its software revenue comes from network computing software.

In 1995, only 10% of IBM's software revenues were from distributed software.

Small and mid-size businesses

Small and mid-size businesses make up 99% of all businesses globally, employ 80% of the world's workforce, and account for 60% of Internet spending and 45% of global IT spending. IBM has homed in on this potential and defines itself as the leading technology vendor to small and mid-size businesses around the world. The growth in this sector is behind the well-conceived and successfully promoted 'e-business' initiative, directed at business growth on the Internet.

The Internet and e-business

IBM recognized the Internet as one of the 'once-per-century revolutions' that transform commerce and communications, like 'the clipper ships, railroads . . . and the interstate highway systems had done in the past'. Electronic commerce is expected to grow from under $8 billion in 1998 to over $100 billion by the turn of the century and through its 'e-business' initiatives and programmes, IBM integrates solutions to get clients up and running.

Java

Seeking a greater stake in networked computing, IBM is investing resources in Sun's Java programming which it sees as an ideal language for a networked world that evolved with networked computers running on unmatched operating systems. A programme written in Java can be structured to run on any and all of the operating systems employed at the same time, from mainframes to laptops. Since it licensed Java from Sun Microsystems, IBM has employed 2,500 Java professionals and invested hundreds of millions of dollars in developing a full Java-based operating system.

Java programmes could even be one of the solutions that break Microsoft's dominance of desktop software, and Lotus has already released 'e-Suite', a set of word-processing and other desktop applications written entirely in Java to run on network systems. IBM is co-developing Java OS for Business with Sun Microsystems, and has teamed up with Intel to work on processors to optimize the possibilities of the system.

Competitive advantage

For the sixth consecutive year, in 1998, IBM was awarded the most US patents, shattering the previous record by more than 40%. The company received 2,658 US patents in 1998 from the US Patent and Trademark Office, earning 934 more patents than it did in 1997, and eclipsing the next closest company by 38%. It started 1998 by winning seven innovation awards at the International Winter Consumer Electronics Show, a pattern of recognition which continues. Mainframes, though a shrinking part of IBM's business, remain a development priority for hardware and software.

Leading-edge microchip technology

In 1997, IBM announced the fastest computer chip ever tested using copper based chip technology, and in 1998 it announced it had perfected an exceptionally high-speed, innovative 'SiGe' technology using a germanium chip which it is moving from the laboratory to the market place.

Multifunction, low-cost, mobile client devices capable of communicating over voice and data networks represent a key element of the future of computing. SiGe technology has the potential to be a new force behind the creation of powerful new micro communications devices, like single-chip watch-sized wireless phones and products combining the capabilities of cellular phones, global positioning and Internet access in one package.

Global brand and resources

As a leading global brand in computer hardware, software and services, IBM leverages off its established name in all markets reaching out to new customer bases. Formidable financial strength is supported by the global network of marketing outlets which is particularly strong in the US and Euroland.

Share buy backs

Committed to buying back its own shares to boost shareholder returns, IBM continues a buy programme which to April 1998 included:

Date Announced	Value (billions)	Stock Close
Jan. 31, 1995	$2.5	$72.125
July 25, 1995	2.5	108.375
Nov. 28, 1995	2.5	97.000
April 30, 1996	2.5	107.750
Nov. 26, 1996	3.5	158.000
April 4, 1997	3.5	158.375
Oct. 28, 1997	3.5	99.375
April 28, 1998	3.5	116.000

Free cash flow for 1998 was $6 billion. IBM spent approximately $9.6 billion on share repurchases in 1998 and will probably do the same again in 1999. The average number of shares outstanding in the quarter was 919.8 million compared with 964.8 million during the same period of 1997.

What can go wrong?

Risks to the share price are mainly from a general softening in equity markets. When market valuations for IBM were more conservative, investors were afforded considerable protection by the formidable financial strength of the group, its strong cash flow and cash resources. Now, as valuations have risen to higher market multiples, the share price will be more vulnerable to sharp corrections in the event of changed equity market conditions.

Monitoring

www.ibm.com is comprehensively informative on developments in the company and current results announcements are clear, well explained and discussed. News about IBM and its major competitors is carried in all the financial media.

SUN MICROSYSTEMS

Share Graph 1997–1998 Sun Microsystems Inc.
Primary Market – NASDAQ – SUNW

Price January 1999 $53.25
Market Value January 1999 $40.58 billion

SECTOR Technology INDUSTRY Computer Hardware
Top Line SUNW Bottom Line S&P 500 Index Relative: Triangle
Marks Split
Left Scale: Top $ Price, Bottom Volume in Thousands
Note: Graphic not rebased for two for one split in 1999.

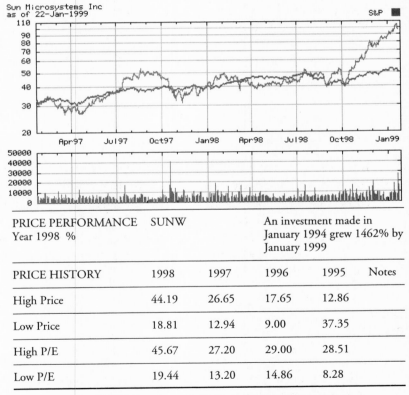

Sun Microsystems Inc
as of 22-Jan-1999   S&P ■

PRICE PERFORMANCE	SUNW		An investment made in
Year 1998 %			January 1994 grew 1462% by January 1999

PRICE HISTORY	1998	1997	1996	1995	Notes
High Price	44.19	26.65	17.65	12.86	
Low Price	18.81	12.94	9.00	37.35	
High P/E	45.67	27.20	29.00	28.51	
Low P/E	19.44	13.20	14.86	8.28	

Chmn/CEO/Pres Scott G. McNealy, www.sun.com
26,300 employees
901 San Antonio Road, Palo Alto, CA 94303
Phone: (650) 960-1300 Fax: (650) 336-0646

Global franchise: Mainframe computing

Since its inception in 1982, Sun's motto has been: 'The Network Is The Computer'. Following a networkcentric strategy, Sun has concentrated on becoming a leading developer and manufacturer of hardware and software for Unix-based workstation computers, storage devices, and servers for powering enterprise-wide intranets. It is the largest Unix computer manufacturer that uses its own chips (SPARC) and operating systems (Solaris). Sun's best-known product among the public is Java, a programming language that creates software that can run unchanged on any kind of computer. Java is now widely used on the Internet for creating graphics and supporting Internet programmes, and is becoming an unofficial industry standard. Workstation sales were the traditional backbone for Sun's revenues, prior to the successful introduction of servers for network computing which now account for 50% of the company's profit. Sun supplies hardware and software to government organizations, telecommunications operators, financial, manufacturing, and educational markets. With more than $10.5 billion in annual revenues, Sun products are supplied in more than 150 countries. Nearly 50% of revenues are earned outside the US.

Setting a rational price

Portfolio 2001 WORKSHEET FOR TARGETING SHARE PRICES OF SUN MICROSYSTEMS IN 1999, 2000, 2001 & 2002 BASED ON FORECASTS MADE IN JANUARY 1999 EPS TO YEAR ENDED JUNE 1988 $0.97

Growth	Year	Estimated EPS	P/E	Share Price Target	+10%	-10%	Notes
22%	1999	$1.40	40	$63	$70	$57	
22%	2000	$1.70	40	$65	$72	$59	
20%	2001	$2.04	37.5	$77	$85	$69	
20%	2002	$2.45	35	$86	$95	$77	

This 'what if' forecast suggests potential earnings and share prices based on current indications. Forecasts must be revised continuously in the light of all company results and industry, market and economic news. Forecasts can be misleading and cannot be treated as investment advice or used to motivate investments. See page 69.

Earnings per share growth expectations

Sun's commitment that 'the network is the computer' is being validated, and it now holds high network ground in several vital hardware and software areas. These include Unix based hardware and software programmes and operating systems, Java and its secondary language Jini supporting communications on network computers, a new association with America on Line which is acquiring Netscape, and an increasing relevance as an Internet company. Sun is promoting its Internet relevance with an extensive '.com' marketing campaign.

Analysts' consensus earnings per share growth of between 20% and 25% are reasonable in relation to current performance and expectations in the industry. The *Portfolio 2001* worksheet projects 22% growth in 1999 and 2000, and scales back to 20% for 2001 and 2002 to allow for increased competition in enterprise computing after the launch of Microsoft NT5.

Earnings multiple expectations

The market price of Sun shares will now depend on whether the market values the company as a computer manufacturer or as an Internet opportunity. A computer manufacturer with earnings per share growth of 22% in the technology sector is likely to trade at an earnings multiple in the 30s, but if Sun is seen by investors as the one-stop source for business users to gain access to e-commerce, e-mail and web serving with Java and Jini software, Sun may be valued as an Internet prospect. In that event, Sun shares might trade at much higher levels in line with other Internet prospects.

The *Portfolio 2001* worksheet is constructed on the basis of Sun being a computer hardware and software supplier with strong profits and excellent scope to accelerate earnings growth as the Internet opportunity develops. The earnings multiple proposed of 40 for 1999 and 2000 follows views taken by analysts in the industry, and multiples are scaled down for 2001 and 2002 to reflect more competition after the launch of Windows NT. Target share prices are at best informed guesstimates, but with companies valued as Internet players, targets have no real chance of being of any predictive value. Internet share values are in uncharted waters.

No adjustment to Earnings Expectations has been factored in for Sun's purchase of Netscape with AOL as sufficient informations is not available.

Past performance indicators

Growth Rates %		SUNW	S&P 500	Industry	Sector	Notes
Earnings per share 5 year		38.99	20.56	40.67	37.02	
1998 last reported vs 1997		1.51	12.25	22.37	25.07	
Sales 5 year 1994-1998		17.84	15.83	22.93	33.80	
Profitability Ratios						
Gross Margin 1998	%	52.06	49.02	31.65	52.36	
5 year average	%	46.27	48.72	32.48	52.29	
Net Profit Margin 1998	%	7.55	10.84	4.20	11.24	
5 year average	%	6.72	10.89	4.28	11.00	
5 Year Returns on:						
Assets	%	12.71	8.29	8.56	12.56	
Investment	%	22.66	13.04	15.32	17.33	
Equity	%	23.44	21.44	19.86	21.28	

The growth story

Recent earnings

Sun Microsystems reported second-quarter earnings for fiscal 1999 with double-digit sales growth and continued success in sales of powerful server computers that host large networks.

For the quarter ended 27 December 1998, net income rose 75% to $261.1 million, or 64 cents a diluted share, from $149.4 million, or 38 cents a share, a year earlier when conditions were depressed by the economic turmoil in Asia. The previous year's reported figures include acquisition-related charges of $12 million in the comparable quarter and $110 million in the year-earlier period. Excluding those charges, Sun's profit rose 22% to $272.3 million, or 67 cents a share, from $223.2 million, or 57 cents a share.

Sun as an Internet company

The growth of Windows NT and the impact of Intel's Pentium microchips started the migration of corporate business away from Unix. In 1997, Sun's performance mirrored the loss of market share by Unix computing to Microsoft NT, but by the quarter ending 29 March 1998, Sun's fortunes had changed and the company was in a strong growth phase. By January 1999, the market started valuing Sun as a 'hot' Internet prospect.

Some analysts who support the Internet valuations compare the current technology revolution to the US gold boom of the nineteenth century, and one has been quoted saying, 'Hitting gold in the gold rush was great, but selling railroad ties was also pretty darn good, and the risk wasn't there.' So too with Sun, he suggests. Internet portal stocks have taken off in value and the more sites that come up on the net, the more servers Sun should be able to sell.

The Internet will continue to expand relentlessly as radio and TV did earlier this century and, once bandwidth problems are resolved, consumers will be inclined to tap into the net for more of their entertainment and information needs. On Sun's credo that the network is the computer, its growth story will be a big one.

Servers and workstations

Sun's Solaris is the leading operating system in the fragmented Unix operating market. Sun's response to increased competition has been to improve its Solaris systems to become the industry benchmark, and to change emphasis from workstations to servers.

One of the effects of fast developing technology has been that when demand for a product matures, prices drop. Following this approach, small businesses and individuals may soon opt to buy their own servers to run their businesses more efficiently and even to service personal web sites instead of renting space on other servers. If so, Sun Microsystems and other computer vendors could have a potential near mass market for servers in small businesses and in homes that create mini-networks with other businesses, or in other homes with more than one computer.

Sun has a revenue stream from licensing its Unix technology and software. For example, there was a deal struck in 1997 with Fujitsu, and its US subsidiary Amdahl, who licensed the Solaris operating environment for use on its Intel architecture-based servers, and in August 1997, Sun made a similar arrangement with NCR Corp., to offer Solaris with NCR servers for big corporate users.

Java software

Apart from Java's success on the Internet, the software has the support of independent and corporate programmers. Over 14,000 programmers have attended Sun Java conferences and, among the corporate developers who are behind Java, IBM has made a significant commitment to programming, and is working with Sun to develop an operating system for server computers which will be entirely based on Java.

Java licensing arrangements have been completed with major companies including Sony, Motorola, Scientific-Atlanta, and Ericsson, in applications from cell phones to TV set top boxes.

Java also attracts supporters because of its potential to lessen Microsoft's dominance in the industry. Sun and the leading database company, Oracle, have a project called 'raw iron', which is working to develop computers that barely use an operating system. The objective is that an Oracle database will run on only the computer's microprocessor.

Competitive advantage

The commitment that the network is the computer proved to be a sound policy, the benefits of which are being seen in the core business of supplying hardware and in success with Java and Solaris software. The association with America on Line in acquiring Netscape further entrenches Sun's position as a leading vendor and player in the Internet support industry.

What can go wrong?

Both 1997 and 1998 have been strong years for Unix workstation and server suppliers, as Year 2000 readiness requirements and the advent of the euro have spurred exceptional demand, and 2000 will probably also lead to similar demand led strength. However, current high levels of business may mask the reality that computer hardware is a very competitive industry and sustained industry growth will depend on a revival of demand globally. Microsoft NT has not yet been accepted as sufficiently powerful and reliable for critical applications but when Microsoft NT5 is launched at the end of 1999 or in 2000, if the power and reliability of the pro-gramme is increased as expected, Sun will face a far more competitive business computing environment that will increasingly challenge its Unix business.

On the hardware side, Dell, Hewlett Packard, IBM and several other large suppliers compete for business in the competitive professional market, and margins will be vulnerable. Also, when Intel's 64 bit Alpha chip is commercialized in 2000 or 2001, the spectrum of competition in the high specification server market will become considerably more competitive.

Sun's alliance with America on Line in acquiring Netscape holds the promise that it will support Sun's operations, and while an enthusiastic Internet investor mentality drives the prices of shares which can benefit from the Internet, at this stage it is early to draw firm investing conclusions.

Similar software programmes to Java are being developed elsewhere. Lucent, for instance, started a programme called Inferno which it has consolidated in a joint venture and intends to exploit, and Microsoft has a programme which it might introduce at any time.

Sun's CEO Scott McNealy, is a vociferous and determined antagonist of both Microsoft and Bill Gates, but he may find at the end of the day that hostilities with Microsoft are not easily won. Microsoft Windows has become a formidably powerful and diverse software resource, and for what it does it is not expensive. Microsoft's value to users and the expansion of the Internet should not be underestimated. Promoters of simpler alternatives will have to persuade consumers to be satisfied with less and it will not be easy to do this.

Monitoring

www.sun.com gives a good picture of Sun's product portfolio and business developments. The introduction of Windows NT5 by 2000, and all the developments in Sun's association with America on Line and Netscape, will be fully covered by financial and industry press and the general media. With Sun now increasingly being valued as an Internet share rather than a computer hardware share, investors will also have the difficult task of reviewing whether soaring share valuations for such shares will prove sustainable.

SAP

Share Graph 1997–1998 SAP AG
Primary Market – Frankfurt – NYSE SAP

Price January 1999 $32.19
Market Value January 1999 $16.8 billion

SECTOR Technology INDUSTRY Software and Programming
Top Line SAP Bottom Line S&P 500 Index Relative
Right Scale: Top $ Price, Bottom Volume in Thousands

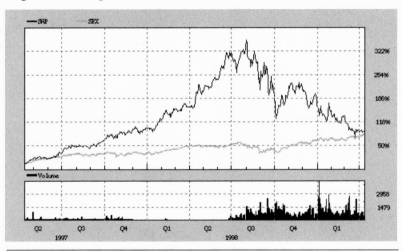

PRICE PERFORMANCE	SAP AOA		An investment made in January 1994 grew 200% by January 1999		
PRICE HISTORY	1998	1997	1996	1995	Notes
High Price	62.25	28.25	12.13	NA	$ ADR
Low Price	25.94	10.65	10.01	NA	
High P/E	NA	69.38	57.36	NA	
Low P/E	NA	26.15	51.15	NA	

Founders/Co-Chairmen Dietmar Hopp, Hasso Plattner, www.sap.com
12,800 employees
Neurottstrasse 16, 69190 Walldorf, Germany
Phone: (212) 815-2367 Fax: (212) 570-3050

Global Franchise: Enterprise Computing Software

The German company SAP is Europe's largest and the world's fifth largest independent software firm after Microsoft, Oracle, Computer Associates Microsoft and IBM. It dominates the market for corporate client/server enterprise resource planning programmes, and services about a third of the market for software used to integrate and process information in areas including product distribution, finance, human resources and manufacturing. SAP's 3/R software programme is used by nearly 9000 companies including global leaders like Chevron, GM, Microsoft, and Nestlé. With the increased use of networks and computer networking the popularity of corporate client/server systems has surged, as has use of SAP's year 2000 complaint software. Three of SAP's founders control about two-thirds of the company. The company operates globally and almost 40% of revenues come from the US.

Setting a rational price

Portfolio 2001 WORKSHEET FOR TARGETING SHARE PRICES OF SAP IN 1999, 2000, 2001 & 2002
BASED ON FORECASTS MADE IN JANUARY 1999
EPS $0.40: 1998

Growth	Year	Estimated EPS	P/E	Share Price Target	+10%	-10%	Notes
15%	1999	$0.46	40	$18	$20	$16	High P/E
25%	2000	$0.57	50	$28	$31	$25	
25%	2001	$0.71	50	$35	$39	$31	
25%	2002	$0.88	50	$44	$49	$40	

This 'what if' forecast suggests potential earnings and share prices based on current indications. Forecasts must be revised continuously in the light of all company results and industry, market and economic news. Forecasts can be misleading and cannot be treated as investment advice or used to motivate investments. See page 69.

1998 profits slow down
SAP shocked the market in January 1999 with an announcement that earnings for the fiscal year 1998 would not be clocked in at the 30 to 35% level which management had indicated, and would only be about 15%. It traced the problem particularly to Japan, where

large orders failed to materialize at the end of the year. SAP has since indicated that earnings above 25% will resume in 1999. Net income rose 63% in 1997, boosted to an extent by a currency gain. With the company's market leadership and its background of past profit growth, the indications of the highly credible management have been accepted by analysts generally, and are the basis for the *Portfolio 2001* forecast.

Earnings per share growth expectations

The earnings multiple to target share prices in the worksheet was taken as 40 times current earnings for 1999 and 50 times current earnings for the following years. Increasing the multiple assumed that management will have put the company back on rails to growth by 2000.

Shares trading at multiples equal to twice the earnings per share growth rate are vulnerable to severe correction on the slimmest disappointments and, in the US market, SAP would be unlikely to command such a high rating without the support of local German investors. SAP is Europe's premier information technology share, and a constituent of the German Dax index, and it attracts substantial institutional support particularly from Germany.

SAP is a doubtful candidate for a low-risk high-reward investment because of the high share price, not because of a setback in earnings growth. The likelihood is that strong earnings will resume in 1999 and when they are entrenched the market price may be higher but the risk for investors will be lower.

Past performance indicators

Growth Rates %		SAP	S&P 500	Industry	Sector	Notes
Earnings per share 5 year		NM	20.71	34.98	37.42	
1998 last reported vs 1997		92.53	12.93	49.98	25.62	
Sales 5 year 1994-1998		NM	16.02	35.81	34.08	
Profitability Ratios						
Gross Margin 1998	%	89.93	49.02	83.54	52.36	
5 year average	%	NA	48.72	81.61	52.29	
Net Profit Margin 1998	%	15.17	10.84	21.93	11.24	
5 year average	%	NA	10.19	19.28	11.00	
5 Year Returns on:						
Assets	%	NA	8.29	18.76	12.56	
Investment	%	NA	13.04	24.66	17.33	
Equity	%	NA	21.44	28.57	21.28	

The growth story

This table, presented by SAP, shows its phenomenal growth to 1997:

Selected Financial Highlights
(in millions of DM, unless otherwise indicated)

	1993	1994	1995	1996	1997
Sales	1,101.7	1,831.1	2,696.4	3,722.2	6,017.5
per employee	0.320	0.414	0.419	0.455	0.521
Personnel expenditure	466.2	675.2	956.7	1,338.5	2,074.9
as % of sales	42.3	36.9	35.5	36.0	34.5
Employees at year-end	3,648	5,229	6,857	9,202	12,856
Development expenditure	267.7	369.6	438.2	588.9	813.3
as % of sales	24.3	20.2	16.3	15.8	13.5
Net income	146.3	281.2	404.8	567.5	925.4
as % of sales	13.3	15.4	15.0	15.2	15.4
Earnings per share (DM)	1.46	2.78	4.00	5.48	8.87
(adjusted according to DVFA/SG method)					

Cash flow (DVFA/SG method)	212.1	386.5	559.0	782.7	1,230.1
as % of sales	19.3	21.1	20.7	21.0	20.4
Balance sheet total	1,306.2	1,749.7	2,218.2	3,367.1	5,070.3
Equity	1,008.6	1,236.2	1,529.5	2,211.3	3,062.4
as % balance sheet total	77.2	70.7	69.0	65.7	60.4
Dividend per ordinary share (DM)	0.44	0.85	1.30	1.80	2.80
Dividend per preference share (DM)	0.48	0.90	1.35	1.85	2.85

The high growth was achieved across all segments of its operations in all the countries it services, with the strongest growth in the US following the launch of a US marketing organization in 1986 and 1987:

SAP 1987	DM	US$	%
Product	4.10 billion	2.29 billion	+56
Consulting	1.25 billion	698 million	+70
Training	580 million	324 million	+90
Other	89 million	50 million	+78
Americas	2.56 billion	1.43 billion	+87
Europe (ex-Germany)	1.4 billion	781 million	+58
Germany	1.15 billion	642 million	+26
Asia-Pacific	785 million	438 million	+69

For the first quarter of 1998, revenues break down as follows:

	DM	US$	%
Product	1,065 million	577 million	+57
Consulting	408 million	221 million	+69
Training	197 million	107 million	+91
Other	12 million	6.5 million	+20
Americas	749 million	406 million	+68
Europe (ex-Germany)	385 million	208 million	+75
Germany	352 million	191 million	+53

Returns to investors

Founders Dietmar Hopp, Professor Dr Hasso Plattner and Dr Klaus E. Tschira control 66% of the company and head its successful management.

SAP went public in November 1988 at an issue price of DM 750 per share. The share has been split several times and shareholders who held one share of common stock when SAP first went public, and reinvested the dividends in additional shares have seen their original investment rise to approximately DM 35,600 by the end of 1997, representing an increase of about 4767%.

A new generation of software products

Enterprise computing in major companies surged in the early 1990s as the Internet opened up easy global connections. At the same time, with the growth in global business, demands were made for greater efficiency in business computing and ease of networking. The Internet and intranets have also led to greater competition across the business spectrum, which in turn encouraged a surge in business process management.

SAP's core and flagship product 'R/3', introduced in 1992, is the core module for a developing family of integrated programmes that combine to form a complete management system which speeds the flow of information, reduces infrastructure costs and empowers managers to oversee and control multiple businesses better. R/3 has been designed to integrate a range of software applications into a single computing resource, to give management control over all functions that make a business work. R/3 has been described as a 'virtual management system' and a 'new generation' of software product.

Growth strategy

By progressively improving established applications, introducing new applications and solutions, and simplifying and accelerating their implementation, SAP builds growth within its client base and inevitably, as the installed base grows, consulting and training revenues also grow. There are now over 1000 software applications which can be introduced within the R/3 framework for a global customer base. SAP claims it has 33% of the enterprise application software market globally, and an installed base of over 12,000 users which underwrites its growth with system upgrades and consulting.

The percentage of business generated by all foreign subsidiaries grew from 48% in 1993 to 81% in 1997.

Treating a business as a single entity

R/3 treats a business as a single entity with all functions and hierarchies including manufacturing, finance, sales, accounting, human resources and other business and management activities working as a cohesive unit. Functions that are often dealt with by different computing regimes in a large business are managed by SAP software to work within a single integrated regime. The software applications can also be customized for specific major industries starting with the R/3 umbrella programme and expanding to cover new uses with add on applications.

Free standing programmes and industry specific programmes

The SAP programmes which start with R/3 and can be built up with additional applications have been developed specifically for major industry groups, including aerospace, automotive, banking, chemicals, consumer products, engineering and construction, health care, high tech electronics, insurance, media, oil and gas and global trading.

Recently SAP has developed a new family of products which function as free standing programmes and can also be integrated in the R/3.4 system. The first of these programmes are for sales data, supply chain management and data warehousing.

In tandem with this more flexible architecture, SAP has set up 15 business units to assemble software systems tailored for15 specific industries. Each industry package has R/3.4 at its core, but the business teams can add software from other companies where this fits the client's requirement best.

New Products

Difficulty and complexity of installing R/3 and allied programmes has been a weakness that has inhibited growth. To meet this difficulty, Release 4 of R/3 (R/3.4) incorporated improvements that simplified installation and operation. With the new programmes, installation time has been reduced from as much as a few years for some installations to as little as a few months for similar new cases.

SAP is also modifying its R/3 software to make it more manageable for smaller businesses, and some 'ready to run' software is being pre-loaded in computer servers as installed programmes.

The millennium bug and the euro

The Year 2000 computer compliance problem has been a focus since it was identified and SAP has been one of the main companies offering solutions globally. The euro has been another growth opportunity. Anyone selling goods and services in EMU countries had to be able to accept payment in euros starting 1 January 1999. Euros and the national currencies of EMU nations are then all in circulation until mid-2002, when national currencies will be withdrawn.

During this transition period, companies in EMU nations will be keeping two sets of books, one in the home currency, the other in euros. While the home currency is expected to remain the preferred method of payment well into the transition period, tax and other government reports will have to be made in euros. Additional software applications will be necessary because in an accountancy method known as triangulation, the Euro will be imposed as an intermediate step in all currency translations. A French company accepting payment in marks will first have to convert the marks into euros and then into francs.

SAP software is multilingual and multi-currency and has been developed to cater for all euro accounting contingencies. According to regulations, euro conversions must be made at a level of precision of six significant figures, which many accounting systems currently can't handle. There are only two ways companies can make their financial software euro-compliant: by fixing their old system or by buying a new one. SAP has been actively seeking business from this new opportunity.

Competitive advantage

In certain applications, including banking, government financial accounting and business applications like airline booking, SAP is recognized has having the world's benchmark products. It follows that unless there is a very good reason, it is unlikely that customers will uninstall R/3 and switch to competitive products. This entrenches SAP's market position and their potential to earn high profits from their installed base, as clients extend existing applications and as new upgrades and applications come on the market.

Management have been astute in working in concert with other industry, technology leaders and professionals to harness their capabilities into new programmes. These include IBM which has a separate SAP service function (see www.ibm.com) and Microsoft where a team of SAP programmers is reportedly stationed. It also has a close working relationship with Intel, developing software for Intel's microprocessors, and the two companies have also launched a joint venture, Pandesic. For $25,000, Pandesic gives small to mid-size businesses a full software programme with everything they need to initiate business on the Internet.

Pandesic seamlessly handles marketing, order processing and fulfilment, inventory pricing, materials management, tax handling, payment processing, shipping and handling logistics, financial reporting, and vendor-payment processes associated with electronic commerce transactions.

Other recent associations are with Arthur Andersen Consulting to create new business solutions for the utilities industry, and PriceWaterhouseCoopers with whom they are working for the chemicals industry.

What can go wrong?

SAP's slower growth in 1998 probably reflected a very ambitious company with a global customer base and global growth potential encountering economic difficulties in Japan, Asia and other emerging economies. Sustained weakness in the global economy will impact on SAP's growth, and the effect could be that the company loses the support of trained programmers and customer support staff who will take time to replace when conditions improve.

Microsoft Windows NT5 is also likely to claim a large share of corporate computing, and encourage more focus on costs when new applications are introduced. This will affect SAP's growth but will not necessarily cut across its entrenched business.

Monitoring

Investors should monitor business strategy followed by SAP as it copes with changes in the market place.

SAP is recognized as the provider of the most powerful suite of software applications for critical business and global corporate applications, well supported by a global sales and maintenance team. Strength of product in the field and a proven record of exceptional profitability all indicate that SAP management will be pragmatic in their response to any tailing off of earnings. However, potential investors should keep in mind the severe set back in 1998 and the high price that SAP trades at compared to similar US companies.

LUCENT

Share Graph 1997–1998 Lucent Technologies
Primary Market – NYSE – LU

Price January 1999 $57.50
Market Value January 1999 $151.9 billion

SECTOR Technology INDUSTRY Communications and Equipment
Top Line LU Bottom Line S&P 500 Index Relative
Left Scale: Top $ Price, Bottom Volume in Thousands
Chart not rebased for two-for-one split April 1999

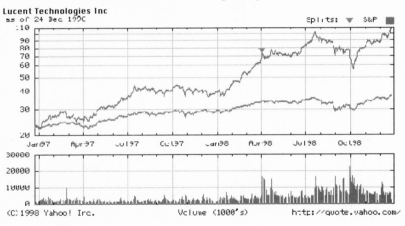

Lucent Technologies Inc
as of 24 Dec 1998

(C) 1998 Yahoo! Inc.   Volume (1000's)   http://quote.yahoo.com/

PRICE PERFORMANCE LU Year 1998			An investment made in April 1996 grew 643% by January 1999		
PRICE HISTORY	1998	1997	1996	1995	Notes
High Price	61	22.69	13.32	NA	
Low Price	18.28	11.19	74.40	NA	
High P/E	156.64	108.04	141.29	NA	
Low P/E	50.29	53.27	79.12	NA	

Chmn/Pres/CEO R. McGinn, www.lucent.com
152,000 employees
600 Mountain Avenue, Murray Hill, NJ 07974
Phone: (908) 582-8500 Fax: (908) 508-2576

Global Franchise: Telephony and communications

Lucent is the eventual successor to the inventor of the telephone, Alexander Graham Bell. Bell Laboratories, which continued in AT&T as the development arm of the enterprise, are now part of Lucent Technologies. Lucent was spun off from AT&T in 1996 and is a leading global contender in all fields of communications infrastructure.

Setting a rational price

Portfolio 2001 WORKSHEET FOR TARGETING SHARE PRICES OF LUCENT TECHNOLOGIES IN 1999, 2000, 2001 & 2002 BASED ON FORECASTS MADE IN JANUARY 1999 YEAR TO SEPTEMBER 1998 $1.73

Growth	Year	Estimated EPS	P/E	Share Price Target	+10%	-10%	Notes
30%	1999	$1.12	50	$56	$62	$55	
30%	2000	$1.47	50	$80	$89	$72	
30%	2001	$1.89	50	$95	$105	$85	
30%	2002	$2.46	45	$111	$122	$99	

This 'what if' forecast suggests potential earnings and share prices based on current indications. Forecasts must be revised continuously in the light of all company results and industry, market and economic news. Forecasts can be misleading and cannot be treated as investment advice or used to motivate investments. See page 69.

Earnings per share growth expectations
Growth indicated by management is 30% and has been forecast for the period to 2002. This does not factor in revenue growth being scaled up by acquisitions which may or may not take place.

Earnings multiple expectations
The telephony sector and Lucent as a company are too volatile to project share price targets sensibly. Information used is certain to be outdated within months or even weeks as Lucent repositions itself strategically to changes and opportunities in the industry. Fifty times earnings is only a number used to complete the above table that fits in with market prices in January 1999, and is consistent with market valuations over the short three years that Lucent has

been listed on the Stock Exchange. Fifity times earnings is a high multiple of current earnings for any share, and where a company is engaged in an industry growing as rapidly as communications, and growing by acquisition as an industry consolidator at the same time, there is no basis for long-range forecasting.

Past performance indicators

Growth Rates %	LU	S&P 500	Industry	Sector	Notes
Earnings per share 5 year	12.85	20.43	24.88	33.15	
1998 last reported vs 1997	69.75	12.34	56.92	25.08	
Sales last reported vs 1998	14.73	11.71	15.39	22.47	
Sales 5 year 1994-1998	NM	NM	NM	NM	
Profitability Ratios					
Gross Margin 1998 %	46.41	46.35	52.1	49.22	
5 year average %	42.70	48.87	41.64	52.01	
Net Profit Margin 1998 %	3.22	10.90	3.39	11.19	
5 year average %	1.01	10.71	2.61	10.75	
5 Year Returns on:					
Assets %	3.87	8.39	4.05	10.85	
Investment %	6.51	13.36	6.22	16.17	
Equity %	5.11	21.46	8.64	20.83	

NM=not meaningful

Past performance comparisons bring little useful information as Lucent is a young company and has changed dramatically from year to year. Detailed accounts highlights published by Lucent for fiscal 1998 are included as a schedule to this report.

Lucent shares have soared in value since it was listed. If markets continue to favour telephony opportunities, and Lucent delivers results in line with forecasts, exceptional investment growth opportunities could continue.

The growth story

The opportunity of a lifetime – reborn free
When Lucent was spun off and floated from AT&T in April

1996, management presented the new company to investors as 'the opportunity of a lifetime'. There were two threads to their presentation.

The first was about the new free standing business and new Stock Exchange listed company. Bell Laboratories innovation and expertise in designing and building communications systems, since the beginnings of telephony time, had moved out of a back room at AT&T. It was as if Bell Laboratories was being reborn, but this time free. The new Lucent could set its sights on being like a Microsoft, a Cisco or an Intel, and management set out to be counted as one of the new breed of technology companies.

AT&T shareholders received a free distribution of 0.324084 of a Lucent share for each AT&T share held in April 1996. By December 1998, the market value of Lucent and AT&T were each about $150 billion. Lucent shares appreciated in value 626% in the first three years, while AT&T appreciated only 113% in the same time. The stellar rise in the value of Lucent's share price compared to AT&T is seen in this comparison chart:

3 year chart showing value growth of Lucent Technologies LU and AT&T

Top line Lucent – Bottom line AT&T = Right scale top % gain: Bottom Volume Lucent in thousands

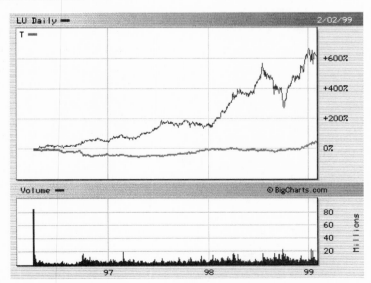

Source: www.wsj.com

The second thread of the opportunity of a lifetime presentation was the exceptional once-in-a lifetime growth opportunity in the telecommunications industry in the late 1990s, discussed later in this report.

By 1998, Lucent reported significant operating earnings. Year on year gains in revenue for its first three years rose from $22.286 billion in 1996 to $26.360 billion in 1997 and $30.147 billion in 1997. In line with the growth in revenues operating earnings per share surged in 1998:

	1998	1997	1996
Operating income (loss) diluted			
Per share in $ cents	*0.73	*0.42	(0.69)

*Excluding one time acquisition related charges

For the first fiscal quarter of 1999, Lucent reported another earnings per share increase of 22% to $1.05, excluding one time events. Lucent's opportunity of a lifetime has already worked out better than expected and investors can feel comfortable that management have the vision to recognize opportunities and the skills to deliver on their promises. For 1999, Lucent is forecasting top line growth of 19 to 20%, and EPS growth of about 35% (excluding one time events).

Growing Lucent capabilities

Lucent's mission has been to position itself as the leading supplier in all key sectors of communications infrastructure. On the road to this goal, a series of fourteen strategic acquisitions has been concluded, with the largest, the $19.2 billion acquisition of Ascend Communications, announced in January 1999.

Wherever possible, operators need to merge their voice, data and video traffic into single networks, because it's cheaper and more efficient than operating several networks. Ascend Communications brings Lucent key technologies that cater for and integrate all kinds of traffic, and is a leader in an important switching technology, ATM.

Acquisitions made by Lucent have filled in gaps in its capacities and strengthened its position as industry consolidators, as seen in this schedule:

DATA NETWORKING ASCEND COMMUNICATIONS	**January 1999 – $19.7 billion** A leading supplier of net access components and high-performance data switches for the Internet and a leader in ATM technology
SOFTWARE KENAN SYSTEMS	**January 1999 – $1.48 billion** A provider of advanced billing and customer care software
DATA NETWORKING YURIE SYSTEMS	**April 1998 – $1.06 billion** A start-up maker of data switches aimed at smaller networks
PROMINET	**December 1997 – $164 million** One of several pioneers in fast switches for corporate networks
VOICE SYSTEMS LIVINGSTON ENTERPRISES	**October 1997 – $610 million** A rival to Ascend and 3Com in net access equipment supplies
OCTEL COMMUNICATIONS	**July 1997 – $1.8 billion** The leading maker of voice-mail systems teams up with the top rival to its own market

Growth in communications

The surging growth in the communications industry globally has been driven by the Internet and the growth in data traffic it introduced. At the same time, wireless telephony traffic has surged and industry deregulation has opened new market opportunities globally.

According to data published by Lucent Internet, traffic is doubling every 100 days and more than 100 million additional Internet users are expected to come on line by 2001. In 1998, 75 million new customers signed up for cellular phone service, bringing the worldwide untethered phone population to roughly 285 million. In 1998, 2.7 trillion e-mails were sent, equal to 5 million every minute, and 900 million voice-mail messages are exchanged each business day.

Lucent claims to have more resources than any other company to make multiple communications networks work, and to make different networks work together. It can integrate wireless, packet, circuit, and enterprise-wide area and local area networks; it can serve customers on multiple levels spanning products, system design and installation; and it can provide the backup services of consulting, network-management, project management and financing.

Global growth
The total global market for Lucent products and services is expected to reach $650 billion by the year 2001, up from $380 billion in 1997. Lucent estimates that the market for communications equipment and support services is growing 15% annually, and as a company it expects to perform well ahead of industry averages, as it has done in its first three years.

Deregulation of the telecoms industry in the US presented the first new growth opportunity for the telecommunications infrastructure industry in the late 1980s. The rest of the world has been deregulating since, and Lucent now expects 60% of its growth opportunity to be outside the United States, where telecommunications privatizations and deregulations are now fashionable. Lucent won more than $2.3 billion in major new contracts as its sales grew 22% outside the United States in 1998. The fourth quarter was particularly strong with a 41% increase over the fourth quarter of 1997.

Networking
Data Networking Equipment Market
(dollars in billions)

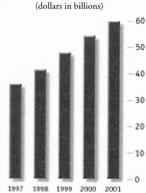

The global data networking equipment market is growing 13% annually (industry estimates)

Source: chart from Lucent annual report

Data networks were once regarded as the poor relations of public voice networks, and were subject to delays, breakdowns and inconsistent transmission performance. With data traffic tripling every year, this had to change and data transmission is demanded of the same quality and reliability as voice. Data is projected to overtake voice as the dominant type of traffic over the world's telecommunications networks by 2005.

Lucent has been actively building the reliability and consistency of data transmissions, and introduced over 300 advanced data networking innovations in 1998. These innovations helped to transform fundamentally the way new networks handle data, and enabled existing voice networks to evolve in the data world. The acquisition of Ascend Communications will strengthen Lucent's resources in data transmission and network service further.

In 1999 and 2000, with the changing structure of the deregulated communications industry, as many as 1,000 new telecommunications carriers will start up in business, and a new 'alphabet' of service providers has appeared around the world. They include these new classes of client for telecommunications suppliers:

CLECs   Competitive local exchange carriers
ISPs   Internet service providers
ILECs   Incumbent local exchange carriers

Established carriers and new start-ups are upgrading and setting up facilities to run data networks with the same quality of service as traditional voice networks. Lucent provides end-to-end networking solutions that include design, product, installation and network-management.

Bandwidth and DWDM technology

Bandwidth is the amount of information that can be transmitted each second over a communications channel, such as a telephone line. The expansion of networks to carry more data has not been at the expense of voice but is in addition to it. With the growth in traffic, the telecommunications industry has developed an insatiable appetite for bandwidth and the increased traffic has been congesting existing networks.

Lucent believes optical networking is emerging as the only way to accommodate the colossal increases in network traffic projected, and this is an area where the legendary Bell Laboratories will again be the pace setter in new innovations for the industry. Dense wave length division multiplexing (DWDM) technology enables carriers to boost the capacity of their existing fibre-optic cables by sending laser pulses of different colours simultaneously over the same fibre. Lucent claims the effect is similar to squeezing 80 lanes of traffic on to a 16-lane highway. Each wavelength or colour of laser light can serve as a separate channel carrying information, boosting the capacity of the fibre up to a hundredfold.

Lucent is the global leader in DWDM technology, and in 1995 was the first to market DWDM products. Since then it has installed going on for 1,500 DWDM systems. Based on Bell Laboratories' patented techniques, the Lucent WaveStar system combines up to 80 optical channels over a single fibre, giving record-breaking capacity of 400 gigabytes per second. This is the equivalent of carrying about five million phone conversations at the same time.

The WaveStar system will be deployed in the global undersea network called Project Oxygen that will link every continent except Antarctica. Lucent's sales of optical networking equipment and other hardware and software to Project Oxygen could result in up to $1 billion in revenues over four years. In February 1999, Lucent licensed several of its fibre optic technologies to the company which has established a new fibre optic cable for the Atlantic Global Crossing (GBLX), and plans to extend its network globally.

The Market for Lucent's Semiconductor Products

(dollars in billions)

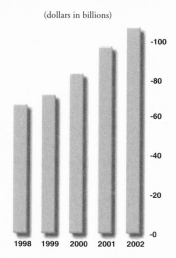

The market for the types of semiconductors sold by Lucent is growing 12% annually

Source: International Data Corp. Chart from Lucent annual report

Half the world's phones will be wireless by 2007
Lucent is among the world's leading manufacturers of data signal processors (DSPs) used in mobile telephony, and, after Texas Instruments, is the largest vendor of DSPs to other manufacturers. Working again at the cutting edge of technology, it is developing a new superchip which incorporates a DSP.

Until now a single microchip has generally performed a single function in telephony applications, but Lucent expects it will be able to put the electronics for entire systems, like cellular phones or disk drives, on a single superchip sliver of silicon. Getting complete systems on one chip will reduce the size of the end product, cut costs and extend battery performance.

Data traffic still makes up only about 3% of wireless network traffic, and the ratio will increase rapidly as the demand for data on wireless follows the growth of the wireless opportunity itself. Lucent is working on mobile wireless systems with transmission rates more than 100 times faster than those of today's cellular phones.

Third-generation, or 3G phones, for which international standards are currently being set, will support voice and additional applications, including Web surfing and even videoconferencing. These standards are being developed by all leading mobile phone companies and are only a few years away from the market.

Optoelectronic devices
In addition to being the leading provider of integrated circuits for the communications industry, Lucent's Microelectronics group is the leading supplier of optoelectronic components for communications. In 1998, it introduced a new group of laser modules, photodetectors and receivers that can quadruple the bandwidth capacity of fibre optic networks, from 2.5 to 10 gigabytes per second.

These Lucent innovations, including the fastest and smallest optical transceivers for use in high-speed voice and data communication systems, make it possible for telecommunications providers to increase four-fold the data they transmit through existing fibre optic networks.

Competitive advantage
The pace of change in the communications industry has been so rapid that Lucent labels it as having reached revolutionary proportions globally. In developed nations there is unprecedented growth

of traffic on public and private networks, as more people work at home, access the Internet, and carry cell phones and laptops. In developing nations, the revolution is driven by the creation of new businesses and rising demand for access to communications.

Lucent claims a unique 'holistic' approach to networking, and that no other company understands how networks work – and work together – better than it does. Its greatest competitive advantage comes from its strength in all segments of communications networking including optical, wireless, software and semiconductor technologies. There will always be many successful companies with niche technologies, but they will find themselves unable to deliver the end-to-end networking solutions that customers need.

Lucent also gains formidable competitive advantage from who it is and what it can do. The credibility and resources that come with its Bell Laboratories and AT&T lineage, and the leading edge technologies it incorporates as an industry consolidator, harness a dynamic combination of forces.

What can go wrong?

A serious declining fortunes scenario for Lucent could emerge if globally the growth in communications were to slow down appreciably, or if global economic conditions were to deteriorate to the extent that major plans to extend communications networks were shelved.

These are unlikely developments. A more likely risk for investors would be short-term damage if Lucent disappointed the market with bad results or product failures, and the valuation of its shares fell.

Highly valued investments are always vulnerable to corrections in market swings and to invest in Lucent with a low-risk high-reward profile, a long investing horizon is necessary.

Monitoring

www.lucent.com is one of the most informative web sites for investors, and much of the information in this report has been extracted from it. Monitoring the growth of the telecommunications industry can be done following news in the financial and daily press on Lucent and its competitors.

Lucent is likely to continue to make acquisitions as a result of which earnings comparisons get distorted and earnings reports must be carefully analysed in relation to ongoing achievements and growth by acquisition.

The headline results for 1998, with explanatary notes on aquisitions, follow:

Schedule Financial Highlights

(dollars in millions, except per share amounts; unaudited)

	Twelve Months Ended 30 Sept. 1998	Twelve Months Ended 30 Sept. 1997	CHANGE
Revenues	$ 30,147	$ 26,360	14.4%
Gross Margin	13,991	(b) 11,470	22.0
Selling, general and administrative	6,436	(b) 5,758	11.8
Research and development	(a) 3,678	(b) 3,102	18.6
Operating income	(a) 3,877	(b) 2,610	48.5
Net income (excluding certain one-time events)	(a) 2,287	(b) 1,507	51.8
Earnings per share – diluted (c) (excluding certain one-time events)	(a) 1.72	(b) 1.17	47.0
Total assets	$ 26,720	$ 23,811	12.2
Working capital	3,650	1,763	107.0
Shareowners' equity	5,534	3,387	63.4
Capital expenditures	$ 1,626	$ 1,635	(0.6%)
Return on assets	(a) 9.3%	(b) 6.5%	2.8 points
Debt to total capital	45.6%	55.4%	(9.8) points
Stock price	$ 69 1/4	$ 40 11/16	70.2%

(a) Excludes impact of $1,416 ($1,412 after tax) of one-time charges associated with the acquisitions of Livingston Enterprises, Prominet Corporation, Yurie Systems Inc., Optimay GmbH, LANNET, SDX Business Systems plc, JNA Telecommunications Limited and MassMedia Communications Inc., as well as $95 (after tax) gain on the sale of Lucent's Advanced Technology Systems business. Including these charges and gain, Lucent reported net income of $970.

(b) Excludes impact of $979 ($966 after tax) of one-time charges associated with the acquisition of Octel Communications. Including the impact of these charges, Lucent reported net income of $541.

(c) All earnings-per-share amounts reflect a two-for-one stock split that became effective 1 April 1998.

TEXAS INSTRUMENTS

Share Graph 1997–1998 Texas Instruments
Primary Market – NASDAQ – TXN

Price January 1999 $46.37
Market Value January 1999 $36.1 billion

SECTOR Technology INDUSTRY Semiconductors
Top Line TXN Bottom Line S&P 500 Index Relative
Left Scale: Top $ Price, Bottom Volume in Thousands
Graphics not rebased for two-for-one split effective August 1999

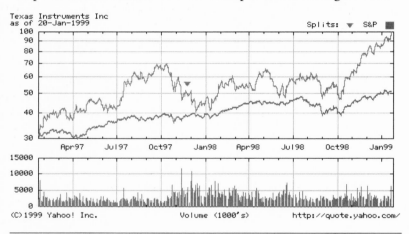

Texas Instruments Inc
as of 20-Jan-1999   Splits: ▼   S&P ■
(C) 1999 Yahoo! Inc.   Volume (1000's)   http://quote.yahoo.com/

PRICE PERFORMANCE	TXN		An investment made in January 1994 grew 563% by January 1999		
Year 1998 %					

PRICE HISTORY	1998	1997	1996	1995	Notes
High Price	45.22	35.62	17.10	20.94	
Low Price	20.12	12.63	10.12	8.59	
High P/E	39.96	40.93	NM	6.67	
Low P/E	84.36	59.59	NM	10.00	

Chairman Thomas Engnobis, **www.ti.com**
35,900 employees
Texas Instruments, 8505 Forest Lane, P.O. Box 600199, Dallas, TX 75266
Phone: (972) 995 3773 Fax: (972) 995-4360

Setting a rational price

Portfolio 2001 WORKSHEET FOR TARGETING SHARE PRICES OF TEXAS INSTRUMENTS IN 1999, 2000, 2001 & 2002 BASED ON FORECASTS MADE IN JANUARY 1999 1988 EPS $1.79 – Q4 1998 $0.59c – 1999 FORECAST BASED ON CONSENSUS

Growth	Year	Estimated EPS	P/E	Share Price Target	+10%	-10%	Notes
Consensus	1999	$3.00	37.5	$112	$124	$88	
20%	2000	$3.67	37.5	$138	$153	$101	
20%	2001	$4.58	37.5	$171	$184	$154	
20%	2002	$5.61	37.5	$210	$224	$189	

This 'what if' forecast suggests potential earnings and share prices based on current indications. Forecasts must be revised continuously in the light of all company results and industry, market and economic news. Forecasts can be misleading and cannot be treated as investment advice or used to motivate investments. See page 69.

Global franchise: Data signal processor microchips

Texas Instruments evolution to becoming the world's largest supplier of data signalling processors, used in mobile telephony, is discussed in the growth and outlook sections following. Annual Revenues exceed $8 billion.

Earnings per share growth expectations

Texas is addressing one of the world's largest growth markets. Digital sensory chips for mobile communications and other applications, and analogue chips, are market leaders and on the basis of current performance, management expectations and market potential, 20% per annum earnings growth is a realistic expectation.

Earnings multiple expectations

With current demand for leading technology shares, a higher market multiple would be likely but, as Texas has had earnings ups and down in the past, markets are likely to be more guarded. In January 1999, an earnings multiple of between 30 and 40 times earnings per share growth is realistic and 37.5 has been used in the *Portfolio 2001* forecast. As Texas succeeds in sustaining targeted earnings growth, this multiple is likely to lift.

Past performance indicators

Growth Rates %		TXN	S&P 500	Industry	Sector	Notes
Earnings per share 5 year		3.90	20.84	36.92	37.05	
1998 last reported vs 1997		35.33	11.42	-3.70	20.63	
Sales 5 year 1994-1998		5.56	32.38	33.92	16.18	
1998 last reported vs 1997		-13.23	12.63	3.59	24.56	
Profitability Ratios						
Gross Margin 1998	%	35.23	49.26	48.91	52.42	
5 year average	%	32.18	48.91	51.44	52.45	
Net Profit Margin 1998	%	4.81	10.63	15.52	11.98	
5 year average	%	4.77	10.21	17.78	11.00	
5 Year Returns on:						
Assets	%	6.56	8.40	18.26	12.71	
Investment	%	9.52	13.20	23.12	17.62	
Equity	%	15.71	21.53	28.07	21.57	

The growth story

Drawing a line in the silicone

Texas recognized data signalling processors – DSP chips – as the best opportunity in the semiconductor industry. The world of electronics is going digital, and digital signal processing solutions are what make it possible. In 1996, to capitalize on exceptional growth prospects, Texas restructured its business and disinvested from a range of other activities to concentrate on manufacturing DSPs. By January 1999, the multi million dollar three-year re-organization which saw it divest 12 operations and acquire seven others over twenty months, was completed. Texas reported that fourth-quarter 1998 semiconductor revenues increased 6% from the third quarter to $1,628 million, driven by record revenues in DSP chips. Its DSP business grew 29% in 1998, somewhat faster than the DSP market overall. Semiconductor orders increased 8% from the third quarter, reflecting gains in almost all semiconductor product lines.

Financial results

In the third quarter of 1998, diluted earnings per share increased to $0.59, compared with $0.41 and $0.55 in the year-ago period, excluding special charges. The increased earnings and improved operating margins reflected the effects of the company's restructuring programme over the last few years and its recent divesting of its memory chip business in the third quarter of 1998.

Revenues were $1,993 million, down $435 million from the year-ago quarter, essentially due to the divestiture of the memory business, but income for the quarter was $237 million, up 8% from the year-ago quarter, excluding special charges, reflecting the company's higher proportion of differentiated analogue and DSP products.

Overall operating margins increased to 16% for the quarter, compared with 9.6% for the third quarter and 12% for the fourth quarter of 1997, excluding special charges.

Following the major corporate restructuring and an internal operational restructuring to increase efficiencies and reduce costs, Texas made several strategic acquisitions to strengthen its expertise in core technologies. 'As reported' figures for results have been confusing, following special charges and one time write downs. The profit figures above reflect the growth of operating earnings and margins.

Outlook

Texas chairman Tom Engnobis, took office as chief executive of a sprawling and largely unprofitable business after the sudden death of founder Jerry Junkins in 1996, and set the company's sights on dominating the DSP market. He has achieved this objective with a market share of DSPs for mobile telephony estimated at 45%, and has reassured investors: 'TI is a much different company today than we were a year ago. We enter 1999 a leader in virtually every market we serve, and we will continue to deliver DSP and analogue solutions that are unparalleled in performance, ease-of-use and value.' Several leading analysts rate chances for the company as exceptional and have made forecasts for operating margins that could pass 20% in 2000, as the DSP business grows at a high rate and company costs associated with divested businesses fade.

The fast growing market for DSPs

In the last quarter of 1998, DSP sales contributed 59% of Texas's total semiconductor sales and 48% of total sales. Growth is fuelled by the growth in wireless and networking applications. Forward Concepts of Tempe, Arizona, who conduct research on the DSP market, have reported that total worldwide sales of DSPs increased by almost 30% from $2.4 billion in 1996 to $3.1 billion in 1997. Texas claims that the market for combined DSPs and analogue chips will reach $50 billion within 5 years.

Unlike microprocessors which undertake varied functions, DSPs are programmed to execute a single job and, being smaller and application specific, they sell in the range $5 to $10. This is a much lower price than for personal-computer microprocessors, but DSPs are smaller, less complex and can be produced in high volume at worthwhile profit margins at these levels. Texas claims that it has the only company in the world with an infrastructure broad enough to serve the industry's entire spectrum of customers, and that it has unique capacity to supply customers with combined digital and analogue solutions.

Texas supplies chips to Nokia and Ericsson, currently the two leaders in cell phones, and Nokia alone was shipping 1 million units a week in September 1998. This could have driven Texas's share of the total DSP market from 45% to 50%.

DSP + analogue

Wherever there is a DSP, Texas claims you will find analogue products as well, and on any day in January 1999 they claim that globally $9.3 million, DSPs and $60 million analogue products were sold. In its web site, Texas gives examples of the dynamic growth potential of the market it is serving, and its own strength in the market:

- Across the globe, more than 1,000 third-party products operate with Texas DSPs
- About 154 million digital wireless phones were sold in 1998, and DSPs powered most of those phones
- 383,000 digital cellular phones are sold every day
- 166 million people have pager services
- There are 18,900 new Internet users every day
- People use products containing a DSP as often as every 10 minutes

- Worldwide DSP sales average $9.3 million per day
- Analogue sales average $60.2 million per day
- Purchases over the Internet are increasing at the rate of $10 billion per year
- A typical hard disk drive currently has a capacity of 3 to 5 gigabytes, and in 5 years will have 10 times the capacity
- Demand for networked products is growing at a rate of 20% annually
- 9,800 digital still cameras are shipped each day, and in four years it will be over 51,780 per day
- At any moment in time a 911 operator (999 in the UK) is having trouble locating a caller in distress. Engineers are working to put Global Position Satellite systems in every digital cell phone
- Digital cellular phone shipments have increased 64% over last year
- Over half the world's population has never made a phone call
- There are 104 million PCs connected to the Internet, and within 4 years that number will triple
- Every day 3,552 high-speed modems are supplied and the next generation of modems will be 100 times faster
- Internet users average 5½ hours on line per week, and there are more than 320 million web pages
- The European Internet market grew 60% in 1998
- In January 1999, every day 21, 600 Europeans connected to the Internet for the first time
- Daily more than $10.5 million worth of goods which include Texas chips, digital TVs, digital cell phones, digital still cameras, fax machines, etc. are purchased over the Internet.

Competitive advantage

Texas Instruments has made substantial investments to pioneer and develop the leading edge technology and efficient manufacturing resources to service the rapacious demand for DSPs, and is the leading supplier of the core product in the shift to digital and wireless communications. The company has also established a leading position in the supply of hard disk drives and components, and it has over 30,000 customers worldwide. Earnings in 1999 are expected to reflect improvement in semiconductor markets and the ongoing benefit of the company's strategic positioning and cost reduction.

Keeping ahead

To maintain its leading position, the company's R&D spend in 1999 will be $1.1 billion, after spending $1.2 billion in 1998. Texas is now the world's leading supplier of DSPs both in terms of dollar sales and breadth of product portfolio. Its strong position in DSPs helps to pull through sales of their other semiconductor products, primarily in their ever-expanding portfolio of analogue chips. The following quotation from Texas's web site further explains its competitive advantage:

> The competitive edge starts with technology with a product line anchored by the world's fastest processors. No matter what the real-world application, there's a TI DSP – and associated products – right for the job. Superior software adds to the value equation for their customers and in 1998 they introduced a new set of software tools that simplifies DSP programming.
>
> DSP is the fastest-growing segment of the semiconductor market and mixed-signal is one of the fastest-growing segments of the total market for processors. This segment is now developing along a faster track than the one the microprocessor followed in the 1980s and 90s and Texas claim they are uniquely positioned to serve this market with their leadership in DSP technology and production and their analog chip manufacturing resources enabling them to supply combined digital analog solutions.
>
> In part, this fast-track growth is driven by the fact that digital signal processors target a broader range of <u>diverse end-use markets</u> than microprocessors: not just personal computers, but also telecom devices, consumer electronics, office equipment, industrial controls and automotive components.
>
> Digital signal processors are much faster (often 10 times faster or more) than general-purpose microprocessors and speed makes them particularly well-suited to handle the demands of processing information from different parts of the world by working in real time. One way to understand how DSPs work is to think about <u>how you experience the world</u>. Every waking moment, your senses

capture a multitude of signals from your surroundings – clues like heat, light, sound and pressure. You use that information to walk, talk, work, play. The same thing is true of digital devices. They can use 'real-world' signals to transmit pictures, record sounds, control heat, adjust pressure. But digital devices are precise. They can only process information that comes in the form of 1s and 0s. That's what it means to be digital. Of course, when digital devices become the brains of electronics and venture out into the world, they encounter the very same ambient information as you do: analog signals, such as heat, light, sound and pressure.

Before the device can do anything useful with those sensations, the signals have to be translated into a language the devices understand. A digital language. This analog-to-digital conversion is handled by companions of the digital signal processor, called mixed-signal/analog products. These products also translate digital signals back to real-world information.

In DSPs, an analog signal such as your voice is digitized by an analog-to-digital converter (A/D). The DSP processes the digital signal, then a digital-to-analog converter (D/A) changes the signal back to analog. When you combine the incredible speed of the digital signal processor . . . with the real-world versatility of the mixed-signal/analog . . . it creates some very interesting possibilities. Texas call those possibilities 'Digital Signal Processing Solutions.'

The future of the digital world depends on DSPs. Texas provides leading DSP technology, products, and system-level solutions needed to cut development time, enhance product applications and speed the time to market.

What can go wrong?

Apart from general economic risks and industry risks facing investors in technology companies, investors will need to keep in mind that Texas has still to prove that it can sustain earnings growth and improve margins even in potentially adverse economic changes. Also, an essential focus for monitoring will be on growth in mobile phones and wireless telephony.

Monitoring

Lack of 'track record' for the restructured Texas keeps monitoring a high priority for researchers and investors. Particular risks to monitor for will include:

1. DSP technology is fast moving and a competitor could develop a better technology
2. The wireless phone market may not grow at expected rates
3. While Texas has improved its operating margins and won back some pricing power, margins could be eroded if the high volumes called for by the market bring excessive competition and pricing power is lost as the product gets commoditized.

Earnings announcements, which can make difficult reading against the background of reorganization and one time charges, have to be studied and operational earnings extracted and evaluated. All company reports will also have to be studied to take a view on whether profit growth remains on course without further exceptional costs.

Investors should also monitor industry news, particularly for mobile communications, wireless telephony and semiconductors. Motorola is entering the DSP market with a chip it claims is superior to other offerings, and Lucent is already a formidable competitor in DSP manufacture.

Texas Instruments' web site www.ti.com is an informative reference point and offers to researchers the facility of a spread sheet download of financial performance which they can monitor and process, and a custom on line news page.

Glossary

Texas includes helpful explanatory material in its web site, including an extremely useful glossary on technical terms relating to its industry. It is too long to reproduce here, but you can find it at www.ti.com

CISCO SYSTEMS

Share Graph 1997–1998 Cisco Systems Inc.
Primary Market – NASDAQ CSCO

Price January 1999 $49.50
Market Value January 1999 $156.4 billion

SECTOR Technology INDUSTRY Computer Networks
Top Line CSCO Bottom Line S&P 500 Index Relative: Triangle
Marks Split
Left Scale: Top $ Price, Bottom Volume in Thousands
Graphic not rebased for two-for-one split effective June 1999.

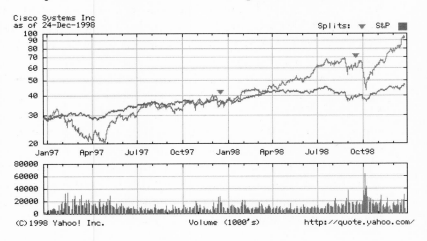

PRICE PERFORMANCE	CSCO		An investment made in January 1994 grew 1463% by January 1999		
PRICE HISTORY	1998	1997	1996	1995	Notes
High Price	48.87	20.19	15.36	9.93	
Low Price	17.16	10.05	17.09	3.59	
High P/E	116.37	59.75	50.12	62.07	
Low P/E	40.87	14.87	23.16	22.48	

Pres/CEO John Chambers, chmn John Morgridge, www.cisco.com
15,000 employees
170 West Tasman Drive, San Jose, CA 951 4
Phone: (408) 526-4000 Fax: (408) 526 4100

Global Franchise: Network routers, switches and equipment

Cisco started business in 1987. Since it became a public company in 1990, its shares have appreciated by 33,000% and annual revenues have increased from $69 million to over $11 billion. Cisco, the largest maker of network routers, which form the backbone of the Internet, has a simple growth strategy: whatever technology its engineers cannot create in-house, it buys. Before 1996, Cisco acquired 8 companies; since then it has added 21.

Cisco networking systems and switches connect people, computing devices and computer networks, enabling the transfer of all kinds of information, including sound and data, irrespective of differences in the type of computer system, time, or place. Cisco was a pioneer developer of routers used to direct and manage the flow of data packets on the Internet and across all kinds of networks, with protocol conversion where necessary. Cisco has dominated the router market from the outset and is also the world's leading supplier of products that link LANs (local area networks) and WANs (wide area networks), with an 85% share of the market for routers used in WANs and a 35% share of the market for switches used in LANs. Other products include dial-up-access servers and network-management software.

Following a vigorous acquisitions strategy, Cisco has been a prominent industry consolidator in a fast growing technology sector. Acquisitions and licensed in technology have been used to improve product line continuously and have led to Cisco having an important presence across the spectrum of WAN and LAN networking. Over 55% of sales are in the US. Revenues exceed $11 million.

Setting a rational price

Portfolio 2001 WORKSHEET FOR TARGETING SHARE PRICES OF CISCO IN 1999, 2000, 2001 & 2002
BASED ON FORECASTS MADE IN JANUARY 1999
EPS FISCAL 1988 TO JULY $0.42

Growth	Year	Estimated EPS	P/E	Share Price Target	+10%	-10%	Notes
consensus	1999	$0.72	60	$63	$48	$39	
30%	2000	$0.94	60	$56	$62	$50	
30%	2001	$1.22	60	$73	$81	$66	
30%	2002	$1.58	60	$95	$105	$85	

This 'what if' forecast suggests potential earnings and share prices based on current indications. Forecasts must be revised continuously in the light of all company results and industry, market and economic news. Forecasts can be misleading and cannot be treated as investment advice or used to motivate investments. See page 69.

Earning per share growth expectations

Earnings per share for the first two quarters of fiscal 1999 ending December 1998 continued to show 30% plus gains year on year (see table on p382).

In the last quarter of 1998, Cisco introduced 13 new products, ahead of its normal annual product introductions, and reported increased levels of orders in all product areas, with some pricing pressure occurring in LAN switching.

With the growth of the Internet, wireless communications and telephony generally, analysts reasonably expect Cisco to continue to show earnings per share growth of above 30% per annum.

Earnings multiple expectations

Cisco's performance has been so consistently strong that, unless it disappoints markets, its share will continue to be highly valued, and multiples in the range of 60 times nominal earnings, double the earnings per share growth rate, can be expected in current strong market conditions. Reported earnings usually include write downs for one time acquisition related charges, and taking these charges into account Cisco has been trading at about 60 times operational earnings.

PRO FORMA STATEMENTS OF OPERATIONS
Excluding Purchased R&D and Realized Gain

(In millions, except per-share amounts)

	Quarters Ended		Six Months Ended	
	23 January 1999	24 January 1998	23 January 1999	24 January 1998
(Unaudited)				
Net sales	$ 2,827	$ 2,016	$ 5,415	$ 3,885
Cost of sales	985	697	1,879	1,349
Gross margin	**1,842**	**1,319**	**3,536**	**2,536**
Operating expenses:				
Research and development	357	239	684	463
Sales and marketing	570	363	1,084	697
General and administrative	90	58	174	114
Total operating expenses	**1,017**	**660**	**1,942**	**1,274**
Operating income	825	659	1,594	1,262
Interest and other income, net	80	44	145	81
Income before provision for income taxes	905	703	1,739	1,343
Provision for income taxes	299	246	574	470
Net income	**$ 606**	**$ 457**	**$ 1,165**	**$ 873**
Net income per share – basic	**$ .38**	**$ .30**	**$ .74**	**$ .57**
Net income per share – diluted	**$ .36**	**$ .29**	**$ .70**	**$ .55**
Shares used in per-share calculation – basic	1,585	1,523	1,578	1,518
Shares used in per-share calculation – diluted	1,679	1,594	1,668	1,589

Note: Earnings per share not adjusted for 1999 split.

If it is rational ever to buy such highly valued shares, it would certainly be rational to buy Cisco shares. Investors in Cisco are buying into one of the most consistently successful business stories, but will be buying shares priced for perfection. Cisco is an industry and market leader supplying key infrastructure for a seemingly unlimited Internet and networking demand and its growth is reflected in the strong momentum in Cisco's earnings growth and share price appreciation.

Past performance indicators

Growth Rates %		CSCO	S&P 500	Industry	Sector	Notes
Earnings per share 5 year		41.52	20.84	38.43	37.05	
1998 last reported vs 1997		1.55*	11.42	5.06	20.36	*Excep-tionals
Sales 5 year 1994-1998		67.11	16.18	73.62	33.92	
Profitability Ratios						
Gross Margin 1998	%	65.58	49.26	62.54	52.42	
5 year average	%	65.87	48.91	63.07	52.45	
Net Profit Margin 1998	%	13.64*	10.63	9.99	11.98	*Excep-tionals
5 year average	%	19.84	10.21	15.14	11.00	
5 Year Returns on:						
Assets	%	28.71	8.40	23.36	12.71	
Investment	%	35.93	13.20	29.45	17.62	
Equity	%	36.31	21.53	32.69	21.57	

The growth story

Cisco has from its inception been the top supplier of computer networking equipment, one of the fastest growing technology industries. At the end of the 1980s, when Cisco started in business, most computers worked as self-sufficient work-stations. Now, practically every computer connects to others in some way, whether through the Internet, networks like America On Line through corporate or private intranets.

Networking fuelled the boom for infrastructure products, including the equipment Cisco manufactures, which connect computers to a network or transfer data from one PC across a network to another PC, mainframe computer or server computer.

As new networks have been built more computers have been connected to them and traffic increases. As is does so, existing networks need faster and more efficient networking equipment and Cisco has the products needed to convey all content, including text, graphics, streaming video and voice telephony.

The expansion of company networks has been another volume driver for Cisco. When they expand they also upgrade to improve speed and capacity, and again Cisco has the necessary products.

Cisco has consistently kept ahead of the competition in delivering new networking technology and cutting-edge networking solutions, by acquiring companies that have new solutions, or licensing in technology from them.

Acquisitions strategy

On its web site www.cisco.com all the acquisitions which have been made since incorporation are listed, with a description of each business acquired. Twenty-three major acquisitions have been made, and with each one two results are achieved. First, Cisco retains its market dominance, and second it introduces the most talented executives and information technology professionals. The key is Cisco's high and ever rising share price. It can afford to pay top price using its highly-valued shares, and can attract management to stay by offering share options. The pace of acquisition continues unabated.

Competitive environment

An important distinction up to now between competition in computer networking, and other technology industries like memory chips, is that price competition hasn't approached the point where profit margins are sacrificed. Cisco earns gross profit margins of 65%, defying expectations that high margins would erode as the market matured. Net profit margins, excluding exceptionals, have held above 20%.

Cisco expects future growth to come from the 'consumer phase' of the Internet revolution, predicting 30 to 50% growth in the data networking markets of countries with strong economies. It has also teamed up with the wireless giant, Motorola, to work together to provide Internet-based services over wireless phones and other wireless devices.

Cisco and Motorola plan to invest jointly as much as $1 billion (£600 million) over four to five years to deliver a wireless Internet. They plan to jump-start a new category of advanced products and services by broadcasting IP (Internet Protocol) signals over the air anytime and anywhere. The idea is to unite the convenience and mobility of wireless devices with the power to access large amounts of information from the Internet, including data, voice and video communications.

Both companies plan to cross-license technology and develop complementary products. The companies also plan to establish four Internet Solutions Centres worldwide, to drive innovation within the wireless industry and encourage other companies that want to provide integrated data, voice and video services over wireless networks.

In a related move, Cisco and French telecoms equipment supplier, Alcatel SA, agreed to develop advanced digital networks for mobile communications.

Lucent Technologies Inc., North America's largest maker of telecom equipment, paid $20.7 billion for number-three data-networking company Ascend Communications Inc., and it will increasingly compete with Cisco. Lucent bought Ascend at the beginning of 1999, for its so-called ATM computer switches that allow telephone companies to shunt data traffic on their own networks. Competition will also come from Lucent's closest rival Northern Telecoms – Nortel – who purchased Bay Networks in 1998. Bay Network specialized in supplying LAN hubs, relatively simple products used by enterprise IT staff to interconnect desktop computers and routers. Nortel and Lucent will now increasingly offer alternative solutions to Cisco and probably attack Cisco's gross margins.

What can go wrong?

Cisco includes the following comment in its most recent report: 'There are a number of market risks that investors and potential investors should consider. For a detailed explanation of the market risks and their potential impact on Cisco, please view Cisco's most recent SEC filings.' In these filings it draws attention to analysts comments on the more significant uncertainties in the industry:

Asia: As a result of recent unfavourable economic and political conditions, sales to certain countries in Asia and the Pacific Rim have declined. If the economic conditions in these markets worsen, or if these unfavourable conditions result in a wider regional or global economic slowdown, this may have a material adverse impact on the business, operations and financial condition of companies in the networking industry.

Year 2000: Many computer systems were not designed to handle any dates beyond the year 1999, which means computer hardware and software will need to be modified prior to the year 2000 in order to remain functional. It is still unknown exactly how the year 2000 will affect computers. It is also unknown how programs to resolve this issue will impact corporate budgets. Companies may need to devote a substantial portion of their information systems' spending in order to become year 2000 compliant. This could result in spending being diverted from networking solutions. Conversely, companies may have already taken corrective measures or may elect to devote smaller portions of their budgets to resolving this issue.

Increased competition: Due to rapid advances in technology and the integration of voice, video, and data networks, large telecommunications equipment players and small start-ups alike are entering the market. Larger companies have the financial strength and market presence to offer a new level of competition, while start-ups have the innovation and freedom necessary to bring new products to market quickly. Because these companies can benefit from one another, there is an increasing trend toward industry consolidation. Cisco expects this trend to continue, creating further competition and potentially impacting organizations' abilities to maintain their competitive advantage.

■■■
Monitoring

Markets are cruel to fallen angels. As long as Cisco performs to the high expectations of investors and analysts, it will be a prized share, but if it disappoints at any stage, the high valuation of the share is vulnerable, in any event in the short term. Investors should monitor Cisco's performance and that of Lucent and Nortel to see the extent to which their competition with Cisco is affecting margins, if any.

Cisco includes on its web site the following useful glossary on technical terms in its industry which is helpful when researching and monitoring:

> There are myriad technologies that go into creating a network. The list below is not intended to be comprehensive. Rather, it provides general explanations of the most common networking components, including links to information about Cisco's products.
>
> Hub – A hub is a hardware component acting as a junction for connecting various networking cables. A hub's primary purpose is to consolidate connectivity requirements for multiple end-users. Cisco's hub products include the FastHub line, 10BaseT hubs, and the 1528 Micro Hub.
>
> LAN – A Local Area Network (LAN) is a high-speed data network that covers a relatively small geographic area. It typically connects workstations, personal computers, printers, and other devices in a single building or other geographically limited area. LANs offer computer users many advantages, including shared access to devices and applications, file exchange between connected users, and communication between users via electronic mail and other applications.
>
> WAN – A Wide Area Network (WAN) is a data communications network that serves users across a relatively broad geographic area. It often uses transmission facilities provided by common carriers such as telephone companies.
>
> Protocol – A protocol is a formal set of rules and conventions that govern how computers exchange information and communicate over the network, much like a language. These technologies can be used to communicate across any set of interconnected networks. Most communication protocols tend to fall into one of the following groups:

- LAN protocols, which define communication over the various LAN media. Examples of LAN protocols include Ethernet and Token Ring.
- WAN protocols, which define communication over the various WAN media. WAN protocols are developed to maximize the ability to move information along greater distances so they generally function at lower speeds than do LAN protocols. An example of WAN protocols include Frame Relay.
- Routing protocols, which determine optimal paths through networks and transport information across these paths.

Router – A router is a device that moves information from one network to another, applying intelligence in the process to ensure that the information reaches its destination securely and in the fastest way possible. Routers support a variety of protocols at the same time. They use intelligence in both hardware and software to offer high functionality for complex networking tasks such as prioritization of data traffic. Cisco offers a broad range of routers, from the <u>Cisco 12000 and 7000 families</u>, which are designed for larger organizations, to the <u>Cisco 1600 series</u>, which is designed for smaller companies. The choice of router depends on the user's specific needs and functionality requirements.

Switch – A switch is a device that moves information between multiple users while maximizing the speed of data transfer. A switch is primarily used in parts of the network to alleviate network congestion and increase bandwidth within the network. Cisco has a variety of switches in its product line. Its LAN switching products are contained in the <u>Catalyst™ family</u>: its WAN switching products include the <u>IGX, BPX, and MGX series</u>. As with routers, the choice of switches depends on the user's specific needs and functionality requirements.

Switch Router – As technology develops at an ever increasing pace, the definitions of switches and routers are becoming increasingly blurred. The industry is now seeing routing and switching functions integrated into a single product called a Switch Router or Layer 3 switch. These products deliver the higher performance associated with traditional switches with some advanced intelligence associated with routers. Cisco recently introduced its <u>8500 family</u> of switch routers.

Remote access – Remote access solutions give groups and individuals who are remotely located the same level of connectivity and information access they would have if they were at the company's main office. Remote access servers are used by smaller workgroups to provide dial-in access to LAN and network resources. Remote access concentrators are used by larger organizations such as Internet Service Providers to provide dial-in access to the Internet and ISP network resources. Cisco offers a broad range of <u>Network Access solutions</u> including the AS5000 family of access servers, DSL solutions, and cable products.

Firewall – Firewalls ensure the security of data on private networks. Firewalls can be software-based, in which case they work with a router or access server, or they can be a standalone hardware solution for higher speed networks. <u>Cisco's firewall products</u> and software provide security solutions for large and small networks, keeping information private from the outside world when connecting to the Internet.

Software – Software functions primarily as the operating system for the network by managing the flow of data throughout the network. Cisco IOS™ software is the standard software that is built into all Cisco products. It provides the connectivity and capabilities required to deliver services and enable applications over the network.

MOTOROLA

Share Graph 1997–1998 – Motorola Inc.
Primary Market – NYSE – MOT

Price January 1999 $65
Market Value January 1999 $39 billion

SECTOR Technology INDUSTRY Communications Equipment
Top Line S&P 500 Index Relative Bottom Line MOT: Triangle
Marks Split
Left Scale: Top $ Price, Bottom Volume in Thousands

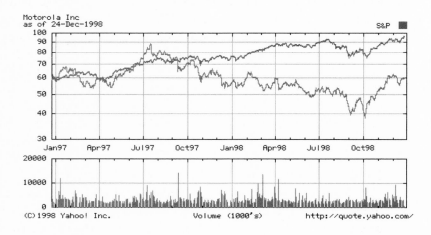

PRICE PERFORMANCE Year 1998	MOT		An investment made in January 1994 grew 38% by January 1999		
PRICE HISTORY	1998	1997	1996	1995	Notes
High Price	65.88	90.50	68.50	82.50	
Low Price	38.38	54.00	44.13	51.50	
High P/E	NM	46.75	36.03	24.47	
Low P/E	NM	29.54	32.22	16.91	

Chairman Gary Tooker, www.motorola.com
150,000 employees
1303 E Algonquin Road, Motorola Center, Schaumburg, IL 60196
Phone: (847) 576-5000 Fax: (847) 576-3258

Global Franchise: Wireless telephony and electronics

Motorola is a titan in the electronics industry, with a significant presence in activities ranging from cheap mobile phones to satellite communications. It is one of the world's largest providers of wireless communications equipment and a leading provider of semiconductors, components and services to the communications, automotive, defence and space industries. It was the first major force in wireless telephony, introduced the famous flip phone, and, until 1998 when Nokia overtook it, Motorola was the world's biggest supplier of mobile phones.

A decade ago, Motorola envisioned a telecommunications system that would harmonize existing land-line and cellular systems with a network of satellites and ground facilities, making global digital communications quick and easy. The Iridium system is the first telecommunications system to offer global access virtually anywhere, anytime, with one phone, one number and one bill. Motorola was the system's inventor, designer, prime contractor, programme manager, integrator and satellite manufacturer. To bring its revolutionary vision to life, Motorola first developed strategic global partnerships by assembling and managing a world-class team of leaders in electronics, aerospace, communications and software, and it owns about 20% of the Iridium communications satellite network.

Cellular products make up nearly 40% of Motorola's sales, and semiconductors account for 24%. It makes digital signal processors, microchips, cable modems, pagers, computers, electronic components and systems, and networking peripherals, and provides wireless telecom services in developing nations including China. Motorola has operations in about 60 countries and 45% of revenues come from outside the US. Annual reserves are $30 billion.

Setting a rational price

Portfolio 2001 WORKSHEET FOR TARGETING SHARE PRICES OF MOTOROLA IN 1999, 2000, 2001 & 2002
BASED ON FORECASTS MADE IN JANUARY 1999
EPS FISCAL 1988 TO DECEMBER $0.58

Growth	Year	Estimated EPS	P/E	Share Price Target	+10%	-10%	Notes
Consensus	1999	$1.95	30	$59	$64	$53	
33%	2000	$2.59	33	$85	$95	$86	
33%	2001	$3.45	30	$103	$114	$93	
30%	2002	$4.48	30	$133	$148	$120	

This 'what if' forecast suggests potential earnings and share prices based on current indications. Forecasts must be revised continuously in the light of all company results and industry, market and economic news. Forecasts can be misleading and cannot be treated as investment advice or used to motivate investments. See page 69.

Earnings per share growth expectations

With the explosive growth in wireless telephony (see the reports of Lucent Technologies and Texas Instrument), Motorola should in any event be in line to grow earnings at between 25% and 30% a year, in line with industry growth. In 1998, earnings were affected by a provision of over $1.5 billion for reorganization and redundancies and comparisons are artificial. Following weakness in the semiconductor market and economic crises in Asia, Motorola commenced reducing its workforce by about 10%, or 15,000 jobs, by June 1999.

Earnings in 1997 were $2.59 and the *Portfolio 2001* forecast follows the assumption that earnings per share growth will be 33% following strength in the mobile phone industry.

Motorola's involvement in the Iridium satellite project makes realistic forecasting problematic, even for short periods, as views differ on when and whether the project will ever be profitable. Iridium is in dire financial circumstances and unless it can do a deal with its creditors may be made formally bankrupt. Losses for Motorola could be severe and revenues for running the service may never materialise.

The forecast prepared does nothing more than slot Motorola earnings into a framework from which monitoring can start.

Earnings multiple expectations

The Iridium project is again a factor that will affect market sentiment and the multiple used of 30 times earnings only lines Motorola's share price up with current marked valuations. If Motorola can reassert its leadership in wireless telephony, a significantly higher multiple can be expected in present market conditions. On the other hand, if management disappoint shareholders again, the share will lack support.

Past performance indicators

Growth Rates %		MOT	S&P 500	Industry	Sector	Notes
Earnings per share 5 year		13.08	20.84	19.21	37.05	
1998 last reported vs 1997		NA	11.42	18.81	20.36	
Sales 5 year 1994-1998		17.50	16.18	19.59	33.92	
Profitability Ratios						
Gross Margin 1998	%	29.78	49.26	43.19	52.42	
5 year average	%	35.44	48.91	41.40	52.45	
Net Profit Margin 1998	%	-3.27	10.63	4.39	11.98	
5 year average	%	5.74	10.21	2.70	12.00	
5 Year Returns on:						
Assets	%	7.64	8.40	4.11	12.71	
Investment	%	11.54	13.20	5.89	17.62	
Equity	%	15.64	21.53	9.11	21.57	

■■■
The growth story

Concentration on analogue phones instead of digital, and falling analogue phone sales, low chip prices, economic problems in Asia and loss of market share to Nokia and Ericsson led Motorola to slash jobs and consolidate operations in 1998. After a wide ranging reorganization, earnings per share plunged from $2.93 in 1995 to $0.52 in 1998. However, the third quarter of 1998 brought a marked improvement in revenue and cost cutting.

Management have identified key growth areas for 1999 in Europe and in digital cellular and have forecast European growth of 50% for the year. According to their projections, the cellular industry in 1999 will grow to 215 million units from 155 million units in 1998, and the analogue's portion of the market will fall to 6% in 1999 from 16% in 1998.

The communications division turned out new digital products in the third quarter of 1998, driving phone revenue up 9%. Although analogue phones still accounted for 40% of Motorola's phone sales, the company released new ranges of digital phones, including a version of its popular StarTAC, and set out to start regaining lost market share.

Also, indications are that Motorola's semiconductor division, which accounts for about a quarter of the company's business, has stopped bleeding. Management halted production of a new chip plant, and there are signs that the semiconductor market has bottomed. International Data Corp., a market research firm in Framingham, Massachusetts, predicts chip sales will grow 8% in 1999, following a 9.2% decline in 1998.

Management plans to slash $750 million in excess costs in 1999. In the third quarter, $140 million was cut, $40 million more than expected. That helped Motorola earn $0.07 a share, an 86% decline from a year earlier, but well ahead of the forecast of $0.01.

Developments in the wireless phone industry

The cellular business accounts for $11.9 billion, about 40% of Motorola's total revenue, and one-half to two-thirds of the cellular business comes from handsets where Motorola has 20 to 25% market share right now. Motorola is hampered by the fact that it makes only base stations, which receive the radio signal when a call is made from a mobile phone, but it does not supply the switches, the brains that coordinate call routing, billing and data traffic, and it has had to outsource these components.

Motorola has now recognized that wireless telephony and the Internet are going to drive the future of communications, and are planning a new business based on a wireless Internet. Among initiatives to achieve this, it is collaborating with Cisco, which supplies the network connectivity products.

The first products of Motorola-Cisco could be ready in two years, and both companies intend to market their wireless Internet products jointly, with Motorola taking the lead.

The aim of the Cisco cooperation is to create a world environ-

ment where the operators of wireless networks can use interchange-
able equipment based on standards, instead of the largely
proprietary equipment used today. Cisco and Motorola say this
will make it easier for the operators of wireless networks to add new
services, such as transferring voice mail to e-mail and smart cards,
and to facilitate electronic commerce. The companies have received
encouragement for their plans from wireless operators including
Sprint Corp., Nextel Communications Inc. and AirTouch Communications Inc.

Motorola and Cisco will collaborate on some products and
have other partners as well. With Alcatel SA of France, Motorola
will develop and market digital network infrastructure for the
wireless protocol CDMA, code-division multiple access. Alcatel
last year purchased DSC Communications Corp. of Plano, Texas,
which makes Motorola's CDMA switch.

Motorola also makes and markets phones in China, the fastest-
growing telecommunications market in the world, adding nearly 1
million cellular-phone users each month. Total subscribers should
reach 22 million by the end of 1999, making it the world's third-
largest cell-phone market after the United States and Japan.

Technological strength
Broadband access opportunities that cable telephony offers are
being exploited now, and Motorola's turnaround should be helped
by this development. It is the leading manufacturer of cable
modems. Market researcher Dataquest has increased its projections
for 1999 shipments of cable modems by 91%, to 1.033 million
units and expects that number to reach 2.44 million in 2000.
Merrill Lynch has raised 1999 revenue estimates for the cable
modem market by 70% from $251 to $428 million.

Data signalling processors
Motorola claims to have developed a new lower-cost, high-speed
DSP (digital signal processor) that can process audio, video and
complex math equations more efficiently than its general-purpose
counterparts. Motorola is currently tied with Analog Devices Inc.
(Norwood, MA) for third place in the DSP market, after Texas
Instruments and Lucent Technologies.

Iridium satellite revenues

By developing a process for satellite mass production, Motorola literally revolutionized the industry, which has led to a shorter production cycle and a record number of satellite launches in the shortest period of time ever. Motorola is also responsible for producing the communications electronics payload – the brains of the satellite – and is the first to use satellite cross-links to relay a signal, allowing satellite to satellite communication.

To link the satellite system with existing land systems, Motorola developed, built and manages the system's ground infrastructure, which integrates the satellite and existing terrestrial phone systems across multiple worldwide standards.

The vision of the Iridium system represents over 40 years of Motorola's innovation in wireless and space communications technology. As the system's designer, developer and prime contractor, Motorola could maintain its position as the leading systems integrator for large-scale global satellite communications systems well into the twenty-first century provided Iridium does not run into trouble.

Commercial service for Iridium commenced in November 1998, when Motorola's service provider business, Motorola Worldwide Information Network Services (M-WINS), received operational and marketing certification to become Iridium North America's first fully integrated service provider for US government customers needing global, mobile Iridium voice and paging services. Earnings prospects are by no means clear, but Motorola could start to see income in 1999, when its investment in Iridium according to some analysts will be fully written off.

Strategic alliances

Motorola and Lucent have entered into an alliance to develop high performance DSPs, and Motorola has formed several additional strategic business alliances. With Numerical Technologies Inc. (NumeriTech) of Santa Clara, California, it established the industry's first alliance for subwavelength design and manufacturing, and the first ever successful fabrication of the 0.1 micron microprocessor using a standard 0.18-micron silicon production process.

This technology breakthrough solves the critical problem facing the semiconductor industry of how to design and manufacture subwavelength integrated circuits necessary to gain further performance and profitability advances.

Fabrication of the 0.1-micron microprocessor was accomplished using phase-shifting and optical proximity correction (OPC) technology from NumeriTech in conjunction with Motorola's advanced processing. Motorola has since incorporated NumeriTech's software into its production design and fabrication processes to produce additional subwavelength integrated circuits.

Motorola claims that the new process represents a significant performance improvement over current industry-standard 0.18-micron processing technology, with consequent smaller die sizes for advanced performance devices such as the PowerPC family.

What can go wrong?

In January 1999, Motorola could not be examined as a low-risk high-reward potential. Over 1999, Motorola should reassert positive earnings growth and bring information into the public domain on current financial prospects for the Iridium project but indications to June 1999 have been poor. Investors will also need to look at the extent of Motorola's involvement in China, where it is manufacturing semiconductors and phones and is the second largest foreign investor in the country after General Motors.

As a wireless phone company, Motorola can be seen as an industry leader with the resources to make a strong comeback and share in the potential of the wireless phone boom.

Motorola attracts easily as a turnaround situation and a speculation, but investors will need to wait until the group picture is less threatening. When this is the case, investing on the back of wireless phone prospects could present as a low-risk high-reward investing opportunity.

Monitoring

Monitoring will be supported by following Texas Instruments, Lucent Technologies, Cisco Systems, Nokia and Ericsson, as well as www.motorola.com to build a more comprehensive picture.

News on the Iridium project and how it may affect Motorola also needs to be monitored.

NORTHERN TELECOM (NORTEL)

Share Graph 1997–1998 Northern Telecom Ltd
Primary Market – NYSE – NT

Price January 1999 $60
Market Value January 1999 $39.8 billion

SECTOR Technology INDUSTRY Communications Equipment
Top Line NT Bottom Line S&P 500 Index Relative: Triangle
Marks Split
Left Scale: Top $ Price, Bottom Volume in Thousands

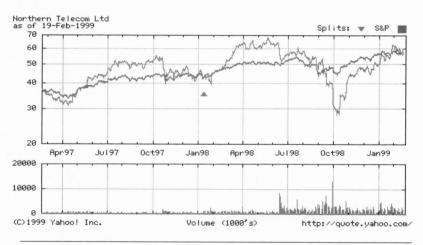

PRICE PERFORMANCE	NT		An investment made in January 1994 grew 327% by January 1999		
Year 1998					

PRICE HISTORY	1998	1997	1996	1995	Notes
High Price	65.88	90.50	68.50	82.50	
Low Price	38.38	54.00	44.13	51.50	
High P/E	NM	46.75	31.03	24.47	
Low P/E	NM	29.54	18.78	16.91	

Chairman D. Schvenke, **www.nortel.com**
80,000 employees
8200 Dixie Road, Suite 100, Brampton, Ontario L6T 56
Phone: (905) 836-0000

Global Franchise: Telephony infrastructure

Northern Telecom, trading as Nortel Networks, is one of the world's leading makers of telecommunications products that include wireless, switching, and broadband network systems for service providers, long-distance telephone systems and local systems for residential and business users. With the acquisition of Bay Networks in 1998, the line was expanded to include voice/data networking equipment, computer telephony integration, multimedia, and telephone network management systems. The US accounts for nearly 60% of sales and Canada, 10%. The Canadian telecom company BCE owns 42% of Nortel. Nortel has customers in more than 150 countries around the world and 80,000 employees worldwide with 20,000 working in Research and Development. Revenues to 31 December were $17.6 billion.

Common shares are listed on the New York, Toronto, Montreal, Vancouver, and London stock exchanges. Revenues for 1998 were 17.6 billion US dollars.

Setting a rational price

Portfolio 2001 WORKSHEET TARGETING SHARE PRICES OF NORTHERN TELECOM IN 1999, 2000, 2001 & 2002
BASED ON FORECASTS MADE IN JANUARY 1999
EPS FISCAL 1988 TO DECEMBER $1.84

Growth	Year	Estimated EPS	P/E	Share Price Target	+10%	-10%	Notes
20%	1999	$2.20	30	$69	$77	$62	
20%	2000	$2.64	30	$79	$87	$71	
20%	2001	$3.16	30	$95	$105	$86	
20%	2002	$3.80	30	$114	$126	$102	

This 'what if' forecast suggests potential earnings and share prices based on current indications. Forecasts must be revised continuously in the light of all company results and industry, market and economic news. Forecasts can be misleading and cannot be treated as investment advice or used to motivate investments. See page 69.

Earnings per share growth expectations

Nortel is a worthy competitor to Lucent, and Lucent's growth was set at 30% consistent with management indications. Nortel is likely to be less aggressive in achieving growth by acquisition. A conservative 20% annual growth, bearing in mind the strong industry demand, is used in the *Portfolio 2001* forecast. In 1998, Nortel grew operational earnings at 22%, above the 20% growth rate in the industry.

Earnings multiple expectations

Thirty times current earnings is, again, a cautious forecast with scope on the upside as Nortel's earnings growth gathers momentum.

Past performance indicators

Growth Rates %		NT	S&P 500	Industry	Sector	Notes
Earnings per share 5 year		4.17	20.73	18.79	36.94	
1998 last reported vs 1997		NA	11.22	17.50	10.13	
Sales 5 year 1994-1998		12.94	16.15	18.79	36.94	
Profitability Ratios						
Gross Margin 1998	%	29.78	49.19	43.93	52.35	
5 year average	%	35.44	48.85	41.41	42.37	
Net Profit Margin 1998	%	-3.27*	10.56	4.18	11.87	*Exceptionals Acquisition
5 year average	%	5.74	10.17	2.62	10.91	
5 Year Returns on:						
Assets	%	7.64	8.29	4.01	10.87	
Investment	%	11.45	13.06	17.38	17.38	
Equity	%	15.64	21.43	9.01	21.31	

The growth story

The growth dynamics of the communications and networking industries have been reviewed extensively in the reports on Lucent and Cisco, and the same growth dynamics create opportunities for Nortel.

Telephony networking is now a $100 billion a year market, deregulation has changed the behaviour of service providers, the Internet has changed consumer behaviour, and boundaries are blurring between data and telephony, wireline and wireless, service provider and enterprise, LAN and WAN. All these changes are creating new market opportunities for Nortel.

Post the acquisition of Bay Networks in 1998, Nortel's capacity to compete with Lucent and Cisco across the spectrum of the industry has been appreciably strengthened, and a share of Nortel's sales now come from data communications and broadband networks for cable systems, both strong growth opportunities.

What can go wrong?

For some time Northern Telecom has been called a tortoise among greyhounds. It was thought to be too closely tied to the conservative telephone company customers that comprise two thirds of its $15 billion revenues, and even its effort to break out of that mould by buying Bay Networks was criticized by analysts at the time. The acquisition was expensive at a cost of $6.7 billion, and raised concerns about Bay's high sales, general and administration expenses, and about culture clashes between Silicon Valley-based Bay and Canadian Nortel, which is headquartered in Ontario. Nortel's share price fell considerably at the time.

Markets incline to be over-critical of Nortel, and the Bay acquisition is working out better than expected. Bay even contributed to Nortel's bottom line by the first quarter of 1999, and recent restructuring moves by management, including 8,000 layoffs, could ultimately reduce Nortel's expenses by up to $300 million a year.

Fundamentally, Nortel has the same exposure to global economic conditions as other major global telecom companies, with almost 40% of its revenues originating overseas. Any weaknesses in Nortel's structure will concern investors and analysts in view of the strong competition from Lucent and Cisco.

Nortel serves a growth industry and is a soundly based successful company which, subject to valuations at the time of investing, could present low-risk high-reward investing opportunities.

Monitoring

Nortel should be monitored with reference to Lucent, Cisco, Texas Instruments and Motorola and `www.nortel.com`.

12

INVESTING IN MILLENNIAL NICHE OPPORTUNITIES

This chapter focuses on companies which are likely to have some special fizz over the millennial years and the millennial celebrations. Tiffany, America's icon jeweller and gift supplier, is superbly well positioned globally to cash in on the gift season and I have high hopes for it. The story for LVMH (Louis Vuitton, Moët & Hennessy), the world's biggest champagne opportunity is similar but not the same. For years it has been picking the grapes to make the millennial fizz of which we are all going to partake, and should have vintage years when the millennial corks start popping. However, LVMH is a complicated investing prospect in need of a good year or two.

The first prospect reviewed in the section, Warren Buffett's Berkshire Hathaway, is an opportunity for very different reasons. Following his merger by acquisition with America's largest insurance company, US Re, at the end of 1998, he has an extra $20 billion-plus cash to invest, and many investors will find the opportunity of another season of share picking with Warren Buffett irresistible.

General Electric, America's top global conglomerate should enter the new century as a wonder company though not a *wunderkind* as its forebear, the Edison Electric Light Company, was at the birth of the twentieth century.

The media giant, Time Warner, should score as the media industry gets into high gear for the millennial celebrations and profits from grand marketing promotions in the run up to the calendar change. Omnicom, the world's largest advertising agency and one of its most consistently profitable companies, should be another great millennial play even though Omnicom is a name most people will not know, and it sounds like a village print shop.

Boeing is a controversial prospect in a cyclical trough and badly affected by the global economic turndown. It is, however, the world's top aircraft manufacturer and space company. As we send missions to Mars and pepper the skies with low earth orbiting satellites, Boeing is very busy making the future happen by launching those satellites.

Vodafone-AirTouch and Nokia need no introduction and it will be obvious to everyone why they are included. The mobile phone revolution is happening. One company is the world's biggest wireless phone service provider and the other is the biggest handset manufacturer.

America On Line (AOL) is also discussed, though at its current price I am not suggesting that it is a low-risk high-reward opportunity. However, with revenues of almost $3 billion a year to its credit and a major acquisition in progress, as we enter the twenty-first century it is very much one of the world's feature companies that could become interesting as an investment prospect in future – and maybe our analyst friends with their feet firmly planted in cyberspace may know more than we do after all. Steve Case, America On Line's inspired founder and driving force, certainly has his feet firmly anchored on terra firma.

Boeing and America On Line being discussed under the same heading, and Berkshire Hathaway and Louis Vuitton sharing an investor's agenda, will be seen by many as a mixture of strange bedfellows. However, there is strength in diversity and *Portfolio 2001*'s Millennial Niche opportunities include interesting research targets for everyone, regardless of their investing styles.

The *Portfolio 2001* web site **www.portfolio2001.com** encourages discussion on Millennial Niches, and more great opportunities will hopefully be revealed by visitors to the site and available for you to access.

BERKSHIRE HATHAWAY

Share Graph 1997–1998 Berkshire Hathaway
Primary Market – NYSE – BRKA

Price January 1999 $59,100
Market Value January 1999 $79.9 billion

SECTOR Financial INDUSTRY Property and Casualty Insurance
Top Line BRKA Bottom Line S&P 500 Index Relative
Left Scale: Top $ Price, Bottom Volume in Thousands

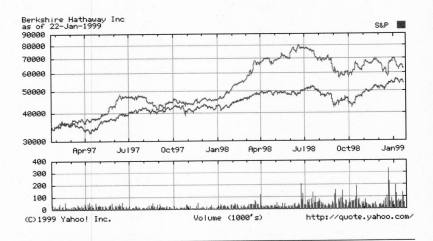

Berkshire Hathaway Inc
as of 22-Jan-1999

(C)1999 Yahoo! Inc.   Volume (1000's)   http://quote.yahoo.com/

PRICE PERFORMANCE	BRKA		An investement made in January 1994 grew 298% by January 1999		
PRICE HISTORY	1998	1997	1996	1995	Notes
High Price	84,000	48,600	38,000	33,400	
Low Price	45,800	33,000	29,800	20,250	
High P/E	NA	31.52	18.40	49.88	
Low P/E	NA	21.40	14.43	30.24	

Chmn/CEO Warren E. Buffett, www.berkshirehathaway.com
38,000 employees
1440 Kiewit Plaza, Omaha, NE 68131
Phone: (402) 346-1400 Fax: (212) 783-3833

Global franchise: Warren Buffett's investing skills

Berkshire Hathaway, 39% owned by Warren Buffet, has investments mainly in insurance companies, but also owns businesses in aviation, manufacturing confectionery products, cleaning systems, footwear, diamonds, furnishing and retailing, among others. Because Buffett is known as the century's greatest stock picker, investors in Berkshire get the best of both worlds: granite-like security and imaginative equity investing which consistently outperforms markets and indexes in good times and bad. Buffett took control of Berkshire in 1965 with its stock at $18 and assets comprising mainly ageing textile plants. The textile plants were soon replaced with more rewarding investments and the same shares now trade at about $60,000.

At the beginning of 1999, Warren Buffett's Berkshire Hathaway holding company completed the acquisition of America's largest reinsurance company, US Re. With Berkshire's $9 billion cash funds the group had about $30 billion for him to invest. If markets are strong Berkshire will be strong with them, and if they are weak, Buffett will make investments which multiply dramatically, as he has done in every market fall for the last three decades.

Setting a rational price

Earnings per share growth and earnings multiple expectations
Berkshire Hathaway is a unique company and analysts are wary forecasting for it. Berkshire shares tend to trade at a substantial premium to asset value which can be difficult to determine with the range of unlisted assets.

With consolidated accounts post the merger with US Re published, analysts will have more scope to construct forecasts based on earnings per share expectations. Investors are inclined to follow Buffett and expect a better return than they would get from other investments.

Past performance indicators
Standardized reporting formats on Berkshire do not give a very

meaningful picture as revenues arise from disposals and provisions are often made on acquisitions.

Past performance indications

Growth Rates %		BRK.A	S&P 500	Industry	Sector	Notes
Earnings per share 5 year		34.13	20.43	20.46	17.50	
1998 last reported vs 1997		NM	12.34	44.30	16.58	
Sales 5 year 1994-1998		28.50	15.68	13.85	13.53	
Profitability Ratios						
Gross Margin 1998 5 year average	% %	NA	NA	NA	NA	
Net Profit Margin 1998 5 year average	% %	23.71 19.17	10.90 10.17	15.56 13.49	15.78 14.90	
5 Year Returns on: Assets Investment Equity	 % % %	 5.73 9.96 9.98	 8.39 13.36 22.98	 3.83 10.62 13.69	 2.16 9.71 16.75	

The growth story

Piling up the earnings growth year after year

Berkshire's earnings per share growth powers ahead year after year, though in 1997 it was lower than the previous year following accounting changes and less realized gains in the fiscal year. Operational earnings advanced from $732 million to $971 million in 1997:

Earnings per share:	1997	1996	1995	1994	1993
Before realized investment gain and cumulative effect of accounting change	$ 971.54	$ 732.96	$ 564.31	$ 417.66 (4)	$449.90 (5)
Realized investment gain (1)	570.47	1,331.83	105.30	51.88	308.50
Cumulative effect of change in accounting for income taxes	–	–	–	–	(28.80)
Net earnings	$1,542.01	$2,064.79	$ 669.61	$ 469.54	$ 729.60

In 1997, Berkshire's net assets increased 34.1%, an achievement
Warren Buffett did not consider noteworthy in a year when the
market advanced at about the same rate. He included these remarks
in his report to shareholders:

> Any investor can chalk up large returns when stocks soar, as they
> did in 1997. In a bull market, one must avoid the error of the
> preening duck that quacks boastfully after a torrential rainstorm,
> thinking that its paddling skills have caused it to rise in the world.
> A right-thinking duck would instead compare its position after the
> downpour to that of the other ducks on the pond . . . though we
> paddled furiously last year, passive ducks that simply invested in the
> S&P Index rose almost as fast as we did. Our appraisal of 1997's
> performance, then: Quack.

Look-through earnings

The only company ever to do so, Berkshire informs shareholders on
both 'reported' earnings and 'look-through' earnings, explained in
this extract from the 1998 report:

> Reported earnings are a poor measure of economic progress at
> Berkshire, in part because the numbers shown in the table
> presented earlier [not shown here] include only the dividends we
> receive from investees – though these dividends typically represent
> only a small fraction of the earnings attributable to our ownership.
> Not that we mind this division of money, since on balance we
> regard the undistributed earnings of investees as more valuable to us
> than the portion paid out. The reason is simple: Our investees often
> have the opportunity to reinvest earnings at high rates of return. So
> why should we want them paid out?
>
> To depict something closer to economic reality at Berkshire than
> reported earnings, though, we employ the concept of 'look-
> through' earnings. As we calculate these, they consist of:
>
> (1) the operating earnings reported in the previous section, plus;
> (2) our share of the retained operating earnings of major
>   investees that, under GAAP accounting, are not reflected in
>   our profits, less;
> (3) an allowance for the tax that would be paid by Berkshire if
>   these retained earnings of investees had instead been
>   distributed to us. When tabulating 'operating earnings' here,

we exclude purchase-accounting adjustments as well as capital gains and other major non-recurring items.

The following table sets forth our 1997 look-through earnings, though I warn you that the figures can be no more than approximate, since they are based on a number of judgment calls. (The dividends paid to us by these investees have been included in the operating earnings itemized on page 11 [not shown here], mostly under 'Insurance Group: Net Investment Income.')

Berkshire's Major Investees	Berkshire's Approximate Ownership at Yearend(1)	Berkshire's Share of Undistributed Operating Earnings (in million $)(2)
American Express Company	10.7%	161
The Coca-Cola Company	8.1%	216
The Walt Disney Company	3.2%	65
Freddie Mac	8.6%	86
The Gillette Company	8.6%	82
The Washington Post Company	16.5%	30
Wells Fargo & Company	7.8%	103
Berkshire's share of undistributed earnings of major investees		743
Hypothetical tax on these undistributed investee earnings (3)		(105)
Reported operating earnings of Berkshire		1,292
Total look-through earnings of Berkshire		$1,930

Competitive advantage

Warren Buffett's skills and track record are Berkshire's competitive advantage. Sure that his investing strategies are sound and market corrections do not affect the intrinsic value of his holdings, Buffett's 1998 shareholders' report discoursed on the difference between investors and disinvestors: 'Rejoice when markets decline and allow [us] . . . to deploy funds more advantageously . . . and . . . smile when you read a headline that says *Investors lose as market falls.* Edit it in your mind to *Disinvestors lose as market falls – but investors gain.* Though writers often forget this truism, there is a buyer for every seller and what hurts one necessarily helps the other. As they say in golf matches: "Every putt makes *someone* happy."'

What can go wrong?

Rejoicing in a market fall will be easier for a billion dollar investor who is on the lookout for buying opportunities than for an investor with modest means fearful of losing his savings. Does Warren Buffett really 'rejoice' when markets fall? The answer could be . . . yes! In the past he has seized opportunities to buy when others followed the herd and sold indiscriminately. And, after saying early in 1998, when markets were over the top, that the margin of safety he looked for before investing was missing, he took responsibility for another $20 billion of cash assets to invest through the US Re transaction.

If there is one person in the world who would not take on another $20 billion plus of assets as an ego booster it is Buffett. In market volatility he will prise out the best opportunities and, short of a global economic disaster, the year 2000 could be a big year for investors in Berkshire.

On the negative side, Berkshire has big holdings in Global Profit Harvesters like Coca-Cola and Gillette which are vulnerable to weaker global growth and, while Buffett has made few mistakes up to now, no one is infallible. He is also in his mid-sixties and some consideration will have to be given to succession.

Monitoring

The annual reports to shareholders published on www.berkshirehathaway.com fully explain the affairs of the group and several books on Buffett strategies detail the multi-billion dollar gains he has scored with a raft of major investments, including Coca-Cola. Whatever major moves Warren Buffett makes are bound to be top stories in the financial press and so investors should find following news on Berkshire is straightforward.

GENERAL ELECTRIC COMPANY

Share Graph 1997–1998 General Electric Company
Primary Market – NYSE – GE

Price January 1999 $104
Market Value January 1999 $332.7 billion

SECTOR Conglomerates INDUSTRY Conglomerates
Top Line GE Bottom Line S&P 500 Index Relative: Triangle
Marks Split
Left Scale: Top $ Price, Bottom Section Volume in Thousands

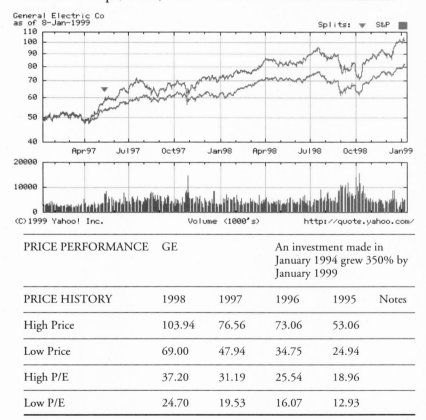

PRICE PERFORMANCE	GE		An investment made in January 1994 grew 350% by January 1999		
PRICE HISTORY	1998	1997	1996	1995	Notes
High Price	103.94	76.56	73.06	53.06	
Low Price	69.00	47.94	34.75	24.94	
High P/E	37.20	31.19	25.54	18.96	
Low P/E	24.70	19.53	16.07	12.93	

Chmn/CEO John F. Welch, www.ge.com
250,000 employees
3135 Easton Turnpike, Fairfield, CT0643
Phone: (203) 373-2816 Fax: (203) 373-3031

Global Franchise: The world's premier industrial group

Business Week introduced an article on GE saying: 'When it comes to investing in as grand an American business as General Electric the question isn't so much why buy the stock, but why not buy it?'

GE Under Jack Welch

MARKET VALUE
BILLIONS OF DOLLARS

NET INCOME
BILLIONS OF DOLLARS

REVENUES
BILLIONS OF DOLLARS

'81 '83 '85 '87 '89 '91 '93 '95 '97 MAY
'98

DATA: COMPANY REPORTS ©BW

Source: *Business Week* chart, May 1998

General Electric Co. was born in 1892 out of the merger of Thomas Edison's Edison General Electric Company and the Thomson Houston Electric Company. It was 'born again' when its CEO 'Jack' Welch took the reins in 1981 and re-invented the corporation as he restructured the GE group. GE is now a diversified technology, manufacturing and services company with almost 250,000 employees and 250 manufacturing plants in over 100 countries, commanding worldwide leadership in twelve businesses. It is the world's largest producer of aircraft engines; owns NBC, the leading US TV network; is one of the world's largest manufacturers of major appliances; and is a leading supplier of lighting products, high performance engineered plastics and industrial materials, industrial control systems, electrical distribution and control products and power systems. GE Information Services is engaged in electronic commerce with over 40,000 trading partners, and GE Medical provides medical diagnostic technology. GE Transport Systems is a leading manufacturer of locomotives and industrial engines, and GE Capital Services embraces a global family of over 30 businesses concentrated on specialized financing and insurance. Global revenues exceed $100 billion with over 50% coming from the US.

Setting a rational price

Portfolio 2001 WORKSHEET FOR TARGETING SHARE PRICES OF GENERAL
ELECTRIC IN 1999, 2000 & 2001
BASED ON FORECASTS MADE IN JANUARY 1999
EPS FISCAL 1998 TO DECEMBER $2.80

Growth	Year	Estimated EPS	P/E	Share Price Target	+10%	-10%	Notes
15%	1999	$3.22	30	$97	$107	$87	
15%	2000	$3.70	30	$111	$123	$100	
15%	2001	$4.25	30	$128	$142	$158	

This 'what if' forecast suggests potential earnings and share prices based on current indications. Forecasts must be revised continuously in the light of all company results and industry, market and economic news. Forecasts can be misleading and cannot be treated as investment advice or used to motivate investments. See page 69.

Earnings per share growth expectations

Analysts take a positive view on: GE's prospects following the strength of the US economy; GE's 14% earnings per share growth in 1998; a net income rise of 17% in GE Capital (including acquisitions); strength in power generation, medical equipment and aircraft engines; and in consistent improvements in productivity across the group plus a rising dividend payment. To increase resources available for acquisition, GE resolved not to continue buying back shares in 1999. Wall Street expects that, in the same way as Jack Welch reinvented the corporation in the 1980s, GE will reinvent any business it acquires and dramatically improve its performance. This intellectual capital plus a healing global economy encourage expectations that GE will find opportunities to flex its financial and management muscle to open a new wave of growth opportunities, particularly in emerging markets. Earnings growth in the *Portfolio 2001* forecast was set at 15% to reflect organic growth and a new wave of acquisitions.

Earnings multiple expectations

Wall Street is convinced that GE management will grow businesses organically and improve performance in both existing operations and in acquisitions. The company's 'Sigma' management disciplines detailed in **www.ge.com** have been used to sustain performance growth decades after structural and managerial improvements in company businesses. In 1998, earnings per share growth was only 14% and GE is priced for perfection at above 30 times 1999 earnings. Investors buying richly valued shares must be vigilant about reviewing their expectations as market conditions and company performances can change for the better or worse. The *Portfolio 2001* forecast has followed market indications in January 1999 on valuations. Conglomerates are an unloved sector and tend to command low valuations, and this makes the rich valuation of GE exceptional.

Past performance indicators

Growth Rates %		GE	S&P 500	Industry	Sector	Notes
Earnings per share 5 year		15.26	20.43	NM	14.90	
1998 last reported vs 1997		14.00	11.71	NM	12.38	
Sales 5 year 1994-1998		11.36	15.68	NM	9.02	
Profitability Ratios						
Gross Margin 1998	%	55.34	49.22	NM	47.31	
5 year average	%					
Net Profit Margin 1998	%	9.25	10.63	8.54	8.54	
5 year average	%	8.99	10.21	8.25	8.25	
5 Year Returns on:						
Assets	%	2.70	8.22	4.01	4.01	
Investment	%	9.66	12.97	9.52	9.62	
Equity	%	22.42	21.46	21.21	21.21	

The growth story

Highlights of 1999 reflect performance true to form

By the end of 1998, GE revenues passed $100 billion for the first time, accompanied by growth in earnings and earnings per share:

	1998	1997
Revenues	$100,469	$90,840
Earnings	$9,296	$8,203
Per Share Earnings		
- Diluted	$2.80 (+14%)	$2.46
- Basic	$2.84 (+13%)	$2.50

Cash generated from operating activities for 1998 was a record $10 billion, up from last year's $9.3 billion.

Earnings per share grew faster than earnings, reflecting the impact of shares repurchased under a six-year $17 billion share repurchase programme initiated in December 1994.

Revenues, including acquisitions, rose 11% to a record $100.5 billion, reflecting continued growth from global activities and product services.

The Six Sigma quality initiative continued to drive GE's operating efficiency measures. Operating margin was a record 16.7% of sales, up from last year's comparable 15.7%.

GE Capital Services earnings were 17% higher at $3.796 billion. The record results reflected the globalization and diversity of GE Capital Services' 28 businesses, with strong double-digit increases in all of its five segments.

In 1998, 108 acquisitions valued at more than $18 billion were made, of which 70 were outside the US, supporting the key initiatives of services growth and globalization.

GE Capital Services announced an agreement to acquire Eagle Star Reinsurance Company Ltd of the United Kingdom, further strengthening its Employers Reinsurance broker business; completed the acquisition of the $4.4 billion consumer loan business of Lake Corporation in Japan; and agreed to acquire WTB Westdeutsche Kreditbank GmbH, a leading German provider of equipment leasing products and services with approximately $670 million in financing assets. GE Capital Services also announced the formation of a $2.6 billion private-label credit card joint venture with First USA.

GE Medical Systems further strengthened its service business with the acquisition of Compagnie Generale des Equipements Medicaux, the largest independent multi-vendor service company in Europe. The previously announced acquisition of Diasonics Vingmed drove a 74% increase in ultrasound revenues in the fourth quarter, including $45 million in cardiac ultrasound sales where GE previously had no presence.

In December, the quarterly dividend was increased by 17% to $0.35 per share, the twenty-third consecutive year of increased dividends by GE.

The house that Jack built

When John F. Welch, 'Jack' Welch, took office as chairman and CEO of GE in 1981, the group was facing a mid-life crisis with challenges from foreign and local competition, and profitability was suffering.

Jack Welch rebuilt the group structurally and conceptually, and his personal legacy is that he is known as the man who reinvented the corporation. Businesses that weren't first or second in their global markets were 'fixed, closed or sold'. GE divested $10 billion of marginal businesses and made $19 billion in acquisitions to strengthen the world-class businesses that would lead it into the nineties and the next century.

The deep and dramatic restructuring initiated in the 1980s foresaw the advent of increased global opportunity and competition. In addition to the 'hardware' changes, GE also set out to instil in its people the 'spirit and soul' of a small company. Self-confidence, simplicity and speed were emphasized and rewarded, and bureaucracy was eliminated, to tap the ideas of those closest to any problem.

The Asia opportunity

GE businesses, particularly GE Capital, continue to make decisive moves to position themselves for strong future growth, and where other corporations saw Asia as a crisis, GE saw an opportunity.

Strategy dictates being in business only where the group business can be a leader, has competitive advantages and can earn an acceptable return.

What can go wrong?

Even in recessionary conditions, GE will probably find growth opportunities, but in a serious global economic downturn it will not escape pressures on earnings. A market revaluation will follow if ever earnings growth stalls or is threatened.

Jack Welch is retiring in 2000 and the succession plan has not yet been announced. With strong management built around him, investors are comfortable that when he leaves 'he will never look over his shoulder'. Nevertheless, when the icon is no longer in charge, markets could be nervous for a while.

Monitoring

www.ge.com is a comprehensive information resource on a large diversified group, and the financial press report fully on GE, Jack Welch and, of course, the various global economic factors that affect the group.

TIFFANY

Share Graph 1997–1998 Tiffany & Company
Primary Market – NYSE – TIF

Price January 1999 $28.75
Market Value January 1999 $1.994 billion

SECTOR Services INDUSTRY Retail – Speciality
Bottom Line TIF intersecting S&P 500 Relative in March 99
Left Scale: Top $ Price, Bottom Volume in Thousands
Graphic not rebased for two-for-one split in June 1999

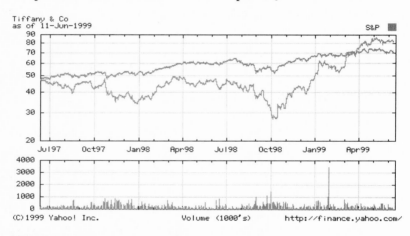

PRICE PERFORMANCE	TIF		An investment made in January 1994 grew 282% by January 1999		
PRICE HISTORY	1998	1997	1996	1995	Notes
High Price	26.00	24.31	21.13	13.72	
Low Price	13.50	16.88	12.34	7.25	
High P/E	25.78	29.36	35.56	29.66	
Low P/E	13.39	20.38	20.78	15.68	

Chmn/CEO William R. Chaney, Pres/COO Michael J. Kowalski,
www.tiffany.com
4,000 employees
727 Fifth Avenue, New York, NY 10022
Phone: (212) 755-8000 Fax: (212) 605-4465

Global Franchise: Jewellery retailing

Tiffany is one of the world's most successful jewellery businesses, on course for a millennial gifts bonanza. If 'tiffany.com' becomes 'tiffan-e' and sells on the Internet, the cybersky is the limit.

Founded in 1837, when Charles Lewis Tiffany opened a store in downtown Manhattan, and with more than 100 Tiffany stores and boutiques worldwide, the group is an internationally renowned designer, manufacturer, marketer and retailer of an extensive selection of fine jewellery (73% of fiscal 1997 sales), timepieces, sterling silverware, china, crystal, stationery, fragrances and accessories. The blue Tiffany box with a white ribbon is almost as famous as the company itself. Tiffany's mission is to be the world's most respected jewellery retailer. Its three channels of distribution are:

1. US representing 48% of fiscal 1997 sales, which includes retail sales in company-operated stores in the US and wholesale sales to independent retailers in the US.

2. Direct marketing and corporate (business-to-business) and catalogue sales.

3. International retail, representing 42% of fiscal 1997 sales. These include retail sales through company-operated stores and boutiques, corporate sales and wholesale sales to independent retailers and distributors in the Asia-Pacific region, Europe, Canada, the Middle East and Latin America.

Headquartered at 727 Fifth Avenue in New York, Tiffany has more than 4,000 employees and annual sales exceeding $1.3 billion.

Setting a rational price

Portfolio 2001 WORKSHEET FOR TARGETING SHARE PRICES OF TIFFANY IN 1999, 2000 & 2001
BASED ON FORECASTS MADE IN JANUARY 1999
EPS FISCAL YEAR TO JANUARY 1998 $0.81

Growth	Year	Estimated EPS	P/E	Share Price Target	+10%	-10%	Notes
20%	1999	$1.5	25	$38	$42	$34	Strong growth
20%	2000	$1.80	25	$45	$50	$41	Millennium peak
20%	2001	$2.16	22.5	$49	$54	$44	Post millennium

This 'what if' forecast suggests potential earnings and share prices based on current indications. Forecasts must be revised continuously in the light of all company results and industry, market and economic news. Forecasts can be misleading and cannot be treated as investment advice or used to motivate investments. See page 69.

Earnings per share growth expectations

Sales and profit growth in 1998 were above expectations and Tiffany is on course for an exceptional year in 1999, when personal and corporate gift buying for the millennial celebrations weigh in. Improved conditions in Asia and Japan, and a stronger yen, would fuel earnings growth further.

www.tiffany.com came on line early in 1998 and the first page invites the viewer to explore the web site and 'afterwards, please visit our store nearest you. Click on the buttons below for information about Tiffany & Co., America's house of design since 1837.' If Tiffany goes 'on line' and the web page message offers a chance to click on the next button and buy directly on the Internet, the impact on trade could be stunning, particularly over the millennial gift season.

The *Portfolio 2001* worksheet forecasts earnings per share growth of 20%. This is based on organic growth of the business through conventional outlets which is higher than analysts' consensus in the range of 18 to 20%. Analysts' forecasts were probably not yet factoring in the millennial gift market bonanza.

Earnings multiple expectations

Analysts' forecasts for earnings multiples were in the region of 18 to 20 times current year's earnings in January 1998. With the higher earnings per share growth suggested, higher earnings multiples have also been applied of 25% in 1999 and 2001, and 30 times current earnings in 2000 to line up with the peak millennial gift buying season.

Portfolio 2001 forecasts follow a bean counter approach. However, if Tiffany ever starts e-trading silverware, gifts, jewellery and diamonds, some zealous analysts will wax poetic along the lines of: 'Twinkle twinkle little Tiffan-e, How much money can you make for me? Your price could go up so very high, you'll be like a diamond in the cybersky.'

Past performance indicators

Growth Rates %		TIF	S&P 500	Industry	Sector	Notes
Earnings per share 5 year		32.28	20.56	31.07	20.48	
1998 last reported vs 1997		18.35	12.25	20.61	21.44	
Sales 5 year 1994-1998		15.91	15.83	21.13	21.84	
Profitability Ratios						
Gross Margin 1998	%	55.73	49.16	27.86	44.44	
5 year average	%	55.31	48.83	27.57	43.27	
Net Profit Margin 1998	%	7.21	10.85	-3.11	6.35	
5 year average	%	4.17	10.21	3.04	5.93	
5 Year Returns on:						
Assets	%	5.50	8.34	-2.44	4.78	
Investment	%	8.00	13.03	11.63	7.72	
Equity	%	12.23	21.49	14.63	14.92	

The growth story

Tiffany has key growth strategies to expand channels of distribution in important markets around the world and ensure that product offerings are superior. Through marketing programmes it enhances customer awareness of the product designs, quality and the value Tiffany offers.

A large scale expansion of outlets was initiated in the early 1990s and over 100 outlets globally now make Tiffany one of the world's largest jewellery and giftware retailers. Though adversely affected by Japan's weak economy and the Asian financial crisis, performance has remained positive, buoyed by American prosperity, the US consumer boom and new stores in the US. Christmas sales in the US in 1998 were outstanding and above expectations. Overall growth was 12%, with a 6% gain in the New York flagship store and a 15% branch store gain. In 1998, new stores opened in the US included Scottsdale, Denver, Las Vegas and Seattle. Sales in Japan also improved. A new store is opening in Paris at the end of 1999.

Focused management have been leveraging the famous American luxury brand and, from small jars of fragrance to expensive jewellery items, Tiffany wares gain competitive advantage with the brand endorsement. The brand goes back 150 years, is a mark of good taste and, in the best American tradition of all, Tiffany products that arrive packaged in the famous blue box with the white ribbon are good value for money.

The www.tiffany.com web site is not yet trading on line, but it is promoting Tiffany wares on the Internet, and a visit to the diamonds page on the site reveals how well advanced the e-trading opportunity is.

What can go wrong?

Short of a global recession or a severe recession in America that takes the wind out of Tiffany's sails, prospects look good.

Monitoring

www.tiffany.com gives a good picture of the company and investors following the site can also monitor developing e-business prospects.

TIME WARNER

Share Graph 1997–1998 – Time Warner Inc.
Primary Market – NYSE – TWX

Price January 1999 $62.50
Market Value January 1999 $69.5 billion

SECTOR Services INDUSTRY Printing and Publishing
Top Line TWX. Bottom Line S&P 500 Index Relative
Left Scale: Top $ Price, Bottom Volume in Thousands

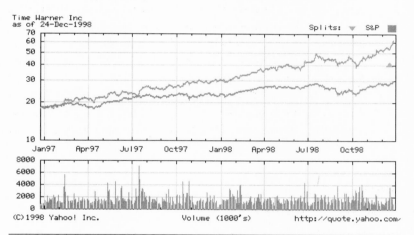

PRICE PERFORMANCE	TWX VS-S&P		An investment made in January 1994 grew 193% by January 1999		
PRICE HISTORY	1998	1997	1996	1995	Notes
High Price	63.13	31.00	22.63	22.81	
Low Price	29.06	18.29	14.88	16.81	
High P/E	NM	NM	NM	NM	
Low P/E	NM	NM	NM	NM	

Chmn/CEO Gerald M. Levin, Vice chairman R. E. Turner,
www.timewarner.com
67,500 employees
75 Rockefeller Plaza, New York, NY 10019
Phone: (212) 484-8000 Fax: (212) 956-2847

Global Franchise: Media & entertainment

Time Warner states that its mission is to be home to the world's best artists and journalists, to offer audiences the highest quality choices, and to bring shareholders a superior return. It has consolidated in a cohesive group enterprise the world's biggest and most important collection of interests in publishing, entertainment and media. These include Turner Entertainment, CNN News Group, Home Box Office, Time Inc., Warner Brothers, Warner Music Group and Time Warner Cable. It is the largest magazine publisher in the US and has leading positions in cable television networks and cable television programming. Warner Brothers is a producer and distributor of movies, TV programmes and videos, and Warner Music Group's Home Box Office is the largest US pay-TV service, with Time Warner Cable the largest US cable system.

Time Warner is positioned to be a key, if not the leading, player in e-commerce as the Internet increasingly is accessed via cable, and it earns subscription and advertising based revenues. The group currently derives $2 billion of revenue from direct marketing, including recordings and Time Life Books, and has 25 million customers on its database.

Setting a rational price

(To reflect realistic earnings, because of the cost of servicing debt, Time Warner is valued on a multiple of earnings before interest, tax, dividends and amortisation (EBITDA), instead of a price earnings multiple.)

Portfolio 2001 WORKSHEET FOR TARGETING SHARE PRICES OF TME WARNER
TWX IN 1999, 2000 & 2001
BASED ON FORECASTS MADE IN JANUARY 1999
EPS FISCAL 1987 TO DECEMBER $3.54(E)

Growth	Year	Estimated EBITDA	Multiple	Share Price Target	+10%	-10%	Notes
17.5%	1999	$4.15	18	$75	$83	$68	
17.5%	2000	$4.87	18	$88	$98	$80	
17.5%	2001	$5.72	18	$102	$114	$92	

This 'what if' forecast suggests potential earnings and share prices based on current indications. Forecasts must be revised continuously in the light of all company results and industry, market and economic news. Forecasts can be misleading and cannot be treated as investment advice or used to motivate investments. See page 69.

EBITDA expectations

EBITDA of $1.368 billion on revenues of $7.464 billion was earned for the fourth quarter of 1998, compared to $1.291 billion on revenues of $6.974 billion for the same period in 1997. For the full year 1998, combined EBITDA was an all-time record $4.462 billion on revenues of $26.838 billion, compared to $4.033 billion on revenues of $24.622 billion in 1997. Revenues grew 9% for the fourth quarter and 11% for 1998, and EBITDA grew 18% for the quarter and 14% for the year. EBITDA results for the fourth quarter and full year follow in a schedule and vary slightly from the headline figures quoted by the group which have been normalized for the effects of certain cable-related transactions that occurred in 1998 and 1997.

An investing opportunity as varied and dynamic as Time Warner is a bad candidate for a long-range forecast and even a forecast for a year would be tentative. EBITDA growth for the *Portfolio 2001* forecast has been set at 17.5%, following the pattern set in the 1999 results. The current importance of the group's cable investments, as evidenced with the January 1999 AT&T transaction, and the millennial entertainment opportunity have not been specially factored in, neither has the effect of debt reduction and lower debt servicing charges.

EBITDA multiple expectations

Time Warner is unique in relation to the strength and breadth of its asset and intellectual property resources and its high debt funding. There are no comparable norms for earnings multiple valuations either as EBITDA, price earnings or other measures. The multiple of 18 used in the forecast reflects the market price in January 1999 based on estimates of EBITDA for the current year.

Past performance indications
1998 TIME WARNER GROUP EDITDA

	Fourth Quarter		Year	
	1998	1997	1998	1997
TIME WARNER	$	$	$	$
Publishing	234	198	607	529
Music	205	153	493	467
Cable Networks – TBS	201	166	706	573
Filmed Entertainment –TBS	98	97	192	200
Cable	96	111	325	427
Intersegment Elimination	(6)	(2)	(27)	(13)
Time Warner EBITDA	**828**	**723**	**2,296**	**2,183**
ENTERTAINMENT GROUP				
Filmed Entertainment-Warner Bros.	100	83	503	404
Broadcasting –The WB Network	(15)	(28)	(93)	(88)
Cable Networks – HBO	115	100	454	391
Cable*	352	425	1,369	1,184
Entertainment Group EBITDA	**552**	**580**	**$2,233**	**1,891**
Intercompany Elimination	(12)	(12)	(67)	(41)
Combined EBITDA	**1,368**	**1,291**	**4,462**	**4,033**

Over recent years, with the build up and consolidation of the group, past performance indicators are of little help as earnings have been affected by acquisition related charges and increments, and interest has taken a toll on earnings. This schedule however illustrates the scope for improvement as management start implementing targets to boost returns on equity to industry norms.

Growth Rates %		TIF	S&P 500	Industry	Sector	Notes
Earnings per share 5 year		NM	21.00	28.01	20.66	
1998 last reported vs 1997		NM	12.19	14.14	24.25	
Sales 5 year 1994-1998		16.08	16.49	11.94	22.17	
Profitability Ratios						
Gross Margin 1998	%	42.76	49.51	48.24	44.79	
5 year average	%	42.14	49.15	48.24	44.79	
Net Profit Margin 1998	%	2.29	10.85	6.93	6.68	
5 year average	%	-0.91	10.27	4.01	5.90	
5 Year Returns on:						
Assets	%	-0.32	8.47	3.70	5.58	
Investment	%	-0.38	13.28	4.71	7.81	
Equity	%	-5.62	21.60	7.04	15.26	

The growth story

The Time Warner Group was built by Ted Turner with a series of mergers and acquisitions, in the course of which substantial debts were incurred. Group debt was $9 billion at the end of 1998, reduced from $11 billion at the beginning of 1998. The cost of servicing the debt has reflected non trading losses and, though earnings per share are positive now, to reflect the operating earnings more realistically analysts usually value Time Warner on a multiple of EBITDA – earnings before interest, tax, dividends and amortisation, instead of a price earnings multiple. Combined pro forma EBITDA growth was 18% for fourth quarter of 1998, 14% for the year 1998. Operating cash flow nearly doubled in 1998, and strong cash flow will continue to fund debt repayment, enhancing profits. A share repurchasing programme has started and will gain momentum as free cash flow grows. In January 1999, Time Warner announced a landmark deal with AT&T which will offer AT&T branded cable telephony service over Time Warner's existing cable television systems. AT&T has over 12 million cable subscribers. Time Warner will have a 22.5% stake in the venture, the funding for which will be provided by AT&T. It will receive about $300 million by way of a one time payment of $15 per telephony-ready household passed on, and a monthly fee of $1.50 per subscriber, climbing to $6 within 6 years. Merrill Lynch initially valued Time Warner's stake in the new joint venture in the range of $5billion. Significantly the transaction illustrates how far Time Warner are on the line to extracting value from their cable infrastructure.

What can go wrong?

While Time Warner is well positioned to capitalize on current opportunities in entertainment and communications, there are risks related to the company and the industries it services. The group's captial structure is complex and the high levels of long-term debt, incurred in the process of building acquisitions, are expected to be paid from earnings, which will be beneficial to shareholders. But, until the debts are extinguished, servicing them is a severe burden, and while they exist they are a potential risk. The entertainment industry is also vulnerable to high profile and costly failures which could impact on earnings. And, while presently Time Warner's cable infrastructure is seen as a potential money spinner, it will be some time before the increased revenues from the cable instrastructure find their way into the earnings stream.

Monitoring

www.timewarner.com is a great Internet resource, and an information gateway to the group's media and publishing empire. By following this web site investors can be kept well informed on group acitivites, potential, and financial performace. Monitoring news and announcements on Time Warner and the industries in which it is engaged through the *Wall Street Journal,* or a similar comprehensive resource for comment and news, will keep investors well informed.

OMNICOM

Share Graph 1997–1998 – Omincom Group Inc.
Primary Market – NYSE – OMC

Price January 1999 $58
Market Value January 1999 $9.7 billion

SECTOR Services INDUSTRY Advertising
Top Line Omnicom Bottom Line S&P 500 Index Relative:
Triangle Marks Split
Left Scale: Top $ Price, Bottom Volume in Thousands

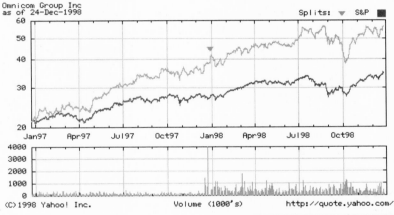

PRICE PERFORMANCE   OMC

An investment made in January 1994 grew 519% by January 1999

PRICE HISTORY	1998	1997	1996	1995	Notes
High Price	58.50	42.38	26.06	18.75	
Low Price	37.00	22.25	17.75	12.47	
High P/E	NA	30.91	23.15	20.20	
Low P/E	NA	16.23	15.76	13.44	

Chmn Bruce Crawford, Pres/CEO John D. Wren, www.omnicom.com
27,200 employees
437 Madison Avenue, New York, NY 10022
Phone: (212) 415-3600 Fax: (212) 415-3530

Global franchise: The world's largest advertising agency group

Omnicom Group Inc. is the world's leading marketing communications company and consists of the advertising agency networks BBDO Worldwide, DDB Needham Worldwide and TBWA Worldwide. Omnicom also includes Diversified Agency Services (DAS), which operates branded independent agencies in public relations, speciality advertising, and direct response and promotional marketing; Optimum Media Direction; Goodby Silverstein & Partners; and Communicade, which manages significant minority investments in several leading Internet and digital media development companies. The group originates and places advertising in various media including television, radio, newspaper and magazines and provides its clients with additional services in the line of marketing consultation, consumer market research, design and production of merchandising and sales promotion programmes and materials, direct mail advertising, corporate indentification, public relations of North America, the United Kingdom, Continental Europe, the Middle East, Africa, Latin America, the Far East and Australia. Revenues exceed $4 billion.

Setting a rational price

Portfolio 2001 WORKSHEET FOR TARGETING SHARE PRICES OF OMNICOM IN
1999, 2000 & 2001
BASED ON FORECASTS MADE IN JANUARY 1999
EPS FISCAL 1998 TO DECEMBER $1.65

Growth	Year	Estimated EPS	P/E	Share Price Target	+10%	-10%	Notes
25%	1999	$2.10	35	$76	$82	$68	
25%	2000	$2.60	35	$91	$101	$82	
25%	2001	$3.25	35	$114	$127	$102	

This 'what if' forecast suggests potential earnings and share prices based on current indications. Forecasts must be revised continuously in the light of all company results and industry, market and economic news. Forecasts can be misleading and cannot be treated as investment advice or used to motivate investments. See page 69.

Earnings per share growth expectations
Analysts' consensus forecasts for growth are currently below 20% a year and at the same time Omnicom earnings per share growth are growing at near 30%. With the expected promotional and marketing surges that will run with the millennial celebrations, forecasting 25% appears to be sensible.

Earnings multiple expectations
The quality and security of Omnicom's earnings in a strong equity market are likely to ensure a market rating of well above 30 times current earnings.

Past performance indicators
Strong earnings growth and good margins are reflected:

Growth Rates %		OMC	S&P 500	Industry	Sector	Notes
Earnings per share 5 year		17.64	15.68	25.86	21.83	
1998 last reported vs 1997		16.84	12.34	23.01	21.19	
Sales 5 year 1994-1998		17.67	15.68	25.86	21.83	
Profitability Ratios						
Gross Margin 1998	%	72.24	49.22	49.32	44.31	
5 year average	%	70.16	48.87	53.36	43.18	
Net Profit Margin 1998	%	7.28	10.90	7.86	6.54	
5 year average	%	6.01	10.17	5.70	5.97	
5 Year Returns on:						
Assets	%	4.27	8.57	5.71	5.11	
Investment	%	14.31	13.65	9.26	7.36	
Equity	%	24.85	23.28	22.09	15.25	

The growth story

Operating results for fiscal year 1998 reflect the earnings growth achieved:

Omnicom Group Inc.

(Unaudited)
(in thousands of dollars, except per share data)

Twelve Months Ended December 31 (Decrease)	1998	1997	Increase
Commission and fee income	$4,092,042	$3,124,813	31%
Operating and interest expenses	3,571,893	2,743,568	30%
Income before income taxes	520,149	381,245	36%
Income taxes	215,808	156,484	38%
Income after income taxes	304,341	224,761	35%
Equity in affiliates	25,069	30,089	17%
Minority interests	(44,342)	(32,435)	(37%)
Net income	$285,068	$222,415	28%
Earnings per share			
Basic	$1.72	$1.40	23%
Diluted	$1.68	$1.37	23%
Dividend declared per share	$0.525	$0.450	17%

What can go wrong?

Omnicom attracts as a low-risk, high-reward opportunity, particularly for investors who expect a millennial spending spree preceded by massive promotion and advertising.

The risks to earning could be a severe global economic setback or extreme market correction. No equity investing is exempt from this danger.

Monitoring

www.omnicom.com is informative on performance and company operations. Investors should keep abreast of company developments and monitor news and global economic events in the *Wall Street Journal* and other financial publications which report on major companies and the global economy.

BOEING

Share Graph 1997–1998 The Boeing Co.
Primary Market – NYSE – BA

Price January 1999 $35.56
Market Value January 1999 $35.5 billion

SECTOR Captial Goods INDUSTRY Aerospace and Defence
Top Line S&P 500 Index Relative Bottom Line Price BA: Triangle
Marks Split
Left Scale: Top $ Price, Bottom Volume in Thousands

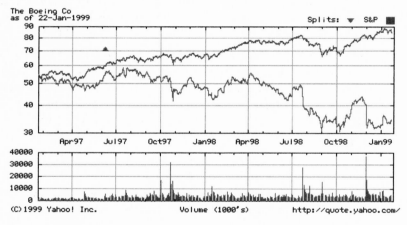

The Boeing Co as of 22-Jan-1999

(C) 1999 Yahoo! Inc.   Volume (1000's)   http://quote.yahoo.com/

PRICE PERFORMANCE   BA

An investment made in January 1994 grew 110% by January 1999

PRICE HISTORY	1998	1997	1996	1995	Notes
High Price	56.25	114.50	107.50	80.00	
Low Price	29.00	43.00	74.13	44.38	
High P/E	43.87	NM	58.05	NM	
Low P/E	28.34	NM	57.51	NM	

Chairman P. M. Condit, www.boeing.com
231,000 employees
7755 East Marginal Way, South Seattle, WA 98108
Phone: (206) 655-2121 Fax: (206) 655-3987

Global Franchise: Jet aeroplanes, space transportation, information and communication systems, defence and missile systems

Prepare for lift off. Boeing will generate $2.2 billion from launch services in 1999 and expects the global space industry to rise over 300% by 2003, from a base of $40 billion in 1998. Boeing is the world's largest manufacturer of commercial aircraft, with a global market share of over 60%, and also the world's leading space industry company. Following a merger with McDonnell Douglas in 1996, the group is the world's leading business in information, space and defence systems company. The information and communication markets addressed by this business segment are projected by industry analysts to more than double within the next ten years, with major growth coming largely from new constellations of communications satellites. Boeing is the principal contractor for NASA and the International Space Station, and the second largest US Department of Defense supplier. In its military aircraft and missiles business unit, Boeing has major products in tactical fighters, trainers, helicopters, military transports, tankers, strike missiles and special purpose airplanes for the US and foreign governments. Of commercial aircraft sales, 64% are outside the United States, and 55% of the commercial aircraft contractual backlog at year-end 1997 was with customers based outside the United States. Of total 1997 revenues of $45.8 billion, commercial aircraft accounted for $27 billion, defence, space and information for $18 billion, and customer finance and other services $700 million.

Setting a rational price

Portfolio 2001 WORKSHEET FOR TARGETING SHARE PRICE RANGE FOR BOEING - BA - IN 1999, 2000 & 2001
BASED ON FORECASTS MADE IN JANUARY 1999
EPS FISCAL 1988 TO DECEMBER $1.08

Growth	Year	Estimated EPS	P/E	Share Price Target	+10%	-10%	Notes
Indication	1999	$1.51	25	$38	$42	$34	
15%	2000	$1.73	25	$43	$48	$39	
15%	2001	$1.98	25	$50	$55	$45	

This 'what if' forecast suggests potential earnings and share prices based on current indications. Forecasts must be revised continuously in the light of all company results and industry, market and economic news. Forecasts can be misleading and cannot be treated as investment advice or used to motivate investments. See page 69.

Earnings per share growth expectations

Sustained growth in airliner demand depends on sustained economic growth and capacity additions by airlines, in line with passenger traffic increases. In Asia, the economic crises in 1997 led to a sharp fall-off in demand that affected plans and led to production cutbacks in 1998.

Taking the view that global economic conditions will start reviving in 1999, earnings growth has been projected ahead at 15%. This will follow several years with low recorded earnings following reorganizations, mergers and the fall-off of business after the Asian economic crisis.

Earnings multiple expectations

Boeing's commercial airliner business is a classic Profit Harvester situation, which will command low multiples unless strong growth is evident. The information, space and technology business could be the world's most diverse and sophisticated technology base and, if it were a free standing business, might attract a higher market valuation.

For the *Portfolio 2001* forecast the current market valuation of Boeing was followed, suggesting a multiple of over twenty-five times earnings.

Past performance indicators

Growth Rates %		BA	S&P 500	Industry	Sector	Notes
Earnings per share 5 year		NM	20.84	27.09	25.94	
1998 last reported vs 1997		NA	11.42	12.74	17.79	
Sales 5 year 1994-1998		-0/75	16.18	5.69	12.33	
Profitability Ratios						
Gross Margin 1998	%	10.82	49.26	14.57	23.61	
5 year average	%	11.13	48.51	14.02	22.72	
Net Profit Margin 1998	%	2.57	10.63	4.04	5.38	
5 year average	%	11.13	10.21	3.32	4.40	
5 Year Returns on:						
Assets	%	2.80	8.40	4.30	5.90	
Investment	%	4.43	13.20	6.65	8.87	
Equity	%	7.42	21.53	10.39	15.20	

The growth story

Flying out of bad weather

With a severe fall off in demand from Asia in 1997 and 1998, Boeing's profits fell out of the sky, and the turbulence encouraged investors to run for the exits.

Source: Microsoft moneycentral.com

When others were selling shares, Boeing had faith in its flight plan and bought back its shares. In the third quarter of 1998, it announced a share repurchase programme to repurchase up to 15% of the company's outstanding shares of common stock. As of year-end 1998, it repurchased 35.2 million shares, approximately 3.5% of outstanding stock, for $1.3 billion.

Results for 1998 indicate that the company is back on course with revenues for the full year of $56.154 billion and net earnings of $1,120 million, or $1.15 per share. Comparable figures for 1997 were sales of $45.8 billion and a net loss of $178 million, or $.18 per share but, excluding a 1997 special charge after the McDonnell acquisition, 1997 earnings would have been $698 million, or $0.71 per share.

	4th Quarter		Year end December 31	
	1998	1997	1998	1997
(Dollars in millions except per share data)				
Sales and other operating revenues	$17,099	$11,727	$56,154	$45,800
Net earnings (loss)	$465	$(498)	$1,120	$(178)
Earnings (loss) per share *	$.48	$(.51)	$1.15	$(.18)
Average shares (millions) *	960.8	985.5	976.7	984.5
* Diluted				

Chairman Phil Condit indicated that the commercial aeroplane production processes continue to demonstrate improvement consistent with plans, and the company continues to make the productivity investments that are key to achieving performance and financial goals. For the second quarter of 1999 Boeing reported markedly improved earnings and the forecasts need to be reviewed.

Boeing's workforce was reduced from a high of 238,000 in 1998 to 231,000 at year-end 1998. Workforce reductions during January 1999 will exceed 3,000. Year-end 1999 and 2000 employment levels are projected to be in the range of 200,000 to 210,000 and 185,000 to 195,000, respectively.

Reports published by Boeing are comprehensive and include business segment data that gives a full picture of a multi division business. The January 1999 report on business segment data follows, and investors wishing to study the company in depth will find full explanations in the comprehensive reports filed in www.boeing.com

The Boeing Company and Subsidiaries
Business Segment Data

(Unaudited)

(Dollars in millions)	Twelve months ended December 31		Three months ended December 31	
	1998	1997	1998	1997
Revenues:				
Commercial Aircraft	$35,545	$26,929	$11,377	$6,681
Military Aircraft and Missile Systems	12,990		3,875	
Space and Communications	6,889		1,686	
Information, Space & Defence Systems	19,879	18,125	5,561	4,832
Customer and Commercial Financing, Other	730	746	161	214
Operating revenues	$56,154	$45,800	$17,099	$11,727
Earnings (loss) from operations:				
Commercial Aircraft	$63	$(1,837)	$218	$(1,244)
Military Aircraft and Missile Systems	1,283		361	
Space and Communications	248		91	
Information, Space & Defence Systems	1,531	1,317	452	309
Customer and Commercial Financing, Other	367	381	34	76
Unallocated expense	(241)	(216)	(55)	(64)
Share-based plans	(153)	99	(47)	141
Earnings (loss) from operations	$1,567	$(256)	$602	$(782)
Other income, principally interest	283	428	64	125
Interest and debt expense	(453)	(513)	(112)	(148)
Earnings (loss) before income taxes	$1,397	$(341)	$554	$(805)
Net earnings (loss)	$1,120	$(178)	$465	$(498)
Effective income tax rate	19.8%	47.8%	16.1%	38.1%
Research and development:				
Commercial Aircraft	$1,021	$1,208	$222	$266
Military Aircraft and Missile Systems	304		91	
Space and Communications	570		151	
Information, Space & Defence Systems	876	716	242	194
Total research and development expence	$1,895	$1,924	$464	$460

Financial outlook for full year 1999 and 2000

Based on current schedules and plans, Boeing has indicated the following performance expectations:

	1999	2000
Consolidated revenues	$58b	
Net earnings	$1.5/1.8	
Commercial aircraft deliveries by number	620	480
Sales by business segment:		
Commercial aircraft	$38b	$28b
Military aircraft and missile systems	$12b	$13b
Space and communication	$ 7b	$7b
Company R&D	$1.6/$1.8b	$1.6./$1.8b
Composite operations margin	4-5%	4-5%

Currently it expects the composite earnings from operations margin for 2000 to be slightly lower than the margin in 1999, due to the model mix of commercial aircraft deliveries. Commercial aircraft deliveries in the year 2000 will be predominantly newer aircraft programmes, which have lower initial gross profit margins than established aircraft programmes.

Commercial aircraft

The strong demand for airliners over the last few decades was boosted by airline deregulation in domestic US markets and in international markets. By 1997, about one-half of the world's air travel was taking place within an open-market environment. The worldwide market for commercial jet aircraft follows long-term trends in airline passenger traffic which depend on sustained economic growth in developed and emerging countries and political stability. While Boeing's airliner business is cylical, its space business has the potential to insulate it from airline cyclicality in the future.

The effects of the Asian economic crisis have been severe for Boeing and have even resulted in its having to store aircraft built for customers who deferred delivery, or were unable to take delivery. After increasing production plans for wide bodied aircraft in 1998, and then scaling them back in view of mounting concern over softening orders from Asia, Boeing made new plans to increase production from 47 to 51 aircraft per month by the first quarter of 1999, followed by 50.5 per month by the second quarter and then back to 48.5 per month from the fourth quarter of 1999.

Production plans will concentrate more on the world's best selling aeroplane, its 737 twinjet, and on smaller, shorter-range models that continue to sell briskly. Worldwide, Boeing is satisfied that overall jetliner output will remain stable for the next two to three years.

Information space and defence systems

Aeroplanes will continue to be over half of Boeing's sales for the foreseeable future, and financial prospects will not improve dramatically until production problems have been resolved and the global economy has regained its vigour. As this happens, space should also become a bigger part of the earnings story.

Commercial space ventures, including the floating Sea Launch rocket platform, and projects such as the International Space Station, can do much to ensure Boeing's viability into the next century. Achieving this position was a major objective of the acquisition of Rockwell in December 1996, and of McDonnell Douglas in July 1997.

Boeing generated over $2 billion from launch services in 1998 and this could rise to possibly $4.55 billion by 2002.

Delta rockets

The Delta II rocket is the workhorse of Boeing's launch business. McDonnell Douglas created the Delta family of rockets in 1960 to support Air Force and NASA programmes, and the Delta II has been in operation since 1989. Iridium World Communications Ltd, the Motorola-backed entity that is offering a global, satellite-based phone and paging service, used Delta II rockets to put 55 satellites into orbit in 1998, more than three-quarters of the total Iridium constellation.

Boeing has a $1.4 billion contract to provide systems integration and build and launch satellites for Ellipso, a 17-satellite constellation that will provide global voice and data communications and is also an industrial partner and investor in Teledesic, a 288-satellite system that will provide high-speed data connections anywhere on the planet.

There have been mishaps with the launch business. The first Delta III rocket failed at lift off, destroying PanAmSat's $225 million Galaxy X communications satellite in the process. Boeing plans to get the Delta III off the ground again in the first quarter of 1999.

Another ambitious Boeing project is Sea Launch. It will use a converted oil rig to send rockets into space from the middle of the Pacific Ocean. By firing payloads from the equator, Sea Launch can leverage the Earth's rotational force to increase the efficiency of its launches. Boeing has a 40% interest in Sea Launch and is the overall project coordinator. The other partners are KB Yuzhnoye/ PO Yuzhmash of Ukraine, which produces the two-stage Zenit launch vehicles for Sea Launch; RSC Energia of Russia, which produces the rocket's upper stage; and Kvaerner Maritime of Norway, which built the Sea Launch command ship and converted the launch platform.

During the fourth quarter of 1998, the first elements of the International Space Station were put in orbit and the Boeing-built Unity module was joined to the Russian-launched Zarya unit by Shuttle astronauts, as part of the Boeing-led, 16-nation effort to establish a permanent research centre in orbit.

The information, space and defence systems business addresses a market expected by industry analysts to surge, with the major growth factor being the rapid expansion of information and communication technologies for satellite-based wireless services. Corporate, business and residential users for these services are expected to grow at a compound annual rate of 7% between 1997 and 2012. Much of this growth is identified with new communications satellite constellations known as the 'Internet in the Sky'. Industry forecasts indicate that up to 2,000 satellites will need to be launched into space in the next two decades, creating a demand for assured access to space and low-cost launch service.

Boeing provides a full family of space launch services and is the prime contractor for NASA's Space Shuttle and the prime contractor for the International Space Station project throughout its lifetime in orbit.

For commercial launch services, which are expected to be the biggest market force affecting the space systems business, Boeing is well positioned with the Sea Launch and Delta family of commercial launch vehicles.

Defence and Ground based 'star wars'

In April 1998, Boeing won a three-year, $1.6 billion contract to be the primary developer of a proposed national United States missile-defence system, one of the Pentagon's most coveted and technically challenging jobs. Boeing's missile-defence contract envisions creating a modest, ground-based version of the hotly debated 'Star Wars' concept which President Ronald Reagan championed more than a decade ago, to protect the US against intercontinental ballistic missiles. Boeing is positioned to receive as much as $5.2 billion over 10 years as the lead coordinator of the programme. At the first stage its main role will be to identify and then coordinate how various radars, ground stations, tracking systems and inter-ceptors can be merged into a single antiballistic-missile system.

Many critics expect that budget and technical problems could end up blocking deployment of a ground based 'star wars' system, but with the award of the US government contract, Boeing's role as the premier integrator of complex, high-profile space projects for the US government has been affirmed.

Competitive advantage

The barriers to entry in both Boeing's aeroplane and space businesses defined by expertise, infrastructure and finance are immense, and the Boeing resources keep it in the pivotal position.

The European consortium, Airbus Industries, is increasing market share in the commercial airlines business, and this com-petition has led to rounds of intense pressure on pricing. Boeing is addressing competition by driving for greater productivity. It is committed to being not only the world's largest but also the most economic and profitable aircraft supplier. Boeing gained econ-omies of scale by mergers and organic industrial growth. Since the mergers, it has been improving processes and introducing cost reduction initiatives to ensure it continues to build aircraft com-petitively at acceptable profit margins.

What can go wrong?

Investors in Boeing will need to have firm views on the direction of the global economy and should keep informed on the activities of competitors. An example of the ever present risks of space technology was the failure of the Delta III launch. Commercial airliner failures could have a severe impact on investor perceptions and even on company earnings. Excessive dollar strength with euro weakness would also give the European Airbus consortium an advantage in jet airliner pricing.

Monitoring

www.boeing.com is informative, and reference to the 10K and 10Q SEC filings flesh out the business's complexities with meaningful explanations.

NOKIA

Share Graph 1997–1998 – Nokia Corporation
Primary Market – HELSINKI – NYSE – ADR NOK

Price January 1999 $138.59
Market Value January 1999 $83.4 billion

SECTOR Technology INDUSTRY Communications Equipment
Top Line Nokia ADR Bottom Line S&P 500 Index Relative
Right Scale: % Growth, Bottom Volume in Thousands

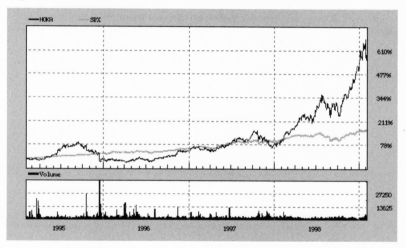

PRICE PERFORMANCE	ADR NOK		An investment made in January 1994 grew 628% by January 1999		
PRICE HISTORY	1998	1997	1996	1995	Notes
High Price	62.72	25.61	14.78	14.78	
Low Price	16.63	13.78	7.78	7.81	
High P/E	NA	24.34	29.20	22.29	
Low P/E	NA	13.10	15.37	11.78	

Chairman Casimir Ehrnrooth, www.nokia.com
42,300 employees
52300 Keilalahdentie 4, PL 226 FIN-00045
Phone: (905) 427-6654 Fax: (358) 065-6388

Global Franchise: Wireless telephony instruments

Nokia is a supplier of telecommunications systems and equipment. Its core businesses include the development, manufacture and delivery of operator-driven infrastructure solutions and end-user-driven mobile phones. It is now a leading global company focused on the key growth areas of wireless and wireline telecommunications. A pioneer in mobile telephony, Nokia is the world's leading mobile phone supplier and a leading supplier of mobile and fixed telecom networks including related customer services.

Nokia also supplies solutions and products for fixed and wireless datacom, as well as multimedia terminals and computer monitors.

Setting a rational price

Portfolio 2001 WORKSHEET FOR TARGETING SHARE PRICES OF NOKIA : NOKA A ADR IN 1999, 2000 & 2001
BASED ON FORECASTS MADE IN JANUARY 1999
EPS FISCAL 1998 TO DECEMBER PER ADR $2.86

Growth	Year	Estimated EPS	P/E	Share Price Target	+10%	-10%	Notes
30%	1999	$1.85	40	$74	$82	$67	
30%	2000	$2.41	40	$97	$107	$87	
30%	2001	$3.13	40	$125	$139	$112	

This 'what if' forecast suggests potential earnings and share prices based on current indications. Forecasts must be revised continuously in the light of all company results and industry, market and economic news. Forecasts can be misleading and cannot be treated as investment advice or used to motivate investments. See page 69.

Earnings per share growth expectations

In January 1999, analysts were re-assessing Nokia after the exceptional results announced for 1998, and increasingly recognized Nokia as one of the world's highest quality stocks with the best prospects over the next five years.

The *Portfolio 2001* forecast has been prepared on the basis of sustained earnings per share growth of 30% per annum. Momentum in Nokia's growth suggests a higher multiple, but achieving 30% growth is a credible achievement for any company, and there are reasons for caution.

Growth in the mobile phones industry is subject to global economic factors and the industry is intensely competitive. If any major markets weaken, competition is certain to erode margins. Nokia management have also indicated that Research and Development spend will increase with the development of G3 phones, third generation cellular products; capital expenditure will grow from 4.3 billion Finnish marks in 1998 to FIM 7 billion in 1999 to cater for production expansion; and 120 million additional shares will be issued, which analysts think may be used to fund acquisitions. Acquisitions can reflect related accounting write downs before they boost profits.

In 1998 there was the first marketing of pay-as-you-use wireless phones, which utilize smart cards and so eliminate the burden of accounts management for service providers. The initial take off of this product appears to have been explosive, and as more information is published, investors in the sector will be in a position to revise industry growth forecasts.

Investors should review Nokia's growth prospects and revised analysts' earnings forecasts and consensus. All forecasts have a short sell-by date, and the more dynamic the opportunity, the greater the need to keep the forecast fresh.

Earnings multiple expectations

The multiple of 40 times earnings used in the *Portfolio 2001* forecast to target Nokia's share and ADR prices appears ungenerous compared to the higher multiples reigning in other technology and telecommunications opportunities. However, the same factors that encouraged caution with earnings per share growth expectations suggest modesty with the price earnings multiple. Nokia has in the past surprised on the upside of best expectations and probably will again. Even with its trail-blazing operating performances and potent technological resources, Nokia is very much a hybrid technology innovator and Global Profit Harvester, and share prices are bound to reflect caution on the global economy until a new round of emerging market growth can be confirmed.

Past performance indicators

Growth Rates %		NOKA	S&P 500	Industry	Sector	Notes
Earnings per share 5 year		89.88	20.71	19.04	37.42	
1998 last reported vs 1997		107.94	12.93	55.08	25.62	
Sales 5 year 1994-1998		89.88	20.71	19.04	37.42	
Profitability Ratios						
Gross Margin 1998	%	35.38	49.02	45.43	52.36	
5 year average	%	30.63	48.72	41.57	52.29	
Net Profit Margin 1998	%	11.61	10.84	3.38	11.24	
5 year average	%	8.61	10.19	2.75	11.00	
5 Year Returns on:						
Assets	%	10.69	8.29	4.00	12.56	
Investment	%	19.66	13.04	5.69	17.33	
Equity	%	24.55	21.44	8.98	21.28	

The growth story

Nokia started in the telecommunications business in the 1960s, and by the late 1970s mobile phones and telecommunications infrastructure products were developed for both domestic and international customers. In the 1980s and 1990s, Nokia became a global leader in digital communications technologies and in 1998 it over took Motorola as the world's largest manufacturer of telephone handsets. Earnings growth has been dramatic:

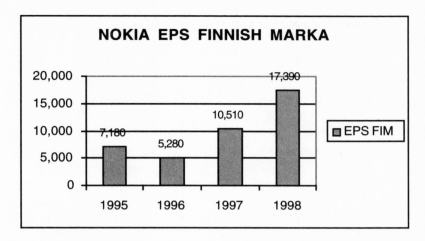

The performance details are even better than the headline. In 1998, operating profit was up 75% and phone sales were up 74%. Nokia replaced Motorola as the world's number one mobile phone company.

Nokia in 1998

1998 EPS FROM CONTINUING
OPERATIONS – FINNISH MARKS

Million FIM	1998	1997	Change %	4Q/1998	4Q/1997
Net sales	79 231	52 612	+ 51	25 877	15 857
Nokia Telecommunications	26 103	18 826	+ 39	8 338	6 368
Nokia Mobile Phones	47 984	27 643	+ 74	16 074	7 505
Other Operations	6 029	7 239	- 17	1 581	2 302
Operating profit	14 799	8 454	+ 75	5 057	2 830
Profit before tax and minority interests	14 603	8 371	+ 74	4 971	2 835
Profit from continuing operations	9 992	5 998	+ 66	3 474	2 018
Net profit	10 408	6 259	+ 66	3 474	2 018
Earnings per share from continuing operations, FIM, basic, split adjusted	17.56	10.59	+ 66	6.09	3.56

What can go wrong?

Apart from the risks of slower market growth following weaker macro economic factors, and the business risk of loss of market share to competitors, wireless telephony is competing in a fast growing technology sector and Nokia's commitment to demanding new G3 European Telecommunications standards will call for large scale investment. Nokia is a latecomer to CDMA, code digital multiple access, and may have to license technology from the US company Qualcomm or Ericsson. The exceptional results in 1998 could also have followed Nokia being fortuitously a few steps ahead of competitors in marketing, particularly Ericsson and Motorola and this advantage may not be enduring. The media from time to time raise a scare about microwaves being a health hazard. Potentially this issue could damage the industry.

Monitoring

As the wireless phone industry powers ahead, monitoring Nokia and growth in the wireless telephone industry should reveal useful buying opportunities. Changed market conditions may also trigger decisive action to protect capital in overvalued markets, if economic or business conditions ever look vulnerable to sharp corrections.

`www.nokia.com` publishes complete financial and performance information and explains the group's products and activities. Competitors' sites including `www.ericsson.com` `www.motorola.com` and `www.qualcomm.com` should also be reviewed. `www.wapforum.org` is important as the mouthpiece of an organization, supported by Nokia and other leading industry companies, which is developing an open standard for wireless phones. Nokia is also working in a joint venture association with the UK mobile computing company Psion, and with competitors including Ericsson and Motorola, to develop an open standard communication platform. Progress in the joint venture will be reported on its web site `www.symbian.com`

G3 – third generation wireless phones, will be able to access the Internet and support interactive communications. This prospect could boost the value of phone manufacturers further on equity markets, but will call for considerable investment in product development first.

AMERICA ON LINE

Share Graph 1997–1998 – America On Line Inc.
Primary Market – NASDAQ AOL

Price January 1999 $158
Market Value January 1999 $74 billion

SECTOR Technology INDUSTRY Computer Services
Top Line AOL: Bottom Line S&P 500 Index Relative: Triangle
Marks Split
Left Scale: Top $ Price, Bottom Volume in Thousands

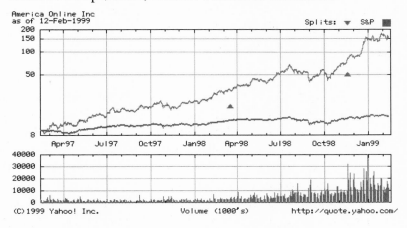

PRICE PERFORMANCE   AOL

An investment made in
January 1994 grew 1142% by
January 1999

PRICE HISTORY	1998	1997	1996	1995	Notes
High Price	160.00	22.84	17.75	11.56	
Low Price	20.63	7.94	5.59	3.08	
High P/E	898.88	NM	253.67	NM	
Low P/E	115.87	NM	79.51	NM	

Pres/COO R. W. Pittman, Chmn/CEO S. M. Case, www.aol.com
8,500 employees
22000 AOL Way, Dulles, VA 20166
Phone: (703) 265-1000 Fax: (703) 265-1101

Global Franchise: Internet access and services

AOL provides subscribers with easy access to services of the Internet. These include electronic mail, conferencing, software, computing support, interactive magazines and newspapers, and on line classes. With 16 million subscribers America On Line is the world's top provider of on line Internet services with a 60% market share in the US and revenues of more than $2.6 million.

AOL Revenues

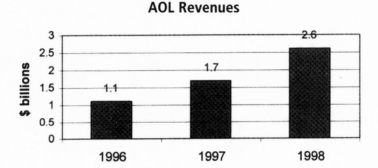

Flat-rate pricing and growing competition in providing Internet access have led AOL to look beyond subscriber fees for revenues. It is successfully selling advertising on its web site, and is forging marketing agreements with other companies and collecting fees on sales to AOL subscribers. AOL is also buying rival Netscape.

AOL Quarterly EPS Sept 97 to Dec 99

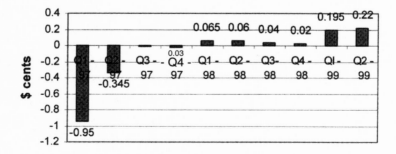

Losses have turned to profits and the market has applauded the achievement:

Value of $10,000 invested – America on Line, Inc. in January 1999

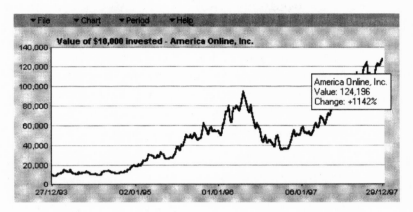

Setting a rational price

There is no information from which to prepare a worksheet, but past performance reflects strong sales and revenue growth.

Past performance indications

Growth Rates %		AOL	S&P 500	Industry	Sector	Notes
Earnings per share 5 year		118.69	16.18	52.29	33.92	
1998 last reported vs 1997		450.59	11.42	15.53	20.36	
Sales 5 year 1994-1998		118.69	16.18	52.20	33.92	
Profitability Ratios						
Gross Margin 1998	%	23.27	49.26	40.36	52.42	
5 year average	%	28.74	48.91	38.24	52.45	
Net Profit Margin 1998	%	7.78	10.63	4.97	11.98	
5 year average	%	-6.11	10.21	-0.15	11.00	
5 Year Returns on:						
Assets	%	-11.15	8.40	-1.08	12.71	
Investment	%	-20.25	13.20	1.92	17.62	
Equity	%	-27.79	21.53	1.94	21.57	

The growth story

There are no conventional yardsticks to value AOL, but revenues approaching $3 million and 16 million subscribers are an epic achievement of management and represent a real asset. With the Netscape acquisition, AOL could become an increasingly interesting investing prospect, particularly if investing measures for Internet prospects become more recognizable.

What can go wrong?

The Internet bubble can burst. AOL is presented as a concept stock and not as a low-risk high-reward investing opportunity currently. Achievements have been substantial and management are no less than brilliant. There is every reason to expect that AOL will continue to succeed as a company and leverage its customer base to great advantage. The valuation of Internet opportunities may, however, be reviewed across the boards.

Any failure by AOL to deliver to the highest expectations would also result in dramatic share price falls.

Monitoring

It will be interesting to monitor AOL for investing opportunities which should arise if Internet shares settle down at levels more in line with other dynamic companies like Microsoft or Lucent.

VODAFONE AIRTOUCH

Share Graph 1997–1998 – Vodafone PLC
Primary Market – London VODFF ADR – NYSE VOD

Price January 1999 ADR $48.75
Market Value January 1999 $60 billion

SECTOR Services INDUSTRY Communications Services
Top Line VOD ADR Bottom Line S&P 500 Index Relative:
Triangle Marks Split
Left Scale: Top $ Price, Bottom Volume in Thousands
Graphic not rebased for four for one split September 1999

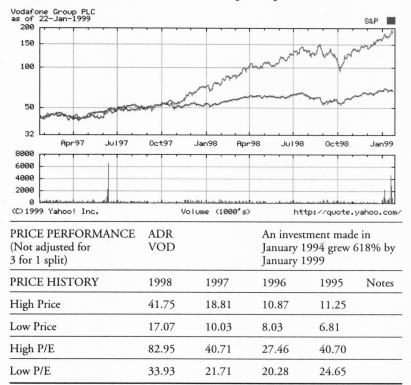

PRICE PERFORMANCE (Not adjusted for 3 for 1 split)	ADR VOD		An investment made in January 1994 grew 618% by January 1999	
PRICE HISTORY	1998	1997	1996	1995	Notes
High Price	41.75	18.81	10.87	11.25	
Low Price	17.07	10.03	8.03	6.81	
High P/E	82.95	40.71	27.46	40.70	
Low P/E	33.93	21.71	20.28	24.65	

Chmn Ian Maclaurin, Non Exec Chmn Sam Ginn, **www.vodaphone.com**
6,051 employees
Headquarters: Newbury, England, with San Francisco serving US/Asia
The Courtyard, 2-4 London Road, Newbury, Berkshire RG14 1JX
Phone: (016) 353-3251 Fax: (016) 354-5713

Share Graph 1997–1998 – Airtouch Communications
Primary Market – NYSE ATI

Price January 1999 ADR $89.19
Market Value January 1999 $51.021 billion

SECTOR Services INDUSTRY Communications Services
Top Line AIRTOUCH Bottom Line S&P 500 Index Relative:
Left Scale: Top $ Price, Bottom Volume in Thousands

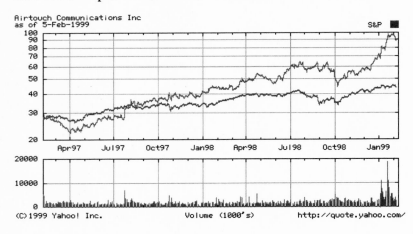

PRICE PERFORMANCE	ATI		An investment made in January 1994 grew 298% by January 1999		
PRICE HISTORY	1998	1997	1996	1995	Notes
High Price	75.00	42.00	33.63	35.63	
Low Price	40.31	22.00	24.88	23.88	
High P/E	NA	53.71	93.92	133.43	
Low P/E	NA	53.15	70.53	105.34	

New name: Vodafone AirTouch PLC

Wireless Wedding: Engagement announced: January 1999
Merger completed 30 June 1999

Investment growth comparison VOD top line ATI bottom line
Vodafone top line: Airtouch bottom line

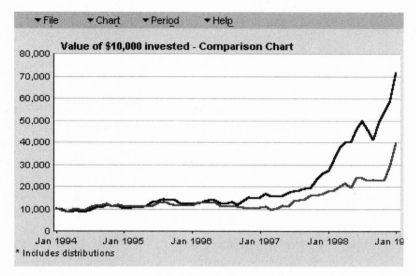

Source: www.moneycentral.com

Global Franchise: global telephony services

In January 1999, Britain's top global wireless phone operator, Vodafone, used its richly valued shares to pay top price and outbid other suitors for AirTouch. Vodafone is paying $58 billion, nearly 17 times AirTouch's cash flow, a price it could afford because its shares trade at more than 20 times cash flow.

At the time of the transaction, AirTouch Communications was the largest company in the world focused on wireless communications, offering a full range of wireless services – cellular, paging, personal communications services (PCS) and in the future, global satellite communications. Vodafone AirTouch will be the world's biggest wireless-communications company, with 23 million mobile-phone customers in four continents and annual revenues of $9.9 billion, cash flow of $3.4 billion and, based on current prices, a stock market value of $110 billion.

Vodafone AirTouch expects to gain competitive advantage by creating extensive 'roaming' agreements for international customers, building cellular networks quicker, and leveraging purchasing power with phone manufacturers.

The transaction is structured as a merger, with each company having seven seats on a board of 14. Shareholders of Vodafone will own slightly more than 50% of the combined company. To ensure that it will hold at least 50%, Vodafone added a cash component to its bid. As a result it will take goodwill write-offs of £2 billion ($3.3 billion) for 10 years. While that will reduce reported earnings, Vodafone and AirTouch shares tend to be valued on cash flow which is not affected by goodwill charges.

Setting a rational price

Pay-as-you talk has unmeasured potential. www.vodafone.com will show you how easily and instantly wireless phone connection can be bought on the Internet from Vodafone itself and several other suppliers. Pay-as-you-talk is a polite way of saying pay before you talk. In addition to getting the cash up front, service providers have no credit risk exposure and very little or no accounts administration. The impact of pay-as-you-talk has not yet been quantified, but if it becomes as popular as early indications show, all forecasts for wireless telephony will have to be substantially raised.

Portfolio 2001 forecasts are intended to identify earnings expectations and target share prices only broadly. Generally, this can be sensibly done, but, pending publication of pro forma projections on Vodafone AirTouch, there is not enough information to prepare a worksheet with any useful ideas.

Analysts' forecasts for AirTouch growth have been lower than for growth achieved by Vodafone. The merged company will doubtless review potential in the US and aim for the higher growth rates being achieved in Europe and the rest of the world for wireless phones.

Investors previously rated Vodafone and AirTouch as the two best cellular phone opportunities, and the attraction of the merged company could be even stronger.

Past performance indicators

Growth Rates %		ADR VOD	S&P 500	Industry	Sector	Notes
Earnings per share 5 year		13.07	20.71	18.42	20.60	
1998 last reported vs 1997			12.93	32.15	21.21	
Sales 5 year 1994-1998		30.05	16.02	18.99	21.96	
Profitability Ratios						
Gross Margin 1998	%		49.52	57.58	44.71	
5 year average	%	70.53	48.72	55.06	43.58	
Net Profit Margin 1998	%	18.09	10.84	3.29	6.61	
5 year average	%	22.14	10.19	6.48	6.03	
5 Year Returns on:						
Assets	%	20.02	8.29	4.54	5.60	
Investment	%	NM	13.04	6.26	7.84	
Equity	%	NM	21.44	17.18	15.35	

What can go wrong?

The main risk for investors will be deterioting global economic conditions and weaker consumer spending. Intense competition in the industry could also erode margins. The media from time to time raise the subject of microwaves as a health hazard. Potentially this issue could damage the industry.

Monitoring

www.vodafone.com gives a complete picture of group activities and monitoring the mobile telephony industry in major financial newspapers will keep investors well informed on current developments, including the global economy.

LOUIS VUITTON MOËT HENNESSY

Share Graph 1997–1998 LVMH Moët Hennessy LV
Primary Market – Paris NASDAQ LVMHY

Price January 1999 $48.25 ADR
Market Value January 1999 $21.23 billion

SECTOR Consumer non-cyclical INDUSTRY Beverages – Alcoholic
Top Line S&P 500 Index Relative Bottom Line LVMHY ADR:
Triangle marks split
Left Scale: Top $ Price, Bottom Volume in Thousands

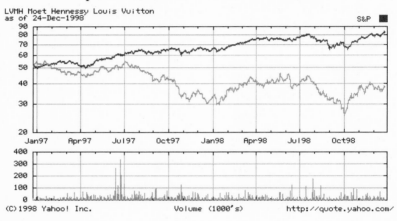

PRICE PERFORMANCE	ADR LVMHY		An investment made in January 1994 grew 96% by January 1999		
PRICE HISTORY	1998	1997	1996	1995	Notes
High Price	46.75	57.13	56.42	41.88	
Low Price	25.50	30.13	40.88	29.75	
High P/E	NA	191.10	59.77	25.80	
Low P/E	NA	110.81	43.43	18.33	

Pres/Chmn Bernard Arnault, www.lvmh.fr and www.lvmh.com
33,511 employees
30 avenue Hoch 75008, Paris
Phone: (314) 413-2222 Fax: +33-1-44-13-21-19

Niche opportunity:
BOTTOMS UP INVESTING
LVMH control the world's greatest champagne brands including Moët & Chandon, Krug, Veuve Clicquot, Dom Perignon, Ponsardin, Canarde Duchene, Ruinart, Mercier, and Pommerv

833 DAYS LEFT *Prepare.* MOËT & CHANDON
CLICK HERE
CHAMPAGNE

15. Do unto others . . . you know the rest . . . 13. Set your watch ahead an hour and celebrate the new century before everyone else . . . 10. Say goodbye to the 1900s 9. Say hello to 2000 7. Stock the bar with fine champagne. 4. Raise your glass. 3. Close your eyes. 2. Make a wish. 1. Witness history in the making.
AS THE CHAMPAGNE CORKS POP OVER THE MILLENNIAL YEARS PROFITS AT LVMH WILL SPARKLE

Global Franchise: Champagne and luxury brands

LVMH is a global conglomerate built by Bernard Arnault of Paris. It was formed by merging the luxury luggage manufacturer Louis Vuitton with the famous champagne house of Moët and the cognac Hennessy. LVHM is involved in the production and distribution of wines, spirits, luggage, leather goods, perfumes, beauty products and fashion. It made an ill-timed near $1 billion purchase in 1996 of 60% of DFS, the largest duty-free retailer in the world, and earnings have been badly affected with the economic slowdown in Asia.

The LVMH group now also hosts other great names including champagnes Dom Perignon, Krug, Veuve Clicquot, Ponsardin, Canarde Duchene, Ruinart, Mercier and Pommery. Perfume brands include Parfums Christian Dior, Guerlain, and Parfums Givenchy, and the company is represented in fashion through Givenchy, Christian Lacroix and Kenzo. In 1997, it acquired the perfumes group Sephora, and in 1998 it acquired Marie-Jeanne,

France's second largest selective fragrances and cosmetics retail chain by sales after Sephora. The French newspaper *La Tribune* is also a subsidiary. In 1999, a 32% holding in Gucci was acquired. LVMH is listed on the Paris Stock Exchange and has an actively traded ADR. The group has a market value of $21 billion and sales of $6 billion.

Interesting group web sites include:
http://www.veuve-clicquot.fr
http://www.clicquot.com
http://www.jwswines.co.jp
http://www.dchandon.com
http://www.lvmh.co.jp
http://www.moet.com
http://www.vuitton.com
http://www.victoire.com
http://www.globeonline.com
http://www.canard-duchene.fr
http://www.sephora.com
http://www.latribune.fr

Setting a rational price

**Portfolio 2001 WORKSHEET FOR TARGETING SHARE PRICES RANGE FOR LVMH
ADR LVMHY IN 1999, 2000 & 2001
BASED ON FORECASTS MADE IN JANUARY 1999
EPS FISCAL 1998 TO DECEMBER $1.33(ADR)
5 ADRs = 1 SHARE**

Growth	Year	Estimated EPS ADR	P/E	Share Price Target	+10%	-10%	Notes
30%	1999	$1.56	30	$47	$52	$42	
25%	2000	$1.95	30	$59	$65	$53	
20%	2001	$2.34	30	$70	$78	$63	

This 'what if' forecast suggests potential earnings and share prices based on current indications. Forecasts must be revised continuously in the light of all company results and industry, market and economic news. Forecasts can be misleading and cannot be treated as investment advice or used to motivate investments. See page 69.

Earnings per share growth expectations
Earnings in 1998 were affected by the economic slowdown in Asia and adverse trading in the duty-free shops, particularly in Asia.

Net sales for 1998 were 6.9 billion euros (45.5 billion French francs), a fall of 5% over the same period in 1997.

After a difficult third quarter showing a 13% fall in sales, the fourth quarter was more positive (+2%) and the group posted record sales figures in December, up 7% over the same period last year. Factors contributing to these results are the successful launch of new products, together with the effects of a stronger yen and the first signs that the Asian situation is now beginning to stabilize.

Broken down by business activity, sales developed as follows:

(million)	1997		1998		% change
	Euro	FRF	Euro	FRF	
Champagne & Wines	1.134	7.440	1.254	8.223	+11%
Cognac & Spirits	762	5.000	663	4.347	-13%
Fashion & Leather Goods	1.837	12.053	1.831	12.011	0%
Fragrances & Cosmetics	1.406	9.220	1.368	8.976	-3%
Selective Retailing	2.170	14.233	1.797	11.786	-17%
Other Activities	14	89	17	116	+20%
TOTAL	7.323	48.035	6.930	45.459	-5%

The performance of the Wines and Spirits groups was mixed. In champagne, sales volumes grew significantly. Volumes are up 5.9% to reach a total of 58 million bottles.

Champagne and gifts should bring LVMH exceptional profits over 1999 and 2000 and probably in 2001. A revival of business in Asia would be a 'double whammy'. Earnings per share growth of 30% is above analysts' consensus, but could still be conservative in relation to the millennium opportunity for LVMH.

Earnings multiple expectations
As the world's largest and most identified French champagne investment, earnings multiples are likely to be bubbly in 1999 and 2000, as investors look for the exciting millennial investing opportunity. For the longer term, LVMH is a vigorously managed company and the world's dominant luxury goods company. Mr Arnault misjudged the purchase of DFS but he is a formidably

successful entrepreneur and, beyond the champagne years, LVMH can be expected to continue to prosper.

Past performance indicators
The DFS purchase has weighed heavily on the figures of past performance.

Growth Rates %			S&P 500	Industry	Sector	Notes
Earnings per share 5 year		-22.39	20.84	7.859	20.99	
1998 last reported vs 1997		-68.23	11.42	6.31	2.87	
Sales 5 year 1994-1998		17.27	16.18	4.54	7.19	
Profitability Ratios						
Gross Margin 1998	%	62.44	49.26	38.35	50.89	
5 year average	%	64.31	48.91	37.27	48.57	
Net Profit Margin 1998	%	10.66	10.63	9.75	9.54	
5 year average	%	12.34	10.21	8.61	8.76	
5 Year Returns on:						
Assets	%	5.78	8.40	8.73	11.09	
Investment	%	8.12	13.20	10.31	17.42	
Equity	%	12.30	21.53	21.81	31.86	

What can go wrong?

There is little risk of champagne going out of fashion for the millennial celebrations, but there are other risks which include the dangers that:

- The Asian economic crisis may linger on longer than expected and leave a profits hole bigger than the champagne can fizz over.

- The global economy may experience a hangover after January 2000, particularly when the Gold Card bills for those cases of champagne have to be paid.

- Earnings per share may rise in 1999 and go flat in 2000.

- As a result of opposition to its bid to acquire Gucci, the bid was blocked and future contention could be damaging.

Monitoring

First focus in 1999 should be on news about champagne supplies for the millennial celebrations, but researching LVMH really involves taking a view on the luxury goods market and a view on Asia's economic situation. With its active ADR exposure, LVMH can be well researched on `www.adr.com` and `www.lvmh.com`.

13

INVESTING IN GLOBAL FINANCIAL SERVICES

Challenges facing the banks

The way we deal with money has changed for all of us over the last few decades. More people invest in equities than before, we are less inclined to leave funds on deposit with banks at low rates of interest, and generally we have less contact with banks. Most of us use cash point machines and credit cards for our regular trans-actions and seldom visit a bank. Habits die hard, however, and we are still inclined to leave surplus funds with traditional banks, often only because we lack the initiative to shop around for the best terms. When we make the effort, we soon discover that other new players like supermarkets pay a few per cent more for our money than the prestigious big-name banks we deal with, also telephone banking with them is cheaper and easier than conventional banking and on line banking is available.

For decades technology has been making conventional banks redundant. US Federal Reserve Board chairman, Dr Alan

Greenspan, has been campaigning for a change in US banking laws to allow banks to conduct insurance business, to keep them profitable and this quotation is from a 1998 speech he made on the subject to a Chamber of Commerce meeting in mid America:

> The same forces that have been reshaping the real economy have also been transforming the financial services industry. Once again, perhaps the most profound development has been the rapid growth of computer and telecommunications technology. The advent of such technology has lowered the cost and broadened the scope of financial services. These developments have made it increasingly possible for borrowers and lenders to transact directly and for a wide variety of financial products to be tailored for very specific purposes. As a result, competitive pressures in the financial services industry are probably greater than ever before.
>
> Technological innovation has accelerated another major trend – financial globalization – that has been reshaping our financial system, not to mention the real economy, for at least three decades. Both developments have expanded cross-border asset holdings, trading, and credit flows. In response, both securities firms and US and foreign banks have increased their cross-border operations. Once again, a critical result has been greatly increased competition both at home and abroad.

Greenspan's comments underline that technology changes have eroded the core profit-making niche from which banks traditionally made their money. Banks were engaged in the business of maturity transformation. In simple terms this means they borrow short term and lend long term and make money on the differential rates.

The diminishing pool of short-term money for banks to access at low rates and lend out at high rates keeps falling because technology shrinks distance and speeds up communications. In the commercial world, businesses have greater direct access to capital markets, individuals borrow long term from mortgage lenders and finance companies and credit card issuers deal with everyday purchases and even supply core lending.

To grow in an environment of increased competition, global banks see their future as financial services providers on a global scale. Also, banks like Citibank have a brand which they can successfully build globally not only for banking, but for insurance and other financial services.

Global personal banking

International US banks have a head start in offering integrated financial services to personal lenders globally. The cheque account is only part of the package which includes credit cards, arranging pensions, equity and fund investments, home and car insurance and all matters financial. US banks started out with an edge in global markets because in their great home market they had already gained unmatched economies of scale, marketing experience and technological and innovative leadership.

The merger of Citicorp and Travelers Group Inc. into Citigroup in 1998, challenged the regulatory barriers between insurance and banking which have existed in the US since the depression years of the 1930s. When fully cleared of these restrictions, US bank assurance companies will become even more formidable competitors globally.

Global investment banking

US investment houses are the world's key corporate deal promoters, and with merger and acquisition activity flourishing, they have been having a field day.

Since 1990 the world's top ten investment banks have almost doubled their share of fee-based and advisory business in global capital markets, according to a study published early in 1999 by the Stern business school in New York. The growing concentration of market share in the hands of the top banks, who now have 77 per cent of the market, has coincided with an explosive growth in global capital markets during the 1990s. From total volume of less than $1,500 billion at the start of the decade, according to the study, volume grew to almost $4,000 billion last year.

Investment banking services are the easiest to export globally as the mechanics of underwriting a global stock or bond offering differ little from country to country, and in 1998 the leading merger and acquisition advisors for deals involving a European entity were US investment banks. By the end of the first half of 1998, the value of mergers and acquisitions in the US exceeded the whole of 1997. Securities Data, a merger and acquisitions consultancy, reported deals worth $931 billion for the period. That compared with deals worth $926 billion in 1997, already a record year for the merger and acquisitions industry. Deals in the US in 1998 eventually topped $1.7 trillion.

The opening months of 1999 were again marked by global mega deals, including the merger of Vodafone and AirTouch, and investment bankers have reported that in spite of the growth in the size of the deals, there has been little pressure on traditional fee structures which are mainly based on the size of each deal.

With the advent of the euro, merger and acquisitions activity in Europe is at an all time high. US investment banks are earning record profits from their active operations in Europe, and also from American firms actively acquiring Asian companies.

Morgan Stanley Dean Witter & Co. is the result of the 1997 merger between investment bank Morgan Stanley and retail brokerage and consumer financial services firm Dean Witter. They have established a model for a modern banking group, spanning global investment banking for corporate and private clients and credit card issuance, which is outlined in the report on the group which follows.

High net worth baby boomers

Managing and investing the savings and inherited wealth of the rich generation of baby boomers has been identified as a prize target for investment bankers. Merrill Lynch published a report in 1998 on the growth of high net worth individuals (HNWI), and their potential as a client base. Outside the United States, western Europe has traditionally been the largest source of global HNWI wealth, and Japan has rapidly emerged as the largest private banking market in the fast-paced Asian region.

In Europe, the current pool of HNWI wealth is estimated to be $5.5 trillion. Three factors were identified as shaping future developments of Europe's wealth markets: a search for higher yields from investment assets; increasing liberalization and convergence of major economies; and declining dependency ratios, that is the ratio of the working population to pensioners.

Investment bankers expect that the euro will stimulate equity and bond markets making European capital markets attractive to issuers. This in turn will increase new supplies of higher yield investments for high net worth individuals. The market will be further boosted by inheritance moneys and equity releases from the businesses of European entrepreneurs.

In Japan, the current pool of HNWI wealth was estimated at about $800 billion. The Japanese have historically placed their wealth in safe onshore investments due partly to the Japanese cultural importance of wealth succession, and hence capital preservation and security. Investment in overseas jurisdictions, and even in non-yen instruments, has traditionally been low. Several forces are beginning to change Japanese investment choices. Following the poor performance of domestic and Asian currencies and markets, global asset diversification is becoming a major factor for Japanese investors.

The European market

The European common currency is narrowing the barriers between Europe and America for bankers. European and global banks will be able to combine operations and offer common products to an extent not possible before.

Japanese banks

The big Japanese banks, which rank among the biggest in the world, are currently on the sidelines, victims of sick balance sheets. Once mighty on the international scene, the Japanese banks barely rate a mention currently.

Shocks after Russia's financial collapse

The collapse of Russia's economy in September 1998 was followed by a chain of stark reminders on how risky global banking can be. Faced with competitive pressures in traditional banking operations, US and European regulated banks were engaging in high-margin high-risk leveraged international lending on a grand scale – activities that often amounted to reckless hedge fund trading.

A great and public crisis for America's banking establishment was revealed when, shortly after Russia's debt default, several of America's top global banks had to get together urgently and fund a $4.5 billion bale out of John Merriweather's Long Term Capital Hedge Fund. If they had failed to do this, in the words of the Federal Reserve chairman Alan Greenspan, the global financial system could have 'seized up' and, no doubt, they would have lost the billions they had loaned to the failed hedge fund. Other banks simply wrote off billions of dollars.

Banks had been lending liberally to hedge funds that were leveraging their capital base by factors of up to 100. As multi-billion-dollar losses were disclosed by banks from their exposure in Russia, it emerged that many top US and European banks were disguising high-risk hedge fund business as proprietary trading.

The losses and disclosures caused a rapid and severe fall in the share prices of banking groups. The instinctive view investors held, that banks were solid safe investments in spite of their mega profits was shattered. On the positive side the global banking industry emerged from the crisis in rude health, even if a little chastened by its errors.

Investors have a range of global banking, insurance and financial services enterprises as prospects to consider. The sequence of events following Russia's financial collapse and the near collapse of the Long Term Capital Hedge Fund should not be forgotten and when investing, you must accept that there are risks inherent in global banking, insurance and financial services industries even though they may be dominated by big names.

The companies reviewed for *Portfolio 2001*

From the wide range of global financial services, *Portfolio 2001* has included headline reports on these ten prospects:

- Charles Schwab, the world's pioneer discount broker and leading Internet broker.

- Morgan Stanley Dean Witter, a premier US investment banking group, now serving corporate and personal clients.
- J. P. Morgan, an icon of US banking, aiming to be one of the world's leading mergers and acquisitions houses.
- The ING Group, the Dutch international banking and assurance model which other financial services want to follow.
- Merrill Lynch, America's top global brokerage, the firm that brought Wall Street to the High Street, with plans to repeat the same act globally and to provide on line broking.
- Citigroup, encompassing the merged businesses of Citibank, the investment bank Salomon Smith Barney and Travelers Insurance.
- Capital One Financial, a specialist US based issuer of credit cards, included as a reminder of how successful specialized banking services can be.
- The AIG Group, America's leading international insurance and financial services company, and a benchmark for performance in the industry.
- Allied Zurich, a combined British/Swiss insurance and financial group that was formed through a merger in 1998 and is listed on the stock exchanges of Zurich, London and, as an ADR, in New York.
- AXA, France's global insurance and financial services giant, which started 1999 with the acquisition of Britain's Guardian Insurance Group.

It is in the nature of companies managing money that investors should pay more attention to details of the financial structure of the prospect than would be the case with a blue-chip commercial company. It was arguably over-ambitious to include a section on global financial services, including banks, insurers and brokers as part of this book: many crucial and radical investing themes affect the sector, and they deserve to be dealt with substantively. Such a discussion is, however, beyond the scope of the present book and comments that follow are only headline reports – profiles to introduce each prospect. The alternative to presenting a selection of companies from across a wide segment of the industry would have been to leave the sector out of Portfolio 2001. That would have been a bad choice, since financial services companies are exciting prospects absolutely tuned in with the times, and the sector provides several potential low-risk high-reward opportunities with the additional attraction that shareholders may benefit in future industry consolidations.

Global financial service companies are now all staking claims to manage the same pool of investors' money, which includes the legendary wealth of the baby boomers. They overlap and they compete with each other and they are acquiring and merging and are also the instruments of acquisitions and mergers for others. If one theme runs through the financial services world it is industry consolidation, regionally, internationally and between different services including banking and insurance.

In a favourable economic climate financial services shares have the potential to perform exceptionally well and be 'must-own' shares. However, there has been so much change over the latter years that in reality there are very few track records. In the headline reports that follow in this section where earnings per share growth is forecast, some consistent previous pattern has been followed. However, in several cases a 'what if' forecast would have given no useful focus to the report and it has been excluded.

What can go wrong? and Monitoring

The 'What can go wrong?' question and monitoring suggestions for all companies point to the importance of the global economy. However financial services companies structure themselves, they keep the characteristics of financial profit harvesters.

CHARLES SCHWAB

Share Graph 1997–1998 Charles Schwab & Co.
Primary Market – NASDAQ SCH

Price January 1999 $69
Market Value January 1999 $27.6 billion

SECTOR Financial INDUSTRY Investment Services
Top Line SCH Bottom Line S&P 500 Index Relatives: Triangle
Marks Split
Left Scale: Top $ Price, Bottom Volume in Thousands

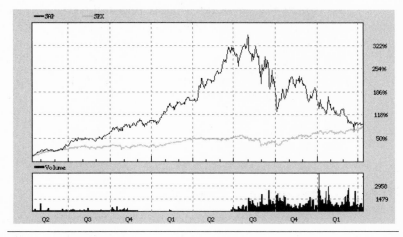

PRICE PERFORMANCE	SCH			An investment made in January 1994 grew 1473% by January 1999	

PRICE HISTORY	1998	1997	1996	1995	Notes
High Price	68.50	29.50	14.61	12.89	
Low Price	18.50	13.50	8.00	4.91	
High P/E	80.68	44.63	25.24	29.97	
Low P/E	21.79	20.42	13.82	11.41	

Chmn/CEO Charles Schwab, www.schwab.com
13,300 employees
120 Kearny Street, San Francisco, CA 94104
Phone: (415) 627-7000 Fax: (415) 627-8538

Global Franchise and growth story: The pioneering and leading on line broker

Charles Schwab's has been business discount brokerage: making trades for clients who make their own investment decisions. Historically hands-off, the company now offers asset allocation advice and refers clients to independent financial advisors. Schwab operates from nearly 275 offices, via telephone, or by PC; the firm dominates the on line trading market. One of the top three mutual fund distributors (with Fidelity and Vanguard), Schwab's popular OneSource sells more than 800 no-load mutual funds from about 120 families. The company is now offering retirement investing packages and working to lure more investment managers as clients. The company has moved into the European market through UK-based Charles Schwab Europe.

Charles Schwab comparison with Merrill Lynch

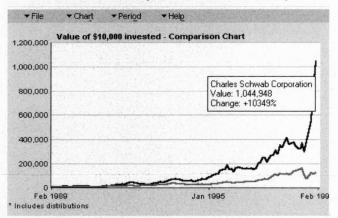

Source: www.moneycentral.com

More than 3 million people were active investors via on line brokerage accounts by the end of 1998. Forrester Research expects the total to top 15 million by 2002. International Data Corp expects nearly one-third of all individual investors in the US will have on line trading accounts by the year 2002, generating $5 billion in commissions. Schwab was the first to tune in to twenty-first century investing, and its market value grew over 10,000% in ten years.

Setting a rational price

Following the dramatic rise in Charles Schwab's share price, setting a realistic price is not 'possible' in January 1999. The following indications from past performance reflect strong earnings growth and net profit margins.

Past performance indicators

Growth Rates %		SCH	S&P 500	Industry	Sector	Notes
Earnings per share 5 year		26.38	20.84	19.46	17.51	
1998 last reported vs 1997		28.44	11.42	15.32	14.20	
Sales 5 year 1994-1998		25.13	16.18	26.91	13.72	
Profitability Ratios						
Gross Margin 1998	%	NM				
5 year average	%	NM				
Net Profit Margin 1998	%	12.74	10.63	9.69	10.63	
5 year average	%	12.43	10.21	11.81	10.21	
5 Year Returns on:						
Assets	%	1.87	8.40	6.02	2.18	
Investment	%	22.88	13.20	15.34	9.74	
Equity	%	28.78	21.53	23.68	16.53	

Current profit reports corresponding with the rise in the share price from December 1998 will be needed to make a useful forecast.

Portfolio 2001 Forecast:

Portfolio 2001 'what if' forecasts are based on assumptions of likely outcomes following past performance trends.

The dynamics of on line broking and asset management affecting Charles Schwab are such that no forecasts can be made running years ahead and investors should review prospects at the time they consider investing in the light of conditions at the time.

What can go wrong?

Schwab have established a commanding position as on line brokers and money managers, and have proved themselves able to withstand competition at lower transaction costs with the support of their core of client investors. The risk to their future success are a weak Wall Street or a change in the flow of funds from equity markets to other investment categories. Any reduction of activity on Wall Street, and progressively in the UK and Europe where Schwab are entrenching themselves, will also be adverse to group prospects.

Monitoring

Investors in Schwab will monitor both the financial performance of the company and the strength of Wall Street and other global markets. With Merrill Lynch entering the business of on line broking the competitive situation should also be monitored.

MORGAN STANLEY DEAN WITTER

Share Graph 1997–1998 Morgan Stanley Dean Witter & Co.
Primary Market – NYSE MWD

Price January 1999 $88.50
Market Value January 1999 $51.1 billion

SECTOR Financial INDUSTRY Investment Services
Top Line MWD: Bottom Line S&P 500 Index Relative: Triangle
Marks Split
Left Scale: Top $ Price, Bottom Volume in Thousands

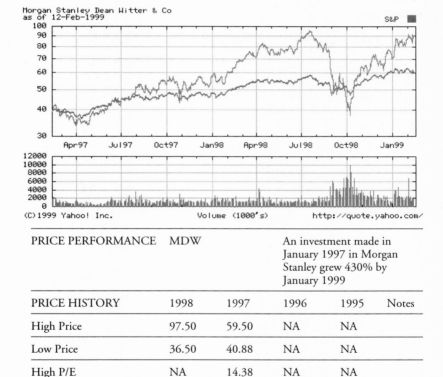

Morgan Stanley Dean Witter & Co
as of 12-Feb-1999

(C) 1999 Yahoo! Inc. Volume (1000's) http://quote.yahoo.com/

PRICE PERFORMANCE	MDW		An investment made in January 1997 in Morgan Stanley grew 430% by January 1999		

PRICE HISTORY	1998	1997	1996	1995	Notes
High Price	97.50	59.50	NA	NA	
Low Price	36.50	40.88	NA	NA	
High P/E	NA	14.38	NA	NA	
Low P/E	NA	9.88	NA	NA	

Chmn/CEO Philip J. Purcell, www.msdw.com
47,200 employees
1585 Broadway, New York, NY 10036
Phone: (212) 761-4000 Fax: (212) 761-0086

Global Franchise and growth story

Morgan Stanley Dean Witter & Co. is a global financial services firm, operating in three segments: securities (underwriting, trading, mergers and related services); asset management; and credit services (issuance and servicing credit cards and real-estate loans). It services institutions and private investors in dedicated business operations which include on line broking. The group is one of the world's top three global financial institutions serving capital markets and institutional investors and has established a model organization servicing financial services at all levels, including Internet broking. In the most recent survey of on line brokers, the newspaper *Barrons* accorded Dean Witter its highest commendation for an on line broker. An outline of the Group's successful and dynamic structure serving institutional and private investors follows at the end of this report.

Setting a rational price

Portfolio 2001 WORKSHEET FOR TARGETING SHARE PRICES OF MORGAN STANLEY DEAN WITTER IN 1999, 2000 & 2001 BASED ON FORECASTS MADE IN FEBRUARY 1999 EPS FISCAL 1988 TO NOVEMBER $4.95

Growth	Year	Estimated EPS	P/E	Share Price Target	+10%	-10%	Notes
15%	1999	$5.69	17.5	$100	$110	$90	
15%	2000	$6.54	17.5	$114	$127	$103	
15%	2001	$7.52	17.5	$132	$147	$118	

This 'what if' forecast suggests potential earnings and share prices based on current indications. Forecasts must be revised continuously in the light of all company results and industry, market and economic news. Forecasts can be misleading and cannot be treated as investment advice or used to motivate investments. See page 69.

Earnings growth and mulitple expectations
Past performance and undemanding earnings multiples in current markets generously support an earnings forecast based on 15% earnings growth and an earnings multiple of 20 for target share prices. Earnings for the first quarter of 1999 were a staggering 60% above 1998.

What can go wrong?

Morgan Stanley's earnings will follow the growth in both global corporate activity and institutional investing and the strength of the US equity market. Weakness in these markets would be likely to impact on earnings prospects.

Monitoring

www.msdw.com is a gateway to the group's activities and is also the best support I know for monitoring the global economy generally. Morgan Stanley's economists file a daily report on macro developments globally.

Investors should monitor the performance of the global banking industry and be mindful of risks to the sector.

J. P. MORGAN

Share Graph 1997–1998 J. P. Morgan & Co. Inc.
Primary Market – NYSE JPM

Price January 1999 $111
Market Value January 1999 $19.5 billion

SECTOR Financial INDUSTRY Money Centre Banks
Top Line S&P 500 Index Relative Bottom Line JPM
Left Scale: Top $ Price, Bottom Volume in Thousands

PRICE PERFORMANCE	JPM		An investment made in January 1994 grew 85% by January 1999		
PRICE HISTORY	1998	1997	1996	1995	Notes
High Price	148.75	125.75	100.13	82.50	
Low Price	72.13	93.13	73.50	56.13	
High P/E	31.77	17.54	13.13	12.85	
Low P/E	15.40	12.99	9.64	8.74	

Chmn/CEO D. A. Warner III, www.jpmorgan.com
15,600 employees
60 Wall Street, New York, NY 10260
Phone: (212) 483-2323 Fax: (212) 648-5545

Global Franchise and growth story: US money centre and global banking

An icon of American banking, J. P. Morgan has a significant global franchise as an investment bank, and in the US has been restructuring from traditional commercial banking to investment banking. It is one of the US's premier international banking companies, and a banker to governments, business enterprises and individuals. Commercial activities include advising on corporate strategy and structure, raising capital, making markets in financial instruments and managing investment assets. Clients include several of the world's leading companies and organizations. Morgan also invests for its own account in promising enterprises, and trades in market opportunities. Core activities include Morgan Guarantee trustee services, investment banking; brokerage services and asset management. Overseas business accounts for almost half of annual revenues of $17.7 billion.

Setting a rational price

Portfolio 2001 WORKSHEET FOR TARGETING SHARE PRICES OF J. P. Morgan
JPM IN 1999, 2000 & 2001
BASED ON FORECASTS MADE IN FEBRUARY 1999
EPS FISCAL 1998 TO NOVEMBER $4.68

Growth	Year	Estimated EPS	P/E	Share Price Target	+10%	-10%	Notes
Consensus	1999	$6.87	17.5	$120	$133	$100	
15%	2000	$7.85	17.5	$137	$152	$123	
15%	2001	$9.02	17.5	$158	$175	$142	

This 'what if' forecast suggests potential earnings and share prices based on current indications. Forecasts must be revised continuously in the light of all company results and industry, market and economic news. Forecasts can be misleading and cannot be treated as investment advice or used to motivate investments. See page 69.

Earnings growth and multiple expectations
Past performance has been patchy and J. P. Morgan has been accident prone in recent emerging market setbacks. While earnings multiples could advance if current equity market strength continues, an earnings forecast based on 15% earnings growth and

an earnings multiple of 17.5 times earnings have been used to target share prices. The consensus earnings estimate for 1999 has been established after taking into account the effect of non trading and one time charges on earnings in 1998.

What can go wrong?

J. P. Morgan's earnings will be strongly affected by global corporate activity and institutional investing. Weakness in these markets would be likely to impact on earnings prospects. The group is also widely exposed to Latin America and will be affected by economic developments in that region.

Monitoring

www.jpmorgan.com reports on group performance and operations in detail. Investors will benefit from following Morgan Stanley's daily economic briefing on www.ms.com to keep abreast of developments in the global macroeconomic arena and monitor the performance of other global banking groups mindful of the risks in the sector.

ING GROUP

Share Graph 1997–1998 ING Group NV
Primary Market – NYSE – ING ADR

Price February 1999 $56.13 ADR
Market Value February 1999 $43.1 billion

SECTOR Financial INDUSTRY Insurance (Life)
Top Line ING ADR Bottom Line S&P 500 Index Relative
Left Scale: Top $ Price, Bottom Volume in Thousands

ING Groep NV
as of 12-Feb-1999   S&P ■

(C)1999 Yahoo! Inc.   Volume (1000's)   http://quote.yahoo.com/

PRICE PERFORMANCE	ING		An investment made in January 1994 grew 98% by January 1999		
PRICE HISTORY	1998	1997	1996	1995	Notes
High Price	76.75	53.00	36.50	NA	
Low Price	36.05	34.88	32.50	NA	
High P/E	NA	15.37	11.59	NA	
Low P/E	NA	10.11	10.32	NA	

CEO Godfried J. A. van der Lugt, http://www.inggroup.com
80,000 employees
Strawinskylaan 2631, P.O. Box 810, Amsterdam, Netherlands
Phone: (00 31 20) 541-5462 Fax: (00 31 20) 541-5452

Global Franchise and growth story: Banking, insurance and integrated financial services

ING Group is a global leader in integrated financial services which include banking, insurance and asset management, with total assets 89 billion US dollars and shareholders' equity of $23 billion. The Group has 80,000 employees in 58 countries, is the largest financial services company in the Netherlands and ranks sixty-fourth in the Fortune Global 500. In insurance, ING covers life, health, personal, marine, commercial, property and casualty risks and undertakes reinsurance. ING Financial Services International, the group's North American operation, owns companies including the insurers Life of Georgia, Security Life of Denver, Security Life Reinsurance, Southland Life, Medical Risk Solutions, The Netherlands Insurance Companies, ING Institutional Markets, Vestax and the Equitable of Iowa Group of companies.

The Group's banking operations include consumer and business banking services throughout Europe, in the US and in Asia, as well as corporate finance, securities, investment and asset management services. ING Group also owns Barings, an investment bank headquartered in the UK, with extensive operations in Asia, and an extensive network of banks throughout the world. In the US, the Group owns the investment bank and broker Furman Selz. A leading global innovator, ING Group's financial services extend to leasing automobiles, aircraft, and satellites.

The global financial crisis depressed profits in 1998 from banking operations, which decreased by 22.6% to NLG 1,635 million. Excluding non-recurring items, an operational net profit remained of NLG 1,035 million (-48%). This decrease attributed entirely to the non-recurring losses from the global financial crisis and the extra additions to the debt provisions. Additions to the provision for loan losses of the banking operations increased by NLG 1,155 million to NLG 2 billion, of which NLG 1 billion related to Asia and Russia.

Setting a rational price

Portfolio 2001 WORKSHEET FOR TARGETING SHARE PRICES OF ING GROUP IN
1999, 2000 & 2001
BASED ON FORECASTS MADE IN JANUARY 1999
EPS/ADR FISCAL 1998 TO DECEMBER = $3.01
ADR=1 SHARE

Growth	Year	Estimated EPS	P/E	ADR Price Target	+10%	-10%	Notes
10%	1999	$3.31	15	$50	$56	$45	
15%	2000	$3.80	15	$57	$63	$51	
15%	2001	$4.37	15	$66	$73	$60	

This 'what if' forecast suggests potential earnings and share prices based on current indications. Forecasts must be revised continuously in the light of all company results and industry, market and economic news. Forecasts can be misleading and cannot be treated as investment advice or used to motivate investments. See page 69.

Earnings growth and multiple expectations

In March 1999 when announcing 1998 results, ING advised that 'due to the uncertain economic conditions in several important markets, the Executive Board considers it premature at this stage to make a firm profit forecast for 1999. However, ING Group has a strong financial and commerical foundation. Therefore the Executive Board faces the future with confidence.'

In June 1999 ING Group earned a profit of 1.385 billion euros (3.052 billion Dutch gilders) following the public offering of 22.5% of the shares in Libertel, a successful telecoms company. The profit contribution resulting from this transaction will form part of the published net profit of ING, but will not be taken into account for determining the profit available for distribution of the dividend. The proceeds will be used for strategic investments.

To complete a 'what if' forecast, earnings growth has been estimated at a modest 10% for 1999 which started as a strong year for the financial services industries and growth has been increased to 15% in 1999 and 2000 in line with expectations for other comparable companies.

An earnings multiple of 15 has been used to target share prices in line with the expected earnings growth rate.

What can go wrong?

ING have been aggressive and imaginative operators globally and have achieved exceptionally high returns. The ethos of the group is likely to continue on similar, if more cautious, lines. Global exposure brings global risks and the global economy is likely to be the strongest influence on ING's earnings prospects.

Monitoring

www.inggroup.com is an informative resource on group activities. As for the other financial services prospects, investors will particularly benefit from following global economic developments reported on www.ms.com and reviewing news and comment in the *Wall Street Journal* and other financial publications. www.adr.com reports new on ING Group and carries updated earnings forecasts.

MERRILL LYNCH

Share Graph 1997–1998 Merrill Lynch & Co. Inc.
Primary Market – NYSE MER

Price January 1999 $69.13
Market Value February 1999 $24.5 billion

SECTOR Financial INDUSTRY Investment Services
Top Line MER Bottom Line S&P 500 Index Relative: Triangle
Marks Split
Left Scale: Top $ Price, Bottom Volume in Thousands

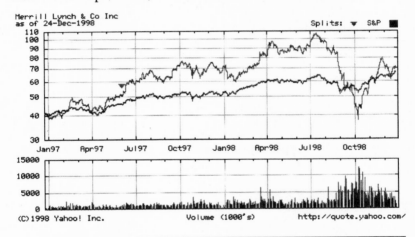

PRICE PERFORMANCE	MER		An investment made in January 1994 grew 314% by January 1999		
PRICE HISTORY	1998	1997	1996	1995	Notes
High Price	109.13	78.19	42.56	32.88	
Low Price	35.77	39.25	24.69	17.31	
High P/E	38.34	16.20	10.35	11.96	
Low P/E	12.56	8.13	6.00	6.40	

Chmn/CEO David H. Komansky, Pres/COO Herbert M. Allison Jr.
www.ml.com
56,600 employees
World Financial Center, North Tower, New York, NY 10281
Phone: (12) 449-1000 Fax: (212) 449-7461

Global Franchise: Broking, investment banking and financial services

Merrill Lynch is the financial services holding company for the world's largest brokerage, with global subsidiaries providing investment banking, brokerage and personal financial services. Group services include cash management accounts, security clearing services, institutional debt sales, trading, financing, corporate financial services and merger and acquisition services. As research-led investors, Merrill Lynch produce extensive research on equities, fixed income investments, economics, and technical market analysis. Brokerage services are supported by financing and market-making services, mutual fund management and insurance services. The group operates globally and has a significant presence outside the US in Europe and in the Far East. In June 1999 they announced they would provide on line broking services.

Setting a rational price

Portfolio 2001 WORKSHEET FOR TARGETING SHARE PRICES OF MERRILL LYNCH IN 1999, 2000 & 2001
BASED ON FORECASTS MADE IN JANUARY 1999
EPS FISCAL 1987 TO DECEMBER

Growth	Year	Estimated EPS	P/E	Share Price Target	+10%	-10%	Notes
Consensus	1999	$4.30	17.5	$75	$83	$66	
15%	2000	$4.94	17.5	$86	$96	$77	
15%	2001	$5.68	17.5	$99	$110	$89	

This 'what if' forecast suggests potential earnings and share prices based on current indications. Forecasts must be revised continuously in the light of all company results and industry, market and economic news. Forecasts can be misleading and cannot be treated as investment advice or used to motivate investments. See page 69.

Earnings per share growth
Merrill's reported earnings per share grew from $2.72 in 1995 to $4.08 in 1996 and $4.79 in 1997. Then in 1998, earnings per share fell to $2.94 as the effect of the global economic crisis took their toll. For the first quarter of 1999 reported earnings per share

were $1.65 basic and $1.44 diluted, compared with $1.44 basic and $1.26 diluted in the 1998 first quarter and $0.97 basic and $0.86 diluted in the 1998 fourth quarter.

Merrill Lynch are the world's largest brokerage and have over $1 trillion under management.

With the surge in on line Internet broking Merrill Lynch have decided to enter this field. 1999 will be a definitive year as Merrill Lynch organize their formidable resources to serve clients on line. The strength of their franchise prevails and earnings can be forecast modestly to grow in line with peers in the industry. An earnings growth rate of 15% has been used in the *Portfolio 2001* forecast and an earnings multiple of 20 times earnings has been used to set conservative price targets, but the effects of low cost on line broking on earnings has not been measured.

What can go wrong?

As the world's largest brokerage and one of the world's top three investment banks, Merrill's fortunes will run parallel with growth in global equity investing. Positive forecasts are based on sustained strength in global markets and sustained profitability in serving private clients notwithstanding the introduction of low cost Internet broking services.

Monitoring

www.merrill-lynch.com is a comprehensive resource on which the group's activities and opinions on markets can be followed.

Investors should also monitor developments in the global economy and the financial services industry in the *Wall Street Journal* and other financial publications and review the reports of the global economics team filed on www.ms.com

The progress of Merrill's on line broking services will also be a top priority on an investors' monitoring list.

CITIGROUP

Share Graph 1997–1998 Citigroup Inc.
Primary Market – NYSE – C

Price January 1999 $36
Market Value January 1999 $117.8 billion

SECTOR Financial INDUSTRY Insurance (Life)
Top Line CITIGROUP: Bottom Line S&P 500 Index Relative:
Triangle Marks Split
Left Scale: Top $ Price, Bottom Volume in Thousands
Note: Graphic not rebased for three for two splits in June 1999

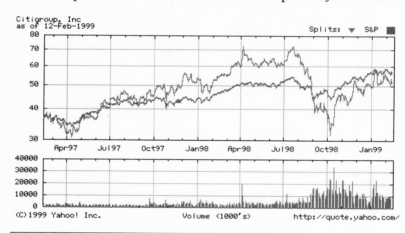

PRICE PERFORMANCE	C		An investment made in January 1994 grew 41% by January 1999		
PRICE HISTORY	1998	1997	1996	1995	Notes
High Price	73.50	76.44	70.59	63.88	
Low Price	28.50	43.75	38.75	32.38	
High P/E	30.43	27.93	24.80	29.25	
Low P/E	11.80	15.98	13.63	14.82	

Co-Chmn/CEO J. Reed, S. Weill, www.citi.com
159,300 employees
399 Park Avenue, New York, NY 10040
Phone: (212) 559-1000 Fax: (212) 816-8913

Global Franchise and growth story: Global banking, insurance and financial services

Citigroup – formed by the merger of Citicorp and Travelers Group has over 100 million customers in 100 countries around the world. The merged companies start with assets of almost $700 billion, net revenues of nearly $50 billion, operating income of over $7.5 billion and shareholders' equity of more than $44 billion. Citicorp's first franchise is as the world's only truly global consumer bank and the world's leading issuer of credit cards, with over 3,400 operations in almost 100 countries providing the same set of banking, savings, and financing services. About half Citicorp's revenues come from its personal banking and card franchise and half from its second franchise which is full scale commercial banking. Travelers Group included the investment bank Salomon Smith Barney and several insurance companies.

Setting a rational price

Portfolio 2001 WORKSHEET FOR TARGETING SHARE PRICES OF CITIGROUP IN 1999, 2000 & 2001
BASED ON FORECASTS MADE IN FEBRUARY 1999
EPS FISCAL TO YEAR TO DECEMBER 1988 $1.75

Growth	Year	Estimated EPS	P/E	Share Price Target	+10%	-10%	Notes
Consensus	1999	$2.71	17.5	$47	$52	$42	
15%	2000	$3.11	17.5	$54	$60	$49	
15%	2001	$3.57	17.5	$62	$69	$56	

This 'what if' forecast suggests potential earnings and share prices based on current indications. Forecasts must be revised continuously in the light of all company results and industry, market and economic news. Forecasts can be misleading and cannot be treated as investment advice or used to motivate investments. See page 69.

Earnings growth and earnings multiple expectations

1999 is the first year of operations for Citigroup following the merger in 1998, and earnings growth expectations have been set at 15%, corresponding with other leading global financial groups. Multiple expectations have also been set in line with peer companies.

What can go wrong

Apart from the spectrum of risks which affect all global financial companies, the integration of Citibank and Salomon Smith Barney could affect performance.

Monitoring

www.citi.com reports on group developments extensively and the *Wall Street Journal* and other financial publications will report fully on all news affecting the group.

Investors should monitor the results of the group and competitors to form an industry picture.

CAPTIAL ONE FINANCIAL

Share Graph 1997–1998 Captial One Financial
Primary Market – NYSE COF

Price January 1999 $40.60
Market Value January 1999 $7.9 billion

SECTOR Financial INDUSTRY Savings Bank
Top Line COF Bottom Line S&P 500 Index Relative
Left Scale: Top $ Price, Bottom Volume in Thousands
Note: Graphic not rebased for two for one share split in 1999.

Capital One Financial Corp
as of 12-Feb-1999

(C) 1999 Yahoo! Inc.   Volume (1000's)   http://quote.yahoo.com/

PRICE PERFORMANCE   COF   An investment made in
                                           January 1994 grew 250% by
                                           January 1999

PRICE HISTORY	1998	1997	1996	1995	Notes
High Price	43.31	18.10	12.29	9.87	
Low Price	16.85	10.17	7.25	5.12	
High P/E	115.00	54.19	36.00	23.88	
Low P/E	12.76	10.90	9.39	8.07	

Chmn/CEO R. D. Fairbank, www.capitalone.com
5,900 employees
2980 Fairview Park Drive, Suite 1300, Falls Church, VA 22042
Phone: (703) 205-1000 Fax: (703) 205-1755

Global Franchise and growth story: Financial services

Capital One Financial is the parent for Capital One Bank, a financial services holding company, one of the US's top 10 credit card companies. Using the information on consumers in its massive databases, the company solicits Visa and MasterCard customers by mail. The company's 3,000 variations of annual percentage rates, credit limits, finance charges, and fees range from platinum and gold cards for preferred customers to secured and unsecured cards for customers with limited credit histories. Other subsidiaries include a federally chartered savings bank that offers credit cards, consumer lending, and deposit services and a company that provides internal support services.

Setting a rational price

Portfolio 2001 WORKSHEET FOR TARGETING SHARE PRICES OF CAPTIAL ONE
IN 1999, 2000 & 2001
BASED ON FORECASTS MADE IN JANUARY 1999
EPS FISCAL YEAR TO DECEMBER 1988 $1.32

Growth	Year	Estimated EPS	P/E	Share Price Target	+10%	-10%	Notes
25%	1999	$1.71	25	$43	$47	$38	
25%	2000	$2.13	25	$53	$59	$48	
25%	2001	$2.67	25	$67	$74	$60	

This 'what if' forecast suggests potential earnings and share prices based on current indications. Forecasts must be revised continuously in the light of all company results and industry, market and economic news. Forecasts can be misleading and cannot be treated as investment advice or used to motivate investments. See page 69.

Earnings growth and multiple expectations
Earnings growth at Capital One keeps exceeding expectations and in the first quarter of 1999 reached 40%. The *Portfolio 2001* earnings forecast has been prepared assuming 25% earnings growth and an earnings multiple in line with growth of 25. As long as the company sustains its growth performance the forecast will be conservative.

What can go wrong?

Capital One earnings are at risk if there is any tightening in monetary policy which would have the effect of tightening money supply which would have the effects of both reducing business volume and increasing bad debts.

Monitoring

www.capitalone.com should be followed for company news. News on the global economy and the US economy should be reviewed.

AIG

Share Graph 1997–1998 American International Group
Primary Market – NYSE AIG SA

Price January 1999 $115
Market Value January 1999 $121.4 billion

SECTOR Financial INDUSTRY Insurance – Property and
Casualty
Top Line AIG Bottom Line S&P 500 Index Relative: Triangle
Marks Split
Left Scale: Top $ Price, Bottom Volume in Thousands

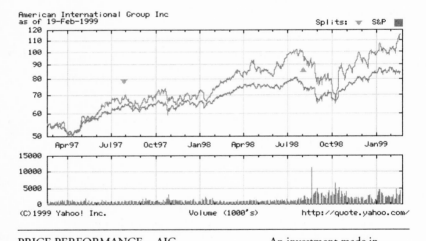

PRICE PERFORMANCE   AIG

An investment made in
January 1994 grew 188% by
January 1999

PRICE HISTORY	1998	1997	1996	1995	Notes
High Price	102.63	75.04	51.72	42.22	
Low Price	64.88	47.33	39.17	28.48	
High P/E	28.78	23.82	18.99	18.09	
Low P/E	18.19	15.02	14.38	12.14	

Chmn/CEO M. Greenberg, www.aig.com
36,000 employees
70 Pine Street, New York, NY 10270
Phone: (212) 770-7000 Fax: (212) 943-1125

Global Franchise and growth story: Global insurance

AIG is one of the world's largest insurance firms. In the US it conducts casualty and life insurance business and develops speciality niches. It is stronger in life insurance outside the US. The group has been built largely from acquisitions and rescue operations of other companies. In 1998, AIG added nearly 10,000 independent agents to its workforce by buying SunAmerica, a fast-growing annuity and investor products firm. AIG's financial services division has a formidable record of achievement and engages in financial trading, currency hedging and aircraft leasing. More than half of AIG's sales come from operations in 130 counties.

Setting a rational price

Portfolio 2001 WORKSHEET FOR TARGETING SHARE PRICES OF AIG IN
1999, 2000 & 2001
BASED ON FORECASTS MADE IN JANUARY 1999
EPS FISCAL 1988 TO DECEMBER $3.53

Growth	Year	Estimated EPS	P/E	Share Price Target	+10%	-10%	Notes
15%	1999	$4.05	25	$101	$112	$91	
15%	2000	$4.65	25	$116	$111	$104	
15%	2001	$5.34	25	$133	$148	$120	

This 'what if' forecast suggests potential earnings and share prices based on current indications. Forecasts must be revised continuously in the light of all company results and industry, market and economic news. Forecasts can be misleading and cannot be treated as investment advice or used to motivate investments. See page 69.

Earnings growth and multiple expectations
AIG has an entrenched track record with five years of earnings growth of 15%. In the light of this performance the share commands a market multiple higher than those financial companies who experienced disruptions over latter years, and its shares are likely to continue to command an earnings multiple of 25 times earnings.

What can go wrong?

While AIG is well insulated from operational risks following its traditional businesses and growth strategies, the shares are vulnerable to correct in any major general market correction, or any weakness in the financial services sector.

Monitoring

Growth will be affected by economic strength, particularly in the US and Europe. www.aig.com reports fully on group activities, and events concerning the company are well covered in the financial press.

ALLIED ZURICH

Share Graph 1997–1998 Allied Zurich
Primary Market – NYSE ADZHY ADR – London ADZ

Price January 1999 $30.25 ADR
Market Value January 1999 $21 billion

SECTOR Financial INDUSTRY Insurance
Top Line AZDHY: Bottom Line S&P 500 Index Relative:
Right Scale: % Gain, Bottom Volume in Thousands

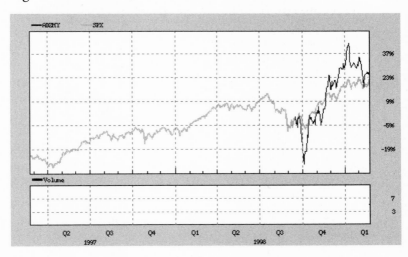

PRICE PERFORMANCE	AZDHY
PRICE HISTORY	1998
High Price	33.3
Low Price	16.75
High P/E	NA
Low P/E	NA

Note: Allied Zurich was not formed until 1998.

Chairman: The Right Honourable the Earl of Cairns CBE
www.alliedzurich.co.uk
22 Arlington Street, London SW1A
Phone 0171-317 3895 Fax: 0171-317 3926

Global Franchise and growth story: Focused financial services

Allied Zurich was formed in September 1998, as a result of the merger of the Zurich Group with the financial services business of BAT Industries. The combined operations form the Zurich Financial Services Group which is a Swiss holding company, in which all the operating entities are now under a single management team. Through a dual holding structure, Zurich Financial Services is 57% owned by Switzerland's Zurich AG – representing the former shareholders of Zurich Insurance Company – and 43% owned by London's Allied Zurich plc – the demerged financial services interests from the former BAT Industries plc. Shares in the Swiss holding company, Zurich Financial Services, or its operating subsidiaries, are not publicly listed on any world stock exchange.

The Zurich Financial Services group is one of the global leaders in the financial services industry, providing its customers with products and solutions in the area of financial protection and asset accumulation, ranging from insurance coverage and retirement plans to mutual funds. The group has a strong focus on specific market or customer segments and is concentrating its activities in four core businesses: non-life and life insurance, reinsurance and asset management.

Headquartered in Zurich, Switzerland, Zurich Financial Services' worldwide presence builds on strong positions in its three home markets, the United States, the United Kingdom and Switzerland, and spreads globally to more than 50 countries, reaching over 30 million customers who are served by more than 68,000 dedicated employees. The group is the largest Swiss based insurance group, the third largest non-life insurer in the UK, and the third largest property and casualty writer in the US. Additionally, the group is one of the world's top ten asset managers with some 375 billion US dollars in assets under management.

In addition to the former Zurich Group, the new organization comprises Eagle Star, Allied Dunbar and Threadneedle, along with their subsidiaries, and the Farmers Group in the USA. Shares of both holding companies, Zurich Allied AG and Allied Zurich plc., began to trade on Tuesday 8 September on the Swiss and the London Stock Exchanges, respectively. Zurich Allied AG is replacing Zurich in the Swiss Market Index (SMI), which represents the 23 most important Swiss companies listed on the Swiss exchange. Allied Zurich plc. is included in the FTSE-100 Share Index in London. The dual listing structure will enable Swiss and UK shareholders to hold their interest in the Zurich Financial Services Group through shares quoted and traded in their respective local currency, quoted from www.cdr.com.

Setting a rational price

Portfolio 2001 WORKSHEET FOR TARGETING SHARE PRICES OF ALLIED ZURICH AZDHY IN 1999, 2000 & 2001 BASED ON FORECASTS MADE IN FEBRUARY 1999 EPS FISCAL 1998 TO JUNE $0.62 ONE ADR = 2 SHARES

Growth	Year	Estimated EPS	P/E	Share Price Target	+10%	-10%	Notes
15%	1999	$1.71	20	$34	$38	$31	
15%	2000	$1.96	20	$39	$43	$35	
15%	2001	$2.25	20	$45	$50	$40	

This 'what if' forecast suggests potential earnings and share prices based on current indications. Forecasts must be revised continuously in the light of all company results and industry, market and economic news. Forecasts can be misleading and cannot be treated as investment advice or used to motivate investments. See page 69.

Earnings growth and multiple expectations

Allied Zurich was listed in 1998 and the first year's results will run to June 1999. The *Portfolio 2001* forecast has been prepared arithmetically, basing 1999 results on analysts' consensus and factoring in 15% growth in line with other leading companies in the sector. The earnings multiple has been set at 20 times earnings in view of the national support which the group will gain from the UK and via its sister company Zurich Allied, based in Switzerland.

What can go wrong?

The well entrenched management skills which came into the company Allied Zurich from both the Allied Dunbar and Zurich Insurance management teams and the high-quality asset base will reassure investors. The main risk to investors will be deterioration in the global economic climate and vulnerability of the share price to any reversal following weakening in markets generally.

Monitoring

`www.alliedzurich.com` presently links to the group's Eagle Star Insurance site which is promoting insurance using the Internet. Financial information on the group is not included. Investors can monitor the group on all UK market services and through the financial press in the UK and the US. `www.adr.com` reviews news and earnings forecasts.

AXA

Share Graph 1997–1998 AXA UAP
Primary Market – NYSE ADR AXA

Price January 1999 $66.25 ADR
Market Value February 1999 $21.9 billion

SECTOR Financial INDUSTRY Insurance
Top Line AXA ADR: Bottom Line S&P 500 Index Relative:
Triangle Marks Split
Left Scale: Top $ Price, Bottom Volume in Thousands

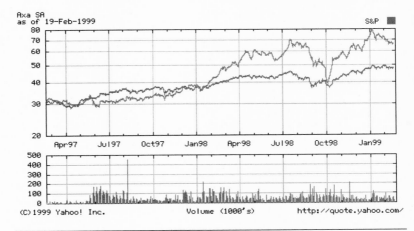

PRICE PERFORMANCE   AXA

An investment made in March 1996 grew 186% by January 1999

PRICE HISTORY	1998	1997	1996	1995	Notes
High Price	72.50	39.88	32.00	NA	
Low Price	36.19	29.25	25.75	NA	
High P/E	NA	39.59	17.55	NA	
Low P/E	NA	29.04	14.12	NA	

Chmn Claude Bebear, www.axa.com
80,600 employees
9 Place Vendome, 75001 Paris
Phone: (212) 314-4176 Fax: (212) 707-1805

Global Franchise and growth story: Global insurance

AXA is the second largest insurance group worldwide in terms of revenues, and the second largest asset manager worldwide in terms of assets under management. It is involved in insurance and related financial services. The company has a worldwide presence, in especially Western Europe, North America and South America.

AXA-UAP provides life, personal and commerical property/casualty insurance, reinsurance, financial services, and real estate investment services. With more than 50 major subsidiaries, primary foreign operations include, in the US, The Equitable Companies (58%), which in turn own most of brokerage and investment bank Donaldson, Lufkin & Jenrette, and a substantial share of Alliance Capital Management. The group also owns National Mutual Life Association of Australasia. Mutuelles AXA, a group of French mutual insurers, owns about a quarter of AXA-UAP.

In February 1999, it was announced that agreement had been reached for the AXA group to acquire the Guardian Royal Exchange through Sun Life and Provincial Holdings (SLPH), the 71.6% UK subsidiary of AXA, for a total consideration of 3,447 million pounds sterling (euro 5.0 billion) in cash and new SLPH shares. GRE is constituent of the FTSE-100 in the UK, and is ranked among the top UK insurance companies.

Setting a rational price

Portfolio 2001 WORKSHEET FOR TARGETING SHARE PRICES OF AXA IN 1999, 2000 & 2001
BASED ON FORECASTS MADE IN MARCH 1999
EPS/ADR FISCAL 1988 TO DECEMBER $2.36
2 ADRs = ONE ORDINARY SHARE

Growth	Year	Estimated EPS	P/E	Share Price Target	+10%	-10%	Notes
15%	1999	$2.71	25	$68	$75	$61	
15%	2000	$3.11	25	$78	$86	$70	
15%	2001	$3.40	25	$85	$94	$76	

This 'what if' forecast suggests potential earnings and share prices based on current indications. Forecasts must be revised continuously in the light of all company results and industry, market and economic news. Forecasts can be misleading and cannot be treated as investment advice or used to motivate investments. See page 69.

Earnings growth and multiple expectations

AXA is engaged in international growth organically and by acquisition. The *Portfolio 2001* forecast has been worked out arithmetically following 15% growth expected by other leading companies in the sector, and a multiple higher than US companies to align the forecast with market conditions at the time it was prepared. The higher earnings multiple follows support for the share from France and higher valuations which are accorded by European companies for national investments than apply for US companies because of local support for national companies.

What can go wrong?

AXA has a proven track record and stands to benefit from the consolidation within the banking and insurance industries. The main risk to investors will be any deterioration in the global economic climate and vulnerability of the share price to a reversal following weakening in markets generally.

Monitoring

`www.axa.com` gives a full picture of group activities and the financial press cover all relevant news and developments. `www.adr.com` is useful for news and financial information.

14

INVESTING IN GLOBAL PROFIT HARVESTERS

Global Profit Harvesters must have growing markets

I invented the name-tag Global Profit Harvesters for companies that operate like efficient money-making machines, and advance like efficient armies from country to country, pursuing new growth opportunities from which they can churn out profits. Season after season after season after season – but what happens in bad seasons? The answer has to be that the Profit Harvesters are cyclical investments, and when times are good they are very, very good and when times are bad they can be horrid. When considering them as prospective investments, there is no escaping a first focus on the global economy.

We all want to own shares in the great global names and expect they will not come cheap, but Global Profit Harvesters are exceptions. They often do come cheap – when global economic growth prospects look bleak so do their share prices.

Is Coca-Cola losing its fizz?

Wall Street loves Coca-Cola for the way it grows profits. The world's top global consumer brand, and the world's largest soft drinks company, reached a milestone in 1997 when consumers refreshed themselves with one billion servings of Coca-Cola products daily. At the time it hardly mattered to Coke that growth in the mature US market was barely 6%. Profit Harvesting in China was increasing their revenues by 30%. Net income for 1997 was $4.1 billion, up 18%, in line with the compound annual investment growth of over 18% scored by shareholders since 1995.

By July 1998, Coca-Cola's share price was showing growth of 330% in three years. Later in the same year, when Coca-Cola issued a profits warning, commentators exclaimed that Coca-Cola had lost its fizz as the share shed over 20% in a week.

Coca-Cola has not been losing its fizz. It is a great drink and the brand is so much part of our lives that we probably get our first urge to taste it as soon as we can mouth its first syllable.

After the fall of the Berlin Wall, Coca-Cola's global growth set off at an unprecedented pace, as top Global Profit Harvesters worked overtime harvesting the opportunities. However, following the Asian crisis in 1998, the climate changed for the worse and expectations for earnings have to be more conservative. The following chart shows how Coca-Cola actually underperformed the S&P 500 index in 1997 and 1998, as it felt the impact of weak global markets:

Top Line S&P 500 Index Relative Bottom Line Coca-Cola

Buying opportunities with cyclical shares

The top global franchises are quality investing prospects, but for an investment to be low-risk and high-reward, getting the timing right is vital. The predictability with which markets move away from cyclical shares can itself present buying opportunities. The following quotation from the Internet site www.motleyfool.com brings a very useful message for long-term investors interested in great industrial companies like Caterpillar and Ford:

> For all the talk of the Information Age economy we supposedly live in, one of the most striking triumphs of the American economy over the last decade has actually been the resurrection of its industrial base. In the late 1970s and early 1980s American manufacturing was out on its feet, devastated by high interest rates, the strong dollar, bloated managerial hierarchies, weak R&D, and rising labour costs. Today, American manufacturing companies tend to be paragons of efficiency, with leaner organisations, more efficient factories, and much-improved management of supply and distribution.

Global markets and industries

This table shows the importance of overseas sales to several of America's top companies:

COMPANY	OVERSEAS SALES AS A % OF REVENUE	ASIA	EUROPE
COCA-COLA	67.4%	22%	34.6%
GILLETTE	61%	17%	32.7%
INTEL	58.4%	30.2%	28.2%
MICROSOFT	57%	25%	32%
CATERPILLAR	46.3%	16.1%	22.2%
BOEING	44.8%	33.1%	9.6%

Source: Morgan Stanley

While working on this book in 1998, I was surprised to see the market value of The Gap (GPS) catching up on Boeing as I researched the companies. When I raised the subject with friends, their responses were polarized. The pragmatic response was: 'so what? The Gap is successful and makes more money and the market capitalization of The Gap should be more than Boeing which is not doing too well.' The doubters' response was: 'Are you sure about your figures? You can't be right?'

The Gap does make more money and the pragmatists have my vote – and so do the doubters. When Boeing's Asian customers could not take up their bookings in 1998, aircraft sales collapsed. However, investors who believe in the strength of industrial leaders like Boeing would focus on prospects for a recovery and would think about investing before a turnaround if they have faith in the future of the aviation industry.

A simple route to investing in Global Profit Harvesters is to buy them when prospects are not looking too bright and the shares are cheap. However, this could prove to be too simplistic if economic conditions do not improve for a long time span, as has happened with Japan's economy. Investments made in Japan in the 1990s have not paid off, regardless of how cheap they looked when they were bought, and the turnaround time for many western companies may be a long time coming if the pattern of traditional business cycles has changed, as many are now suggesting.

Growth cycles in the traditional industrial economies were driven by capital investment. Eventually, increased industrial capacity would lead to overcapacity and a tightening of economic conditions followed, during which the overcapacity was absorbed or wound down. In the slowdown, less building of new factories resulted in less demand for cement, steel, finance, services and transportation etc. In tune with each other, cycles of capital spending, employment and consumer confidence have tended to turn round in time frames of five to ten years, sufficient time for much of the economy to get into the same pattern. Recognizable patterns supported reliable economic forecasting and with their backing informed cyclical buying decisions could be made.

Nowadays, corrections in the global economy are showing less synchronization between the services and the manufacturing sectors, between construction and industrial investment, inflation and growth, and between the developed and the emerging worlds. One reason given for this change is that structurally the information economy is different. It is more efficient and computer guided to gain scalability and to support 'just in time' manufacturing and inventory control. If this is correct, it indicates we should rethink whether traditional investing paradigms are still meaningful.

Deflation

Inflation has usually been good for Global Profit Harvesters, but deflation would be a menace. Even without deflation, flagging earnings may continue to depress them for longer than we expect as there are already gluts on the market of all commodities including oil, which is trading at its lowest prices for twenty-five years. With falling commodity prices, manufacturers find it more difficult to raise their product prices and they lose pricing power. In the worst case scenario, this will result in a general deflation and call for a rethink on all investment strategies.

Watching commodity markets for opportunities

The range of investing prospects in Global Profit Harvesters includes classic cyclical industries, commodity based opportunities and more general prospects.

As the world begins to get back its economic wind in 1999, we have seen a meaningful rebound in commodity prices, and monetary policy concerns could even move from deflation to reflation. If this happens, depressed commodity cyclical shares will have their day again. With this prospect in mind, *Portfolio 2001* includes research on RTZ, the world's leading base minerals mining company; Shell, the world's largest integrated oil company; and Volkswagen, Germany's largest car manufacturer.

Timing investments in tune with markets

It is always tempting to try and make a killing by being a step or two ahead of the market. You may read that Warren Buffett is buying silver, or that George Soros is selling gold, and think you will make money doing the same. However, the rumours you hear are probably not true, and even Soros and Buffett are not infallible. Speculating against the markets on commodity prices is unlikely to pay off and, if you ignore the weather reports, the chances increase that your investments will get blown off course.

Serious investors anticipate cyclical changes by making balancing adjustments to their holdings from time to time. It is a hard strategy to beat.

The Global Profit Harvester prospects

The ten Global Profit Harvesters in *Porfolio 2001* are prospects investors may consider when rotating investments for a more prosperous global economy. The first five are Disney, Sony, The Gap, Gillette and Unilever.

Disney is arguably the world's premier entertainment group, but is not doing brilliantly at present. Sony, though not the world's largest, is one of the top consumer electronics businesses and is also having an uninspiring time, with earnings in a trough as Asian markets have weakened and competition in the West has intensified. However, Sony has a vital position in the world of audio visual entertainment and, when overall economies improve, Sony's fortunes should change.

The Gap has had a different experience of economic conditions. Importing clothing from Asia and selling it with brilliant marketing flare in the US and Europe has made it into one of the world's most successful businesses. Gillette has lived through both worlds – early in 1998 it experienced its profits setback from global markets, by the end of that year it was gaining ground and in 1999 growth was stalling again.

Unilever, one of the world's most successful non cyclical consumer companies, is returning a cash mountain of $8 billion to shareholders because it does not need the money for growth!

The next four global profit harvesters are Caterpillar, Royal Dutch Shell, Rio Tinto (RTZ) and Volkswagen. Caterpillar is the world's leading earthmoving and construction equipment manufacturer and had to be affected by a weak global economy, but earnings have been robust and the earth will move for Caterpillar investors again. Royal Dutch Shell has been affected by the lowest oil prices in three decades, and Rio Tinto by the lowest industrial base minerals prices, and they will only recover lost earnings when demand starts to exceed supply again.

I included Volkswagen as the automobile manufacturer after hours spent trying to find the *Portfolio 2001* company most linked to a global economic recovery in the sector outside Japan. General Motors and Ford are prospering on the US market, and are investments that I suggest should be seen as more than cyclicals. I see signs of 'reinvented' corporations – businesses that Jack Welch of GE would be proud to own. Jaguar may also come to be a great earner for Ford if its new mid-range models succeed as expected. Daimler, which was one of my original portfolio of 20 companies, is now Daimler Chrysler and, exceptional as I still think the company is, the next few years will be a post-merger synergy story as much as a cylical auto company story. Alas Honda, brilliant as it is, is too much of a currency hostage, like other Japanese auto companies, and is subject also to Japan's complex macro economic dynamics. Global production is changing this for Honda.

The world automobile industry is facing a global over-production problem, and to form any picture of the industry it is useful to know the size of each company at the end of 1998:

COMPANY	COUNTRY	MARKET CAP $ billion
1. Toyota Motor Corp	Japan	96.38
2. Ford Motor Co	USA	68.71
3. General Motors Corp	USA	66.30
4. Daimler Chrysler AG	Germany	58.76
5. Honda Motor Co Ltd	Japan	34.88
6. Volkswagen AG	Germany	34.85
7. BMW	Germany	17.28
8. Fiat SpA	Italy	14.50
9. Renault SA	France	12.35
10.Volvo AB	Sweden	11.95

		COMPANY SALES $ billion
1. General Motors Corp	USA	178.17
2. Ford Motor Co	USA	153.63
3. Daimler Chrysler	Germany	134.76
4. Toyota Motor Corp	Japan	100.98
5. Volkswagen AG	Germany	66.29
6. Fiat SpA	Italy	52.56
7. Honda Motor Co Ltd	Japan	51.88
8. Renault SA	France	36.22
9. BMW	Germany	35.12
10.Peugeot	France	32.54
11.Mitsubishi Motors Corp	Japan	32.30
12.Nissan Motor Co Ltd	Japan	30.63
13.Volvo AB	Sweden	23.77

Volkswagen was chosen as the auto prospect from Europe over BMW, mainly because Volkswagen has an ADR listing and BMW does not. Volkswagen is also a classic Global Profit Harvester and uninspiring performance in 1999 will give investors an opportunity to study the prospect with a view to recognising buying opportunities in future.

The last Global Profit Harvester is America's Wal-Mat Group, the world's most successful retailer.

DISNEY

Share Graph 1997–1998 Disney
Primary Market – NYSE DIS

Price January 1999 $34.13
Market Value January 1999 $72.6 billion

SECTOR Services INDUSTRY Recreational Activities
Top Line S&P 500 Relative: Bottom Line DISNEY: Triangle
Marks Split
Left Scale: Top $ Price, Bottom Volume in Thousands

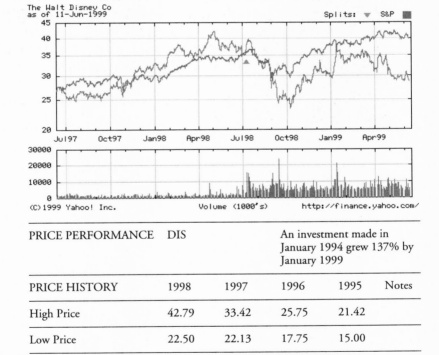

The Walt Disney Co
as of 11-Jun-1999

Splits: ▼ S&P ■

(C) 1999 Yahoo! Inc.   Volume (1000's)   http://finance.yahoo.com/

PRICE PERFORMANCE	DIS		An investment made in January 1994 grew 137% by January 1999		
PRICE HISTORY	1998	1997	1996	1995	Notes
High Price	42.79	33.42	25.75	21.42	
Low Price	22.50	22.13	17.75	15.00	
High P/E	48.08	35.03	39.37	24.67	
Low P/E	25.28	23.19	27.14	17.28	

Chmn/CEO M. D. Eisner, www.disney.com
117,000 employees
500 South Buena Vista Street, Burbank, CA 91521
Phone: (818) 560-1000 Fax: (818) 560-1930

Global Franchise Entertainment:

The Disney Brothers studio was formed in 1923, and the world of entertainment changed for ever when, in 1926, Mickey and Minnie Mouse made their debut. Pluto and Goofy followed soon afterwards and Donald Duck made his first appearance in 1934. The fantasy characters entered the psyche of the twentieth century through films, records and books and in 1955 the first Disneyland theme park opened in California. The Disney fantasy keeps growing in size and profitability. There are three business divisions – theme parks and resorts, content creation and broadcasting, Theme parks are now global and include animal life parks and cruise liners. The Walt Disney company is now the world's second-largest media conglomerate after Time Warner, with major franchises in films, the ABC TV and radio stations, cable channels, Disneyland Epcot and Animal Kingdom Theme Parks and publication companies, including Disney Hachette Press, Disney Press, Hyperion Press and Mouse Works. Disney acquired 48% of the Internet portal Infoseek, and its own web site www.disney.com is one of the most visited on the net and a leading e-commerce business. ABC Radio has 40 million listeners, the wholly owned Disney Channel has 30 million subscribers, ESPN (80% owned) has 72 million US subscribers, A&E (35% owned) has 78 million subscribers, and Lifetime Entertainment (50% owned) has 69 million subscribers.

However, disappointing profit growth has led to concern that Mickey Mouse and friends may be having a mid-life crisis, or worse that they may be terminally ill.

With a view to reviving market values, in July 1999 Disney announced plans to acquire the shares in Infoseek it did not already own and merge its Internet interests in Infoseek, at the same time promoting the shares in Infoseek as an Internet company.

Setting a rational price

**Portfolio 2001 WORKSHEET FOR TARGETING SHARE PRICE RANGE DISNEY IN 1999, 2000 & 2001
BASED ON FORECASTS MADE IN JANUARY 1999
EPS FISCAL 1988 TO SEPTEMBER $0.88**

Growth	Year	Estimated EPS	P/E	Share Price Target	+10%	-10%	Notes
Consensus	1999	0.72	35	25	28	23	
20%	2000	0.86	35	30	33	27	
20%	2001	1.03	35	36	40	32	

This 'what if' forecast suggests potential earnings and share prices based on current indications. Forecasts must be revised continuously in the light of all company results and industry, market and economic news. Forecasts can be misleading and cannot be treated as investment advice or used to motivate investments. See page 69.

Past performance indications

Growth Rates %	DIS	S&P 500	Industry	Sector	Notes
Earnings per share 5 year	21.92	16.18	21.53	22.04	
1998 last reported vs 1997	-13.51	11.42	0.02	24.70	
Sales 5 year 1994–1998	21.92	16.18	21.53	22.04	
Profitability Ratios					
Gross Margin 1998 %	17.48	49.26	28.79	44.62	
5 year average %	18.86	48.91	28.47	43.47	
Net Profit Margin 1998 %	7.39	10.63	12.32	6.56	
5 year average %	9.13	10.21	12.14	5.85	
5 Year Returns on:					
Assets %	4.27	8.57	6.42	5.11	
Investment %	5.26	13.65	7.76	7.36	
Equity %	9.10	23.28	12.08	15.25	

The growth story

The Disney global empire projects itself both as the world's leading family entertainment company and as a pace setting investment with a management commitment to deliver 20% compound annual growth in earnings per share. Earnings growth was on track until September 1998 when the effects of the Asian recession were felt and Disney also announced earnings below forecasts:

SEGMENT RESULTS
For the Year Ended 30 September 1998

(Unaudited; in millions)

	1998	1997 (Pro Forma)	% Change
Revenues:			
Creative Content	$10.302	$10.098	2%
Broadcasting	7,142	6,501	10%
Theme Parks & Resorts	5,532	5,014	10%
Total	$22,976	$21,613	6%
Operating Income: (1) (2)			
Creative Content	$1,403	$1,693	(17)%
Broadcasting	1,325	1,285	3%
Theme Parks & Resorts	1,287	1,136	13%
	$4,015	$4,114	2%
Gain on Sale of KCAL	–	–	n/m
Total Operating Income	$4,015	$4,114	(2)%

Results for the quarter to December 1998 were also disappointing.

Disney has experienced a downturn in the film industry, but management expect earnings to be back on track from 1999.

20% compound earnings per share growth target
Disney's economic objective is to create shareholder value as the world's premier entertainment company from a creative, strategic and financial standpoint, building on the Disney name and franchise. The primary financial objective is 20% compound annual earnings per share growth over future five-year periods, and steady improvement in return on equity.

Creative Content
The acquisition of the ABC broadcast and television network provided the opportunity to combine some of Disney's similar

businesses under the name Creative Content, which captures the spirit of the creative engine behind the film and merchandise operations. In the Creative Content segment, Disney produces animated and live-action features for worldwide theatrical, home video and television distribution, licenses its characters, operates The Disney Store network, releases Disney-branded records, and manages the ABC Inc. publishing operations. The Creative Content segment accounts for some 50% of pro forma revenues and 44% of pro forma operating income.

Broadcasting
Broadcasting became a major part of the Walt Disney company with the acquisition of Capital Cities/ABC. This new segment comprises ABC's businesses and the Disney Channel. This segment accounts for 29% of pro forma revenues and 29% of pro forma operating income.

Theme parks and resorts
The Walt Disney company designs, builds and operates theme parks and hotels and manages its real estate holdings through its Theme Parks and Resorts segment. This sector has reported strong profits growth and will be further boosted by cruise liner revenues.

Competitive advantage
In segments of its business Disney competes with other companies on equal terms, but business from its cartoon characters has no meaningful competitors.

Earnings growth expectations

In spite of current flat earnings growth investors clearly expect Disney to revert to earnings per share growth in the range of 20% in line with past performance and sustained management commitments.

Earnings multiple expectations

Management have explained their flat earnings as an effect of the Asian economic crisis and claim a single year's financial accounts at times is not a meaningful period to reflect the benefits of new business developments. Investors clearly accept the validity of these explanations and continue to support a high valuation of the shares based on 40 times current earnings. Substantial revenues could also result from the independent flotation of parts of the group which have been mooted by management. The quality of Disney's intellectual property assets, the width of its distribution and the strength of elements of the business such as theme parks are likely to continue to support high earnings multiples as long as management demonstrate that they are steering the group back to sustained high growth.

What can go wrong?

'The best laid plans of mice and men' can go wrong. Mickey Mouse and Donald Duck must be suffering the mid life crisis and the investment has lost sparkle. Theme parks and cruise liners hold the best promise currently. The launch of cruise ships, successful animal safari theme parks cruises and a revival of demand in Asia might help kick start profits back to life. There are also plans to restructure its significant Internet business to give additional value to shareholders.

If Disney does not restore expected levels of prosperity investors will loose interest – and in show business that is the last thing anyone wants. Currently the sum of the parts is greater than Disney's current value.

Monitoring

Many influences will affect the fortunes of Disney and investors should monitor particularly the extent of which management deliver on their promises to restore 20% earnings growth. Their achievements will be influenced by the global economic climate but the diversity of the group is such that well run, it should produce strong results in most conditions, excepting severe economic misfortunes.

SONY

Share Graph 1997–1998 Sony Corporation
Primary Market – TOKYO: ADR NYSE – SNE

Price January 1999 $69.06
Market Value January 1999 $28.1 billion

SECTOR Consumer Cyclical INDUSTRY Audio and Video
Equipment
Top Line S&P 500 Index Relative: Bottom Line Sony ADR SNE
Left Scale: Top $ Price, Bottom Volume in Thousands

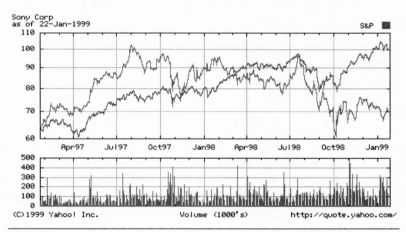

PRICE PERFORMANCE	ADR SNE		An investment made in January 1994 grew 51% by January 1999		
PRICE HISTORY	1998	1997	1996	1995	Notes
High Price	97.19	103.69	67.88	61.50	
Low Price	60.25	63.88	57.38	42.50	
High P/E	22.95	38.28	57.81	NM	
Low P/E	14.23	23.40	48.87	NM	

Pres/CEO Nobuyuti Idei, www.sony.com
173,000 employees
7-35, Kitashinagawa 6-Chome, Shinagawa - Ku, Tokyo 141-0001 Japan
Phone: (212) 833-6800 Fax: (212) 833-6938

Global Franchise: Consumer electronics

After Matsushita, Sony is the world's second largest consumer electronics manufacturer. Its product line includes PlayStation home video games, DVD – digital video disc players, TVs, cameras, MiniDisc systems, computer monitors, flat screen TVs, telephones, semiconductors and batteries. The company's TVs, VCRs, stereos, PlayStations, and other electronics products account for some 70% of revenues.

Entertainment assets in the group include Columbia TriStar Motion Picture Group and record labels Columbia and Epic. The group also includes insurance and finance businesses. Global revenues exceed $7 billion.

Setting a rational price

Portfolio 2001 WORKSHEET FOR TARGETING SHARE PRICES OF SONY ADR IN
1999, 2000 & 2001
BASED ON FORECASTS MADE IN JANUARY 1999
EPS FISCAL 1988 TO MARCH $3.66(E)
1 ADR = 1 SHARE

Growth	Year	Estimated EPS	P/E	Share Price Target	+10%	-10%	Notes
-5%	1999	$3.47	20	$69	$77	$62	
-20%	2000	$2.74	25	$69	$77	$62	
+33%	2001	$3.66	25	$91	$102	$82	

This 'what if' forecast suggests potential earnings and share prices based on current indications. Forecasts must be revised continuously in the light of all company results and industry, market and economic news. Forecasts can be misleading and cannot be treated as investment advice or used to motivate investments. See page 69.

Earnings per share growth expectations
Sony is uniquely well positioned to supply digital-ready content and to benefit from the union of digital technology and entertainment taking place globally now. It is restructuring and upgrading existing lines and introducing new ones like the DVD-video players and software it is already marketing. Sony technology and products will experience another surge in demand with the proliferation of digital satellite broadcasting and wireless telephony. Sony's intellectual property assets should also benefit from a

content boom, with its movie picture library now available as digital content.

In line with the profits warning made in January 1999, earnings forecasts have been scaled back. Forecasting earnings that only return to 1998 levels in 2001 is probably modest, and prices forecast are below market levels at the time this report goes to press.

Earnings multiple expectations

Sony's importance in consumer electronics should result in higher valuations on the market, but investors have difficulty in understanding the sources of earnings across the wide range of Sony businesses, and in coping with the 'special effects' from ancillary businesses which include film making and insurance. Market valuations in February 1999, at a little above 20 times earnings, were modest but when the restructuring was announced in March 1999 the ADR jumped about 25% from range $75 to range $95 in a few days and lifted the Tokyo Stock Exchange with it.

Backed by their strong brand, global marketing and leading digital technologies, Sony should benefit appreciably from the new focus on profitability and restructuring to reduce over-staffing. Growth is also expected from computers and wireless phones and Sony are engaged in various uniform global standards initiatives to secure future competitive advantages in wireless telephony.

Sony stands to benefit from a revival of consumer demand in emerging markets when it takes place and from its relevance in the digital age. It is also an important manufacturer of wireless phones and is engaged in the various uniform standards initiatives in the industry to secure its position. Positive news could stimulate Sony's share price dramatically.

Past performance indicators

Growth Rates %		SNE	S&P 500	Industry	Sector	Notes
Earnings per share 5 year		39.29	20.71	23.35	18.92	
1998 last reported vs 1997		56.33	12.93	17.05	56.33	
Sales 5 year 1994-1998		11.09	16.02	55.26	10.72	
Profitability Ratios						
Gross Margin 1998	%	27.19	49.02	62.64	30.99	
5 year average	%	8.87	22.17	-21.69	13.19	

Net Profit Margin 1998	%	3.54	10.84	24.57	7.03
5 year average	%	0.19	10.19	-20.68	4.18

5 Year Returns on:					
Assets	%	0.37	8.29	-30.78	5.00
Investment	%	0.62	13.04	-61.18	7.69
Equity	%	1.11	21.44	1.01	19.13

The growth story

In January 1998, Sony warned investors of a downward revision of earnings estimates following the soft market for consumer electronics in Japan and the loss of markets in Asia, Russia and Latin America. In the US and Europe, the strengthening yen was eroding margins. Revised earnings estimates in line with indications are:

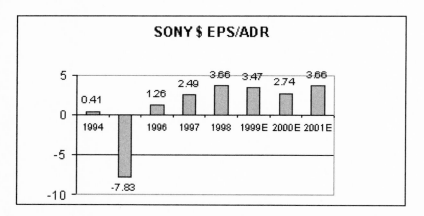

Sony's PlayStation home video game system continues to gain ground in the US and Europe and accounts for 10% of the electronics and entertainment giant's worldwide sales. When the economic climate improves, Sony's exceptional product range should assure a strong earnings rebound. Sony is engaged in audiovisual businesses in all its applications, and globally it enjoys exceptional growth prospects.

What can go wrong?

Earnings are at risk from both sustained weakness in global markets and from any surges in the value of the Japanese yen that affect its competitiveness.

Monitoring

Studying the company and monitoring must start with www.sony.com which is an essential and inspiring gateway to Sony's brilliant product range and marketing flare. A visit to a retail electronics outlet will add information on the product range and its competitiveness in your own market. Investors will need to monitor that management can deliver improved results following the reconstruction and that the global economy supports sustained growth in consumer spending.

THE GAP

Share Graph 1997–1998 The Gap Inc.
Primary Market – NYSE GPS

Price January 1999 $31.12
Market Value January 1999 $34.64 billion

SECTOR Retail INDUSTRY Apparel
Top Line GPS: Bottom Line S&P 500 Index Relative: Triangle
Marks Split
Left Scale: Top $ Price, Bottom Volume in Thousands
Graphic not rebased for two for one split in June 1999

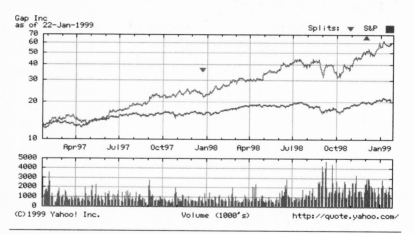

PRICE PERFORMANCE	ACTUAL GPS		An investment made in January 1994 grew 627% by January 1999		
PRICE HISTORY	1998	1997	1996	1995	Notes
High Price	$40.92	17.15	10.81	7.56	
Low Price	$15.31	8.26	6.22	4.41	
High P/E	$70.71	36.38	29.39	22.90	
Low P/E	$26.45	17.52	16.91	13.36	

President/CEO M. S. Drexler, Chmn D. G. Fisher, www.thegap.com
8,100 employees
One Harrison Street, San Francisco, CA 94105
Phone: (415) 952-4400 Fax: (415) 427-7007

Global Franchise: Clothing retailing

The Gap is an international speciality retailer, operating 2,143 stores selling casual apparel, personal care and other accessories for all age groups. Brands include Gap, GapKids, babyGap, Banana Republic and Old Navy. They are among the strongest and best managed globally and the company's profits set performance benchmarks. Managed growth is achieved through promotion, remodelling and store upgrading, expanding advertising and building on a successful e-business franchise. Revenues exceed $9 billion.

Setting a rational price

Portfolio 2001 WORKSHEET FOR TARGETING SHARE PRICES OF THE GAP IN 1999, 2000 & 2001
BASED ON FORECASTS MADE IN JANUARY 1999
EARNINGS FOR FISCAL YEAR ENDING JANUARY 1999 $1.38

Growth	Year	Estimated EPS	P/E	Share Price Target	+10%	-10%	Notes
25%	1999	$1.72	40	$69	$76	$62	
25%	2000	$2.15	40	$86	$96	$77	
25%	2001	$2.68	40	$116	$128	$100	

This 'what if' forecast suggests potential earnings and share prices based on current indications. Forecasts must be revised continuously in the light of all company results and industry, market and economic news. Forecasts can be misleading and cannot be treated as investment advice or used to motivate investments. See page 69.

Earnings per share growth expectations
Analysts' consensus indicates 20% plus earnings per share growth for the next three to five years. The *Portfolio 2001* forecast has been prepared assuming 25%, following the strong growth in the US economy and a resumption of positive global growth in the second half of 1998.

Earnings multiple expectations
The Gap is a favoured investment for institutions and individuals. Its straightforward growth story with strong predictable earnings attracts high market multiples and is likely to continue to do so,

unless there is a general market correction. With investments made at lofty market valuations, low-risk high-reward investing demands long-term holding strategies.

Past performance indicators

Growth Rates %		GPS	S&P 500	Industry	Sector	Notes
Earnings per share 5 year		21.41	21.00	18.31	20.66	
1998 last reported vs 1997		53.92	12.19	47.72	24.25	
Sales 5 year 1994-1998		36.27	12.79	25.46	12.79	
Profitability Ratios						
Gross Margin 1998	%	40.82	36.70	44.79	49.51	
5 year average	%	36.86	33.55	43.62	49.15	
Net Profit Margin 1998	%	8.87	10.85	8.42	6.68	
5 year average	%	8.25	10.27	6.09	5.90	
5 Year Returns on:						
Assets	%	17.17	8.47	13.33	5.58	
Investment	%	23.33	13.28	21.35	7.81	
Equity	%	27.04	21.60	21.84	15.26	

The growth story

The Gap has concentrated on retailing own brand apparel and by developing its own outlets, acquisitions and direct marketing, including business concluded on the Internet. From the outset The Gap has consistently grown earnings, with exceptional growth achieved in 1998. An account of The Gap growth story is included in Chapter 4, pages 61.

What can go wrong?

The Gap has potential to grow its brands and branches globally. Emerging markets have not yet been included in the retail network as penetration in Europe is still small and the US is far from saturated. Nevertheless, developments in the US and global economies will affect the company, and if US consumer spending were to fall, it would impact on revenues very visibly. Currency volatility is also a risk as The Gap imports extensively from Asia, and a weakening of the US dollar, or strengthening of other currencies, might impact profitability. The greatest risk is a market correction which would affect all highly valued shares indiscriminately.

The Gap product design, selection, merchandising and retailing are a class act, and are likely to reward investors over the long term, even if there are market ups and downs.

Monitoring

www.thegap.com is an increasingly important company marketing tool and information resource for investors. The main focus of monitoring will be on company results and announcements, and on the global and US economies – as with all other Global Profit Harvesters.

GILLETTE

Share Graph 1997–1998 Gillette Co.
Primary Market – NYSE G

Price January 1999 $58.50
Market Value January 1999 $58 billion

SECTOR Consumer non-cyclical INDUSTRY Personal and household
Bottom Line GILLETTE Top Line S&P 500 Index Relative: Triangle Marks Split
Left Scale: Top $ Price, Bottom Volume in Thousands

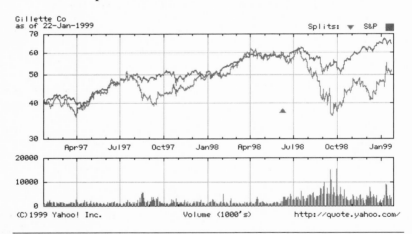

Gillette Co as of 22-Jan-1999   Splits: ▼ S&P ■

(C) 1999 Yahoo! Inc.   Volume (1000's)   http://quote.yahoo.com/

PRICE PERFORMANCE	G		An investment made in January 1994 grew 320% by January 1999		
PRICE HISTORY	1998	1997	1996	1995	Notes
High Price	62.66	53.19	38.88	27.69	
Low Price	35.31	36.00	24.13	17.69	
High P/E	65.88	42.79	46.72	29.33	
Low P/E	37.13	28.96	29.00	18.74	

Chmn/CEO A. M. Zeien, www.gillette.com
65,000 employees
Prudential Tower Building, Boston, MA 02199
Phone: (617) 421-7000 Fax: (617) 421-7123

Global Franchise: Fast moving consumer goods

Gillette is the world's biggest soaps and cosmetics group, embracing its famous name razors and shaving preparations; Duracell batteries, Parker, Paper Mate and Waterman's pens, and a wide range of deodorants and everyday cosmetics. It is a top global consumer goods marketer, poised to pounce as world markets revive. Revenues exceed $10 billion.

Setting a rational price

Portfolio 2001 WORKSHEET FOR TARGETING SHARE PRICES OF GILLETTE IN 1999, 2000 & 2001
BASED ON FORECASTS MADE IN JANUARY 1999
EPS FISCAL YEAR TO DECEMBER 1997 $1.235 1998 £0.955

Growth	Year	Estimated EPS	P/E	Share Price Target	+10%	-10%	Notes
Consensus	1999	$1.35	40	$50	$55	$45	
15%	2000	$1.58	37.5	$56	$62	$50	
15%	2001	$1.74	36	$63	$70	$57	

This 'what if' forecast suggests potential earnings and share prices based on current indications. Forecasts must be revised continuously in the light of all company results and industry, market and economic news. Forecasts can be misleading and cannot be treated as investment advice or used to motivate investments. See page 69.

Earnings per share growth expectations

Gillette has been a star performer in growing earnings and rewarding investors for a decade, but in 1998 revenues and profits fell, affected particularly by Asian economic problems. By the third quarter of 1998 Gillette was back on a growth tack, and a revival in the strength of the global economy from late 1999 was expected to set the stage for Gillette to regain ground lost in 1998. Analysts expect earnings per share growth for 1999 of 16 to 18%, bearing in mind that the comparison will be with 1998 when earnings fell. *Portfolio 2001* forecasts growth of 19% in 2000, assuming there will be a revival of growth in Asia and other emerging markets from the end of 1999. In 1998, Gillette also undertook a restructuring and took a charge of $400 million to improve operating performance from 1999, which should result in improved margins and earnings.

Earnings multiple expectations

Gillette's reports results in 1999, after its Mach 3 razor was successfully launched at the end of 1998, were disappointing. Earnings per share were $0.24 per share. Gillette has been a leading Global Profit Harvester for decades, and in liquidity driven markets its share is likely to command an earnings multiple in the range of twice its earnings growth, as long as indications stay positive. The group has also been built with strategic acquisitions, the last of which was Duracell Batteries in 1996, and investors tend to factor into the value of Gillette its potential to create value with strategic acquisitions.

Portfolio 2001 has followed the market's valuation in January 1999 of forecast earnings, but high valuations, particularly with momentum shares, are vulnerable to extreme volatility and investors should be cautious.

If the US equity market were to be less liquidity driven, or soften for any other reason, forecasting Gillette at an earnings multiple in the range of 36 to 40 times earnings would be very ambitious.

Past performance indicators

Growth Rates %		G	S&P 500	Industry	Sector	Notes
Earnings per share 5 year		16.51	21.00	41.08	20.89	
1998 last reported vs 1997		-26.22	12.19	-1.26	4.40	
Sales 5 year 1994-1998		14.28	8.11	7.18	16.49	
Profitability Ratios						
Gross Margin 1998	%	61.60	49.51	47.55	50.98	
5 year average	%	62.36	49.15	46.88	48.67	
Net Profit Margin 1998	%	10.75	10.85	8.84	9.50	
5 year average	%	11.11	10.27	7.86	8.75	
5 Year Returns on:						
Assets	%	13.01	8.47	10.06	11.06	
Investment	%	18.86	13.28	15.09	17.32	
Equity	%	35.46	21.60	28.99	31.87	

The growth story

For almost a decade, Gillette successfully achieved high double digit earnings per share growth. Growth was built on its position as a leading global brand manufacturer and distributor with product leadership, marketing resources and infrastructure globally. These strengths encourage expectations for strong revenue and earnings growth. Gillette's cutting edge Mach 3 razor was successfully launched in the US in 1998, but commercializing it, and re-stimulating Gillette's growth globall, will be challenging until economic growth revives in markets outside the US and Europe.

What can go wrong?

Gillette will certainly need stable and sustainable global growth to maintain its performance, and loss of momentum in global markets will be certain to damage both earnings per share growth and market valuation.

Investors need to decide top down that they want to be in the global consumer non-cyclicals sector, and invested in as highly priced a share as Gillette, before they make their investment. Gillette has been a great name for investors in the past and probably will be in future, but market volatility could take a severe toll on the share price. If earnings growth were to disappoint at the same time an extreme price correction could result.

Monitoring

Investors must monitor both the company performance and the global and US economy to ensure that their investment remains low-risk high-reward.

UNILEVER

Share Graph 1997–1998 Unilever PLC
Primary Market – LONDON – ADR NYSE UL

Price January 1999 $80
Market Value January 1999 $51.2 billion

SECTOR Consumer Non-Cyclical INDUSTRY Food Processing
Top Line UNILEVER ADR Bottom Line S&P 500 Index
Relative: Triangle Marks Split
Left Scale: Top $ Price, Bottom Volume in Thousands

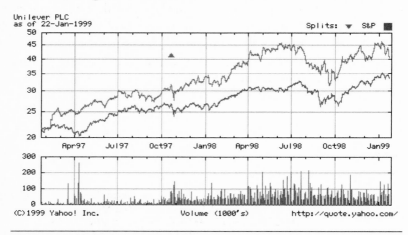

PRICE PERFORMANCE	ADR UL			An investment made in January 1994 grew 213% by January 1999	
PRICE HISTORY	1998	1997	1996	1995	Notes
High Price	46.38	39.94	24.38	21.31	
Low Price	30.31	22.00	17.97	17.75	
High P/E	NA	20.07	39.11	19.75	
Low P/E	NA	12.64	28.83	16.44	

Chmn Niall Fitzgerald, www.unilever.com
38,000 employees
Weena 455, PO Box 760 3000 DK, Rotterdam
Phone: (212) 906-4240 Fax: (212) 906-4666

Global Franchise: Packaged consumer goods

Unilever was created in 1929 when Margarine Unie merged with Lever Brothers Limited. Both were in the business of supplying goods for household needs but were competing for supplies of oils and fats. Unilever is the now world's second-largest packaged consumer goods company after Proctor & Gamble

Unilever has identified five food categories of key importance: culinary, frozen foods, ice cream, tea and yellow fats. In addition the group has eight key home and personal care (HPC) categories: laundry, personal wash, mass skin, hair, oral, deodrants, household care and prestige. Together these account for over a third of Unilever's annual turnover, with combined sales totalling US$20bn. DiverseyLever is Unilever's global professional cleaning and hygiene business with annual sales of over US$1.8 billion dollars. It focuses on cleaning and hygiene solutions for institutional and industrual customers throughout the world. Unilever is the world's biggest yellow fats business, including margarine and ice cream. Annual revenues exceed $30 billion.

Setting a rational price

Portfolio 2001 WORKSHEET FOR TARGETING SHARE PRICE RANGE UNILEVER ADR UL IN 1999, 2000 & 2001
BASED ON FORECASTS MADE IN FEBRUARY 1999
EPS FISCAL 1998 TO DECEMBER $1.53
ONE ADR = 4 SHARES

Growth	Year	Estimated EPS	P/E	Share Price Target	+10%	-10%	Notes
	1999	$1.71	20	$34	$38	$31	
15%	2000	$1.96	20	$39	$43	$35	
15%	2001	$2.25	20	$45	$50	$40	

This 'what if' forecast suggests potential earnings and share prices based on current indications. Forecasts must be revised continuously in the light of all company results and industry, market and economic news. Forecasts can be misleading and cannot be treated as investment advice or used to motivate investments. See page 69.

Earnings multiple expectations

The *Portfolio 2001* forecast has followed analysts' forecasts for earnings growth and market related valuation of the shares at a multiple of 20 times forecast earnings.

Past performance indicators

Growth Rates %		UL	S&P 500	Industry	Sector	Notes
Earnings per share 5 year		22.09	20.71	9.08	20.34	
1998 last reported vs 1997		250.83	12.93	19.80	9.97	
Sales 5 year 1994-1998		4.32	16.02	6.27	7.14	
Profitability Ratios						
Gross Margin 1998	%	44.65	49.02	40.58	50.93	
5 year average	%	42.94	48.72	39.01	48.59	
Net Profit Margin 1998	%	11.89	10.84	5.30	9.56	
5 year average	%	6.42	10.19	5.42	8.67	
5 Year Returns on:						
Assets	%	10.61	8.29	7.66	10.97	
Investment	%	17.38	13.04	11.14	17.19	
Equity	%	20.41	21.44	23.42	31.83	

The growth story

Following the disposal of their chemicals business a few years earlier and successful operations resulting from the businesses they have focussed on, Unilever announced a record net profit in 1998 and a special dividend amounting to $8.5 billion.

With the special dividend the equivalent of 10.6% of Unilever's market capitalization, the company fulfilled its promise that the proceeds of the sale of its special chemical operations in 1997 would be spent in two to three years with benefits to shareholders.

Analysts expect that Unilever will still have scope to make acquisitions despite the special dividend. Unilever chairman Niall Fitzgerald said the captial return would increase shareholder value, while also leaving the group well placed for acquisitions. The group will continue to evaluate and examine potential acquisitions in line with their strategic priorities capable of creating sustainable value.

What can go wrong?

Unilever has proved its ability to gain profitability by focusing on core and profitable businesses but substantial growth will require sustained strength in the economies in the US and Europe and the support of a revival in emerging markets.

Monitoring

Unilever can be followed as an ADR on `www.adr.com` in the UK and on the Amsterdam Stock Exchange. Investors will be kept well informed on all major developments in the company by the financial press. Revival of economic growth globally should stimulate profit growth and Unilever are likely to make requisitions which will affect future earnings when emerging market growth appears secure.

CATERPILLAR

Share Graph 1997–1998 Caterpillar
Primary Market – NYSE

Price January 1999 $43.25
Market Value January 1999 $15.5 billion

SECTOR Capital Goods INDUSTRY Construction and
Agricultural Machinery
Top Line CATERPILLAR Bottom Line S&P 500 Index Relative:
Triangle Marks Split
Left Scale: Top $ Price, Bottom Volume in Thousands

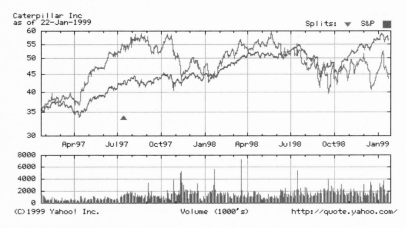

PRICE PERFORMANCE	CAT		An investment made in January 1994 grew 112% by January 1999		
PRICE HISTORY	1998	1997	1996	1995	Notes
High Price	60.75	61.63	40.50	37.63	
Low Price	39.06	36.25	27.00	24.13	
High P/E	14.82	14.09	11.56	13.26	
Low P/E	9.53	8.29	7.71	8.50	

Chmn/CEO G. A Bowton, www.caterpillar.com
59,863 employees
100 NE Adams Street, Peoria, IL 61629
Phone: (309) 675-1000 Fax: (309) 675-6155

Global Franchise: Heavy machinery

Caterpillar is the world's leading maker of earth-moving machinery, including Caterpillar earth-moving equipment. Products include a variety of construction, mining, and agricultural machinery, as well as engines for trucks, locomotives, and electrical power-generation systems. It also provides financing and insurance for its dealers and customers. 70% of sales are from machinery, 25% from engines, and 4% from financial services. It maintains some 40 plants and more than 190 dealerships around the world. Caterpillar is expanding its products range in the power-generation equipment, small engine, and agricultural equipment areas. Global revenues exceed $21 billion.

Setting a rational price

**Portfolio 2001 WORKSHEET FOR TARGETING SHARE PRICES OF CATERPILLAR
IN 1999, 2000 & 2001
BASED ON FORECASTS MADE IN JANUARY 1999
EPS FISCAL 1998 TO DECEMBER $4.11**

Growth	Year	Estimated EPS	P/E	Share Price Target	+10%	-10%	Notes
0%	1999	$4.11	12	$49	$55	$44	
10%	2000	$4.56	12	$55	$60	$50	
10%	2001	$50.16	12	$60	$67	$54	

This 'what if' forecast suggests potential earnings and share prices based on current indications. Forecasts must be revised continuously in the light of all company results and industry, market and economic news. Forecasts can be misleading and cannot be treated as investment advice or used to motivate investments. See page 69.

Earnings per share growth expectations

Caterpillar is a particularly well managed business at grass roots and a model of corporate and industrial efficiency. However, to forecast for it as a Global Profit Harvester, *Portfolio 2001* research has been focused on global economic prospects. Even assuming that 1999 will be what many economists are describing as a year of healing, with growth reviving in Asia in the second half of the year, there is no foundation to forecast earnings per share growth in 1999. Indeed, to avoid a further fall Caterpillar will need the US economy to stay buoyant. Analysts' consensus is for earnings to fall a further

5% to 7.5% in 1999, but their response could be knee jerk. The *Portfolio 2001* forecast assumes level earnings with 1998 and, with a range of 20% between high and low expectations, unless more global economic disruption erupts, earnings should stabilize and commence climbing again.

Earnings multiple expectations

The multiple of 12 times earnings per share projected is demanding by traditional yardsticks for cyclical shares. When demand is weak, cyclicals trade at multiples as low as five or six times earnings. Setting a high multiple assumes continued strength of the US equity market, and continued support for Caterpillar as a cyclical blue chip and dividend paying share.

Past performance indicators

Growth Rates %		CAT	S&P 500	Industry	Sector	Notes
Earnings per share 5 year		27.03	20.71	47.82	28.43	
1998 last reported vs 1997		6.98	12.93	8.49	2.45	
Sales 5 year 1994-1998		13.17	16.02	14.78	12.68	
Profitability Ratios						
Gross Margin 1998	%	29.08	49.02	27.95	23.56	
5 year average	%	28.56	48.72	25.90	22.66	
Net Profit Margin 1998	%	7.90	10.84	7.05	5.34	
5 year average	%	7.16	10.19	6.35	4.29	
5 Year Returns on:						
Assets	%	6.61		6.25	5.79	
Investment	%	9.93		10.69	8.78	
Equity	%	36.73		29.16	15.19	

Growth story

With weakness in 1998 in emerging markets globally, Caterpillar as the world's largest manufacturer of earth-moving, construction and materials-handling machinery, was bound to feel the pain. An impressive five-year rising earnings per share growth pattern was broken.

Earnings per share of $4.11 for 1999, only 7% lower than 1997, reflected a credible performance, taking into account Caterpillar's exposure as a Global Profit Harvester. When the global economy revives, earnings should start to stack up higher and higher again. Caterpillar is one of the world's top brands and part of the global landscape. Disappointments early in 1999 followed slow revival in emerging markets but expectations for growth revival remain strong.

What can go wrong?

In its report for the last quarter of 1998, Caterpillar drew attention to price-cutting by competitors in the US, particularly in the agricultural machinery sector. With weak emerging markets and increased competition in the US, Caterpillar may start losing pricing power over a wide spectrum of business.

Monitoring

Quarterly earnings reports and all relevant company and industry news and announcements must be carefully monitored and, if the earth has moved the wrong way for Caterpillar, investors following a buying strategy of 'bottom fishing' could fall in a hole. Deflation could make investments in capital equipment manufacturers unattractive in the long term, and an overstrong US currency would unhelpfully move the prospects of an earnings recovery at Caterpillar a few years further down the line. Investors will need to look at the competitive market in the US, global economic prospects and valuations generally on Wall Street.

ROYAL DUTCH PETROLEUM (SHELL)

Share Graph 1997–1998 Royal Dutch Petroleum
Primary Markets – AMSTERDAM/LONDON – ADR NYSE RD

Price January 1999 $43.25 (June 1999 $60.00)
Market Value January 1999 $92.7 billion

SECTOR Energy INDUSTRY Oil and Gas Integrated
Top Line S&P 500 Index Relative: Bottom Line RD ADR
Right Scale: Top $ Price, Bottom Volume in Thousands

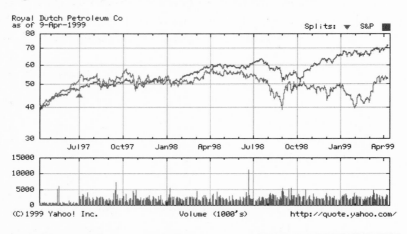

Royal Dutch Petroleum Co
as of 9-Apr-1999   Splits: ▼ S&P ■

(C) 1999 Yahoo! Inc.   Volume (1000's)   http://quote.yahoo.com/

PRICE PERFORMANCE	RD-ADR		An investment made in January 1994 grew 80% by January 1999		
PRICE HISTORY	1998	1997	1996	1995	Notes
High Price	60.38	59.44	43.47	35.44	
Low Price	39.75	42.00	33.41	26.81	
High P/E	61.6	27.39	17.49	18.30	
Low P/E	40.5	19.35	13.44	13.84	

Pres. Maarter A. van der Bergh, www.shell.com
105,000 employees
30 Carel van Bylandtlaan, 2596 HR The Hague, Netherlands
Phone: (212) 261-5660 Fax: (212) 261-5663
Shell Transport & Trading Shell Centre, London SE1 7NA
www.shell.com

Global Franchise: Oil and petroleum products

Royal Dutch Petroleum, a holding company, own 60% of Royal Dutch/Shell Group, and owns, directly or indirectly, investments in numerous companies, known as Royal Dutch/Shell Group of Companies. The group is one of the world's top three oil and gas conglomerates and it explores for, and produces, oil and natural gas, manufacturers chemicals and retails petroleum products. It trades as Royal Dutch Petroleum on the Amsterdam Exchange. The UK holding company Shell Transport & Trading Plc owns 40% of the Group and trades on the London Stock Exchange. Both companies have ADR listings on the New York Stock Exchange.

In 1998 Royal Dutch Shell earnings were affected by both the falling oil price and the weaker global economy. In 1998, the Brent crude price averaged $12.75 per barrel compared to $19.10 per barrel a year earlier.

For the last quarter of 1998, Shell Group results on an adjusted CCS earnings basis (an estimated current cost of supplies basis, excluding special items) were $5,146 million, 36% below the 1997 level. Following a 33% fall in crude oil prices and the impact of the recession in Asia-Pacific on the earnings of chemicals world-wide. Reported net income for the year to December 1998 fell 95% to $210 million. This included the impact of special charges totalling $4,245 million after tax covering writing down down of assets and to restructuring and redundancy charges.

In May 1999 the Shell Group announced encouraging first quarter results with earnings adjusted to the current costs of supplies, excluding special items, of $1,436 million. This resulted in earnings per share for Royal Dutch Shell of $0.40 for the quarter. In spite of the oil price weakness which continued during the period results improved following cuts in capital expenditure from $3.8 billion to $1.7 billion in the same period last year, reduced exploration expenses and sales of under-performing and non-strategic assets.

Management also claim operational performance has improved across the board with cost reduction initiatives succeeding. The target is $2.5 billion reduction by 2001 to secure future group profitability. The group is aiming to produce 14% return on capital employed by 2001 assuming a $14 Brent oil price and to pay dividends in line with inflation. Global revenues exceed $56 billion.

Setting a rational price

Portfolio 2001 WORKSHEET FOR TARGETING SHARE PRICES OF ROYAL DUTCH
SHELL ADR IN 1999, 2000 & 2001
BASED ON FORECASTS MADE IN JANUARY 1999
EPS/ADR FISCAL 1988 TO DECEMBER $2.46
ONE ADR = ONE SHARE

Share price volatility related to expectations for the oil industry, management initiatives in Shell and possibly to corporate activity negate the usefulness of a *Portfolio 2001* forecast based on earnings growth and earnings multiples.

After the write downs and provisions made at the end of 1998 earnings reported per share/adr were only $0.13. Earnings for the first quarter of 1999 were $0.40 per share/adr.

A more useful picture of prospects emerges examining earnings per share/adr from December 1994 to December 2000:

2000	1999	1998	1997	1996	1995	1994
est	est					
2.26	$1.78	$0.13	$2.30	$2.66	$2.04	$1.84

Following analysts, forecasts for 1999 earnings of of $1.78 with its share price at $60 it is trading at a multiple of 33 times earnings.

It is not possible to make a rational forecast currently based on price earnings multiples.

Earnings per share growth expectations

Shell has several earnings streams, including dominant positions in oil exploration, production and marketing and processing of by-products. It is also one of the world's major liquid gas suppliers.

Management have a target of 14% return on capital employed by 2000, with a possible target of 20% in mind for later. This will mean reviewing the full range of projects and businesses in which it is engaged, and concentrating on lower cost/higher margin production resources and rationalizing lower margin businesses, including refining and petrochemicals production.

Earnings multiple expectations

Investors are not valuing Shell using price earnings relationships as a meaningful measure. Several other analytical tools are being employed including discounted cash flow, sum of the parts valuations and dividend yield. There are also expectations that management initiatives at improving the cost base will be successful and the return to global growth will encourage analysts to revise earnings. Optimism on the share price is likely to prevail, even if overall conditions remain punishing as the Shell Group has a cash mountain which, at the end of 1996, stood at over $11.2 billion. Recycling this cash back to investors is a regular topic that encourages speculation, apart from a general belief that the oil price will come right and Shell will reinvent itself to be more visionary in its assett management.

Past performance indicators

Growth Rates %		SC ADR	S&P 500	Industry	Sector	Notes
Earnings per share 5 year		7.63	20.71	14.42	17.50	
1998 last reported vs 1997		-12.58	12.93	-20.35	-21.10	
Sales 5 year 1994-1998		5.81	16.02	2.42	6.38	
Profitability Ratios						
Gross Margin 1998	%	21.66	49.02	46.05	43.44	
5 year average	%	21.75	48.72	45.85	42.68	
Net Profit Margin 1998	%	6.08	10.84	5.41	5.96	
5 year average	%	6.23	10.19	4.74	5.68	
5 Year Returns on:						
Assets	%	6.21	8.29	6.31	5.84	
Investment	%	8.40	13.04	8.26	7.66	
Equity	%	11.91	21.44	15.34	13.53	

What can go wrong?

The main risk to investors will be if the improved oil price which has come from a tightening of supplies by OPEC in 1999 cannot be sustained.

Monitoring

There are three strands to monitoring: the oil price, the global economy and management performance. Results are well explained and documented in `www.shell.com`

Shell has the potential to be a low-risk high-reward investing opportunity for investors who are comfortable taking a positive view on global growth, supported by an understanding of the oil industry.

The web site of the American Petroleum Institute `www.api.com` will support informed monitoring of the oil industry. Monitoring should also include monitoring for buying opportunities if markets overreact to a weakening in the oil price in future.

RIO TINTO (RTZ)

Share Graph 1997–1998 Rio Tinto
Primary Market – LONDON – RIO – ADR NYSE RTP

Price January 1999 $48
Market Value January 1999 $12.8 billion

SECTOR Basic Materials INDUSTRY Metal Mining
Top Line S&P 500 Index Relative Bottom Line RTZ
Left Scale: Top $ Price, Bottom Volume in Thousands

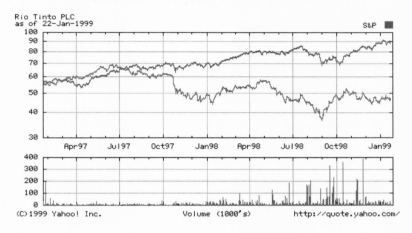

PRICE PERFORMANCE	RTP ADR		An investment made in January 1994 grew 7% by January 1999		
PRICE HISTORY	1998	1997	1996	1995	Notes
High Price	60.75	73.13	67.83	60.00	
Low Price	37.44	47.31	54.25	45.50	
High P/E	NA	24.44	23.32	15.66	
Low P/E	NA	15.81	18.71	11.87	

Chmn Robert P. Wilson, **www.riotinto.com**
28,500 employees
6 Saint James Square, London SW1Y 4LD
Phone: (0171) 930-2399 Fax: (0171) 930-3249

■■■

Global Franchise: Mining metals and minerals

Rio Tinto plc, formed in 1995 by the merger of RTZ and CRA, Australia, is the world's largest mining company engaged in long life projects supplying mainly commodity raw materials. Commodity prices have been falling over recent years. Some commodities reached all time lows. Copper fell to 65 cents a pound, in real terms lower than it was during the depression of the 1930s. Demand for copper collapsed in 1997 and 1998, when Asian producers cut back and cancelled orders. The inevitable effect has been overcapacity and falling prices with reduced earnings.

In spite of market weakness for its products, Rio Tinto's financial and operational strengths underpinned robust earnings per share, with only small percentage declines recorded and expected. Growth expected again in 2000 should revive flagging earnings. Global revenues exceed $4 billion.

■■■

Setting a rational price

Portfolio 2001 WORKSHEET FOR TARGETING SHARE PRICES OF RIO TINTO ZINC RTP IN 1999, 2000 & 2001
BASED ON FORECASTS MADE IN JANUARY 1999
EPS FISCAL 1988 TO DECEMBER $3.21
1 ADR = 4 SHARES

Growth	Year	Estimated EPS	P/E	Share Price Target	+10%	-10%	Notes
0%	1999	$3.30	15	$50	$55	$45	
10%	2000	$3.63	15	$54	$60	$49	
15%	2001	$4.17	17.5	$73	$81	$66	

This 'what if' forecast suggests potential earnings and share prices based on current indications. Forecasts must be revised continuously in the light of all company results and industry, market and economic news. Forecasts can be misleading and cannot be treated as investment advice or used to motivate investments. See page 69.

Earnings per share growth expectations
Significant earnings growth will only be possible when global growth rates of 3.5% to 4% are experienced again. The 1.5% to 2% forecast for 1999 will probably keep earnings stable.

Earnings multiple expectations
Current forecasts for global economic growth point to a sustainable

revival in 1999 and acceleration in 2000. Cyclical stocks have in the past bottomed out six months to a year before the economy starts performing strongly. Rio Tinto is a core holding for institutions and the value of the share is underpinned by a dividend currently yielding 4% and cost savings which management have implemented.

While there is optimism on the prospects for the global economy to revive, Rio Tinto should be well supported at an earnings multiple of fifteen which reflects expectations for higher earnings. If expectations for global revival turn pessimistic, the share price will be vulnerable to correction. At below $40 per share Rio has been buying in shares for cancellation.

Investors recognize Rio Tinto as the global leader in mining commodity metals, especially copper.

Past performance indicators

Growth Rates %		RTP	S&P 500	Industry	Sector	Notes
Earnings per share 5 year		30.72	20.71	77.35	21.49	
1998 last reported vs 1997		NM	12.93	1.12	-4.81	
Sales 5 year 1994-1998		18	16.02	7.99	7.20	
Profitability Ratios						
Gross Margin 1998	%	15.21	49.02	24.13	30.09	
5 year average	%	20.37	48.72	19.29	31.86	
Net Profit Margin 1998	%	26.15	10.84	6.97	5.52	
5 year average	%	25.95	10.19	6.29	5.72	
5 Year Returns on:						
Assets	%	10.60	8.29	5.21	5.87	
Investment	%	13.66	13.04	6.29	7.70	
Equity	%	17.19	21.44	8.88	15.68	

The growth story

The Rio Tinto Company was formed in 1873 to mine copper in Spain. The Consolidated Zinc Corporation was incorporated in 1905, initially to treat zinc bearing tailings at Broken Hill in New South Wales, Australia which soon expanded into mining.

Rio Tinto plc (then the Rio Tinto-Zinc Corporation) was formed in 1962 by the merger of two British companies, the Rio Tinto Company and the Consolidated Zinc Corporation. Following the 1962 merger, RTZ developed a number of major projects including Palabora (copper) in South Africa, Rössing (uranium) in Namibia, and Neves Corvo (copper and tin) in Portugal. It also grew through acquisitions, including the Borax group in 1968.

A major review of corporate strategy between 1987 and 1988 led to a series of disposals and acquisitions which refocused the company on mining and related activities. As a result, between 1988 and 1994, non-mining businesses were sold as going concerns, and interests in mining acquired. These included the 1989 acquisition of the major part of British Petroleum's international minerals businesses, and the 1993 acquisition of the Nerco and Cordero coal mining businesses in the US.

In mid-1995 an approximately 12% shareholding in Freeport-McMoRan Copper & Gold was also acquired, together with a 40% direct interest in the expansion potential of its Grasberg copper mine in Indonesia.

Since 1962, CRA also grew through the development of several important mineral discoveries, at Hamersley (iron ore) in Australia; Bougainville (copper) in Papua New Guinea; Comalco (bauxite, alumina refining and aluminium smelting) in Australia and New Zealand; Argyle (diamonds), and Blair Athol and Tarong (coal) in Australia; and Kelian (gold) and Kaltim Prima (coal) in Indonesia. Acquisitions included the Australian coal assets of BP minerals in 1989 and a 70.7% interest in Coal & Allied Industries' New South Wales operations.

Since 1995, exploration, research and technology have been refocused on a global basis, and the management structure has been reorganized to capture the potential of the merger for the future. Rio Tinto has also acquired additional coal interests in South America in 1996 and in the US in 1997.

The downside for investors is that capital expenditure has been at record levels on Rio Tinto's wide range of projects, where excess capacity has been created, and the payoff could be a long time coming until renewed global economic growth takes up what?

What can go wrong?

There are no certainties that global demand for commodities will revive in the short term, and there is a risk that with some commodities, including copper, new mines have resulted in excess capacity which will depress prices in the long term. Rio Tinto is now heavily geared to global metal prices and, with a spread of production principally in aluminium, copper, energy, gold and other industrial minerals, Rio is a classic cyclical share in spite of the strength of its resources, its lead in exploration, and excellence in mining technologies.

Monitoring

www.riotinto.com gives a very full overview of company operations and includes factsheets, which can also be obtained printed, on the main commodities mined.

Monitoring growth in economics globally and demand for industrial materials will be necessary for investors in RTZ.

VOLKSWAGEN

Share Graph 1997–1998 Volkswagen
Primary Market – FRANKFURT VDW – ADR NASDAQ VLKAY

Price January 1999 $16.38
Market Value January 1999 $25.3 billion

SECTOR Consumer Cyclical INDUSTRY Auto and Truck Manufacture
Top Line VOLKSWAGEN Bottom Line S&P 500 Index Relative
Right Scale: % Growth, Bottom Volume in Thousands

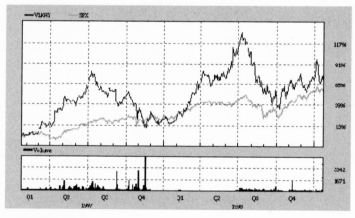

Source: www.adr.com

PRICE PERFORMANCE	VLKAY		An investment made in January 1994 grew 137% by January 1999		
PRICE HISTORY	1998	1997	1996	1995	Notes
High Price	22.25	17.50	8.48	NA	
Low Price	10.40	8.15	7.58	NA	
High P/E	NA	33.62	29.79	NA	
Low P/E	NA	15.66	26.17	NA	

Chmn Ferdinand Piech, www.vw.de
280,000 employees
Volkswagen AG Finanz-Publizitat und Statisik D-38436 Wolfsburg
Phone: (800) 822-8987

Global Franchise: Car manufacturing

Europe's biggest car manufacturer, Volkswagen is engaged in major product line expansion and increasing capacity globally. Volkswagen has held the number one slot in western Europe for passenger cars since 1985. Its global vehicle deliveries rose 7.5% to a record 4.58 million units in 1998. Western European market share for Volkswagen brand passenger cars rose to 12.8% in January from 10.0% one year ago. New registrations in western Europe for Volkswagen cars in January rose to 160,882 from 126,484, a 27% increase on the year.

Audi AG, the luxury car unit of Volkswagen lifted sales to a record 27 billion marks ($15.65 billion) last year from 22.4 billion in 1997. Since 1994, turnover has more than doubled. Audi group deliveries worldwide climbed 9.7% to 599,509 units. Volkswagen is the strongest of Germany's auto makers in the Asia-Pacific region.

In 1999, Volkswagen purchased the Rolls-Royce Motor Car Company and other global prestige brands. Global revenues exceed $70 billion.

Setting a rational price

Portfolio 2001 **WORKSHEET FOR TARGETING SHARE PRICES OF VOLKSWAGEN ADR VALKY IN 1999, 2000 & 2001**
BASED ON FORECASTS MADE IN JANUARY 1999
EPS/ADR FISCAL 1998 TO DECEMBER $1.13
FIVE ADR = ONE ORDINARY SHARE

Growth	Year	Estimated EPS	P/E	Share Price Target	+10%	-10%	Notes
12.5%	1999	$1.35	12.5	$17	$19	$15	
12.5%	2000	$1.51	12.5	$19	$21	$17	
12.5%	2001	$1.69	12.5	$21	$23	$19	

This 'what if' forecast suggests potential earnings and share prices based on current indications. Forecasts must be revised continuously in the light of all company results and industry, market and economic news. Forecasts can be misleading and cannot be treated as investment advice or used to motivate investments. See page 69.

Earnings per share growth expectations
For the fiscal year ended March 1997 group net sales rose 13% to 113.25 billion marks. Net income was DM1.36 billion, up from

678 million. Revenues reflect increased Audi deliveries in western Europe and Germany, and earnings also reflect improvements in cost structures.

Management have indicated strong earnings growth is expected for the fiscal year ending March 1999, and sustained 10% earnings per share growth consistent with management indications and analysts' forecasts can be expected.

Earnings multiple expectations

US auto companies tend to trade at lower earnings multiples than European auto shares. The reason is entrenched German and European investor support, and with Volkswagen's strong product, market and earnings growth, a multiple of 12.5 times earnings is probably not ambitious.

Past performance indicators

Growth Rates %		VLKAY	S&P 500	Industry	Sector	Notes
Earnings per share 5 year		52.68	20.71	33.85	18.92	
1998 last reported vs 1997		9.63	12.93	-32.65	1.82	
Sales 5 year 1994-1998		5.81	16.02	8.59	10.72	
Profitability Ratios						
Gross Margin 1998	%	NA	49.02	25.30	30.99	
5 year average	%	NA	48.72	23.45	29.73	
Net Profit Margin 1998	%	NA	10.84	9.32	7.03	
5 year average	%	NA	10.19	3.34	4.18	
5 Year Returns on:						
Assets	%	NA	8.29	2.33	5.00	
Investment	%	NA	13.04	5.84	7.69	
Equity	%	NA	21.44	30.93	19.13	

The growth story

	1 YEAR	3 YEARS	5 YEARS
Sales %	13.11	12.26	5.81
Eps %	79.74	101.06	52.68
Dividend %	33.33	58.74	43.10

VW sold around 4.6 million vehicles worldwide in 1998 with a western Europe market share of 19.5%. Western Europe is VW's biggest market. The company is also heavily exposed in Brazil and Latin America.

In April 1999, Volkswagen announced that its Volkswagen of America subsidiary raised first quarter sales 60.6% to 63,525 units. The company also aims to sell 15% of its vehicles worldwide in Asia in the future. The Asia-Pacific region accounted for only 0.4% of the company's turnover in 1997.

What can go wrong?

A slowing in the global economy and a weaker dollar would affect Volkswagen's earnings. Apart from these macro considerations Volkswagen cars enjoy strong demand and, with the enhanced brand marketing initiatives of the group, enhanced earnings are likely to follow. Intense competition in the automotive industry and a weak European market could damage Volkswagen's prospects for an earnings growth recovery for some time.

Monitoring

The automotive industry is cyclical and investors have to monitor closely the market and the performance of the company in which they are invested. While Volkswagen does have an ADR listing, and a full share quote in the US, reporting is still difficult to follow at times and can be opaque. News on the company is extensively reported on `www.adr.com` and in the financial press. However, no Volkswagen web site carries meaningful investor information.

WAL-MART

Share Graph 1997–1998 Wal-Mart Stores Inc.
Primary Market – NYSE – WMT

Price January 1999 $47.50
Market Value April 1999 $211.2 billion

SECTOR Retail INDUSTRY Retail – Department and Discount
Top Line WAL-MART Line S&P 500 Index Relative: Triangle
Marks Split
Left Scale: Top $ Price, Bottom Volume in Thousands

Note: Graphic reflects prices pre April 1999 2 for 1 stock split.
The other prices in this report are adjusted for the split.

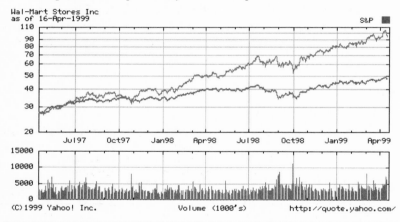

PRICE PERFORMANCE	WMT		An investment made in January 1994 grew 231% by January 1999		
PRICE HISTORY	1998	1997	1996	1995	Notes
High Price	82.75	41.94	28.25	27.63	
Low Price	37.56	22.00	19.09	20.50	
High P/E	4.90	31.51	23.70	23.67	
Low P/E	19.02	16.53	16.02	17.57	

Chmn S. Robson Walton, www.walmart.com and
www.samsclub.com
920,000 employees
702 Southwest 8th Street, Bentonville, AR 72716
Phone: (501) 273-4000 Fax: (501) 273-4053

Global Franchise: The world's number one retailer

The late Sam Walton opened the first Wal-Mart store in 1962, starting a retailing revolution and success story that brought customers flocking to his discount stores for their wide ranges, low prices, and good service, and made Walton America's (then) richest man. Now, with 3600 stores, Wal-Mart serves almost 100 million customers a week, and is the world's number one retailer, bigger than Sears, K-mart, and J. C. Penney combined.

The group has diversified into grocery (Wal-Mart Supercenters), international operations, membership warehouse clubs (Sam's Clubs), and deep discount warehouse outlets (Bud's Discount City). Most stores are in the US, where Wal-Mart is upgrading operations and converting older outlets into Supercenters. Operations extend to Canada, Latin America, Asia, and Europe. On 19 June Wal-Mart acquired the UK supermarket group Asda for $10.72 billion, also adding to its growing European operations in Germany. Sam's Club is the second largest US chain of warehouse clubs, behind Costco. Annual group revenues exceed $137 million.

Setting a rational price

Portfolio 2001 WORKSHEET FOR TARGETING SHARE PRICES OF WAL-MART WMT IN 1999, 2000 & 2001
BASED ON FORECASTS MADE IN APRIL 1999
EPS FISCAL 1998 TO JANUARY 1999 $0.99

Growth	Year	Estimated EPS	P/E	Share Price Target	+10%	-10%	Notes
Consensus	1999	$1.13	40	$45	$50	$40	
15%	2000	$1.29	40	$51	$57	$51	
15%	2001	$1.48	40	$59	$66	$53	

This 'what if' forecast suggests potential earnings and share prices based on current indications. Forecasts must be revised continuously in the light of all company results and industry, market and economic news. Forecasts can be misleading and cannot be treated as investment advice or used to motivate investments. See page 69.

Earnings per share growth expectations
Growth in 1998 exceeded 24%. Analysts' consensus view is for growth of 14% per annum. With high levels of consumer spending in the US and vigorous growth globally, 15% earnings per share growth can be sensibly forecast.

Earnings multiple expectations

By April 1999, after announcing two exceptionally strong quarters and in a soaring stock market, Wal-Mart shares were trading at almost 50 times earnings. Investors will need substantial ongoing positive information to support these high expectations for a retail business. The historic trading range for the company was substantially lower.

	1998	1997	1996	1995
High P/E	4.90	31.51	23.70	23.67
Low P/E	19.02	16.53	16.02	17.57

40 times earnings has been used for the *Portfolio 2001* forecast, well above the peak 31.5 times earnings recorded in 1997. This high multiple has been adopted on the basis of the strength in consumer spending in the US and on the assumption that the global economy is recovering and Wal-Mart's international expansion will start to pay off. It is expected that Wal-Mart's earnings growth will continue to attract strong institutional and private investor support. It is in line with the multiples commanded by France's Carrefour and is supported by the group's e-trade strength and potential, and by its information technology resources. But is an ambitious target which investors should review critically at the time of considering an investment and when monitoring their holdings.

Past performance indicators

Growth Rates %		WMT	S&P 500	Industry	Sector	Notes
Earnings per share 5 year		12.37	20.26	11.72	21.73	
1998 last reported vs 1997		27.76	12.25	20.32	26.52	
Sales 5 year 1994-1998		16.34	17.63	14.50	25.35	
Profitability Ratios						
Gross Margin 1998	%	20.99	49.08	24.37	42.50	
5 year average	%	20.54	48.79	24.08	42.26	
Net Profit Margin 1998	%	3.26	10.91	3.23	4.61	
5 year average	%	3.10	10.45	3.01	4.93	
5 Year Returns on:						
Assets	%	8.65	8.36	7.31	4.51	
Investment	%	12.33	13.24	10.35	7.58	
Equity	%	21.33	21.72	18.89	14.33	

The growth story

Discounting

Sam Walton credited a manufacturer's agent, 'Harry', with his most important lesson about discount pricing:

> 'Harry was selling ladies' panties for $2 a dozen. We'd been buying similar panties from Ben Franklin for $2.50 a dozen and selling them at three pair for $1. Well, at Harry's price of $2, we could put them out at four for $1 and make a great promotion for our store. Here's the simple lesson we learned ... say I bought an item for 80 cents. I found that by pricing it at $1.00, I could sell three times more of it than by pricing it at $1.20. I might make only half the profit per item, but because I was selling three times as many, the overall profit was much greater. Simple enough. But this is really the essence of discounting: by cutting your price, you can boost your sales to a point where you earn far more at the cheaper retail than you would have by selling the item at the higher price. In retailer language, you can lower your mark-up but earn more because of the increased volume.'

Wal-Mart has rigidly adhered to the strategy of buying at keen prices and passing the savings on to the customer.

Information system – the just-in-time pioneer

To hone its competitive advantage, Wal-Mart invested in information technology ahead of its competitors. It now utilizes computer disk storage systems and databases with a total capacity of 43 terabytes – more computer disk storage than the US Internal Revenue System. This enabled it to pioneer and capitalize on just-in-time inventory management. Now it is analysing data accumulated on its customers and their buying preferences, and using the information to fine-tune inventory control and marketing. Individual store managers can choose which items to display, and how much shelf space to give to a product category, or to individual brands within a category. The result is that this gigantic retailer is fast on its feet and customizes its product offerings to optimize returns by reducing slow-moving inventory and building revenue through increased sales.

Electronic commerce

Like The Gap, Wal-Mart are using their strong market positions and marketing resources to launch e-trading from catalogues on their web site. Their product range and marketing resources put them in a favourable position vis-à-vis competitors marketing similar offerings through the web only.

What can go wrong?

Wal-Mart is likely to continue to maintain its dominant position in large scale discount retailing. Risks to investors come mainly from any slowing of consumer spending in the US or of global economic recovery, and from any fall in overall stock exchange levels.

Monitoring

www.walmart.com gives the full picture of the company, including its e-trading offerings. Investors will need to keep themselves well informed and reassure themselves that the high price they are likely to have to pay for shares are supported by fundamentals. Shares which trade at exceptionally high multiples are most vulnerable to steep market corrections.

THE 3I GROUP

Europe's leading venture capital company

With global growth set to gather pace again, the twenty-first century should present exceptional opportunities to entre-preneurial investors. In this context the UK-based and increasingly international 3i Group, an acronym for 'investors in industry', would have fitted as a millennial niche or financial services prospect but, as it does not yet have a US ADR listing, it was not included in either of these sections. It is also a paradox to propose a low-risk, high-reward venture capital opportunity, but assuming a buoyant and growing global economy, the 3i group is indeed such an opportunity.

Well-established as Britain's leading venture capital company, the group owes its origins to a consortium of Britain's clearing banks who in the 1970s pooled resources to build a venture capital business with specialist managerial skills. In July 1994 the 3i Group floated on the London Stock Exchange with its shares trading at 272p. By June 1999 its shares traded at 770p. Total return to investors from flotation in 1994 to their March 1999 financial year end was 21.3% per annum, including the share price rise of 130% at the time.

3i is now also one of Europe's leading quoted companies with a market capitalisation above £5 billion and is a member of the FTSE 100 and FTSE Eurotop 300 indices. Apart from the increase in share price, the value of net assets per share almost doubled from 313p to 601p in the five years ending March 1999. The total return of £177.1 million for the financial year to March 1999 comprised both capital and revenue profits including realised capital profits of £180.1 million on the sale of investments, which made the signifi-cant contribution to the group's results. Following a doggedly conservative valuation policy, discussed again below, a change in valuation of unrealised investments resulted in a reduction of £90 million accounted for in the year , following a a 22% fall in the price earnings ratios used in valuing the UK portfolio. For the year ending March 1999, revenue profit before tax was £136.6 million, an increase of 10.2% from the previous year. Revenue profit after tax increased only by 2.8% as a result of a higher tax charge.

Europe's leading venture capital company

The 3i Group claims to be Europe's leading venture capital company investing over £1 billion annually in a full range of venture capital transactions, generally below £250 million per transaction. In 1998 3i's investment, including co-investment funds in continental Europe, doubled from £121.1 million to £240.6 million in 152 businesses, representing more than 20% of the Group's total investment during the year. A beneficiary of the level playing field for investors ushered in by the euro currency, they plan to hold at least 20% of their investments in continental Europe by 2003.

3i have the experience and managerial skills to focus on technology and plan to build their portfolio of investments in technology companies to around 30% of investment assets by 2003. In 1998 the 3i Group invested £291 million, including co-investment funds, in 240 technology businesses representing an increase of almost 80% on the previous year. 3i's technology portfolio has grown to 542 investments and at the end of 1998 it was valued at £974 million, representing 21% of 3i's total portfolio.

Combination of money, top management and managerial skills

Venture capital is a money and management business and 3i qualify as an attractive opportunity on both scores. A recognised company achiever, Chief Executive Officer Brian Larcombe was promoted to his present position in 1997 from the key post of Financial Director and he is now leading the group into increased exposure in Europe, the United States and Asia. Larcombe recognizes the Group's key resource is people and is building an integrated European business with the necessary skills, language capabilities and knowledge to maximize opportunities. He is also placing more emphasis on the management of the group's extensive portfolio of investments and has directed the objectives of the Corporate Finance team to adding value to 3i's portfolio.

The 3i Group has appreciable financial strength endorsed by long-term credit ratings of Aa3 from Moody's and AA- from Standard & Poor's, which facilitates borrowings on favourable terms. In the year to March 1999 net borrowings reduced by £79.5 million to £1,034.6 million and represented 28.7% of shareholders' funds.

Valuation

Venture capitalists earn their money essentially when they sell investments or when unquoted investments are successfully listed on stock exchanges, since both risk and value can easily be masked in unquoted investments. Because of this the most telling measure of performance is the average uplift in the value at which equity investments were held at the start of a period compared with the proceeds received when investments were sold. The 3i Group have achieved a potent 40% uplift over each of the last five years.

In view of the masked value in unrealised investments, the 3i Group is not an investment that can be valued using the same yardsticks that are usually applied, and a significant gap between its net asset value and its share price is often cited as evidence that the share is overpriced. Though shares in investment trusts usually trade at substantial discounts to net asset value, 3i tends to trade at a premium, often in the range of 20%.

Excessive focus on the premium over asset value can mask the crucial question of how the asset backing is calculated. The annual uplift of 40% quoted above indicates the conservative and intentionally understated valuation of the unlisted portfolio of holdings.

Another concern which investors in venture capital companies will have is that it may be difficult to offload investments. 3i's strong track record of picking winners, specialist acquisition teams and regional management resources give every encouragement that the group can enjoy steady growth. Flotations during the last financial year – 12 in the UK and 11 in continental Europe – made a significant contribution to the increase in the value of the quoted equity portfolio and, over the year, realizations exceeded cash outflow on investment by a small margin.

Monitoring

As a business enterprise relying on meaningful communications between investors and investees, 3i treats its shareholders with the same respect is expects from its investees. www.3igroup.com keeps investors meaningfully informed and includes an ongoing free subscription service which brings e-mails on all group developments.

The more difficult side of monitoring 3i relates to monitoring the global economy. Venture capital valuations and prospects, even with an accent on technology, are bound to be victims of a deteriorating global growth scenario.

15

DEMOGRAPHIC
DESTINY

Portfolio 2001 has two messages. One is on a rigorous, research-led investing strategy with prospects drawn from among the world's best shares. The other is that investors should look at a 'market of shares' and not a 'share market'. The stock market is only the aggregate of the movements of individual stocks. It often conceals the dynamics that are driving it and masks value. An overall advance can disguise considerable sector rotation, with some market sectors rising while others fall. A rising market that starts to stall may be a warning, but if your investments are doing well it need not encourage you to change your long-term strategy. On the other hand, if the market is rising and your portfolio is not, you should review your portfolio and consider making changes to investing in more positive sectors.

Company specific research
In 1995 I first selected a portfolio of twenty of the world's best growth companies for investors to hold into the new millennium. At the time I reasoned deductively – and felt intuitively – that global blue chips were going to prove to be exciting low-risk, high-reward, investing opportunities. The companies I picked at the time, with very few exceptions, performed extremely well year after year. However, at the time I was so positive about prospects, I made two seriously flawed assumptions about the global economy.

First, I had expected that Asian economies would be the front runners in the global economic stakes and instead they became casualties. And second, by the time I had expected the Dow Jones

Industrial index to be climbing past the 7000 mark, in fact it was vaulting towards 9000.

The strength of the US economy in 1998, notwithstanding the dire economic problems in Asia and Russia's economic collapse, has surprised economists, analysts and all doubters including me. Evidently there are two US economies – manufacturing and services. The manufacturing economy faces oversupply problems, loss of pricing power and the effects on exports and imports of a strong dollar. But the services industry has boomed on regardless, supported by high employment, high personal earnings and ageing baby boomers investing and spending their vast wealth.

The world's top companies are part of our lives

I believe there are good reasons why top global companies will continue to be investments that outperform the markets. The first is that they are omnipresent – we do not live a day without doing business directly or indirectly with global leaders. Before writing this paragraph I changed from my office clothes for an evening's writing – I am working at my computer wearing a comfortable pair of Gap trousers and adidas leisure shoes. My PC has Intel inside and uses Microsoft software. I have just been using the Internet and it is a safe bet that my call was connected using Lucent or Cisco switches and routers. I am going on a business visit to Germany tomorrow and will drive my BMW to the airport and fly on a Boeing aircraft with flight insurance cover from a company in the ING Group. I plan to leave for the flight early because I saw some Caterpillars on the road last week (the big yellow ones that dig the streets up, not the sneaky brown ones that anger my wife by eating her garden plants). Yesterday I bought some Monsanto herbicide for her to eliminate them. When I am at the airport tomorrow I will visit Louis Vuitton's Duty Free Store (DFS) and buy some Moët champagne for our wedding anniversary next month and maybe treat myself to some of their Hennessy cognac. I also want to buy my wife a gift from Tiffany packaged in the famous blue box with the white ribbon as an anniversary surprise. On the way home from the airport I will probably stop at the Shell garage and fill up with petrol and treat myself to a refreshing ice cream made by a Unilever company. Then I should walk across the road to the late-night chemist and pick up a scrip for the Merck medication I take. I must also buy some of Gillette's Duracell batteries at the garage or the chemist.

The Asia crisis and the global economy

Post mortems on what sparked the economic problems that spread across Asia in 1997 and 1998 have confirmed that over-investment in manufacturing capacity led to over-production, loss of pricing power and eventually the economic declines that plagued the affected emerging economies. Several Asian leaders have also been accused of supporting crony capitalism, and international bankers, fund managers and speculators have been accused of blasting into countries loaded with opportunist money and get-rich-quick schemes. They are also accused of blasting out again as soon as the party started to slow down, clutching whatever capital they could lay their hands on and so exacerbating the downturn with their opportunism.

Analysts now agree that there was no question that emerging Asia's speculative bubble had to burst – and yet one crucial question remains unanswered. If, as we are told now, a speculative bubble was bound to burst – why did it come as such a shock when it did? Part of the answer could be that it was unrealistic to forecast relentless Asian economic growth without any upsets on the way. Western industrialized nations took centuries to build their economies, which have been strongly prone to cycles of boom and bust. We should have been more realistic than to believe that emerging economies would not encounter comparable setbacks along the way.

Asia, globalization and demography

To quote a popular cliché, demography is destiny. The dynamics of demography and globalization will continue to drive economic growth in Asia's emerging economies. These countries have young, intelligent and hardworking people who aspire to improved standards of living. When Asian economic growth resumes, the positive stimulus to the global economy will be dramatic.

I quoted Bryan and Farrel's ventriloquist's dummy 'Professor' Lau in Chapter 2 on the year 2000 as 'an approximate marking point for the emergence of a truly global economy' which would usher in 'several decades of economic growth unparalleled in human history'.

Asia's domestic economic potential is still untapped and, in the context of an expanding global free market, the wealth of the rich baby boomers in the developed world will be channelled to fund new growth opportunities in emerging economies. Banks and managed funds will certainly be part of this wealth transfusion for emerging nations, but there is a strong case to make that the main thrust in the next investing cycle directed at emerging economies will be through major global businesses. They are not as opportunist as banks are bound to be, and they have the experience and resources to build businesses and markets to support investments. And, if they need extra capital for new enterprises, they will certainly have no difficulty raising it.

General Electric Capital know better than any banker or fund manager how to put money to work, and are vigorously growing their presence in Asia. GlaxoWellcome are launching their new blockbuster drug for hepatitis B in China. The digital age brings worldwide demand for the products of Microsoft and Intel. The wireless boom does the same for Motorola, Lucent and Nokia. And so on.

Investors who were sold on attractively packaged speculative opportunities in emerging markets may have overlooked the long-term commitments of major global companies to building markets and businesses. I expect investors will increasingly realize that a great way to buy a stake in the global economy is to buy a stake in a great global company. Well-informed and well-timed buying of these shares will still produce low-risk, high-reward opportunities for long-term investors.

A banker's view of Asian recovery

Stephen Roach, Morgan Stanley's respected global strategist, contributed this analysis of Asia's prospects in www.ms.com in July 1998:

'A year into the Asian crisis, and investors and policy makers are still desperate for a way out. According to research recently conducted by the International Monetary Fund, the wait is far from over. In an analysis of financial crises in over 50 countries over the 1975-97 period, the IMF found that a return to trend GDP growth in emerging economies that had been battered by currency crises or crashes took an average of 1.5 to 1.9 years. Add in a banking crisis, and the average recovery time rose to 2.6 years. On the basis of these historical findings, little improvement in Asia can be expected until the first half of 1999, at the soonest . . . And so the chain of events that might lead to the end of the Asian crisis is now coming into view . . . If that's the case, then the history of past financial crises may be a good guide as to what lies ahead: The beginnings of an Asian recovery might just be possible in the first half of 1999.'

From poverty to prosperity

In October 1999, shortly after publication of this book, the six-billionth earthling is going to be entering the population statistics. According to figures released by the US Census Bureau, it took 123 years from 1884 to 1927 for the world population to grow from from 1 billion to 2 billion. Now it only takes about 12 years to add a billion:

Year	Population	Years taken to add a billion:
1927	2 Billion	123
1960	3 Billion	33
1974	4 Billion	14
1987	5 Billion	13
1999	6 Billion	12

Source: US Census Bureau

Lifetime prospects for earthling number 6 billion will depend on which side of the tracks he or she is born. In the developed world we enjoy unprecedented wealth while billions of the world's population endure lives of abject misery. Globally, poverty is so extreme that over half the world's population may at times wish they had never had been born. 1.3 billion people live on less than $1 a day; 3 billion live on under $2 a day; 1.3 billion have no access to clean water; 3 billion have no access to sanitation; 2 billion have no access to power.

On October 6th 1998, in a watershed address to the Governors of the World Bank, its President James D. Wolfensohn warned of 'a crisis of world population (growth) that will add 3 billion more people to the planet over the next twenty-five years. A crisis of global water that will see 2 billion people suffering from chronic water shortages by 2025. A crisis of urbanization that will mean that urban populations will treble over the next thirty years . . . a crisis of food security that will mean that over the next thirty years food production will have to double . . . a human crisis from which the developed world will not be able to insulate itself . . . [and which] will not be resolved unless we address the fundamental issue of the essential interdependence of the developed and the developing worlds. A human crisis that will not be met unless we begin to take a holistic approach . . .'

Wolfensohn's address to the representatives of the rich and poor countries within his bank closed with these themes : 'We succeed or we suffer together. We owe it to our children to recognize now that their world is one world linked by communications and trade, linked by markets, linked by finance, linked by environment and shared resources, linked by common aspirations. If we act now with realism and with foresight, if we show courage, if we think globally and allocate our resources accordingly, we can give our children a more peaceful and equitable world – one where poverty and suffering will be reduced. Where children everywhere will have a sense of hope. This is not just a dream – this is our responsibility.'

The beginnings of a true global economy

Historians may yet come to mark Wolfensohn's initiatives as one of the defining events that led to a truly global economy. Our fictional friend Professor Lau, quoted earlier in this book, spoke of the year 2000 as the approximate marking point for the emergence of a truly global economy and praised the role of global capitalism in ushering in decades of unprecedented prosperity.

As Wolfensohn's initiatives succeed, the great global growth opportunity promises to become a compelling opportunity for investors. His credentials could not be better for the investing community. Before joining the World Bank in 1996, he was one of the world's most successful investment bankers. The mergers and acquisitions firm he built continues in the Bankers Trust stable as 'BT Wolfensohn'. When investment bankers speak of a crisis of global water supply they also focus on the opportunity to build reservoirs. A crisis in electricity supplies is an opportunity to install infrastructure, and a crisis in food production is an opportunity for farmers. As one of the leading figures in global finance, Wolfensohn helped steer a turnaround from global economic meltdown to global healing in 1998 to 1999 and, since launching his strategy for a holistic approach, he has again acted decisively.

Towards a comprehensive global development framework

In January 1999 'A Proposal for a Comprehensive Development Framework – A Discussion Draft' was circulated within the World Bank and to the development community, fleshing out the initiative introduced in October 1998. If applied, over a 10-15 year time-frame, the holistic approach will represent a radically different way for the Bank to fulfil its development mandate and will concentrate on having the country in the driver's seat. The debate is holistic in that it goes beyond economics and social concepts. We can all keep informed on its progress and even participate on www.worldbank.org. In May 1999 the World Bank launched an eight-week public electronic discussion of the Framework paper. Similar dialogue with us, our fellow earthlings and our representatives and organisations will continue

Wolfensohn's October 1998 Speech 'The Other Crisis' and the progress of the Comprehensive Development Framework initiatives for a new global financial architecture are accessible on www.worldbank.org

A great bull market and decades of unprecedented growth

Portfolio 2001 is first and foremost a book about investment *research*. My predictions for the Dow Jones or other market indexes a few years down the line are and should be irrelevant. They would, in any event, prove to be as flawed as those of any other commentator unwise enough to stick his or her neck out too far. The forecast that currently attracts me most is from a fiercely independent and often insightful economist Martin Armstrong, the founder of Princeton Economics (www.princetoneconomics.com.). Armstrong expects a 'bull market in volatility' for the early years of the twenty-first century.

Mainstream forecasts are for global growth to revive, and my view is that as the growth trend gathers pace, the world's top companies are going to prosper more and more. From the onset of the Asian crisis until mid 1999 I was apprehensive about the publication date of this book, concerned that surging equity markets were not pricing in risks. While fundamentals and earnings growth potential will eventually set share prices, there are times when markets are too volatile or excessively driven by fear or greed and as such they are too dangerous to enter.

The Wall Street Crash of 1929 was followed by a triad of deflation, competitive devaluations and protectionism that led to and sustained the Great Depression of the 1930s. In 1998, when an equally threatening global crisis erupted, the leaders of the world's economies set a course that steered away from past mistakes. In October 1998, America's awesomely strong and robust economy was spurred by interest rate cuts intended to head off the dangers of recession and deflation both domestically and globally. Loose monetary policy encouraged consumers to adopt a 'shop till you drop' mode, and surging American imports helped sustain the economies of several developing countries over the crisis days. By mid 1999, a process of global healing was widely recognised by economists and the US Federal Reserve moved to a bias towards tightening monetary policy. The initial move upwards in June 1999 and the prospect of higher interest rates should contribute to stabilising markets.

I will be concentrating on how to manage risk to bring rewards and will closely follow the debate on Wolfensohn's Comprehensive Development Framework for sustainable global economic growth.

Stock Exchange yardsticks

In a way Stock Exchange Indexes resemble the lines we often make on a wall marking the height of our children as they grow up. We expect them to be higher while they are growing and to be much higher while they are growing fast.

Moore's Law helps explain why markets use different yardsticks at times. In 1965, while preparing a graph on growth in memory chip performance, Intel's co-founder Gordon Moore identified a trend. Each new chip contained roughly twice as much capacity as its predecessor and was released within 18 to 24 months of the previous chip. If the trend continued, he argued, computer power would rise exponentially over relatively brief periods of time as prices fell. Moore's observation, now part of technology legend and widely known as Moore's Law, described a trend which has continued for thirty five years, has changed the way the world works and will continue to well into the next century. The following graphic tracks the number of transistors on an Intel microprocessor chip increasing more than 3,200 times from 2000 in 1971 to over ten million by 1999.

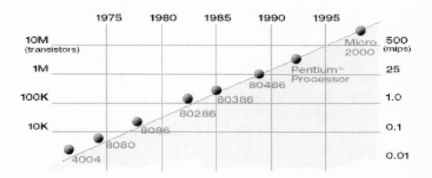

Source: **www.intel.com**

The effects of Moore's Law and the progress of technology have boosted productivity, efficiency and competitiveness. World Bank initiatives aimed at turning poverty to prosperity could achieve benefits of greater magnitude. For our children's height, we can use the same tape measure year after year – but for markets we cannot. Market measures that do not recognise the effects of great intangibles or expectations – like Moores Law and Wolfensohn's holistic initiatives – might as well have invisible letters. The 'children' markets measure, unlike ours, are not certain to get taller year after year. At times they may get be getting shorter – hence the volatility **and risk that is inherent in investment.**

12,500 on the Dow by 2000 or 15,000, or more, within a few years? Why not – if the new millennium corresponds with ushering in years of strong global economic growth, technological advance, free competitive markets, low inflation and low interest rates.

Portfolio 2001 has acted as your navigator on to the information highway, and has marked some stop-off points you will turn to good account. But you – and only you – are in the driver's seat. You will have to make difficult decisions, as valuations of global blue chips are at historic highs and may often be over-stretched. Unexpected events like Russia's default in 1998 and Asia's crisis in 1997 could upset markets and prospects again, and you have to take into account such major risk factors when you decide what to pay for a share. Remember, when you decide what to pay for a share, that the risks are priced in as far as possible.

Time invested in company-specific research will be a good investment
Free enterprise and the information age are ushering in years of exceptional global economic growth. In the early dawn of the post cold war era some of the worst imaginable excesses of unbridled capitalism ran riot and there were casualties. Top global companies experienced slowdowns, but they emerged mainly unscathed, and armed with even more competitive advantage and financial muscle than before.

Timing will always be the most crucial element of investing, and the way to start the investing process is with research – starting now. Then – when you find an opportunity that meets your requirements – you'll be ready to pounce.

16

INDEX

V
valuation rules 115–116
Venture Capital (3i)
563–566
Viagra 157
Vodafone Airtouch 455–459
Volkswagen 554–557

W
Wal–Mart Stores Inc.
558–562
Wall Street, predominance of
31–34
Wall Street Journal 106–107,
108–109, 119–120, 124
Wall Street Research Net
110–112
web browsers 297
see also internet
Welch, John F (Jack) GE 411,
416
'what if?' forecasting 69, 121,
141, 307–308, 477

Wintel duopoly 294–297
Wolfensogn, James D. 117
World Bank sustainable
development initiative
571–573
world depression 15–18
world wide web 291–294
see also internet

X
Xenotransplantation 170, 237,
239

Y
Yahoo 53
Y2K (Year 2000)
and the millenium bug
136–137, 355
software industry and 300

Z
Zantac 255ff